MEI STRUCTURED MATHEMATICS

THIRD EDITION

AS Pure Mathematics

Val Hanrahan
Jean Matthews
Roger Porkess
Peter Secker

Series Editor: Roger Porkess

HODDER
EDUCATION
AN HACHETTE UK COMPANY

Acknowledgements

We are grateful to the following companies, institutions and individuals who have given permission to reproduce photographs in this book. Every effort has been made to trace and acknowledge ownership of copyright. The publishers will be glad to make suitable arrangements with any copyright holders whom it has not been possible to contact.

OCR, AQA and Edexcel accept no responsibility whatsoever for the accuracy or method of working in the answers given.

Papers used in this book are natural, renewable and recyclable products. They are made from wood grown in sustainable forests. The logging and manufacturing processes conform to the environmental regulations of the country of origin.

Orders: please contact Bookpoint Ltd, 130 Milton Park, Abingdon, Oxon OX14 4TD. Telephone: (44) 01235 827720, Fax: (44) 01235 400454. Lines are open from 9 am to 5 pm, Monday to Saturday, with a 24-hour message-answering service. You can also order through our website at *www.hoddereducation.co.uk*.

British Library Cataloguing in Publication Data
A catalogue record for this title is available from the The British Library.

ISBN: 978 0 340 813973

First Edition Published 1994
Second Edition Published 2000
Third Edition Published 2004
Impression number 16
Year   2013

Typeset by Pantek Media, Maidstone, Kent.
Printed in Great Britain for Hodder Education, an Hachette UK company, 338 Euston Road, London NW1 3BH by CPI Group (UK) Ltd, Croydon CR0 4YY.

MEI Structured Mathematics

Mathematics is not only a beautiful and exciting subject in its own right but also one that underpins many other branches of learning. It is consequently fundamental to the success of a modern economy.

MEI Structured Mathematics is designed to increase substantially the number of people taking the subject post-GCSE, by making it accessible, interesting and relevant to a wide range of students.

It is a credit accumulation scheme based on 45 hour units which may be taken individually or aggregated to give Advanced Subsidiary (AS) and Advanced GCE (A Level) qualifications in Mathematics and Further Mathematics. The units may also be used to obtain credit towards other types of qualification.

The course is examined by OCR (previously the Oxford and Cambridge Schools Examination Board) with examinations held in January and June each year.

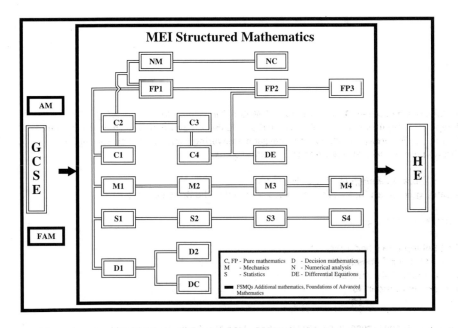

This is one of the series of books written to support the course. Its position within the whole scheme can be seen in the diagram above.

Mathematics in Education and Industry is a curriculum development body which aims to promote the links between Education and Industry in Mathematics at secondary school level, and to produce relevant examination and teaching syllabuses and support material. Since its foundation in the 1960s, MEI has provided syllabuses for GCSE (or O Level), Additional Mathematics and A Level.

For more information about MEI Structured Mathematics or other syllabuses and materials, write to MEI Office, Albion House, Market Place, Westbury, Wiltshire, BA13 3DE or visit www.mei.org.uk.

Introduction

The twelve chapters of this book cover the pure mathematics required for the AS subject criteria. The material is divided into the two units (or modules) for MEI Structured Mathematics: C1, *Introduction to Advanced Mathematics* and C2, *Concepts for Advanced Mathematics*. It is the first in a series of pure mathematics books for AS and A Levels in Mathematics and Further Mathematics.

Since their total content is the same, this book also covers the requirements of all the other specifications for AS Mathematics, and it is also suitable for other courses at this level.

Throughout the series the emphasis is on understanding rather than mere routine calculations, but the various exercises do nonetheless provide plenty of scope for practising basic techniques. Extensive on-line support is available via the MEI site, www.mei.org.uk.

This book is written on the assumption that you have at least grade C in GCSE Mathematics. You may, of course, know more mathematics than that; if so some of the early chapters will be partly revision for you but it is still important to check that you understand the basic work, particularly the algebra, and can handle it fluently and accurately.

This is the third edition of this series. Much of the content in this book was previously in *Pure Mathematics 1* and *2* but it has now been reorganised to meet the requirements of the new specification being first taught in September 2004. The original authors would like to thank Jean Matthews for her work in updating this book, and for her original contributions. We would also like to thank the various examination boards who have given permission for their past questions to be included in the exercises.

Roger Porkess
Series Editor

Key to symbols in this book

? This symbol means that you want to discuss a point with your teacher. If you are working on your own there are answers in the back of the book. It is important, however, that you have a go at answering the questions before looking up the answers if you are to understand the mathematics fully.

! This is a warning sign. It is used where a common mistake, misunderstanding or tricky point is being described.

This is the ICT icon. It indicates where you should use a graphic calculator or a computer.

e This symbol and a dotted line down the right-hand side of the page indicates material which is beyond the criteria for the unit but which is included for completeness.

☆☆ Harder questions are indicated with stars. Many of these go beyond the usual examination standard.

Contents

Introduction to Advanced Mathematics

1

Basic algebra

Sherlock Holmes: "Now the skillful workman is very careful indeed ... He will have nothing but the tools which may help him in doing his work, but of these he has a large assortment, and all in the most perfect order."

A. Conan Doyle

Manipulating algebraic expressions

You will often wish to tidy up an expression, or to rearrange it so that it is easier to read its meaning. The following examples show you how to do this. You should practise the techniques for yourself on the questions in Exercise 1A.

Collecting terms

Very often you just need to collect like terms together, in this example those in x, those in y and those in z.

❓ What are 'like' and 'unlike' terms?

EXAMPLE 1.1

Simplify the expression $2x + 4y - 5z - 5x - 9y + 2z + 4x - 7y + 8z$.

SOLUTION

Expression $= 2x + 4x - 5x + 4y - 9y - 7y + 2z + 8z - 5z$ ← Collect like terms

$= 6x - 5x + 4y - 16y + 10z - 5z$ ← Tidy up

$= x - 12y + 5z$ ← This cannot be simplified further and so it is the answer.

Removing brackets

Sometimes you need to remove brackets before collecting like terms together.

EXAMPLE 1.2

Simplify the expression $3(2x - 4y) - 4(x - 5y)$.

SOLUTION

Expression $= 6x - 12y - 4x + 20y$ ← *Open the brackets*

Notice $(-4) \times (-5y) = +20y$

$= 6x - 4x + 20y - 12y$ ← *Collect like terms*

$= 2x + 8y$ ← *Answer*

EXAMPLE 1.3

Simplify $x(x + 2) - (x - 4)$.

SOLUTION

Expression $= x^2 + 2x - x + 4$ ← *Open the brackets*

$= x^2 + x + 4$ ← *Answer*

EXAMPLE 1.4

Simplify $a(b + c) - ac$.

SOLUTION

Expression $= ab + ac - ac$ ← *Open the brackets*

$= ab$ ← *Answer*

Factorisation

It is often possible to rewrite an expression as the product of two or more numbers or expressions, its *factors*. This usually involves using brackets and is called *factorisation*. Factorisation may make an expression easier to use and neater to write, or it may help you to interpret its meaning.

EXAMPLE 1.5

Factorise $12x - 18y$.

SOLUTION

6 is a factor of both 12 and 18.

Expression $= 6(2x - 3y)$

EXAMPLE 1.6

Factorise $x^2 - 2xy + 3xz$.

SOLUTION

x is a factor of all three terms.

Expression $= x(x - 2y + 3z)$

Multiplication

Several of the previous examples have involved multiplication of variables: cases like

$$a \times b = ab \quad \text{and} \quad x \times x = x^2.$$

In the next example the principles are the same but the expressions are not quite so simple.

EXAMPLE 1.7

Multiply $\quad 3p^2qr \times 4pq^3 \times 5qr^2$.

SOLUTION

You might well do this line in your head.

$$\begin{aligned} \text{Expression} &= 3 \times 4 \times 5 \ \times \ p^2 \times p \ \times \ q \times q^3 \times q \ \times \ r \times r^2 \\ &= 60 \times p^3 \times q^5 \times r^3 \\ &= 60p^3q^5r^3 \end{aligned}$$

Fractions

The rules for working with fractions in algebra are exactly the same as those used in arithmetic.

EXAMPLE 1.8

Simplify $\dfrac{x}{2} - \dfrac{2y}{10} + \dfrac{z}{4}$.

SOLUTION

As in arithmetic you start by finding the common denominator. For 2, 10 and 4 this is 20.

Then you write each part as the equivalent fraction with 20 as its denominator, as follows.

This line would often be left out.

$$\begin{aligned} \text{Expression} &= \frac{10x}{20} - \frac{4y}{20} + \frac{5z}{20} \\ &= \frac{10x - 4y + 5z}{20} \end{aligned}$$

EXAMPLE 1.9

Simplify $\dfrac{x^2}{y} - \dfrac{y^2}{x}$.

SOLUTION

The common denominator is xy.

$$\begin{aligned} \text{Expression} &= \frac{x^3}{xy} - \frac{y^3}{xy} \\ &= \frac{x^3 - y^3}{xy} \end{aligned}$$

EXAMPLE 1.10   Simplify $\dfrac{3x^2}{5y} \times \dfrac{5yz}{6x}$.

SOLUTION

Since the two parts of the expression are multiplied, terms may be cancelled top and bottom as in arithmetic. In this case 3, 5, x and y may all be cancelled.

Expression

EXAMPLE 1.11   Simplify $\dfrac{(x-1)^3}{4x(x-1)}$.

SOLUTION

$(x-1)$ is a common factor of both top and bottom, so may be cancelled. However, x is not a factor of the top (the numerator), so may not be cancelled.

$$\text{Expression} = \frac{(x-1)^2}{4x}$$

EXAMPLE 1.12   Simplify $\dfrac{24x+6}{3(4x+1)}$.

SOLUTION

When the numerator (top) and/or the denominator (bottom) are not factorised, first factorise them as much as possible. Then you can see whether there are any common factors which can be cancelled.

$$\begin{aligned}\text{Expression} &= \frac{6(4x+1)}{3(4x+1)} \\ &= 2\end{aligned}$$

EXERCISE 1A

 The work in this exercise is almost completely routine. If you have access to a computer algebra system, use it to check your answers. By doing so you will also be learning how to use the system.

1 Simplify the following expressions by collecting like terms.

(i) $8x + 3x + 4x - 6x$

(ii) $3p + 3 + 5p - 7 - 7p - 9$

(iii) $2k + 3m + 8n - 3k - 6m - 5n + 2k - m + n$

(iv) $2a + 3b - 4c + 4a - 5b - 8c - 6a + 2b + 12c$

(v) $r - 2s - t + 2r - 5t - 6r - 7t - s + 5s - 2t + 4r$

2 Factorise the following expressions.

(i) $4x + 8y$

(ii) $12a + 15b - 18c$

(iii) $72f - 36g - 48h$

(iv) $p^2 - pq + pr$

(v) $12k^2 + 144km - 72kn$

3 Simplify the following expressions, factorising the answers where possible.

(i) $8(3x + 2y) + 4(x + 3y)$

(ii) $2(3a - 4b + 5c) - 3(2a - 5b - c)$

(iii) $6(2p - 3q + 4r) - 5(2p - 6q - 3r) - 3(p - 4q + 2r)$

(iv) $4(l + w + h) + 3(2l - w - 2h) + 5w$

(v) $5u - 6(w - v) + 2(3u + 4w - v) - 11u$

4 Simplify the following expressions, factorising the answers where possible.

(i) $a(b + c) + a(b - c)$

(ii) $k(m + n) - m(k + n)$

(iii) $p(2q + r + 3s) - pr - s(3p + q)$

(iv) $x(x - 2) - x(x - 6) + 8$

(v) $x(x - 1) + 2(x - 1) - x(x + 1)$

5 Perform the following multiplications, simplifying your answers.

(i) $2xy \times 3x^2y$

(ii) $5a^2bc^3 \times 2ab^2 \times 3c$

(iii) $km \times mn \times nk$

(iv) $3pq^2r \times 6p^2qr \times 9pqr^2$

(v) $rs \times 2st \times 3tu \times 4ur$

6 Simplify the following fractions as much as possible.

(i) $\dfrac{ab}{ac}$

(ii) $\dfrac{2e}{4f}$

(iii) $\dfrac{x^2}{5x}$

(iv) $\dfrac{4a^2b}{2ab}$

(v) $\dfrac{6p^2q^3r}{3p^3q^3r^2}$

7 Simplify the following as much as possible.

(i) $\dfrac{a}{b} \times \dfrac{b}{c} \times \dfrac{c}{a}$

(ii) $\dfrac{3x}{2y} \times \dfrac{8y}{3z} \times \dfrac{5z}{4x}$

(iii) $\dfrac{p^2}{q} \times \dfrac{q^2}{p}$

(iv) $\dfrac{2fg}{16h} \times \dfrac{4gh^2}{4fh} \times \dfrac{32fh^3}{12f^3}$

(v) $\dfrac{kmn}{3n^3} \times \dfrac{6k^2m^3}{2k^3m}$

8 Write the following as single fractions.

(i) $\dfrac{x}{2} + \dfrac{x}{3}$

(ii) $\dfrac{2x}{5} - \dfrac{x}{3} + \dfrac{3x}{4}$

(iii) $\dfrac{3z}{8} + \dfrac{2z}{12} - \dfrac{5z}{24}$

(iv) $\dfrac{2x}{3} - \dfrac{x}{4}$

(v) $\dfrac{y}{2} - \dfrac{5y}{8} + \dfrac{4y}{5}$

9 Write the following as single fractions.

(i) $\dfrac{3}{x} + \dfrac{5}{x}$

(ii) $\dfrac{1}{x} + \dfrac{1}{y}$

(iii) $\dfrac{4}{x} + \dfrac{x}{y}$

(iv) $\dfrac{p}{q} + \dfrac{q}{p}$

(v) $\dfrac{1}{a} - \dfrac{1}{b} + \dfrac{1}{c}$

10 Write the following as single fractions.

(i) $\dfrac{x+1}{4} + \dfrac{x-1}{2}$

(ii) $\dfrac{2x}{3} - \dfrac{x-1}{5}$

(iii) $\dfrac{3x-5}{4} + \dfrac{x-7}{6}$

(iv) $\dfrac{3(2x+1)}{5} - \dfrac{7(x-2)}{2}$

(v) $\dfrac{4x+1}{8} + \dfrac{7x-3}{12}$

11 Simplify the following expressions.

(i) $\dfrac{x+3}{2x+6}$

(ii) $\dfrac{6(2x+1)^2}{3(2x+1)^5}$

(iii) $\dfrac{2x(y-3)^4}{8x^2(y-3)}$

(iv) $\dfrac{6x-12}{x-2}$

(v) $\dfrac{(3x+2)^2}{6x} \times \dfrac{x^4}{6x+4}$

Equations

 What is a variable?

You will often need to find the value of the variable in an expression in a particular case, as in the following example.

EXAMPLE 1.13

A polygon is a closed figure whose sides are straight lines. Figure 1.1 shows a seven-sided polygon (a heptagon).

Figure 1.1

An expression for $S°$, the sum of the angles of a polygon with n sides, is

$$S = 180(n-2).$$

 How is this expression obtained?
Try dividing a polygon into triangles, starting from one vertex.

Find the number of sides in a polygon with an angle sum of (i) 180° (ii) 1080°.

SOLUTION

(i) Substituting 180 for S gives $\qquad$ $180 = 180(n-2)$

Dividing both sides by 180 $\quad\Rightarrow\quad 1 = n-2$

Adding 2 to both sides $\qquad\Rightarrow\quad 3 = n$

> This is an equation which can be solved to find n.

The polygon has three sides: it is a triangle.

(ii) Substituting 1080 for S gives $\quad 1080 = 180(n-2)$

Dividing both sides by 180 $\quad\Rightarrow\quad 6 = n-2$

Adding 2 to both sides $\qquad\Rightarrow\quad 8 = n$

The polygon has eight sides: it is an octagon.

Example 1.13 illustrates the process of solving an equation. An *equation* is formed when an expression, in this case $180(n-2)$, is set equal to a value, in this case 180 or 1080, or to another expression. *Solving* means finding the value(s) of the variable(s) in the equation.

Since both sides of an equation are equal, you may do what you wish to an equation provided that you do exactly the same thing to both sides. If there is only one variable involved (like n in the above examples), you aim to get that on one side of the equation, and everything else on the other. The two examples which follow illustrate this.

In both of these examples the working is given in full, step by step. In practice you would expect to omit some of these lines by tidying up as you went along.

 Look at the statement $5(x-1) = 5x-5$.

What happens when you try to solve it as an equation?

This is an *identity* and not an equation. It is true for *all* values of x.

For example, try $x = 11$: $5(x-1) = 5 \times (11-1) = 50$; $5x-5 = 55-5 = 50$ ✓,

or try $x = 46$: $5(x-1) = 5 \times (46-1) = 225$; $5x-5 = 230-5 = 225$ ✓,

or try $x =$ anything else and it will still be true.

To distinguish an identity from an equation, the symbol $\equiv$ is sometimes used.

Thus $5(x-1) \equiv 5x-5$.

EXAMPLE 1.14

Solve the equation $\quad 5(x-3) = 2(x+6)$.

SOLUTION

Open the brackets	$\Rightarrow$	$5x - 15 = 2x + 12$
Subtract $2x$ from both sides	$\Rightarrow$	$5x - 2x - 15 = 2x - 2x + 12$
Tidy up	$\Rightarrow$	$3x - 15 = 12$
Add 15 to both sides	$\Rightarrow$	$3x - 15 + 15 = 12 + 15$
Tidy up	$\Rightarrow$	$3x = 27$
Divide both sides by 3	$\Rightarrow$	$\dfrac{3x}{3} = \dfrac{27}{3}$
	$\Rightarrow$	$x = 9$

CHECK

When the answer is substituted in the original equation both sides should come out to be equal. If they are different, you have made a mistake.

Left-hand side	**Right-hand side**
$5(x-3)$	$2(x+6)$
$5(9-3)$	$2(9+6)$
5×6	2×15
30	30 (as required).

EXAMPLE 1.15

Solve the equation $\frac{1}{2}(x+6) = x + \frac{1}{3}(2x-5)$.

SOLUTION

Start by clearing the fractions. Since the numbers 2 and 3 appear on the bottom line, multiply through by 6 which cancels both of them.

Multiply both sides by 6 $\Rightarrow$	$6 \times \frac{1}{2}(x+6) = 6 \times x + 6 \times \frac{1}{3}(2x-5)$
Tidy up $\Rightarrow$	$3(x+6) = 6x + 2(2x-5)$
Open the brackets $\Rightarrow$	$3x + 18 = 6x + 4x - 10$
Subtract $6x$, $4x$, and 18 from both sides $\Rightarrow$	$3x - 6x - 4x = -10 - 18$
Tidy up $\Rightarrow$	$-7x = -28$
Divide both sides by $(-7) \Rightarrow$	$\dfrac{-7x}{-7} = \dfrac{-28}{-7}$
$\Rightarrow$	$x = 4$

CHECK

Substituting $x = 4$ in $\frac{1}{2}(x+6) = x + \frac{1}{3}(2x-5)$ gives:

Left-hand side	**Right-hand side**
$\frac{1}{2}(4+6)$	$4 - \frac{1}{3}(8-5)$
$\frac{10}{2}$	$4 + \frac{3}{3}$
5	5 (as required).

EXERCISE 1B

The first question in this exercise involves routine solution of equations. Good calculators and computer algebra systems will do this work for you. If you have either of these facilities to hand, use them to check your answers.

In the final eight questions, you are asked to set up the equations as well as solve them, and this is something which a machine will not do for you.

1 Solve the following equations.

(i) $5a - 32 = 68$

(ii) $4b - 6 = 3b + 2$

(iii) $2c + 12 = 5c + 12$

    (iv) $5(2d + 8) = 2(3d + 24)$

    (v) $3(2e - 1) = 6(e + 2) + 3e$

    (vi) $7(2 - f) - 3(f - 4) = 10f - 4$

    (vii) $5g + 2(g - 9) = 3(2g - 5) + 11$

    (viii) $3(2h - 6) - 6(h + 5) = 2(4h - 4) - 10(h + 4)$

    (ix) $\frac{1}{2}k + \frac{1}{4}k = 36$

    (x) $\frac{1}{2}(\ell - 5) + \ell = 11$

    (xi) $\frac{1}{2}(3m + 5) + 1\frac{1}{2}(2m - 1) = 5\frac{1}{2}$

    (xii) $n + \frac{1}{3}(n + 1) + \frac{1}{4}(n + 2) = \frac{5}{6}$

2 The largest angle of a triangle is six times as big as the smallest. The third angle is 75°.

    (i) Write this information in the form of an equation for a, the size in degrees of the smallest angle.

    (ii) Solve the equation and so find the sizes of the three angles.

3 Beth and Polly are twins and their sister Louise is 2 years older than them. The total of their ages is 32 years.

    (i) Write this information in the form of an equation for ℓ, Louise's age in years.

    (ii) What are the ages of the three girls?

4 The length, d m, of a rectangular field is 40 m greater than the width. The perimeter of the field is 400 m.

    (i) Write this information in the form of an equation for d.

    (ii) Solve the equation and so find the area of the field.

5 Simon can buy three pencils and have 49p change, or he can buy five pencils and have 15p change.

    (i) Write this information as an equation for x, the cost in pence of one pencil.

    (ii) How much money did Simon have to start with?

6 A train has 8 coaches, f of which are first class and the rest standard class. A first class coach seats 48 passengers, a standard class 64.

    (i) Write down an expression in terms of f for the seating capacity of the train.

    (ii) The seating capacity of the train is 480. Form an equation for f and solve it. How many standard class coaches does the train have?

7 In a multiple-choice examination of 25 questions, four marks are given for each correct answer and two marks are deducted for each wrong answer. One mark is deducted for any question which is not attempted. A candidate attempts q questions and gets c correct.

    (i) Write down an expression for the candidate's total mark in terms of q and c.

    (ii) James attempts 22 questions and scores 55 marks. Write down and solve an equation for the number of questions which James gets right.

8 Joe buys 18 kg of potatoes. Some of these are old potatoes at 22 p per kilogram, the rest are new ones at 36p per kilogram.

(i) Denoting the weight of old potatoes he buys by w kg, write down an expression for the total cost of Joe's potatoes.

(ii) Joe pays with a £5 note and receives 20p change. What weight of new potatoes does he buy?

9 In 18 years' time Halley will be five times as old as he was 2 years ago.

(i) Write this information in the form of an equation involving Halley's present age, a years.

(ii) How old is Halley now?

Changing the subject of an equation

The area of a trapezium is given by

$$A = \tfrac{1}{2}(a + b)h$$

where a and b are the lengths of the parallel sides and h is the distance between them (see figure 1.2). An equation like this is often called a *formula*.

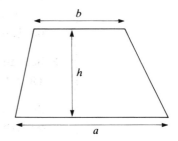

Figure 1.2

The variable A is called the subject of this formula because it only appears once on its own on the left-hand side. You often need to make one of the other variables the subject of a formula. In that case, the steps involved are just the same as those in solving an equation, as the following examples show.

EXAMPLE 1.16

Make a the subject in $A = \tfrac{1}{2}(a + b)h$.

SOLUTION

It is usually easiest if you start by arranging the equation so that the variable you want to be its subject is on the left-hand side.

$$\tfrac{1}{2}(a + b)h = A$$

Multiply both sides by 2 $\quad \Rightarrow \quad (a + b)h = 2A$

Divide both sides by h $\quad \Rightarrow \quad a + b = \dfrac{2A}{h}$

Subtract b from both sides $\quad \Rightarrow \quad a = \dfrac{2A}{h} - b$

EXAMPLE 1.17

Make T the subject in the simple interest formula $I = \dfrac{PRT}{100}$.

SOLUTION

Arrange with T on the left-hand side $\quad \dfrac{PRT}{100} = I$

Multiply both sides by 100 $\qquad \Rightarrow \quad PRT = 100I$

Divide both sides by P and R $\qquad \Rightarrow \quad T = \dfrac{100I}{PR}$

EXAMPLE 1.18

Make x the subject in the formula $v = \omega\sqrt{a^2 - x^2}$. (This formula gives the speed of an oscillating point.)

SOLUTION

Square both sides $\qquad\qquad\qquad \Rightarrow \qquad v^2 = \omega^2(a^2 - x^2)$

Divide both sides by ω^2 $\qquad\qquad \Rightarrow \qquad \dfrac{v^2}{\omega^2} = a^2 - x^2$

Add x^2 to both sides $\qquad\qquad\quad \Rightarrow \qquad \dfrac{v^2}{\omega^2} + x^2 = a^2$

Subtract $\dfrac{v^2}{\omega^2}$ from both sides $\quad \Rightarrow \qquad x^2 = a^2 - \dfrac{v^2}{\omega^2}$

Take the square root of both sides $\;\Rightarrow \qquad x = \pm\sqrt{a^2 - \dfrac{v^2}{\omega^2}}$

EXAMPLE 1.19

Make m the subject of the formula $mv = I + mu$. (This formula gives the momentum after an impulse.)

SOLUTION

Collect terms in m on the left-hand side
and terms without m on the other. $\qquad \Rightarrow \qquad mv - mu = I$

Factorise the left-hand side $\qquad\qquad \Rightarrow \qquad m(v - u) = I$

Divide both sides by $(v - u)$ $\qquad\quad \Rightarrow \qquad m = \dfrac{I}{v - u}$

EXERCISE 1C

1 Make **(i)** a **(ii)** t the subject in $v = u + at$.

2 Make h the subject in $V = \ell wh$.

3 Make r the subject in $A = \pi r^2$.

4 Make **(i)** s **(ii)** u the subject in $v^2 - u^2 = 2as$.

5 Make h the subject in $A = 2\pi rh + 2\pi r^2$.

6 Make a the subject in $s = ut + \frac{1}{2}at^2$.

7 Make b the subject in $h = \sqrt{a^2 + b^2}$.

8 Make g the subject in $T = 2\pi\sqrt{\frac{\ell}{g}}$.

9 Make m the subject in $E = mgh + \frac{1}{2}mv^2$.

10 Make R the subject in $\frac{1}{R} = \frac{1}{R_1} + \frac{1}{R_2}$.

11 Make h the subject in $bh = 2A - ah$.

12 Make u the subject in $f = \frac{uv}{u + v}$.

13 Make d the subject in $u^2 - du + fd = 0$.

14 Make V the subject in $p_1VM = mRT + p_2VM$.

❓ All the equations in Exercise 1C refer to real situations. Can you recognise them?

Quadratic equations

EXAMPLE 1.20

The length of a rectangular field is 40 m greater than its width, and its area is 6000 m². Form an equation involving the length, x m, of the field.

SOLUTION

Since the length of the field is 40 m greater than the width,

the width in m must be $x - 40$

and the area in m² is $x(x - 40)$.

So the required equation is $x(x - 40) = 6000$

or $\qquad x^2 - 40x - 6000 = 0$.

Figure 1.3

This equation, involving terms in x^2 and x as well as a constant term (i.e. a number, in this case 6000), is an example of a *quadratic equation*. This is in contrast to a linear equation. A linear equation in the variable x involves only terms in x and constant terms.

It is usual to write a quadratic equation with the right-hand side equal to zero. To solve it, you first factorise the left-hand side if possible, and this requires a particular technique.

Quadratic factorisation

EXAMPLE 1.21

Factorise $xa + xb + ya + yb$.

SOLUTION

$$xa + xb + ya + yb = x(a + b) + y(a + b)$$

Notice $(a + b)$ is a common factor.

$$= (x + y)(a + b)$$

The expression is now in the form of two factors, $(x + y)$ and $(a + b)$, so this is the answer.

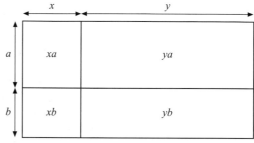

You can see this result in terms of the area of the rectangle in figure 1.4. This can be written as the product of its length $(x + y)$ and its width $(a + b)$, or as the sum of the areas of the four smaller rectangles, xa, xb, ya and yb.

Figure 1.4

The same pattern is used for quadratic factorisation, but first you need to split the middle term into two parts. This gives you four terms, which correspond to the areas of the four regions in a diagram like figure 1.4.

EXAMPLE 1.22

Factorise $x^2 + 7x + 12$.

SOLUTION

Splitting the middle term, $7x$, as $4x + 3x$ you have

$$x^2 + 7x + 12 = x^2 + 4x + 3x + 12$$
$$= x(x + 4) + 3(x + 4)$$
$$= (x + 3)(x + 4).$$

How do you know to split the middle term, $7x$, into $4x + 3x$, rather than say $5x + 2x$ or $9x - 2x$?

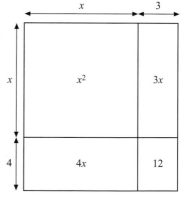

Figure 1.5

The numbers 4 and 3 can be added to give 7 (the middle coefficient) and multiplied to give 12 (the constant term), so these are the numbers chosen.

The coefficient of x is 7.   The constant term is 12.

$$x^2 + 7x + 12$$

$4 + 3 = 7$ $4 \times 3 = 12$

EXAMPLE 1.23   Factorise $x^2 - 2x - 24$.

SOLUTION

First you look for two numbers that can be added to give −2 and multiplied to give −24:

$$-6 + 4 = -2 \qquad -6 \times (+4) = -24.$$

The numbers are −6 and +4 and so the middle term, −2x, is split into −6x + 4x.

$$
\begin{aligned}
x^2 - 2x - 24 &= x^2 - 6x + 4x - 24 \\
&= x(x - 6) + 4(x - 6) \\
&= (x + 4)(x - 6).
\end{aligned}
$$

This example raises a number of important points.

1 It makes no difference if you write $+4x - 6x$ instead of $-6x + 4x$. In that case the factorisation reads:

$$
\begin{aligned}
x^2 - 2x - 24 &= x^2 + 4x - 6x - 24 \\
&= x(x + 4) - 6(x + 4) \\
&= (x - 6)(x + 4) \qquad \text{(clearly the same answer).}
\end{aligned}
$$

2 There are other methods of quadratic factorisation. If you have already learned another way, and consistently get your answers right, then continue to use it. This method has one major advantage: it is self-checking. In the last line but one of the solution to the example, you will see that $(x + 4)$ appears twice. If at this point the contents of the two brackets are different, for example $(x + 4)$ and $(x - 4)$, then something is wrong. You may have chosen the wrong numbers, or made a careless mistake, or perhaps the expression cannot be factorised. There is no point in proceeding until you have sorted out why they are different.

3 You may check your final answer by multiplying it out to get back to the original expression. There are two common ways of setting this out.

(i) Long multiplication

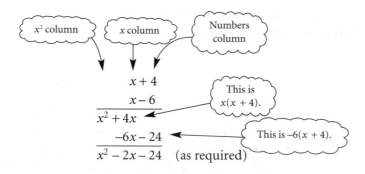

(ii) Multiplying term by term

$$(x + 4)(x - 6) = x^2 - 6x + 4x - 24$$

$$= x^2 - 2x - 24 \quad \text{(as required)}$$

You would not expect to draw the lines and arrows in your answers. They have been put in to help you understand where the terms have come from.

EXAMPLE 1.24

Factorise $x^2 - 20x + 100$.

SOLUTION

$$\begin{aligned} x^2 - 20x + 100 &= x^2 - 10x - 10x + 100 \\ &= x(x - 10) - 10(x - 10) \\ &= (x - 10)(x - 10) \\ &= (x - 10)^2 \end{aligned}$$

Notice:
$(-10) + (-10) = -20$
$(-10) \times (-10) = +100$

Note

The example above was a *perfect square*. It is helpful to be able to recognise the form of such expressions.

$$(x + a)^2 = x^2 + 2ax + a^2 \quad \text{(in this case } a = 10)$$
$$(x - a)^2 = x^2 - 2ax + a^2$$

EXAMPLE 1.25

Factorise $x^2 - 49$.

SOLUTION

Notice this is $x^2 - 7^2$

$x^2 - 49$ can be written as $x^2 + 0x - 49$.

$$\begin{aligned} x^2 + 0x - 49 &= x^2 - 7x + 7x - 49 \\ &= x(x - 7) + 7(x - 7) \\ &= (x + 7)(x - 7) \end{aligned}$$

$-7 + 7 = 0$
$(-7) \times 7 = -49$

This one was an example of *the difference of two squares* which may be written in more general form as

$$a^2 - b^2 = (a + b)(a - b).$$

? What would help you to remember the general results from Examples 1.24 and 1.25?

The previous examples have all started with the term x^2, that is the coefficient of x^2 has been 1. This is not the case in the next example.

EXAMPLE 1.26

Factorise $6x^2 + x - 12$.

SOLUTION

The technique for finding how to split the middle term is now adjusted. Start by multiplying the two outside numbers together:

$$6 \times (-12) = -72.$$

Now look for two numbers which add to give $+1$ (the coefficient of x) and multiply to give -72 (the number found above).

$$(+9) + (-8) = +1 \qquad\qquad (+9) \times (-8) = -72$$

Splitting the middle term gives

$$6x^2 + 9x - 8x - 12$$

3x is a factor of both $6x^2$ and $9x$.

$$= 3x(2x + 3) - 4(2x + 3)$$

$$= (3x - 4)(2x + 3)$$

−4 is a factor of both $-8x$ and -12.

Note

The method used in the earlier examples is really the same as this. It is just that in those cases the coefficient of x^2 was 1 and so multiplying the constant term by it had no effect.

 Before starting the procedure for factorising a quadratic, you should always check that the terms do not have a common factor as for example in

$$2x^2 - 8x + 6.$$

This can be written as $2(x^2 - 4x + 3)$ and factorised to give $2(x - 3)(x - 1)$.

EXAMPLE 1.27

Simplify $\dfrac{x^2 - 5x + 6}{x^2 + x - 12}$.

SOLUTION

First factorise the numerator and denominator. Then you can see which factors will cancel.

$$\frac{x^2 - 5x + 6}{x^2 + x - 12} = \frac{(x - 2)(x - 3)}{(x + 4)(x - 3)}$$

$$= \frac{x - 2}{x + 4}$$

EXAMPLE 1.28

Simplify $\dfrac{x^2 - 7x + 6}{(x-1)^2} \div \dfrac{x+1}{2x-2}$.

SOLUTION

$$\dfrac{x^2 - 7x + 6}{(x-1)^2} \div \dfrac{x+1}{2x-2} = \dfrac{(x-6)(x-1)}{(x-1)^2} \div \dfrac{x+1}{2(x-1)}$$

Factorise first.

$$= \dfrac{(x-6)(x-1)}{(x-1)^2} \times \dfrac{2(x-1)}{x+1}$$

Remember: To divide by a fraction, invert it and multiply.

$$= \dfrac{2(x-6)}{x+1}$$

Solving quadratic equations

It is a simple matter to solve a quadratic equation once the quadratic expression has been factorised. Since the product of the two factors is zero, it follows that one or other of them must equal zero, and this gives the solution.

EXAMPLE 1.29

Solve $x^2 - 40x - 6000 = 0$.

SOLUTION

$$\begin{aligned}
x^2 - 40x - 6000 &= x^2 - 100x + 60x - 6000 \\
&= x(x - 100) + 60(x - 100) \\
&= (x + 60)(x - 100)
\end{aligned}$$

$$\Rightarrow \quad (x + 60)(x - 100) = 0$$
$$\Rightarrow \quad \text{either } x + 60 = 0 \quad \Rightarrow \quad x = -60$$
$$\Rightarrow \quad \text{or } x - 100 = 0 \quad \Rightarrow \quad x = 100$$

The solution is $x = -60$ or 100.

Note

The *solution* of the equation in the example is $x = -60$ or 100.
The *roots* of the equation are the values of x which satisfy the equation, in this case one root is $x = -60$ and the other root is $x = 100$.

Equations that cannot be factorised

The method of quadratic factorisation is fine so long as the quadratic expression can be factorised, but not all of them can. In the case of $x^2 - 6x + 2$, for example, it is not possible to find two whole numbers which add to give -6 and multiply to give $+2$.

There are other techniques available for such situations, as you will see in the next few pages.

Graphical solution

If an equation has a solution, you can always find an approximate value for it by drawing a graph. In the case of

$$x^2 - 6x + 2 = 0$$

you draw the graph of

$$y = x^2 - 6x + 2$$

and find where it cuts the x axis.

x	0	1	2	3	4	5	6
x^2	0	1	4	9	16	25	36
$-6x$	0	−6	−12	−18	−24	−30	−36
$+2$	+2	+2	+2	+2	+2	+2	+2
y	+2	−3	−6	−7	−6	−3	+2

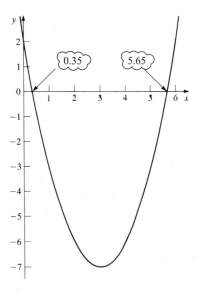

Figure 1.6

From figure 1.6, x is approximately 0.35 or 5.65.

Clearly the accuracy of the answer is dependent on the scale of the graph but, however large a scale you use, your answer will never be completely accurate.

Completing the square

If a quadratic equation has a solution, this method will give it accurately. It involves adjusting the left-hand side of the equation to make it a perfect square. The steps involved are shown in the following example.

EXAMPLE 1.30

Solve the equation $x^2 - 6x + 2 = 0$ by completing the square.

SOLUTION

Subtract the constant term from both sides of the equation:

$$\Rightarrow \quad x^2 - 6x \quad = -2$$

Take the coefficient of x: $\quad -6$
Halve it: $\quad -3$
Square the answer: $\quad +9$

Explain why this makes the left-hand side a perfect square.

Add it to both sides of the equation:

$$\Rightarrow \quad x^2 - 6x + 9 = -2 + 9$$

Factorise the left-hand side. It will be found to be a perfect square:

$$\Rightarrow \quad (x - 3)^2 = 7$$

Take the square root of both sides:

$$\Rightarrow \quad x - 3 = \pm\sqrt{7}$$
$$\Rightarrow \quad x = 3 \pm \sqrt{7}$$

This is an exact answer.

Using your calculator to find the value of $\sqrt{7}$

This is an approximate answer.

$$\Rightarrow \quad x = 5.646 \text{ or } 0.354, \text{ to 3 decimal places.}$$

Completing the square is a powerful method because it can be used on any quadratic equation. However it is seldom used to solve an equation in practice because it can be generalised to give a formula which is used instead. The derivation of this follows exactly the same steps.

The quadratic formula

To solve a general quadratic equation $ax^2 + bx + c = 0$ by completing the square, we follow the steps in the last example.

First divide both sides by a: $\Rightarrow x^2 + \dfrac{bx}{a} + \dfrac{c}{a} = 0.$

Subtract the constant term from both sides of the equation:

$$\Rightarrow \quad x^2 + \frac{bx}{a} = -\frac{c}{a}$$

Take the coefficient of x: $\quad +\dfrac{b}{a}$

Halve it: $\quad +\dfrac{b}{2a}$

Square the answer: $\quad +\dfrac{b^2}{4a^2}$

Add it to both sides of the equation:

$$\Rightarrow \quad x^2 + \frac{bx}{a} + \frac{b^2}{4a^2} = \frac{b^2}{4a^2} - \frac{c}{a}$$

Factorise the left-hand side and tidy up the right-hand side:

$$\Rightarrow \quad \left(x + \frac{b}{2a}\right)^2 = \frac{b^2 - 4ac}{4a^2}$$

Take the square root of both sides:

$$\Rightarrow \quad x + \frac{b}{2a} = \pm \frac{\sqrt{b^2 - 4ac}}{2a}$$

$$\Rightarrow \quad x = \frac{-b \pm \sqrt{b^2 - 4ac}}{2a}$$

This important result, known as the quadratic formula, has significance beyond the solution of awkward quadratic equations, as you will see later. The next two examples, however, demonstrate its use as a tool for solving equations.

EXAMPLE 1.31

Use the quadratic formula to solve $3x^2 - 6x + 2 = 0$.

SOLUTION

Comparing this to the form $ax^2 + bx + c = 0$
gives $a = 3$, $b = -6$ and $c = 2$.

Substituting these values in the formula $x = \dfrac{-b \pm \sqrt{b^2 - 4ac}}{2a}$

gives $x = \dfrac{6 \pm \sqrt{36 - 24}}{6}$

$\qquad = 0.423 \text{ or } 1.577 \qquad$ (to 3 d.p.).

EXAMPLE 1.32

Solve $x^2 - 2x + 2 = 0$.

SOLUTION

The first thing to notice is that this cannot be factorised. The only two whole numbers which multiply to give 2 are 2 and 1 (or -2 and -1) and they cannot be added to get -2.

Comparing $x^2 - 2x + 2$ to the form $ax^2 + bx + c = 0$
gives $a = 1$, $b = -2$ and $c = 2$.

Substituting these values in $x = \dfrac{-b \pm \sqrt{b^2 - 4ac}}{2a}$

gives $x = \dfrac{2 \pm \sqrt{4 - 8}}{2}$

$\qquad = \dfrac{2 \pm \sqrt{-4}}{2}.$

Trying to find the square root of a negative number creates problems.
A positive number multiplied by itself is positive: $+2 \times +2 = +4$.
A negative number multiplied by itself is also positive: $-2 \times -2 = +4$.
Since $\sqrt{-4}$ can be neither positive nor negative, no such number exists, and so the equation has no solution.

Note

It is not quite true to say that a negative number has no square root. Certainly it has none among the real numbers but mathematicians have invented an imaginary number, denoted by j, with the property that $j^2 = -1$. Numbers like $1 + j$ and $-1 - j$ (which are in fact the solutions of the equation above) are called complex numbers. Complex numbers are extremely useful in both pure and applied mathematics; they are covered in FP1 and FP2.

To return to the problem of solving the equation $x^2 - 2x + 2 = 0$, look what happens if you draw the graph of $y = x^2 - 2x + 2$. The table of values is given below and the graph is shown in figure 1.7. As you can see, the graph does not cut the x axis and so there is indeed no real solution to this equation.

x	-1	0	1	2	3
x^2	$+1$	0	$+1$	$+4$	$+9$
$-2x$	$+2$	0	-2	-4	-6
$+2$	$+2$	$+2$	$+2$	$+2$	$+2$
y	$+5$	$+2$	$+1$	$+2$	$+5$

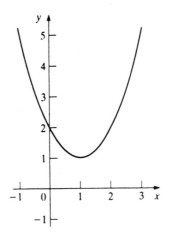

Figure 1.7

The part of the quadratic formula which determines whether or not there are real roots is the part under the square root sign. This is called the *discriminant*.

$$x = \frac{-b \pm \sqrt{b^2 - 4ac}}{2a}$$

The discriminant, $b^2 - 4ac$

If $b^2 - 4ac > 0$, the equation has two real roots (see figure 1.8).

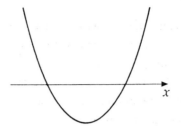

Figure 1.8

If $b^2 - 4ac < 0$, the equation has no real roots (see figure 1.9).

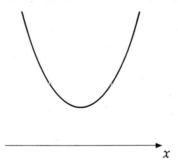

Figure 1.9

If $b^2 - 4ac = 0$, the equation has one repeated root (see figure 1.10).

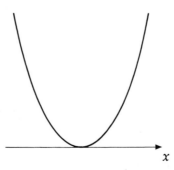

Figure 1.10

More on completing the square

The process of completing the square can be used not only for solving quadratic equations, but also as a source of valuable information about a quadratic expression and its graph.

Take, for example, the expression $x^2 - 5x + 9$.

Rewrite the expression with the constant term moved to one side

$$\Rightarrow \quad x^2 - 5x \qquad\qquad + 9$$

Take the coefficient of x: $\quad -5$

Divide it by 2: $\qquad\qquad -2\frac{1}{2}$

Square it: $\qquad\qquad +6\frac{1}{4}$

Add this to the left-hand part and compensate by subtracting it from the constant term on the right:

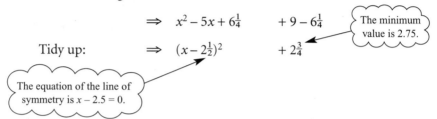

$$\Rightarrow \quad x^2 - 5x + 6\tfrac{1}{4} \qquad + 9 - 6\tfrac{1}{4}$$

The minimum value is 2.75.

Tidy up: $\qquad\qquad \Rightarrow \quad (x - 2\tfrac{1}{2})^2 \qquad + 2\tfrac{3}{4}$

The equation of the line of symmetry is $x - 2.5 = 0$.

This means that the graph of $y = x^2 - 5x + 9$ has a minimum value of $y = 2.75$ ocurring when $x = 2.5$ and its line of symmetry is given by $x = 2.5$. This is shown in figure 1.11.

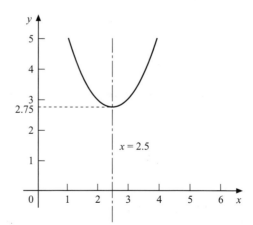

Figure 1.11

1 Factorise the following expressions.

(i) $al + am + bl + bm$

(ii) $px + py - qx - qy$

(iii) $ur - vr + us - vs$

(iv) $m^2 + mn + pm + pn$

(v) $x^2 - 3x + 2x - 6$

(vi) $y^2 + 3y + 7y + 21$

(vii) $z^2 - 5z + 5z - 25$

(viii) $q^2 - 3q - 3q + 9$

(ix) $2x^2 + 2x + 3x + 3$

(x) $6v^2 + 3v - 20v - 10$

2 Multiply out the following expressions and collect like terms.

(i) $(a + 2)(a + 3)$

(ii) $(b + 5)(b + 7)$

(iii) $(c - 4)(c - 2)$

(iv) $(d - 5)(d - 4)$

(v) $(e + 6)(e - 1)$

(vi) $(g - 3)(g + 3)$

(vii) $(h + 5)^2$

(viii) $(2i - 3)^2$

(ix) $(a + b)(c + d)$

(x) $(x + y)(x - y)$

3 Factorise the following quadratic expressions.

(i) $x^2 + 6x + 8$

(ii) $x^2 - 6x + 8$

(iii) $y^2 + 9y + 20$

(iv) $r^2 + 2r - 15$

(v) $r^2 - 2r - 15$

(vi) $s^2 - 4s + 4$

(vii) $x^2 - 5x - 6$

(viii) $x^2 + 2x + 1$

(ix) $a^2 - 9$

(x) $(x + 3)^2 - 9$

4 Factorise the following expressions.

(i) $2x^2 + 5x + 2$

(ii) $2x^2 - 5x + 2$

(iii) $5x^2 + 11x + 2$

(iv) $5x^2 - 11x + 2$

(v) $2x^2 + 14x + 24$

(vi) $4x^2 - 49$

(vii) $6x^2 - 5x - 6$

(viii) $9x^2 - 6x + 1$

(ix) $t_1^2 - t_2^2$

(x) $2x^2 - 11xy + 5y^2$

5 Simplify the following expressions. Leave your answers in factorised form.

(i) $\dfrac{x^2 + 4x + 3}{x + 1}$

(ii) $\dfrac{x^2 - 25}{x - 5}$

(iii) $\dfrac{x^2 - x - 6}{x^2 + x - 12}$

(iv) $\dfrac{(x + 4)^6 \, (x + 1)}{x^2 + 5x + 4}$

(v) $\dfrac{2x + 6}{3x - 1} \times (3x^2 + 8x - 3)$

(vi) $\dfrac{4x + 8}{3} \div \dfrac{x^2 - 3x - 10}{4}$

6 Solve the following equations.

(i) $x^2 - 11x + 24 = 0$ **(ii)** $x^2 + 11x + 24 = 0$

(iii) $x^2 - 11x + 18 = 0$ **(iv)** $x^2 - 6x + 9 = 0$

(v) $x^2 - 64 = 0$

7 Solve the following equations.

(i) $3x^2 - 5x + 2 = 0$ **(ii)** $3x^2 + 5x + 2 = 0$

(iii) $3x^2 - 5x - 2 = 0$ **(iv)** $25x^2 - 16 = 0$

(v) $9x^2 - 12x + 4 = 0$

8 Use your calculator to solve the following equations, where possible.

(i) $x^2 + 8x + 5 = 0$ **(ii)** $x^2 + 2x + 4 = 0$

(iii) $x^2 - 5x - 19 = 0$ **(iv)** $(x - 2)^2 = 5$

(v) $(2x + 1)^2 = \frac{3}{4}$

9 The length of a rectangular field is 30 m greater than its width, w metres.

(i) Write down an expression for the area $A\,\text{m}^2$ of the field, in terms of w.

(ii) The area of the field is $8800\,\text{m}^2$. Find its width and perimeter.

10 The height h metres of a ball at time t seconds after it is thrown up in the air is given by the expression

$$h = 1 + 15t - 5t^2.$$

(i) Find the times at which the height is $11\,\text{m}$.

(ii) Use your calculator to find the time at which the ball hits the ground.

(iii) What is the greatest height the ball reaches?

11 A cylindrical tin of height h cm and radius r cm, has surface area, including its top and bottom, $A\,\text{cm}^2$.

(i) Write down an expression for A in terms of r, h and π.

(ii) A tin of height 6 cm has surface area $54\pi\,\text{cm}^2$. What is the radius of the tin?

(iii) Another tin has the same diameter as height. Its surface area is $150\pi\,\text{cm}^2$. What is its radius?

12 When the first n positive integers are added together, their sum is given by

$$\tfrac{1}{2}n(n + 1).$$

(i) Demonstrate that this result holds for the case $n = 5$.

(ii) Find the value of n for which the sum is 105.

(iii) What is the smallest value of n for which the sum exceeds 1000?

13 The shortest side AB of a right-angled triangle is x cm long. The side BC is 1 cm longer than AB and the hypotenuse, AC, is 29 cm long.

Form an equation for x and solve it to find the lengths of the three sides of the triangle.

14 The cost of an anorak rose by £6. As a result a shop could buy 5 fewer anoraks for £600. If the cost of the anorak was £x before the rise, find expressions, in terms of x, for the number of anoraks which could be bought before and after the rise. Hence form an equation in x and show that it reduces to $x^2 + 6x - 720 = 0$. Solve this equation and state the original cost of the anorak.

[MEI]

15 A grower planned to plant 160 fruit trees in a new orchard. He planted n equal rows. Write down an expression for the number of trees in each row.

He noticed that if he had had ten more trees he could have planted two more rows, but with three trees fewer in each row. Write down an equation involving n.

Show that the equation can be rewritten as

$$3n^2 + 16n - 320 = 0.$$

Solve this equation, and hence find the number of rows of trees that he actually planted.

[MEI]

16 (i) Show by substituting numbers for a and b that $(a + b)^2$ does not equal $a^2 + b^2$.

(ii) What does $(a + b)^2$ equal?

(iii) The lengths in this figure are as shown.

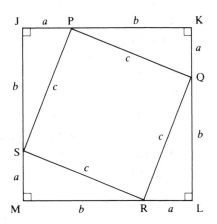

Find the area of JKLM in these two ways:

(a) as a square (in terms of a and b);

(b) as square PQRS (in terms of c) and four triangles.

(iv) Make an equation by putting your answers to (iii) equal to each other and simplify it.

(v) What well known theorem have you proved?

Simultaneous equations

There are many situations which can only be described mathematically in terms of more than one variable. When you need to find the values of the variables in such situations, you need to solve two or more equations simultaneously (i.e. at the same time). Such equations are called *simultaneous equations*. If you need to find values of two variables, you will need to solve two simultaneous equations; if three variables, then three equations, and so on. The work here is confined to solving two equations to find the values of two variables, but most of the methods can be extended to more variables if required.

EXAMPLE 1.33

At a poultry farm, six hens and one duck cost £40, while four hens and three ducks cost £36. What is the cost of each type of bird?

SOLUTION

Let the cost of one hen be £h and the cost of one duck be £d.

Then the information given can be written as:

$$6h + d = 40 \qquad ①$$
$$4h + 3d = 36. \qquad ②$$

There are several methods of solving this pair of equations.

Method 1: Elimination

Multiplying equation ① by 3	$\Rightarrow$	$18h + 3d = 120$
Leaving equation ②	$\Rightarrow$	$4h + 3d = 36$
Subtracting	$\Rightarrow$	$14h = 84$
Dividing both sides by 14	$\Rightarrow$	$h = 6$

Substituting $h = 6$ in equation ① gives		$36 + d = 40$
	$\Rightarrow$	$d = 4$

Therefore a hen costs £6 and a duck £4.

Note

1 The first step was to multiply equation ① by 3 so that there would be a term $3d$ in both equations. This meant that when equation ② was subtracted, the variable d was eliminated and so it was possible to find the value of h.

2 The value $h = 6$ was substituted in equation ① but it could equally well have been substituted in the other equation. Check for yourself that this too gives the answer $d = 4$.

Before looking at other methods for solving this pair of equations, here is another example.

EXAMPLE 1.34

Solve $\qquad$ $3x + 5y = 12$ $\qquad$ ①

$\qquad\qquad\quad$ $2x - 6y = -20$ $\qquad$ ②

SOLUTION

$$
\begin{array}{rlrr}
① \times 6 & \Rightarrow & 18x + 30y = & 72 \\
② \times 5 & \Rightarrow & 10x - 30y = & -100 \\
\text{Adding} & \Rightarrow & 28x \quad\quad = & -28 \\
\\
\text{Giving} & & x \quad = & -1
\end{array}
$$

Substituting $x = -1$ in equation ① $\quad\Rightarrow\qquad -3 + 5y = \quad 12$

Adding 3 to each side $\qquad\qquad\qquad\Rightarrow\qquad\qquad 5y = \quad 15$

Dividing by 5 $\qquad\qquad\qquad\qquad\quad\Rightarrow\qquad\qquad y = \quad 3$

Therefore $x = -1$, $y = 3$.

Note

In this example, both equations were multiplied, the first by 6 to give $+30y$ and the second by 5 to give $-30y$. Because one of these terms was positive and the other negative, it was necessary to add rather than subtract in order to eliminate y.

Returning now to the pair of equations giving the prices of hens and ducks,

$$
\begin{array}{rl}
6h + d & = 40 \qquad ① \\
4h + 3d & = 36 \qquad ②
\end{array}
$$

here are two alternative methods of solving them.

Method 2: Substitution

The equation $6h + d = 40$ is rearranged to make d its subject:

$$d = 40 - 6h.$$

This expression for d is now substituted in the other equation, $4h + 3d = 36$, giving

$$
\begin{array}{rl}
& 4h + 3(40 - 6h) = 36 \\
\Rightarrow & 4h + 120 - 18h = 36 \\
\Rightarrow & -14h = -84 \\
\Rightarrow & h = 6
\end{array}
$$

Substituting for h in $d = 40 - 6h$ gives $d = 40 - 36 = 4$.

Therefore a hen costs £6 and a duck £4 (the same answer as before, of course).

Method 3: Intersection of the graphs of the equations

Figure 1.12 shows the graphs of the two equations, $6h + d = 40$ and $4h + 3d = 36$. As you can see, they intersect at the solution, $h = 6$ and $d = 4$.

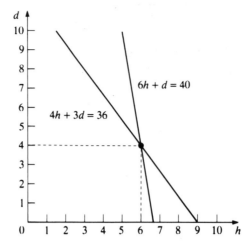

Figure 1.12

Non-linear simultaneous equations

The simultaneous equations in the examples so far have all been *linear*, that is their graphs have been straight lines. A linear equation in, say, x and y contains only terms in x and y and a constant term. So $7x + 2y = 11$ is linear but $7x^2 + 2y = 11$ is not linear, since it contains a term in x^2.

You can solve a pair of simultaneous equations, one of which is linear and the other not, using the substitution method. This is shown in the next example.

EXAMPLE 1.35

Solve
$$x + 2y = 7 \qquad ①$$
$$x^2 + y^2 = 10 \qquad ②$$

SOLUTION

Rearranging equation ① gives $x = 7 - 2y$.
Substituting for x in equation ②:

$$(7 - 2y)^2 + y^2 = 10$$

Multiplying out the $(7 - 2y) \times (7 - 2y)$

gives $49 - 14y - 14y + 4y^2 = 49 - 28y + 4y^2$,

so the equation is

$$49 - 28y + 4y^2 + y^2 = 10.$$

This is rearranged to give

$$5y^2 - 28y + 39 = 0$$
$$\Rightarrow \quad 5y^2 - 15y - 13y + 39 = 0$$
$$\Rightarrow \quad 5y(y - 3) - 13(y - 3) = 0$$
$$\Rightarrow \quad (5y - 13)(y - 3) = 0$$

A quadratic in y which you can now solve using factorisation or the formula.

Either $5y - 13 = 0 \Rightarrow y = 2.6$
Or $y - 3 = 0 \Rightarrow y = 3$

Substituting in equation ①, $x + 2y = 7$:

$$y = 2.6 \Rightarrow x = 1.8$$
$$y = 3 \Rightarrow x = 1$$

The solution is either $x = 1.8, y = 2.6$ or $x = 1, y = 3$.

 Always substitute into the linear equation. Substituting in the quadratic will give you extra answers which are *not* correct.

EXERCISE 1E

 For the routine questions (numbers 1 and 5), solve the pairs of simultaneous equations, and if possible use a calculator or a computer algebra system to check your answers.

1 Solve the following pairs of simultaneous equations.

(i) $2x + 3y = 8$
    $3x + 2y = 7$

(ii) $x + 4y = 16$
     $3x + 5y = 20$

(iii) $7x + y = 15$
      $4x + 3y = 11$

(iv) $5x - 2y = 3$
     $x + 4y = 5$

(v) $8x - 3y = 21$
     $5x + y = 16$

(vi) $8x + y = 32$
     $7x - 9y = 28$

(vii) $4x + 3y = 5$
      $2x - 6y = -5$

(viii) $3u - 2v = 17$
       $5u - 3v = 28$

(ix) $4l - 3m = 2$
     $5l - 7m = 9$

2 A student wishes to spend exactly £10 at a second-hand bookshop. All the paperbacks are one price, all the hardbacks another. She can buy five paperbacks and eight hardbacks. Alternatively she can buy ten paperbacks and six hardbacks.

(i) Write this information as a pair of simultaneous equations.
(ii) Solve your equations to find the cost of each type of book.

3 The cost of a pear is 5p greater than that of an apple. Eight apples and nine pears cost £1.64.

(i) Write this information as a pair of simultaneous equations.
(ii) Solve your equations to find the cost of each type of fruit.

4 A car journey of 380 km lasts 4 hours. Part of this is on a motorway at an average speed of $110 \, \text{km h}^{-1}$, the rest on country roads at an average speed of $70 \, \text{km h}^{-1}$.

(i)   Write this information as a pair of simultaneous equations.

(ii) Solve your equations to find how many kilometres of the journey is spent on each type of road.

5 Solve the following pairs of simultaneous equations.

(i) $x^2 + y^2 = 10$
       $x + y = 4$

(ii) $x^2 - 2y^2 = 8$
       $x + 2y = 8$

(iii) $2x^2 + 3y = 12$
       $x - y = -1$

(iv) $k^2 + km = 8$
       $m = k - 6$

(v) $t_1^2 - t_2^2 = 75$
       $t_1 = 2t_2$

(vi) $p + q + 5 = 0$
       $p^2 = q^2 + 5$

(vii) $k(k - m) = 12$
       $k(k + m) = 60$

(viii) $p_1^2 - p_2^2 = 0$
       $p_1 + p_2 = 2$

6 The diagram shows the net of a cylindrical container of radius r cm and height h cm. The full width of the metal sheet from which the container is made is 1 m, and the shaded area is waste. The surface area of the container is $1400\pi \, \text{cm}^2$.

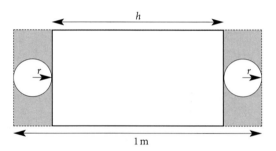

(i)   Write down a pair of simultaneous equations for r and h.

(ii) Find the volume of the container, giving your answers in terms of π. (There are two possible answers.)

7 A large window consists of six square panes of glass as shown. Each pane is x m by x m, and all the dividing wood is y m wide.

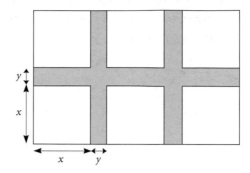

(i) Write down the total area of the whole window in terms of x and y.

(ii) Show that the total area of the dividing wood is $7xy + 2y^2$.

(iii) The total area of glass is 1.5 m², and the total area of dividing wood is 1 m². Find x, and hence find an equation for y and solve it.

[MEI]

KEY POINTS

Each chapter in this series of books ends with *Key points*: a summary of the essential ideas that you should have understood in the chapter. Chapter 1 of this book, however, is so fundamental that it is impossible to draw out individual key points from it. You will need to be confident on all the techniques covered in this chapter if you are to understand the rest of your course.

Co-ordinate geometry

2

A place for everything, and everything in its place

Samuel Smiles

Co-ordinates

Co-ordinates are a means of describing a position relative to some fixed point, or origin. In two dimensions you need two pieces of information; in three dimensions, you need three pieces of information.

In the Cartesian system (named after René Descartes), position is given in perpendicular directions: x, y in two dimensions; x, y, z in three dimensions (see figure 2.1). This chapter concentrates exclusively on two dimensions.

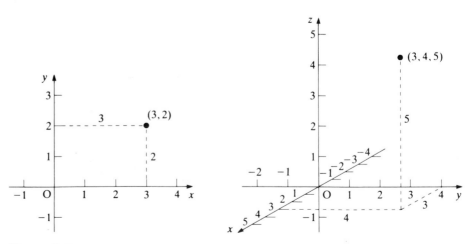

Figure 2.1

Plotting, sketching and drawing

In two dimensions, the co-ordinates of points are often marked on paper and joined up to form lines or curves. A number of words are used to describe this process.

Plot (a line or curve) means mark the points and join them up as accurately as you can. You would expect to do this on graph paper and be prepared to read information from the graph.

Sketch means mark points in approximately the right positions and join them up in the right general shape. You would not expect to use graph paper for a sketch and would not read precise information from one. You would however mark on the co-ordinates of important points, like intersections with the x and y axes and points at which the curve changes direction.

Draw means that you are to use a level of accuracy appropriate to the circumstances, and this could be anything between a rough sketch and a very accurately plotted graph.

The gradient of a line

In everyday English the word *line* is used to mean a straight line or a curve. In mathematics it is usually understood to mean a straight line. If you know the co-ordinates of any two points on a line, then you can draw the line.

The slope of a line is measured by its *gradient*. It is often denoted by the letter m.

In figure 2.2, A and B are two points on the line. The gradient of the line AB is given by the increase in the y co-ordinate from A to B divided by the increase in the x co-ordinate from A to B.

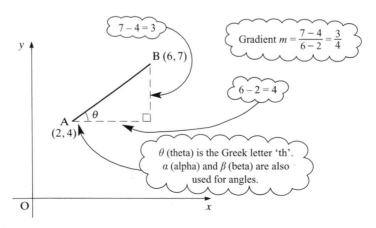

Figure 2.2

In general, when A is the point (x_1, y_1) and B is the point (x_2, y_2), the gradient is

$$m = \frac{y_2 - y_1}{x_2 - x_1}.$$

When the same scale is used on both axes, $m = \tan\theta$ (see figure 2.2).

Figure 2.3 shows four lines. Looking at each one from left to right: line A goes uphill and its gradient is positive; line B goes downhill and its gradient is negative. Line C is horizontal and its gradient is 0; the vertical line D has an infinite gradient.

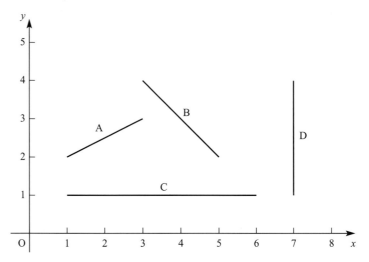

Figure 2.3

ACTIVITY 2.1   On each line in figure 2.3, take any two points and call them (x_1, y_1) and (x_2, y_2). Substitute the values of x_1, y_1, x_2 and y_2 in the formula

$$m = \frac{y_2 - y_1}{x_2 - x_1}$$

and so find the gradient.

?   Does it matter which point you call (x_1, y_1) and which (x_2, y_2)?

Parallel and perpendicular lines

If you know the gradients m_1 and m_2, of two lines, you can tell at once if they are either parallel or perpendicular – see figure 2.4.

parallel lines: $m_1 = m_2$ perpendicular lines: $m_1 m_2 = -1$

Figure 2.4

Lines which are parallel have the same slope and so $m_1 = m_2$. If the lines are perpendicular, $m_1 m_2 = -1$. You can see why this is so in the activities below.

ACTIVITY 2.2 Draw the line L_1 joining $(0, 2)$ to $(4, 4)$, and draw another line L_2 perpendicular to L_1. Find the gradients m_1 and m_2 of these two lines and show that $m_1 m_2 = -1$.

ACTIVITY 2.3

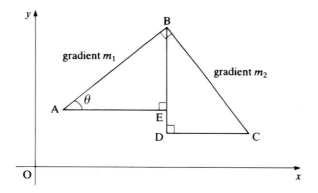

Figure 2.5

The lines AB and BC in figure 2.5 are equal in length and perpendicular. By showing that triangles ABE and BCD are congruent prove that the gradients m_1 and m_2 must satisfy $m_1 m_2 = -1$.

 Lines for which $m_1 m_2 = -1$ will only look perpendicular if the same scale has been used for both axes.

The distance between two points

When the co-ordinates of two points are known, the distance between them can be calculated using Pythagoras' theorem, as shown in figure 2.6.

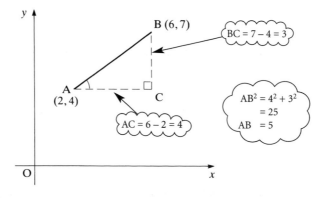

Figure 2.6

This method can be generalised to find the distance between any two points, $A(x_1, y_1)$ and $B(x_2, y_2)$, as in figure 2.7.

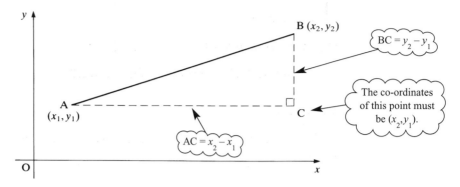

Figure 2.7

The length of the line AB is $\sqrt{(x_2 - x_1)^2 + (y_2 - y_1)^2}$.

The mid-point of a line joining two points

Look at the line joining the points A(2, 1) and B(8, 5) in figure 2.8. The point M(5, 3) is the mid-point of AB.

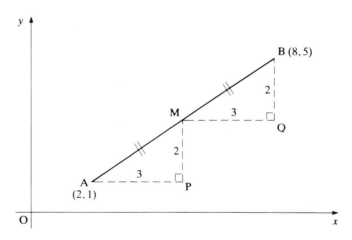

Figure 2.8

Notice that the co-ordinates of M are the means of the co-ordinates of A and B.

$$5 = \tfrac{1}{2}(2 + 8); \qquad 3 = \tfrac{1}{2}(1 + 5).$$

This result can be generalised as follows. For any two points $A(x_1, y_1)$ and $B(x_2, y_2)$, the co-ordinates of the mid-point of AB are the means of the co-ordinates of A and B so the mid-point is

$$\left(\frac{x_1 + x_2}{2}, \frac{y_1 + y_2}{2} \right).$$

EXAMPLE 2.1

A and B are the points (2, 5) and (6, 3) respectively (see figure 2.9). Find:

(i) the gradient of AB

(ii) the length of AB

(iii) the mid-point of AB

(iv) the gradient of the line perpendicular to AB.

SOLUTION

Taking A(2, 5) as the point (x_1, y_1), and B(6, 3) as the point (x_2, y_2) gives $x_1 = 2$, $y_1 = 5$, $x_2 = 6$, $y_2 = 3$.

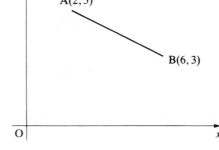

(i) Gradient $= \dfrac{y_2 - y_1}{x_2 - x_1}$

$= \dfrac{3 - 5}{6 - 2} = -\dfrac{1}{2}$

(ii) Length AB $= \sqrt{(x_2 - x_1)^2 + (y_2 - y_1)^2}$

$= \sqrt{(6 - 2)^2 + (3 - 5)^2}$

$= \sqrt{16 + 4} = \sqrt{20}$

Figure 2.9

(iii) Mid-point $= \left(\dfrac{x_1 + x_2}{2}, \dfrac{y_1 + y_2}{2} \right)$

$= \left(\dfrac{2 + 6}{2}, \dfrac{5 + 3}{2} \right) = (4, 4)$

(iv) Gradient of AB $= m_1 = -\frac{1}{2}$.

If m_2 is the gradient of the line perpendicular to AB, then $m_1 m_2 = -1$

$\Rightarrow -\frac{1}{2} m_2 = -1$

$m_2 = 2$.

EXAMPLE 2.2

Using two different methods, show that the lines joining P(2, 7), Q(3, 2) and R(0, 5) form a right-angled triangle (see figure 2.10).

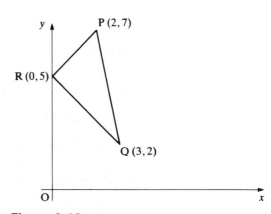

Figure 2.10

SOLUTION

Method 1

Gradient of RP $= \dfrac{7-5}{2-0} = 1$

Gradient of RQ $= \dfrac{2-5}{3-0} = -1$

$\Rightarrow$ product of gradients $= 1 \times (-1) = -1$

$\Rightarrow$ sides RP and RQ are at right angles.

Method 2

Pythagoras' theorem states that for a right-angled triangle whose hypotenuse has length a and whose other sides have lengths b and c, $a^2 = b^2 + c^2$.

Conversely, if you can show that $a^2 = b^2 + c^2$ for a triangle with sides of lengths a, b, and c, then the triangle has a right angle and the side of length a is the hypotenuse.

This is the basis for the alternative proof, in which you use

$$\text{length}^2 = (x_2 - x_1)^2 + (y_2 - y_1)^2.$$

$$PQ^2 = (3-2)^2 + (2-7)^2 = 1 + 25 = 26$$

$$RP^2 = (2-0)^2 + (7-5)^2 = 4 + 4 = 8$$

$$RQ^2 = (3-0)^2 + (2-5)^2 = 9 + 9 = 18$$

Since $26 = 8 + 18$, $\quad PQ^2 = RP^2 + RQ^2$

$\Rightarrow \quad$ sides RP and RQ are at right angles.

EXERCISE 2A

1 For the following pairs of points A and B, calculate:

  (a) the gradient of the line AB
  (b) the mid-point of the line joining A to B
  (c) the distance AB
  (d) the gradient of the line perpendicular to AB.

  (i) A(0, 1)   B(2, −3)   (ii) A(3, 2)   B(4, −1)
  (iii) A(−6, 3)   B(6, 3)   (iv) A(5, 2)   B(2, −8)
  (v) A(4, 3)   B(2, 0)   (vi) A(1, 4)   B(1, −2)

2 The line joining the point P(3, −4) to Q(q, 0) has a gradient of 2. Find the value of q.

3 The three points X(2, −1), Y(8, y) and Z(11, 2) are collinear (i.e. they lie on the same straight line).

  Find the value of y.

4 The points A, B, C and D have co-ordinates $(1, 2)$, $(7, 5)$, $(9, 8)$ and $(3, 5)$.

   (i) Find the gradients of the lines AB, BC, CD and DA.

   (ii) What do these gradients tell you about the quadrilateral ABCD?

   (iii) Draw a diagram to check your answer to part (ii).

5 The points A, B and C have co-ordinates $(2, 1)$, $(b, 3)$ and $(5, 5)$, where $b > 3$ and $\angle ABC = 90°$. Find:

   (i) the value of b

   (ii) the lengths of AB and BC

   (iii) the area of triangle ABC.

6 The triangle PQR has vertices $P(8, 6)$, $Q(0, 2)$ and $R(2, r)$. Find the values of r when the triangle:

   (i) has a right angle at P

   (ii) has a right angle at Q

   (iii) has a right angle at R

   (iv) is isosceles with RQ = RP.

7 The points A, B, and C have co-ordinates $(-4, 2)$, $(7, 4)$ and $(-3, -1)$.

   (i) Draw the triangle ABC.

   (ii) Show by calculation that the triangle ABC is isosceles and name the two equal sides.

   (iii) Find the mid-point of the third side.

   (iv) By calculating appropriate lengths, calculate the area of the triangle ABC.

8 For the points $P(x, y)$, and $Q(3x, 5y)$, find in terms of x and y:

   (i) the gradient of the line PQ

   (ii) the mid-point of the line PQ

   (iii) the length of the line PQ.

9 A quadrilateral has vertices $A(0, 0)$, $B(0, 3)$, $C(6, 6)$, and $D(12, 6)$.

   (i) Draw the quadrilateral.

   (ii) Show by calculation that it is a trapezium.

   (iii) Find the co-ordinates of E when EBCD is a parallelogram.

10 Three points A, B and C have co-ordinates $(1, 3)$, $(3, 5)$, and $(-1, y)$. Find the values of y when:

   (i) AB = AC

   (ii) AC = BC

   (iii) AB is perpendicular to BC

   (iv) A, B and C are collinear.

11 The diagonals of a rhombus bisect each other at 90°, and conversely, when two lines bisect each other at 90°, the quadrilateral formed by joining the end points of the lines is a rhombus.

Use the converse result to show that the points with co-ordinates $(1, 2)$, $(8, -2)$, $(7, 6)$ and $(0, 10)$ are the vertices of a rhombus, and find its area.

The equation of a straight line

The word *straight* means going in a constant direction, that is with fixed gradient. This fact allows you to find the equation of a straight line from first principles.

EXAMPLE 2.3

Find the equation of the straight line with gradient 2 through the point $(0, -5)$.

SOLUTION

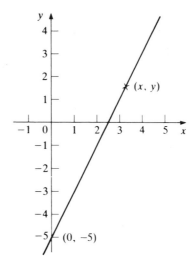

Figure 2.11

Take a general point (x, y) on the line, as shown in figure 2.11. The gradient of the line joining $(0, -5)$ to (x, y) is given by

$$\text{gradient} = \frac{y - (-5)}{x - 0} = \frac{y + 5}{x}.$$

Since we are told that the gradient of the line is 2, this gives

$$\frac{y + 5}{x} = 2$$

$$\Rightarrow \qquad y = 2x - 5.$$

Since (x, y) is a general point on the line, this holds for any point on the line and is therefore the equation of the line.

The example above can easily be generalised (see pages 46 to 47) to give the result that the equation of the line with gradient m cutting the y axis at the point $(0, c)$ is

$$y = mx + c.$$

(In the example above, m is 2 and c is -5.)

This is a well-known standard form for the equation of a straight line.

Drawing a line, given its equation

There are several standard forms for the equation of a straight line, as shown in figure 2.12.

When you need to draw the graph of a straight line, given its equation, the first thing to do is to look carefully at the form of the equation and see if you can recognise it.

(a) Equations of the form x = a

(b) Equations of the form y = b

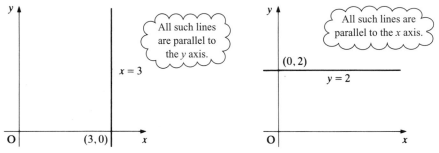

(c) Equations of the form y = mx

(d) Equations of the form y = mx + c

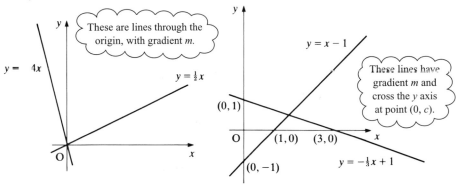

(e) Equations of the form px + qy + r = 0

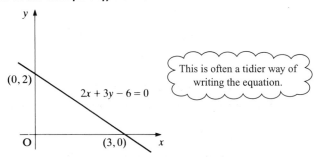

Figure 2.12

(a), (b): *Lines parallel to the axes*

Lines parallel to the x axis have the form $y =$ constant, those parallel to the y axis the form $x =$ constant. Such lines are easily recognised and drawn.

(c), (d): *Equations of the form y = mx + c*

The line $y = mx + c$ crosses the y axis at the point $(0, c)$ and has gradient m. If $c = 0$, it goes through the origin. In either case you know one point and can complete the line either by finding one more point, for example by substituting $x = 1$, or by following the gradient (e.g. 1 along and 2 up for gradient 2).

(e): *Equations of the form px + qy + r = 0*

In the case of a line given in this form, like $2x + 3y - 6 = 0$, you can either rearrange it in the form $y = mx + c$ (in this example $y = -\frac{2}{3}x + 2$), or you can find the co-ordinates of two points that lie on it. Putting $x = 0$ gives the point where it crosses the y axis, $(0, 2)$, and putting $y = 0$ gives its intersection with the x axis, $(3, 0)$.

EXAMPLE 2.4

Sketch the lines $x = 5$, $y = 0$ and $y = x$ on the same axes.
Describe the triangle formed by these lines.

SOLUTION

The line $x = 5$ is parallel to the y axis and passes through $(5, 0)$.
The line $y = 0$ is the x axis.
The line $y = x$ has gradient 1 and goes through the origin.

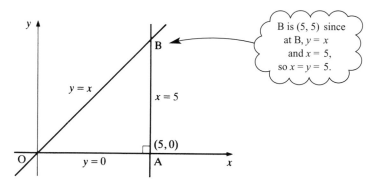

B is (5, 5) since at B, $y = x$ and $x = 5$, so $x = y = 5$.

Figure 2.13

The triangle obtained is an isosceles right-angled triangle, since OA = AB = 5 units, and $\angle$OAB = 90°.

EXAMPLE 2.5

Sketch $y = x - 1$ and $3x + 4y = 24$ on the same axes.

SOLUTION

(i) The line $y = x - 1$ has gradient 1, and passes throught the point $(0, -1)$.
Substituting $y = 0$ gives $x = 1$, so the line also passes through $(1, 0)$.

(ii) Find two points on the line $3x + 4y = 24$.
Substituting $x = 0$ gives $4y = 24$ i.e. $y = 6$
substituting $y = 0$ gives $3x = 24$ i.e. $x = 8$.

The line passes through (0, 6) and (8, 0).

Figure 2.14

In this exercise, you should sketch the lines by hand. You can use a graphic calculator or computer graphics package to check your results.

1 Sketch the following lines.

(i)	$y = -2$	**(ii)**	$x = 5$
(iii)	$y = 2x$	**(iv)**	$y = -3x$
(v)	$y = 3x + 5$	**(vi)**	$y = x - 4$
(vii)	$y = x + 4$	**(viii)**	$y = \frac{1}{2}x + 2$
(ix)	$y = 2x + \frac{1}{2}$	**(x)**	$y = -4x + 8$
(xi)	$y = 4x - 8$	**(xii)**	$y = -x + 1$
(xiii)	$y = -\frac{1}{2}x - 2$	**(xiv)**	$y = 1 - 2x$
(xv)	$3x - 2y = 6$	**(xvi)**	$2x + 5y = 10$
(xvii)	$2x + y - 3 = 0$	**(xviii)**	$2y = 5x - 4$
(xix)	$x + 3y - 6 = 0$	**(xx)**	$y = 2 - x$

2 By calculating the gradients of the following pairs of lines, state whether they are parallel, perpendicular or neither.

(i)	$y = -4$	$x = 2$
(ii)	$y = 3x$	$x = 3y$
(iii)	$2x + y = 1$	$x - 2y = 1$
(iv)	$y = 2x + 3$	$4x - y + 1 = 0$
(v)	$3x - y + 2 = 0$	$3x + y = 0$
(vi)	$2x + 3y = 4$	$2y = 3x - 2$
(vii)	$x + 2y - 1 = 0$	$x + 2y + 1 = 0$
(viii)	$y = 2x - 1$	$2x - y + 3 = 0$
(ix)	$y = x - 2$	$x + y = 6$
(x)	$y = 4 - 2x$	$x + 2y = 8$
(xi)	$x + 3y - 2 = 0$	$y = 3x + 2$
(xii)	$y = 2x$	$4x + 2y = 5$

45

Finding the equation of a line

The simplest way to find the equation of a straight line depends on what information you have been given.

(i) *Given the gradient, m, and the co-ordinates (x_1, y_1) of one point on the line*

Take a general point (x, y) on the line, as shown in figure 2.15.

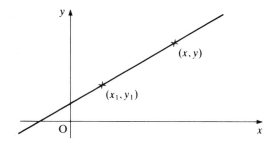

Figure 2.15

The gradient, m, of the line joining (x_1, y_1) to (x, y) is given by

$$m = \frac{y - y_1}{x - x_1}$$

$$\Rightarrow \quad y - y_1 = m(x - x_1).$$

This is a very useful form of the equation of a straight line. Two positions of the point (x_1, y_1) lead to particularly important forms of the equation.

(a) When the given point (x_1, y_1) is the point $(0, c)$ where the line crosses the y axis, the equation takes the familiar form

$$y = mx + c$$

as shown in figure 2.16.

(b) When the given point (x_1, y_1) is the origin, the equation takes the form

$$y = mx$$

as shown in figure 2.17.

Figure 2.16

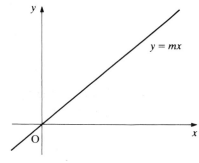

Figure 2.17

EXAMPLE 2.6

Find the equation of the line with gradient 3 which passes through the point $(2, -4)$.

SOLUTION

Using $y - y_1 = m(x - x_1)$
$\Rightarrow y - (-4) = 3(x - 2)$
$\Rightarrow \quad y + 4 = 3x - 6$
$\Rightarrow \quad\quad y = 3x - 10.$

(ii) *Given two points, (x_1, y_1) and (x_2, y_2)*

The two points are used to find the gradient:

$$m = \frac{y_2 - y_1}{x_2 - x_1}.$$

This value of m is then substituted in the equation

$$y - y_1 = m(x - x_1).$$

This gives $\quad y - y_1 = \left(\dfrac{y_2 - y_1}{x_2 - x_1}\right)(x - x_1).$

Rearranging the equation gives

$$\frac{y - y_1}{y_2 - y_1} = \frac{x - x_1}{x_2 - x_1} \quad \text{or} \quad \frac{y - y_1}{x - x_1} = \frac{y_2 - y_1}{x_2 - x_1}.$$

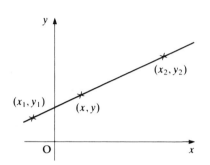

Figure 2.18

EXAMPLE 2.7

Find the equation of the line joining $(2, 4)$ to $(5, 3)$.

SOLUTION

Taking (x_1, y_1) to be $(2, 4)$ and (x_2, y_2) to be $(5, 3)$, and substituting the values in

$$\frac{y - y_1}{y_2 - y_1} = \frac{x - x_1}{x_2 - x_1}$$

gives

$$\frac{y - 4}{3 - 4} = \frac{x - 2}{5 - 2}.$$

This can be simplified to

$$x + 3y - 14 = 0.$$

❓ Show that the equation of the line in figure 2.19 can be written

$$\frac{x}{a} + \frac{y}{b} = 1.$$

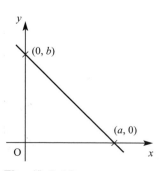

Figure 2.19

Different techniques to solve practical problems

The following examples illustrate the different techniques, and show how these can be used to solve a practical problem.

EXAMPLE 2.8

Find the equations of the lines (a) – (e) in figure 2.20.

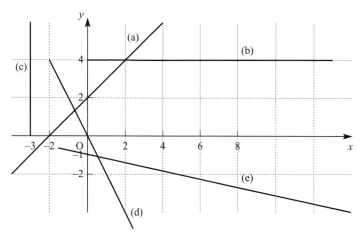

Figure 2.20

SOLUTION

Line (a) passes through $(0, 2)$ and has gradient 1
$\Rightarrow$ equation of (a) is $y = x + 2$.

Line (b) is parallel to the x axis and passes through $(0, 4)$
$\Rightarrow$ equation of (b) is $y = 4$.

Line (c) is parallel to the y axis and passes through $(-3, 0)$
$\Rightarrow$ equation of (c) is $x = -3$.

Line (d) passes through $(0, 0)$ and has gradient -2
$\Rightarrow$ equation of (d) is $y = -2x$.

Line (e) passes through $(0, -1)$ and has gradient $-\frac{1}{5}$
$\Rightarrow$ equation of (e) is $y = -\frac{1}{5}x - 1$.

This can be rearranged to give $x + 5y + 5 = 0$.

EXAMPLE 2.9

Two sides of a parallelogram are the lines $2y = x + 12$ and $y = 4x - 10$. Sketch these lines on the same diagram.

The origin is a vertex of the parallelogram. Complete the sketch of the parallelogram, and find the equations of the other two sides.

SOLUTION

The line $2y = x + 12$ has gradient $\frac{1}{2}$ and passes through the point $(0, 6)$

(since dividing by 2 gives $y = \frac{1}{2}x + 6$).

The line $y = 4x - 10$ has gradient 4 and passes through the point $(0, -10)$.

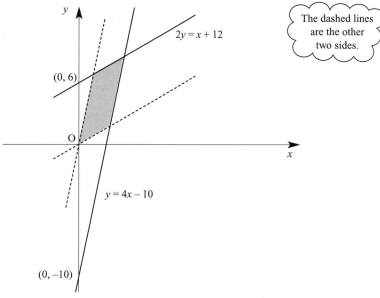

The dashed lines are the other two sides.

Figure 2.21

The other two sides are lines with gradients $\frac{1}{2}$ and 4 which pass through $(0, 0)$,

i.e. $y = \frac{1}{2}x$ and $y = 4x$.

EXAMPLE 2.10

Find the equation of the perpendicular bisector of the line joining P$(-4, 5)$ to Q$(2, 3)$.

SOLUTION

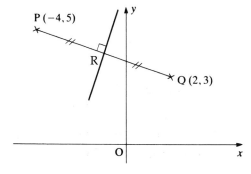

Figure 2.22

The gradient of the line PQ is

$$\frac{3-5}{2-(-4)} = \frac{-2}{6} = -\frac{1}{3}$$

and so the gradient of the perpendicular bisector is $+3$.

The perpendicular bisector passes throught the mid-point, R, of the line PQ. The co-ordinates of R are

$$\left(\frac{2+(-4)}{2}, \frac{3+5}{2}\right) \text{ i.e. } (-1, 4).$$

Using $y - y_1 = m(x - x_1)$, the equation of the perpendicular bisector is
$$y - 4 = 3(x - (-1))$$
$$y - 4 = 3x + 3$$
$$y = 3x + 7.$$

EXAMPLE 2.11

The diameter of a snooker cue varies uniformly from 9 mm to 23 mm over its length of 140 cm. (*Varying uniformly* means that the graph of diameter against distance from the tip is a straight line.)

(i) Sketch the graph of diameter (y mm) against distance (x cm) from the tip.

(ii) Find the equation of the line.

(iii) Use the equation to find the distance from the tip at which the diameter is 15 mm.

SOLUTION

(i) The graph passes through the points $(0, 9)$ and $(140, 23)$

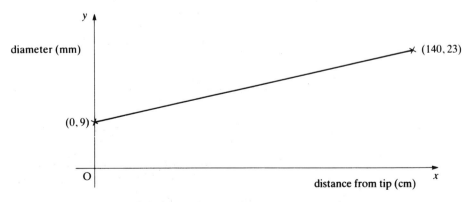

Figure 2.23

(ii) Gradient $= \dfrac{y_2 - y_1}{x_2 - x_1}$

$$= \frac{23 - 9}{140 - 0} = 0.1$$

Using the form $y = mx + c$, the equation of the line is $y = 0.1x + 9$.

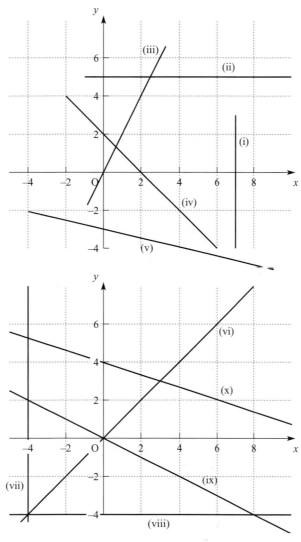

(iii) Substituting $y = 15$ into the equation gives

$$15 = 0.1x + 9$$
$$0.1x = 6$$
$$x = 60$$

$\Rightarrow$ the diameter is 15 mm at a point 60 cm from the tip.

EXERCISE 2C

1 Find the equations of the lines (i) – (x) in the diagrams below.

2 Find the equations of the following lines.

  (i) parallel to $y = 2x$ and passing through $(1, 5)$
  (ii) parallel to $y = 3x - 1$ and passing through $(0, 0)$
  (iii) parallel to $2x + y - 3 = 0$ and passing through $(-4, 5)$
  (iv) parallel to $3x - y - 1 = 0$ and passing through $(4, -2)$
  (v) parallel to $2x + 3y = 4$ and passing through $(2, 2)$
  (vi) parallel to $2x - y - 8 = 0$ and passing through $(-1, -5)$

3 Find the equations of the following lines.

    (i) perpendicular to $y = 3x$ and passing through $(0, 0)$
    (ii) perpendicular to $y = 2x + 3$ and passing through $(2, -1)$
    (iii) perpendicular to $2x + y = 4$ and passing through $(3, 1)$
    (iv) perpendicular to $2y = x + 5$ and passing through $(-1, 4)$
    (v) perpendicular to $2x + 3y = 4$ and passing through $(5, -1)$
    (vi) perpendicular to $4x - y + 1 = 0$ and passing through $(0, 6)$

4 Find the equations of the line AB in each of the following cases.

    (i) A$(0, 0)$ B$(4, 3)$
    (ii) A$(2, -1)$ B$(3, 0)$
    (iii) A$(2, 7)$ B$(2, -3)$
    (iv) A$(3, 5)$ B$(5, -1)$
    (v) A$(-2, 4)$ B$(5, 3)$
    (vi) A$(-4, -2)$ B$(3, -2)$

5 Triangle ABC has an angle of 90° at B. Point A is on the y axis, AB is part of the line $x - 2y + 8 = 0$, and C is the point $(6, 2)$.

    (i) Sketch the triangle.
    (ii) Find the equations AC and BC.
    (iii) Find the lengths of AB and BC and hence find the area of the triangle.
    (iv) Using your answer to (iii), find the length of the perpendicular from B to AC.

6 A median of a triangle is a line joining one of the vertices to the mid-point of the opposite side.

In a triangle OAB, O is at the origin, A is the point $(0, 6)$, and B is the point $(6, 0)$.

    (i) Sketch the triangle.
    (ii) Find the equations of the three medians of the triangle.
    (iii) Show that the point $(2, 2)$ lies on all three medians. (This shows that the medians of this triangle are concurrent.)

7 A quadrilateral ABCD has its vertices at the points $(0, 0)$, $(12, 5)$, $(0, 10)$ and $(-6, 8)$ respectively.

    (i) Sketch the quadrilateral.
    (ii) Find the gradient of each side.
    (iii) Find the length of each side.
    (iv) Find the equation of each side.
    (v) Find the area of the quadrilateral.

8 A sum of £5 000 is invested and simple interest is paid at a rate of 8%.

    (i) Calculate the interest received after 1, 2, and 3 years, and hence sketch the graph of interest against time, and find its equation.

    (ii) Use the equation to find the length of time for which the money must be invested for the total interest to reach £2500.

Adding the interest to the sum invested gives the *amount* of the investment after a period of time.

    (iii) Sketch the graph of *amount* against time and find its equation.

9 Use your calculator for this question.

For the tax year 1998–99 the Personal Allowance set against tax was £4045 for a single person. After this and any other allowances were deducted, the first £4300 of income was taxed at 20%, the next £22 800 was taxed at 23%, and the rest at 40%. Anyone earning less than £4045 per annum (p.a.) did not pay tax.

For a single person with no other allowances to deduct:

    (i) calculate the tax paid on a salary of

        (a) £8345 p.a.

        (b) £15 000 p.a.

    (ii) sketch the graph of tax paid against salary for salaries up to £30 000 (put salary on the horizontal axis)

    (iii) using the symbols S for salary and T for tax, and writing each equation in the form $T = mS + c$, find the equations of the lines corresponding to salaries:

        (a) between £4045 and £8345

        (b) between £8345 and £30 000

    (iv) use the equations to find the tax paid on salaries of

        (a) £8000   **(b)** £18 000   **(c)** £25 000.

10 A firm manufacturing jackets finds that it is capable of producing 100 jackets per day, but it can only sell all of these if the charge to the wholesalers is no more than £20 per jacket. On the other hand, at the current price of £25 per jacket, only 50 can be sold per day.

Assuming that the graph of price P against number sold per day N is a straight line:

    (i) sketch the graph, putting the number sold per day on the horizontal axis (as is normal practice for economists)

    (ii) find its equation.

Use the equation to find:

    (iii) the price at which 88 jackets per day could be sold

    (iv) the number of jackets that should be manufactured if they were to be sold at £23.70 each.

11 Use your calculator for this question.

When the interest rate for deposits is 7%, a small building society attracts £35 million of savings. When the rate is increased to 8.5%, the savings increase by £2 million. Assuming that the graph of savings against interest rates is linear for interest rates between 5% and 12%:

(i) sketch the graph of savings (in £million) against interest rates (%) in this interval with interest rates on the horizontal axis

(ii) find the equation of the line

(iii) find the value of savings attracted by a rate of 11.5%

(iv) find the interest rate needed to attract savings of £40 million.

12 A spring has an unstretched length of 10 cm. When it is hung with a load of 80 g attached, the stretched length is 28 cm. Assuming that the extension of the spring is proportional to the load:

(i) draw a graph of extension E against load L and find its equation

(ii) find the extension caused by a load of 48 g

(iii) find the load required to extend the spring to a length of 20 cm.

This particular spring passes its elastic limit when it is stretched to four times its original length. (This means that if it is stretched more than that it will not return to its original length.)

(iv) Find the load which would cause this to happen.

13 To clean the upstairs window on the side of a house, it is necessary to position the ladder so that it just touches the edge of the lean-to shed as shown in the diagram. The co-ordinates represent distances from O in metres, in the x and y directions shown.

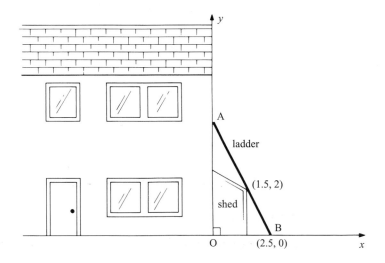

(i) Find the equation of the line of the ladder.

(ii) Find the height of the point A reached by the top of the ladder.

(iii) Find the length of the ladder to the nearest centimetre.

The intersection of two lines

The intersection of any two curves (or lines) can be found by solving their equations simultaneously. In the case of two distinct lines, there are two possibilities: (i) they are parallel, or (ii) they intersect at a single point.

EXAMPLE 2.12

Sketch the lines $x + 2y = 1$ and $2x + 3y = 4$ on the same axes, and find the co-ordinates of the point where they intersect.

SOLUTION

The line $x + 2y = 1$ passes through $(0, \frac{1}{2})$ and $(1, 0)$.

The line $2x + 3y = 4$ passes through $(0, \frac{4}{3})$ and $(2, 0)$.

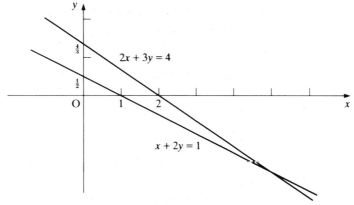

Figure 2.24

①: $x + 2y = 1$ ① × 2: $2x + 4y = 2$
②: $2x + 3y = 4$ ②: $2x + 3y = 4$
                    Subtract: $y = -2$.

Substituting $y = -2$ in ①: $x - 4 = 1$
                                 $\Rightarrow x = 5$.

The co-ordinates of the point of intersection are $(5, -2)$.

EXAMPLE 2.13

Find the co-ordinates of the vertices of the triangle whose sides have the equations $x + y = 4$, $2x - y = 8$ and $x + 2y = -1$.

SOLUTION

A sketch will be helpful, so first find where each line crosses the axes.

① $x + y = 4$ crosses the axes at $(0, 4)$ and $(4, 0)$.
② $2x - y = 8$ crosses the axes at $(0, -8)$ and $(4, 0)$.
③ $x + 2y = -1$ crosses the axes at $(0, -\frac{1}{2})$ and $(-1, 0)$.

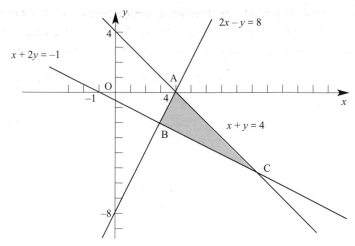

Figure 2.25

Since two lines pass through the point $(4, 0)$ this is clearly one of the vertices. It has been labelled A on figure 2.25.

Point B is found by solving ② and ③ simultaneously:

$$
\begin{array}{ll}
②\times 2: & 4x - 2y = 16 \\
③: & \underline{x + 2y = -1} \\
\text{Add} & 5x \quad\;\; = 15 \\
\Rightarrow & x \quad\;\; = \;\; 3.
\end{array}
$$

Back-substituting in ② gives $y = -2$, so B is the point $(3, -2)$.

Point C is found by solving ① and ③ simultaneously:

$$
\begin{array}{ll}
①: & x + \;\;y = \;\; 4 \\
③: & \underline{x + 2y = -1} \\
\text{Subtract} & -y = \;\; 5 \quad \text{so} \quad y = -5.
\end{array}
$$

Back-substitution gives $x = 9$, so C is the point $(9, -5)$.

❓ The line ℓ has equation $2x - y = 4$ and the line m has equation $y = 2x - 3$.

What can you say about the intersection of these two lines?

Historical note

René Descartes was born near Tours in France in 1596. At the age of eight he was sent to a Jesuit boarding school where, because of his frail health, he was allowed to stay in bed until late in the morning. This habit stayed with him for the rest of his life and he claimed that he was at his most productive before getting up.

After leaving school he studied mathematics in Paris before becoming in turn a soldier, traveller and optical instrument maker. Eventually he settled in Holland where he devoted his time to mathematics, science and philosophy, and wrote a number of books on these subjects.

In an appendix, entitled *La Géométrie*, to one of his books, Descartes made the contribution to co-ordinate geometry for which he is particularly remembered.

In 1649 he left Holland for Sweden at the invitation of Queen Christina but died there, of a lung infection, the following year.

EXERCISE 2D

1 **(i)** Find the vertices of the triangle ABC whose sides are given by the lines AB: $x - 2y = -1$, BC: $7x + 6y = 53$ and AC: $9x + 2y = 11$.

(ii) Show that the triangle is isosceles.

2 Two sides of a parallelogram are formed by parts of the lines $2x - y = -9$ and $x - 2y = -9$.

(i) Show these two lines on a graph.

(ii) Find the co-ordinates of the vertex where they intersect.

Another vertex of the parallelogram is the point $(2, 1)$.

(iii) Find the equations of the other two sides of the parallelogram.

(iv) Find the co-ordinates of the other two vertices.

3 A$(0, 1)$, B$(1, 4)$, C$(4, 3)$ and D$(3, 0)$ are the vertices of a quadrilateral ABCD.

(i) Find the equations of the diagonals AC and BD.

(ii) Show that the diagonals AC and BD bisect each other at right angles.

(iii) Find the lengths of AC and BD.

(iv) What type of quadrilateral is ABCD?

4 The line with equation $5x + y = 20$ meets the x axis at A and the line with equation $x + 2y = 22$ meets the y axis at B. The two lines intersect at a point C.

(i) Sketch the two lines on the same diagram.

(ii) Calculate the co-ordinates of A, B and C.

(iii) Calculate the area of triangle OBC where O is the origin.

(iv) Find the co-ordinates of the point E such that ABEC is a parallelogram.

5 Two rival taxi firms have the following fare structures:

firm A: fixed charge of £1 plus 40p per kilometre;
firm B: 60p per kilometre, no fixed charge.

(i) Sketch the graph of price (vertical axis) against distance travelled (horizontal axis) for each firm (on the same axes).

(ii) Find the equation of each line.

(iii) Find the distance for which both firms charge the same amount.

(iv) Which firm would you use for a distance of 6 km?

6 The diagram shows the *supply* and *demand* of labour for a particular industry in relation to the wage paid per hour.

Supply is the number of people willing to work for a particular wage, and this increases as the wage paid increases.
Demand is the number of workers that employers are prepared to employ at a particular wage: this is greatest for low wages.

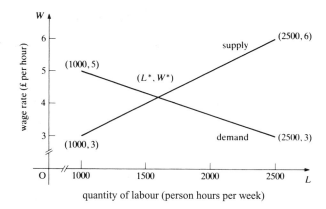

quantity of labour (person hours per week)

(i) Find the equation of each of the lines.
(ii) Find the values of L^* and W^* at which the market 'clears', i.e. at which *supply* equals *demand*.
(iii) Although economists draw the graph this way round, mathematicians would plot wage rate on the horizontal axis. Why?

7 A median of a triangle is a line joining a vertex to the mid-point of the opposite side. In any triangle, the three medians meet at a point.
The centroid of a triangle is at the point of intersection of the medians.

Find the co-ordinates of the centroid for each triangle shown.

(i)

(ii)

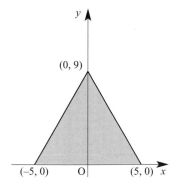

8 When the market price £p of an article sold in a free market varies, so does the number demanded, D, and the number supplied, S.
In one case $D = 20 + 0.2p$ and $S = -12 + p$.

(i) Sketch both of these lines on the same graph. (Put p on the horizontal axis.)

The market reaches a state of equilibrium when the number demanded equals the number supplied.

(ii) Find the equilibrium price and the number bought and sold in equilibrium.

9 You are given the co-ordinates of the four points

  A(6, 2), B(2, 4), C(–6, –2) and D(–2, –4).

(i) Calculate the gradients of the lines AB, CB, DC and DA.
Hence describe the shape of the figure ABCD.

(ii) Show that the equation of the line DA is $4y - 3x = -10$, and find the length DA.

(iii) Calculate the gradient of a line which is perpendicular to DA, and hence find the equation of the line l through B which is perpendicular to DA.

(iv) Calculate the co-ordinates of the point P where l meets DA.

(v) Calculate the area of the figure ABCD.

[MEI]

10 The diagram shows a triangle whose vertices are A(–2, 1), B(1, 7) and C(3, 1). The point L is the foot of the perpendicular from A to BC, and M is the foot of the perpendicular from B to AC.

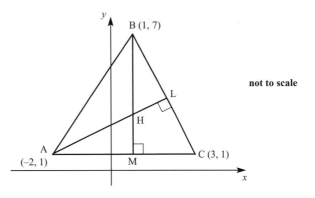

not to scale

(i) Find the gradient of the line BC.

(ii) Find the equation of the line AL.

(iii) Write down the equation of the line BM.

The lines AL and BM meet at H.

(iv) Find the co-ordinates of H.

(v) Show that CH is perpendicular to AB.

(vi) Find the area of the triangle BLH.

[MEI]

Curves

You can always plot a curve, point by point, if you know its equation. Often, however, all you need is a general idea of its shape and a sketch is quite sufficient.

Figures 2.26 and 2.27 show some common curves of the form $y = x^n$ for $n = 1, 2, 3$ and 4 and $y = \dfrac{1}{x^n}$ for $n = 1$ and 2.

Curves of the form $y = x^n$ for $n = 1, 2, 3$ and 4

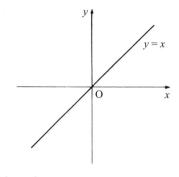

(a) $n = 1, y = x$

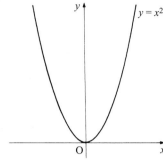

(b) $n = 2, y = x^2$

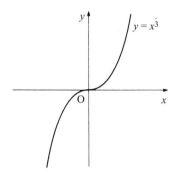

(c) $n = 3, y = x^3$

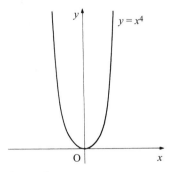

(d) $n = 4, y = x^4$

Figure 2.26

❓ How are the curves for even values of n different from those for odd values of n?

Curves of the form $y = \frac{1}{x^n}$ (for $x \neq 0$)

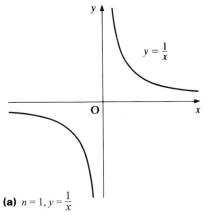

(a) $n = 1, y = \frac{1}{x}$

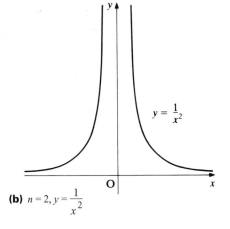

(b) $n = 2, y = \frac{1}{x^2}$

Figure 2.27

The curves for $n = 3, 5, \ldots$ are not unlike that for $n = 1$, those for $n = 4, 6, \ldots$ are like that for $n = 2$. In all cases the point $x = 0$ is excluded because $\frac{1}{0}$ is undefined.

An important feature of these curves is that they approach both the x and the y axes ever more closely but never actually reach them. These lines are described as *asymptotes* to the curves. Asymptotes may be vertical (e.g. the y axis), horizontal, or lie at an angle, when they are called oblique.

Asymptotes are usually marked on graphs as dotted lines but in the cases above the lines are already there, being co-ordinate axes. The curves have different branches which never meet. A curve with different branches is said to be *discontinuous*, whereas one with no breaks, like $y = x^2$, is *continuous*.

ACTIVITY 2.4

Using a graphic calculator sketch the curves

$$y = \frac{1}{x-1} + 2 \quad \text{and} \quad y = \frac{1}{(x-1)^2} + 2.$$

State the equations of the asymptotes in each case.

The circle

You are of course familiar with the circle, and have probably done calculations involving its area and circumference. In this section you are introduced to the *equation* of a circle.

The circle is defined as the *locus* of all the points in a plane which are at a fixed distance (the radius) from a given point (the centre). (Locus means path.)

As you have seen, the length of a line joining (x_1, y_1) to (x_2, y_2) is given by

$$\text{length} = \sqrt{(x_2 - x_1)^2 + (y_2 - y_1)^2}.$$

This is used to derive the equation of a circle.

In the case of a circle of radius 3, with its centre at the origin, any point (x, y) on the circumference is distance 3 from the origin. Since the distance of (x, y) from $(0, 0)$ is given by $\sqrt{(x - 0)^2 + (y - 0)^2}$, this means that $\sqrt{(x - 0)^2 + (y - 0)^2} = 3$ or $x^2 + y^2 = 9$ and this is the equation of the circle.

Similarly a point (x, y) on the circumference of the circle with centre $(9, 5)$ and radius 4, is such that $\sqrt{(x - 9)^2 + (y - 5)^2} = 4$ or $(x - 9)^2 + (y - 5)^2 = 16$, the equation of the circle.

These two circles are shown in figure 2.28.

Figure 2.28

 ❓ How would you draw these curves on a graphic calculator or computer so that they are displayed as circles?

These results can be generalised to give the equation of a circle as follows:

centre $(0, 0)$, radius r: $x^2 + y^2 = r^2$
centre (h, k), radius r: $(x - h)^2 + (y - k)^2 = r^2$.

Multiplying out the second of these equations gives

$$x^2 - 2hx + h^2 + y^2 - 2ky + k^2 = r^2.$$

Rearranging this gives

$$x^2 + y^2 - 2hx - 2ky + (h^2 + k^2 - r^2) = 0.$$

Note

In this form, the equation highlights some of the important characteristics of the equation of a circle. In particular:

(i) the coefficients of x^2 and y^2 are equal

(ii) there is no xy term.

EXAMPLE 2.14

Find the centre and radius of the circle $(x-3)^2 + (y+5)^2 = 49$.

SOLUTION

Comparing with the general equation for a circle with radius r and centre (h, k), $(x-h)^2 + (y-k)^2 = r^2$, you have $h = 3$, $k = -5$, $r = 7$

$\Rightarrow$ the centre is $(3, -5)$, the radius is 7.

Circle geometry

There are some right-angle facts about a circle which are useful when solving co-ordinate geometry problems.

1 The angle in a semi-circle is a right angle (see figure 2.29).

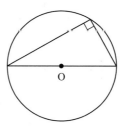

Figure 2.29

2 The perpendicular from the centre of a circle to a chord bisects the chord (see figure 2.30).

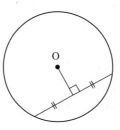

Figure 2.30

3 The tangent to a circle at a point is perpendicular to the radius through that point (see figure 2.31).

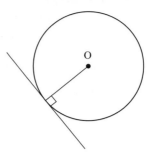

Figure 2.31

? How could you prove these facts are true?

The converses of these statements are also true. The following examples show two being used.

? What is the converse of a geometrical statement or theorem?
How could you prove that the converses of these theorems are true?

EXAMPLE 2.15

A circle has a radius of 5 units, and passes through the points $(0, 0)$ and $(0, 8)$. Sketch the two possible positions of the circle, and find their equations.

SOLUTION

The line joining $(0, 0)$ to $(0, 8)$ is a chord of the circle, and the mid-point of the chord is $(0, 4)$. The centre must lie on the perpendicular bisector of the chord, the line $y = 4$.

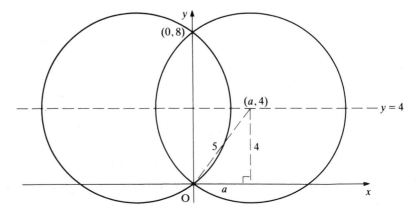

Figure 2.32

Let the centre be the point $(a, 4)$.

Using Pythagoras' theorem $a^2 + 16 = 25$

$$\Rightarrow \qquad a^2 = 9$$
$$\Rightarrow \qquad a = 3 \quad \text{or} \quad a = -3.$$

Possible equations are therefore

$$(x - 3)^2 + (y - 4)^2 = 25 \quad \text{and} \quad (x - (-3))^2 + (y - 4)^2 = 25$$
$$(x + 3)^2 + (y - 4)^2 = 25.$$

EXAMPLE 2.16

Show that OB is a diameter of the circle which passes through the points O(0, 0), A(2, 6) and B(8, 4). Find also the equation of the circle.

SOLUTION

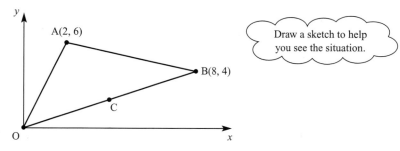

Draw a sketch to help you see the situation.

Figure 2.33

Gradient of OA $= \dfrac{6}{2} = 3$

Gradient of AB $= \dfrac{6 - 4}{2 - 8} = \dfrac{2}{-6} = -\dfrac{1}{3}$

Product of gradients $= 3 \times -\dfrac{1}{3} = -1$

$\Rightarrow$ Lines OA and AB are perpendicular and angle OAB $= 90°$.

$\Rightarrow$ A is the angle in a semi-circle where OB is the diameter, as required, by the converse of the theorem that the angle in a semi-circle is a right angle.

The centre C of the circle is the mid-point of OB and so has co-cordinates

$\left(\dfrac{0 + 8}{2}, \dfrac{0 + 4}{2}\right) = (4, 2).$

The radius of the circle, CO $= \sqrt{4^2 + 2^2} = \sqrt{20}$.

For any point P(x, y) on the circle, PC $= \sqrt{20}$

$$\Rightarrow \qquad\qquad\qquad PC^2 = 20$$

$\Rightarrow \quad (x - 4)^2 + (y - 2)^2 = 20$, which is the equation of the circle.

EXAMPLE 2.17

A(3, 5) and B(9, −3) lie on a circle. Show that the centre of the circle lies on the line with equation $4y − 3x + 14 = 0$.

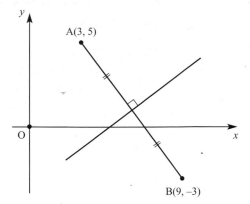

Figure 2.34

SOLUTION

AB is a chord of the circle, so the centre lies on the perpendicular bisector of AB.

Gradient of AB $= \dfrac{-3 - 5}{9 - 3} = \dfrac{-8}{6} = -\dfrac{4}{3}$.

So the gradient of its perpendicular bisector is $\frac{3}{4}$.

The mid-point of AB has co-ordinates $\left(\dfrac{3 + 9}{2}, \dfrac{5 + -3}{2} \right) = (6, 1)$.

So the centre of the circle lies on the line passing through (6, 1) with gradient $\frac{3}{4}$.

Using $y − y_1 = m(x − x_1)$, the equation of the line is

$$y − 1 = \tfrac{3}{4}(x − 6)$$

$\Rightarrow \qquad\qquad 4y − 4 = 3x − 18$

$\Rightarrow \qquad 4y − 3x + 14 = 0$, as required.

❓ What further information would you need to find the centre of the circle?

EXERCISE 2E

1 Find the equations of the following circles.

    (i) centre $(1, 0)$, radius 4   **(ii)** centre $(2, −1)$, radius 3

    (iii) centre $(1, −3)$, radius 5   **(iv)** centre $(−2, −5)$, radius 1

2 For each of the following circles state
    (a) the co-ordinates of the centre
    (b) the radius.

    (i) $x^2 + y^2 = 9$ **(ii)** $x^2 + (y − 2)^2 = 25$

    (iii) $(x − 3)^2 + (y + 1)^2 = 16$ **(iv)** $(x + 2)^2 + (y + 2)^2 = 4$

    (v) $(x + 4)^2 + y^2 = 8$

3 Find the equation of the circle with centre $(1, 7)$ passing through the point $(-4, -5)$.

(Hint: Use the co-ordinates of these two points to find the radius.)

4 Sketch the circle $(x - 4)^2 + (y - 5)^2 = 16$.

5 Show that the equation $x^2 + y^2 + 2x - 4y + 1 = 0$ can be written in the form $(x + 1)^2 + (y - 2)^2 = r^2$, where the value of r is to be found.
Hence give the co-ordinates of the centre and the radius of the circle.

6 **(i)** Find the mid-point, C, of AB where A and B are $(1, 8)$ and $(3, 14)$ respectively. Find also the distance AC.

(ii) Hence find the equation of the circle which has AB as a diameter.

7 Sketch the circle of radius 4 units which touches the positive x and y axes, and find its equation.

8 A circle passes through the points $(2, 0)$ and $(8, 0)$ and has the y axis as a tangent. Find the two possible equations.

9 A$(1, -2)$ is a point on the circle $(x - 3)^2 + (y + 1)^2 = 5$.

(i) State the co-ordinates of the centre of the circle and hence find the co-ordinates of the point B where AB is a diameter of the circle.

(ii) C$(2, 1)$ also lies on the circle.
Use co-ordinate geometry to verify that angle ACB = $90°$.

10 A$(6, 3)$ and B$(10, 1)$ are two points on a circle with centre $(11, 8)$. Calculate

(i) the co-ordinates of the mid-point of the chord

(ii) the distance of the chord AB from the centre of the circle

(iii) the radius of the circle.

11 A circle passes through the points A$(3, 2)$, B$(5, 6)$ and C$(11, 3)$.

(i) Calculate the lengths of the sides of the triangle ABC.

(ii) Hence show that AC is a diameter of this circle. State which theorems you have used, and in each case whether you have used the theorem or its converse.

(iii) Calculate the area of triangle ABC.

12 A$(6, 6)$, B$(6, -2)$, C$(-1, -1)$ and D$(-2, 2)$ are four points on a circle.

(i) Find the equations of the perpendicular bisectors of AB and CD.

(ii) Hence find the co-ordinates of the centre of the circle.

(iii) Find the equation of the circle.

13 Using the fact that a tangent to a circle is perpendicular to the radius passing through the point of contact, find the equation of the tangent to the circle $x^2 + (y + 4)^2 = 25$ at the point $(-4, -1)$.

The intersection of a line and a curve

When a line and a curve are in the same plane, there are three possible situations.

(i) *All points of intersection are distinct* (see figure 2.35).

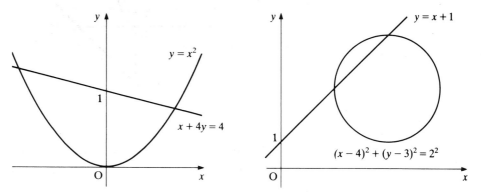

Figure 2.35

(ii) *The line is a tangent to the curve at one (or more) point(s)* (see figure 2.36).

In this case, each point of contact corresponds to two (or more) co-incident points of intersection. It is possible that the tangent will also intersect the curve somewhere else (as in the second part of figure 2.36).

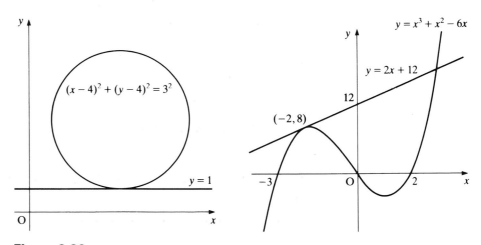

Figure 2.36

(iii) *The line and the curve do not meet* (see figure 2.37).

The co-ordinates of the point of intersection can be found by solving the two equations simultaneously. If you obtain an equation with no roots, the conclusion is that there is no point of intersection.

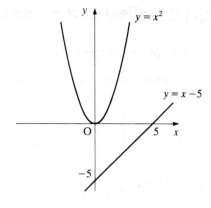

Figure 2.37

The equation of the straight line is, of course, linear and that of the curve non-linear. The examples which follow remind you how to solve such pairs of equations.

EXAMPLE 2.18

Find the co-ordinates of the points where the circle $(x-5)^2 + (y-8)^2 = 73$ intersects the x axis.

SOLUTION

The equation of the x axis is $y = 0$. Substituting $y = 0$ in the equation of the circle gives

$$(x-5)^2 + (0-8)^2 = 73$$
$$\Rightarrow x^2 - 10x + 25 + 64 = 73$$
$$\Rightarrow \quad x^2 - 10x + 16 = 0$$
$$\Rightarrow \quad (x-2)(x-8) = 0$$
$$\Rightarrow \quad x = 2 \text{ or } x = 8.$$

The circle meets the x axis at $(2, 0)$ and $(8, 0)$.

 There is a neater method of handling the algebra in the last example. Can you find it?

EXAMPLE 2.19

Find the co-ordinates of the points where the line $x + y = 9$ meets the circle $(x-2)^2 + (y-3)^2 = 16$.

Sketch the line and the circle on the same diagram and label the two points of intersection.

SOLUTION

From the equation of the line, $x = 9 - y$.

Substituting $(9 - y)$ for x in the equation of the circle gives

$$(9 - y - 2)^2 + (y - 3)^2 = 16$$
$$\Rightarrow \qquad (7 - y)^2 + (y - 3)^2 = 16$$
$$\Rightarrow 49 - 14y + y^2 + y^2 - 6y + 9 = 16$$
$$\Rightarrow \qquad 2y^2 - 20y + 42 = 0$$
$$\Rightarrow \qquad 2(y^2 - 10y + 21) = 0$$
$$\Rightarrow \qquad 2(y - 3)(y - 7) = 0$$
$$\Rightarrow \qquad y = 3 \text{ or } y = 7.$$

Since $x = 9 - y$, the points are $(6, 3)$ and $(2, 7)$.

In figure 2.38, you will see that:

– the line $x + y = 9$ passes through $(0, 9)$ and $(9, 0)$;

– the circle $(x - 2)^2 + (y - 3)^2 = 16$ has centre $(2, 3)$ and radius 4.

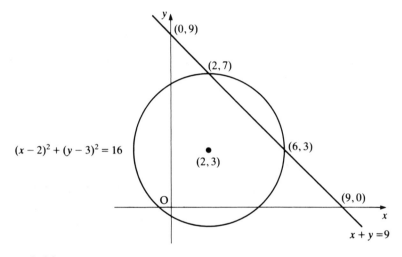

Figure 2.38

EXAMPLE 2.20

Show that the line $x + y = 2$ is a tangent to the circle $x^2 + y^2 = 2$.

SOLUTION

From the equation of the line, $y = 2 - x$.

Substituting this into the equation of the circle,

$$x^2 + (2 - x)^2 = 2$$
$$\Rightarrow x^2 + 4 - 4x + x^2 = 2$$
$$\Rightarrow \qquad 2x^2 - 4x + 2 = 0$$
$$\Rightarrow \qquad 2(x^2 - 2x + 1) = 0$$
$$\Rightarrow \qquad 2(x - 1)^2 = 0$$
$$\Rightarrow \qquad x = 1 \text{ (twice)}.$$

When $x = 1$, $y = 1$.

The repeated solution implies that there are two co-incident points of intersection, i.e. the line is a tangent to the circle at $(1, 1)$.

EXAMPLE 2.21 Show that the line $y = 4x$ is a tangent to the curve $y = x^2 + 4$, and find the co-ordinates of the point of contact.

SOLUTION

Substituting $y = 4x$ in the equation of the curve gives

$$4x = x^2 + 4$$
$$\Rightarrow \quad x^2 - 4x + 4 = 0$$
$$\Rightarrow \quad (x - 2)(x - 2) = 0$$
$$\Rightarrow \quad x = 2 \text{ (twice)}.$$

The line is therefore a tangent.

Substituting $x = 2$ in the equation of the line gives $y = 8$, so the point of contact is $(2, 8)$.

 How many different methods do you know for finding the intersection of a curve and a line?

The intersection of two curves

The same principles apply to finding the intersection of two curves, but it is only in simple cases that it is possible to solve the equations simultaneously using algebra (rather than a numerical or graphical method).

EXAMPLE 2.22 Find the points of intersection of the circle $x^2 + y^2 = 16$ and the curve $y = x^2 - 4$.

SOLUTION

Because x^2 appears in both equations and x occurs in neither, it is possible to eliminate x by rewriting $y = x^2 - 4$

as $\qquad x^2 = y + 4$

and substituting in the equation of the circle

$$y + 4 + y^2 = 16$$
$$y^2 + y - 12 = 0$$
$$\Rightarrow \quad (y - 3)(y + 4) = 0.$$
Either $\qquad y = 3 \Rightarrow x^2 = 7$
$$x = \pm \sqrt{7}$$
or $\qquad y = -4 \Rightarrow x^2 = 0$
$$x = 0 \text{ (twice)}.$$

The points of intersection are $(-\sqrt{7}, 3)$, $(\sqrt{7}, 3)$ and $(0, -4)$ (twice). The circle and the curve are shown in figure 2.39.

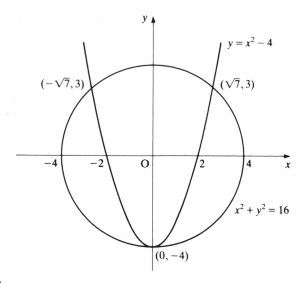

$y = x^2 - 4$

$(-\sqrt{7}, 3)$ $(\sqrt{7}, 3)$

$x^2 + y^2 = 16$

$(0, -4)$

Figure 2.39

EXERCISE 2F

 You may wish to use a graphic calculator or computer graphics package to check your answers where appropriate.

1 Show that the line $y = 3x + 1$ crosses the curve $y = x^2 + 3$ at (1, 4) and find the co-ordinates of the other point of intersection.

2 **(i)** Show that the line $x + y = 6$ is a tangent to the circle $x^2 + y^2 = 18$.
   (ii) Show the line and circle on a diagram.
   Find the point of contact of the tangent parallel to the line $x + y = 6$, and the equation of the tangent.

3 Sketch the circle $(x + 2)^2 + (y - 3)^2 = 16$, and find the equations of the four tangents to the circle which are parallel to the co-ordinate axes.

4 Find the co-ordinates of the points A and B where the line $y = 2x - 1$ cuts the curve $y = x^2 - 4$.

5 **(i)** Find the co-ordinates of the points of intersection of the line $y = 2x$ and the curve $y = x^2 + 6x - 5$.
   (ii) Show also that the line $y = 2x$ does not cross the curve $y = x^2 + 6x + 5$.

6 Find the co-ordinates of the points A and B where the line $x - 3y + 15 = 0$ cuts the circle $x^2 + y^2 + 2x - 6y + 5 = 0$.

7 Find the co-ordinates of the points where the line $y = x + 1$ meets the curve $y = x^3 - 3x^2 + 3x + 1$.

8 The diagram shows the cross-section of a goldfish bowl. The bowl can be thought of as a sphere with its top removed and its base flattened.
Assume the base is on the x axis and the y axis is a line of symmetry.

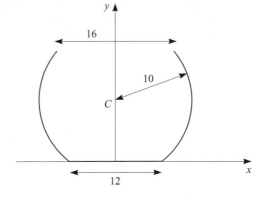

all dimensions
in centimetres

(i)   Find the height of the bowl.
(ii) Find the equation of the circular part of the cross-section.
(iii) The bowl is filled with water to a depth of 12 cm.
      Find the area of the surface of the water.

9 The line $3x + 4y = 24$ cuts the x axis at point A and the y axis at point B.
The point C is the mid-point of AB.

(i)   Find the co-ordinates of A, B and C. Find also the length of AB.
(ii) Find the equation of the circle with centre C which passes through A and
      B. Show that this circle also passes through the origin.
(iii) The tangent to the circle at B meets the straight line through O and C at
      the point D. Find the co-ordinates of D.

[MEI]

10 A circle has the two points P(−1, 3) and Q(5, 11) as ends of a diameter.

(i)   Find the equation of the line PQ.
(ii) Find the co-ordinates of C, the centre of the circle.
(iii) Find the length of the radius of the circle.
(iv) Write down the equation of the circle in the form $(x - a)^2 + (y - b)^2 = r^2$.
(v)   The line $y = -7x - 4$ cuts the circle at P and at another point R.
      Find the co-ordinates of R.
(vi) Prove that the line RC is perpendicular to the line PQ.

[MEI]

11 The points A(−1, 0), B(3, 2), C(5, −2) are joined to form a triangle.

(i)   Show that AB = BC.
(ii) Find the gradients of AB and BC and show that ABC is a right angle.
(iii) Find the exact area of the triangle.
(iv) Find the equation of the line of symmetry of the triangle.
(v)   Show that the equation $x^2 + y^2 + 2x - 39 = 0$ represents the circle, with
      centre A, passing through C.
(vi) Use your calculator to find the x co-ordinates of the points where this
      circle cuts the line of symmetry of the triangle.

[MEI]

12 Sanchia, a member of her college mathematical society, was asked to design a logo in the form of a sloping letter M, as shown in the diagram, on a circular background.

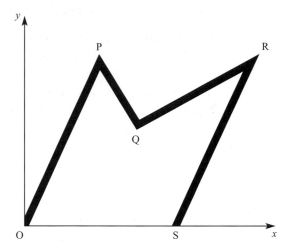

Using x and y axes on graph paper she drew a line from the origin O to the point P with co-ordinates $(2, 4)$.

(i) Calculate the gradient of OP.

She then drew SR parallel to OP and with the same length.

(ii) Given that S had co-ordinates $(4, 0)$, write down the co-ordinates of R.

To locate the point Q she drew a line from P with gradient -2, and a line from R perpendicular to this line from P. The point Q was where these lines met.

(iii) Find the equation of the line PQ.
(iv) Find the co-ordinates of the point Q.

For the background Sanchia drew the smallest circle which would contain the whole of her letter M.

(v) Find the equation of this circle.

[MEI]

13 The diagram shows a triangle with vertices $O(0, 0)$, $A(2, 6)$ and $B(12, 6)$. The perpendicular bisectors of OA and AB meet at C.

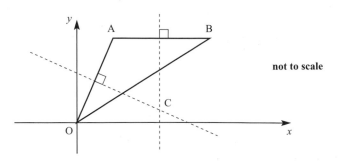

not to scale

(i)   Write down the equation of the perpendicular bisector of AB.
(ii) Find the equation of the perpendicular bisector of OA.
(iii) Hence show that the co-ordinates of C are (7, 1).

The point C is the centre of the circle which passes through O, A and B.

(iv) Find the equation of this circle.
(v)   Find the y co-ordinate of the point other than O where the circle cuts the y axis.
(vi) Write down the area of triangle OAB.
(vii) Hence or otherwise show that the length of the perpendicular from A to OB is $\sqrt{20}$.
(viii) Deduce that angle AOB is exactly 45°.

[MEI]

INVESTIGATION

A company is to manufacture brooches from metal or metal and enamel. The steps in the manufacture are:

(i)   the shape of the brooch is cut out from sheet metal
(ii) if required, a ridge is superimposed to contain the enamel sections.

A computer is to be programmed to operate the equipment which cuts the metal and adds the ridge. For each brooch design the computer is programmed using the equations of the lines or curves.

Figure 2.40 shows the equations and the necessary ranges of x which are required to make a simple brooch in the shape of a rhombus with the maximum dimensions 4 cm by 2 cm.

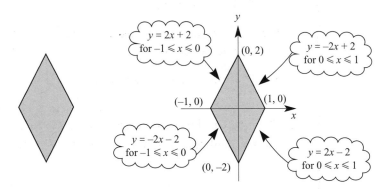

Figure 2.40

Design some brooches of your own, using the equations of lines, circles or any other curve that you have met. For each design you should specify all the necessary equations, and give ranges of x where appropriate. Figure 2.41 shows some possible designs to get you started.

Figure 2.41

1 The gradient of the straight line joining the points (x_1, y_1) and (x_2, y_2) is given by

$$\text{gradient} = \frac{y_2 - y_1}{x_2 - x_1}.$$

2 Two lines are parallel when their gradients are equal.

3 Two lines are perpendicular when the product of their gradients is −1.

4 When the points A and B have co-ordinates (x_1, y_1) and (x_2, y_2) respectively, then

$$\text{distance AB} = \sqrt{(x_2 - x_1)^2 + (y_2 - y_1)^2}$$

$$\text{mid-point of line AB is} \left(\frac{x_1 + x_2}{2}, \frac{y_1 + y_2}{2} \right).$$

5 The equation of a straight line may take any of the following forms:

- line parallel to the y axis: $x = a$
- line parallel to the x axis: $y = b$
- line through the origin with gradient m: $y = mx$
- line through $(0, c)$ with gradient m: $y = mx + c$
- line through (x_1, y_1) with gradient m: $y - y_1 = m(x - x_1)$
- line through (x_1, y_1) and (x_2, y_2):

$$\frac{y - y_1}{y_2 - y_1} = \frac{x - x_1}{x_2 - x_1} \quad \text{or} \quad \frac{y - y_1}{x - x_1} = \frac{y_2 - y_1}{x_2 - x_1}.$$

6 The equation of a circle with centre (h, k) and radius r is

$$(x - h)^2 + (y - k)^2 = r^2.$$

When the centre is at the origin $(0, 0)$, this simplifies to

$$x^2 + y^2 = r^2.$$

3 Polynomials

No, it [1729] is a very interesting number. It is the smallest number expressible as the sum of two cubes in two different ways.

Srinivasa Ramanujan

A brilliant mathematician, Ramanujan was largely self-taught, being too poor to afford a university education. He left India at the age of 26 to work with G.H. Hardy in Cambridge on number theory, but fell ill in the English climate and died six years later in 1920. On one occasion when Hardy visited him in hospital, Ramanujan asked about the registration number of the taxi he came in. Hardy replied that it was 1729, an uninteresting number; Ramanujan's instant response is quoted above.

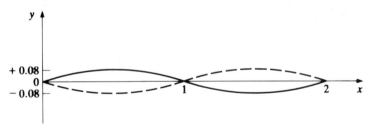

The photograph shows the Tamar Railway Bridge. The spans of this bridge, drawn to the same horizontal and vertical scales, are illustrated on the graph as two curves, one drawn solid, the other broken.

 How would you set about trying to fit equations to these two curves?

You will already have met quadratic expressions, like $x^2 - 5x + 6$, and solved quadratic equations, such as $x^2 - 5x + 6 = 0$. Quadratic expressions have the form

$ax^2 + bx + c$ where x is a variable, a, b and c are constants and a is not equal to zero. This work is covered in Chapter 1.

An expression of the form $ax^3 + bx^2 + cx + d$, which includes a term in x^3, is called a *cubic* in x. Examples of cubic expressions are

$$2x^3 + 3x^2 - 2x + 11, \qquad 3y^3 - 1 \qquad \text{and} \qquad 4z^3 - 2z.$$

Similarly a *quartic* expression in x, like $x^4 - 4x^3 + 6x^2 - 4x + 1$, contains a term in x^4; a *quintic* expression contains a term in x^5 and so on.

All these expressions are called *polynomials*. The *order* of a polynomial is the highest power of the variable it contains. So a quadratic is a polynomial of order 2, a cubic is a polynomial of order 3 and $3x^8 + 5x^4 + 6x$ is a polynomial of order 8 (an *octic*).

Notice that a polynomial does not contain terms involving $\sqrt{x}, \frac{1}{x}$, etc. Apart from the constant term, all the others are multiples of x raised to a positive integer power.

Operations with polynomials

Addition of polynomials

Polynomials are added by adding like terms, for example you add the *coefficients* of x^3 together (i.e. the numbers multiplying x^3), the coefficients of x^2 together, the coefficients of x together and the numbers together. You may find it easiest to set this out in columns.

EXAMPLE 3.1

Add $(5x^4 - 3x^3 - 2x)$ to $(7x^4 + 5x^3 + 3x^2 - 2)$.

SOLUTION

$5x^4$	$-3x^3$		$-2x$	
$+ (7x^4$	$+5x^3$	$+3x^2$		$-2)$
$12x^4$	$+2x^3$	$+3x^2$	$-2x$	-2

Note

This may alternatively be set out as follows:

$(5x^4 - 3x^3 - 2x) + (7x^4 + 5x^3 + 3x^2 - 2) = (5 + 7)x^4 + (-3 + 5)x^3 + 3x^2 - 2x - 2$
$$= 12x^4 + 2x^3 + 3x^2 - 2x - 2.$$

Subtraction of polynomials

Similarly polynomials are subtracted by subtracting like terms.

EXAMPLE 3.2

Simplify $(5x^4 - 3x^3 - 2x) - (7x^4 + 5x^3 + 3x^2 - 2)$.

SOLUTION

$$
\begin{array}{llllll}
5x^4 & -3x^3 & & -2x & & \\
-(7x^4 & +5x^3 & +3x^2 & & -2) \\
\hline
-2x^4 & -8x^3 & -3x^2 & -2x & +2
\end{array}
$$

 Be careful of the signs when subtracting. You may find it easier to change the signs on the bottom line and then go on as if you were adding.

This, too, may be set out as follows:

$$(5x^4 - 3x^3 - 2x) - (7x^4 + 5x^3 + 3x^2 - 2) = (5 - 7)x^4 + (-3 - 5)x^3 - 3x^2 - 2x + 2$$
$$= -2x^4 - 8x^3 - 3x^2 - 2x + 2.$$

Multiplication of polynomials

When you multiply two polynomials, you multiply each term of the one by each term of the other, and all the resulting terms are added. Remember that when you multiply powers of x, you add the indices: $x^5 \times x^7 = x^{12}$.

EXAMPLE 3.3

Multiply $(x^3 + 3x - 2)$ by $(x^2 - 2x - 4)$.

SOLUTION

Arranging this in columns, so that it looks like an arithmetical long multiplication calculation you get:

$$
\begin{array}{lllllll}
 & & x^3 & & +3x & -2 \\
 & & & x^2 & -2x & -4 \\
\hline
\text{Multiply top line by } x^2 & x^5 & & +3x^3 & -2x^2 & & \\
\text{Multiply top line by } -2x & & -2x^4 & & -6x^2 & +4x & \\
\text{Multiply top line by } -4 & & & -4x^3 & & -12x & +8 \\
\hline
\text{Add} & x^5 & -2x^4 & -x^3 & -8x^2 & -8x & +8
\end{array}
$$

Note

Alternatively:

$$(x^3 + 3x - 2) \times (x^2 - 2x - 4) = x^3(x^2 - 2x - 4) + 3x(x^2 - 2x - 4) - 2(x^2 - 2x - 4)$$
$$= x^5 - 2x^4 - 4x^3 + 3x^3 - 6x^2 - 12x - 2x^2 + 4x + 8$$
$$= x^5 - 2x^4 + (-4 + 3)x^3 + (-6 - 2)x^2 + (-12 + 4)x + 8$$
$$= x^5 - 2x^4 - x^3 - 8x^2 - 8x + 8.$$

Division of polynomials

Division of polynomials is usually set out rather like arithmetical long division.

EXAMPLE 3.4

Divide $2x^3 - 3x^2 + x - 6$ by $x - 2$.

SOLUTION

> Found by dividing $2x^3$ (the first term in $2x^3 - 3x^2 + x - 6$) by x (the first term in $x - 2$).

$$\begin{array}{r} 2x^2 \\ x - 2 \overline{\smash{)}2x^3 - 3x^2 + x - 6} \\ 2x^3 - 4x^2 \end{array}$$

> $2x^2(x-2)$

Now subtract $2x^3 - 4x^2$ from $2x^3 - 3x^2$, bring down the next term (i.e. x) and repeat the method above:

> $x^2 \div x$

$$\begin{array}{r} 2x^2 + x \\ x - 2 \overline{\smash{)}2x^3 - 3x^2 + x - 6} \\ \underline{2x^3 - 4x^2} \\ x^2 + x \\ x^2 - 2x \end{array}$$

> $x \times (x - 2)$

Continuing gives:

> This is the answer.

$$\begin{array}{r} 2x^2 + x + 3 \\ x - 2 \overline{\smash{)}2x^3 - 3x^2 + x - 6} \\ \underline{2x^3 - 4x^2} \\ x^2 + x \\ \underline{x^2 - 2x} \\ 3x - 6 \\ \underline{3x - 6} \\ 0 \end{array}$$

> The final remainder of zero means that $x - 2$ divides exactly into $2x^3 - 3x^2 + x - 6$.

Thus $(2x^3 - 3x^2 + x - 6) \div (x - 2) = (2x^2 + x + 3)$.

Alternatively this may be set out as follows if you know that there is no remainder.

SOLUTION

Let $(2x^3 - 3x^2 + x - 6) \div (x - 2) = ax^2 + bx + c$

> The polynomial here must be of order 2 because $2x^3 \div x$ will give an x^2 term.

Multiplying both sides by $(x - 2)$ gives

$(2x^3 - 3x^2 + x - 6) = (ax^2 + bx + c)(x - 2)$.

Multiplying out the expression on the right

$2x^3 - 3x^2 + x - 6 \equiv ax^3 + (b - 2a)x^2 + (c - 2b)x - 2c$

> The identity sign is used here to emphasise that this is an identity and true for all values of x.

Comparing coefficients of x^3

$$2 = a$$

Comparing coefficients of x^2

$$-3 = b - 2a$$
$$= b - 4$$
$$\Rightarrow b = 1$$

Comparing coefficients of x

$$1 = c - 2b$$
$$= c - 2$$
$$\Rightarrow c = 3$$

Checking the constant term

$$-6 = -2c \text{ (which agrees with } c = 3\text{)}.$$

So $ax^2 + bx + c$ is $2x^2 + x + 3$

i.e. $(2x^3 - 3x^2 + x - 6) \div (x - 2) \equiv 2x^2 + x + 3$.

With practice you may be able to do this method 'by inspection'. The steps in this would be as follows.

SOLUTION

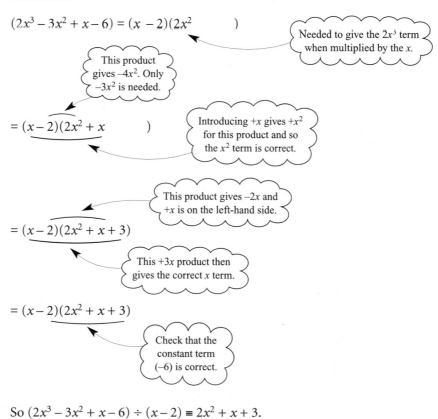

$$(2x^3 - 3x^2 + x - 6) = (x - 2)(2x^2 \qquad)$$

Needed to give the $2x^3$ term when multiplied by the x.

This product gives $-4x^2$. Only $-3x^2$ is needed.

$$= (x - 2)(2x^2 + x \qquad)$$

Introducing $+x$ gives $+x^2$ for this product and so the x^2 term is correct.

This product gives $-2x$ and $+x$ is on the left-hand side.

$$= (x - 2)(2x^2 + x + 3)$$

This $+3x$ product then gives the correct x term.

$$= (x - 2)(2x^2 + x + 3)$$

Check that the constant term (-6) is correct.

So $(2x^3 - 3x^2 + x - 6) \div (x - 2) \equiv 2x^2 + x + 3$.

1 State the orders of the following polynomials.

    (i) $x^3 + 3x^2 - 4x$ **(ii)** x^{12} **(iii)** $2 + 6x^2 + 3x^7 - 8x^5$

2 Add $(x^3 + x^2 + 3x - 2)$ to $(x^3 - x^2 - 3x - 2)$.

3 Add $(x^3 - x)$, $(3x^2 + 2x + 1)$ and $(x^4 + 3x^3 + 3x^2 + 3x)$.

4 Subtract $(3x^2 + 2x + 1)$ from $(x^3 + 5x^2 + 7x + 8)$.

5 Subtract $(x^3 - 4x^2 - 8x - 9)$ from $(x^3 - 5x^2 + 7x + 9)$.

6 Subtract $(x^5 - x^4 - 2x^3 - 2x^2 + 4x - 4)$ from $(x^5 + x^4 - 2x^3 - 2x^2 + 4x + 4)$.

7 Multiply $(x^3 + 3x^2 + 3x + 1)$ by $(x + 1)$.

8 Multiply $(x^3 + 2x^2 - x - 2)$ by $(x - 2)$.

9 Multiply $(x^2 + 2x - 3)$ by $(x^2 - 2x - 3)$.

10 Multiply $(x^{10} + x^9 + x^8 + x^7 + x^6 + x^5 + x^4 + x^3 + x^2 + x^1 + 1)$ by $(x - 1)$.

11 Simplify $(x^2 + 1)(x - 1) - (x^2 - 1)(x - 1)$.

12 Simplify $(x^2 + 1)(x^2 + 4) - (x^2 - 1)(x^2 - 4)$.

13 Simplify $(x + 1)^2 + (x + 3)^2 - 2(x + 1)(x + 3)$.

14 Simplify $(x^2 + 1)(x + 3) - (x^2 + 3)(x + 1)$.

15 Simplify $(x^2 - 2x + 1)^2 - (x + 1)^4$.

16 Divide $(x^3 - 3x^2 - x + 3)$ by $(x - 1)$.

17 Divide $(x^3 + x^2 - 6x)$ by $(x - 2)$.

18 Divide $(2x^3 - x^2 - 5x + 10)$ by $(x + 2)$.

19 Divide $(x^4 + x^2 - 2)$ by $(x - 1)$.

20 Divide $(2x^3 - 10x^2 + 3x - 15)$ by $(x - 5)$.

Polynomial curves

It is useful to be able to look at a polynomial and to visualise immediately the general shape of its curve. The most important clues to the shape of the curve are the order of the polynomial and the sign of the highest power of the variable.

Turning points

A turning point is a place where a curve changes from increasing (curve going up) to decreasing (curve going down), or vice versa. A *turning point* may be described as a *maximum* (change from increasing to decreasing) or a *minimum* (change from decreasing to increasing). In general, the curve of a polynomial of order n has $n - 1$ turning points as shown in figure 3.1.

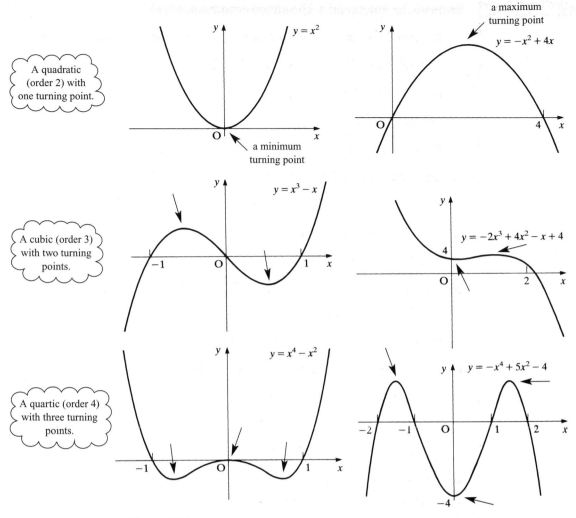

A quadratic (order 2) with one turning point.

A cubic (order 3) with two turning points.

A quartic (order 4) with three turning points.

Figure 3.1

There are some polynomials for which not all the turning points materialise, as in the case of $y = x^4 - 4x^3 + 5x^2$ (whose curve is shown in figure 3.2). To be accurate, you say that the curve of a polynomial of order n has *at most* $n - 1$ turning points.

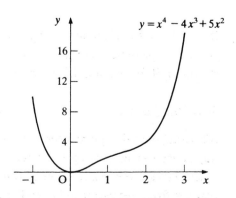

Figure 3.2

Behaviour for large x (positive and negative)

What can you say about the value of a polynomial for large positive values and large negative values of x? As an example, look at

$$f(x) = x^3 + 2x^2 + 3x + 9,$$

and take 1000 as a large number.

$$f(1000) = 1\,000\,000\,000 + 2\,000\,000 + 3000 + 9$$
$$= 1\,002\,003\,009$$

Similarly,

$$f(-1000) = -1\,000\,000\,000 + 2\,000\,000 - 3000 + 9$$
$$= -998\,002\,991.$$

Note

1 The term x^3 makes by far the largest contribution to the answers. It is the *dominant* term.
  For a polynomial of order n, the term in x^n is dominant as $x \to \pm\infty$.

2 In both cases the answers are extremely large numbers. You will probably have noticed already that away from their turning points, polynomial curves quickly disappear off the top or bottom of the page.
  For all polynomials as $x \to \pm\infty$, either $f(x) \to +\infty$ or $f(x) \to -\infty$.

When investigating the behaviour of a polynomial of order n as $x \to \pm\infty$, you need to look at the term in x^n and ask two questions.

(i) Is n even or odd?
(ii) Is the coefficient of x^n positive or negative?

According to the answers, the curve will have one of the four types of shape illustrated in figure 3.3.

ACTIVITY 3.1

Find an equation to fit each of the four cases shown in figure 3.3 overleaf, and check the shape of its curve using a graphic calculator or a computer graphics package.

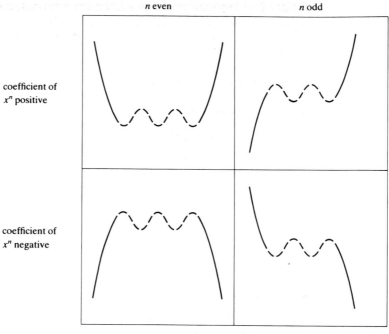

n even   *n* odd

coefficient of
x^n positive

coefficient of
x^n negative

Figure 3.3

Intersections with the *x* and *y* axes

The constant term in the polynomial gives the value of *y* where the curve intersects the *y* axis. So $y = x^8 + 5x^6 + 17x^3 + 23$ crosses the *y* axis at the point (0, 23). Similarly, $y = x^3 + x$ crosses the *y* axis at (0, 0), the origin, since the constant term is zero.

When the polynomial is given, or known, in factorised form you can see at once where it crosses the *x* axis. The curve $y = (x-2)(x-8)(x-9)$, for example, crosses the *x* axis at $x = 2$, $x = 8$ and $x = 9$. Each of these values makes one of the brackets equal to zero, and so $y = 0$.

EXAMPLE 3.5   Sketch the curve $y = x^3 - 3x^2 - x + 3 = (x+1)(x-1)(x-3)$.

SOLUTION

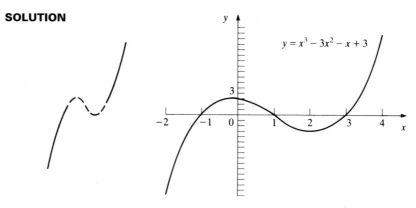

$y = x^3 - 3x^2 - x + 3$

Figure 3.4

Since the polynomial is of order 3, the curve has up to two turning points. The term in x^3 has a positive coefficient (+1) and 3 is an odd number, so the general shape is as shown on the left of figure 3.4.

The actual equation

$$y = x^3 - 3x^2 - x + 3 = (x+1)(x-1)(x-3)$$

tells you that the curve:

– crosses the y axis at $(0, 3)$
– crosses the x axis at $(-1, 0)$, $(1, 0)$ and $(3, 0)$.

This is enough information to sketch the curve (see the right of figure 3.4).

In this example the polynomial $x^3 - 3x^2 - x + 3$ has three factors, $(x+1)$, $(x-1)$ and $(x-3)$. Each of these corresponds to an intersection with the x axis, and to a root of the equation $x^3 - 3x^2 - x + 3 = 0$. Clearly a cubic polynomial cannot have more than three factors of this type, since the highest power of x is 3. A cubic polynomial may, however, cross the x axis fewer than three times, as in the case of $f(x) = x^3 - x^2 - 4x + 6$ (see figure 3.5).

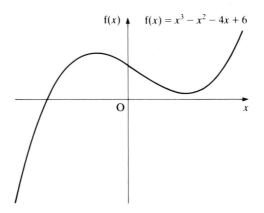

Figure 3.5

Note

This illustrates an important result. If $f(x)$ is a polynomial of degree n, the curve with equation $y = f(x)$ crosses the x axis at most n times, and the equation $f(x) = 0$ has at most n roots.

An important case occurs when the polynomial function has one or more repeated factors, as in figure 3.6. In such cases the curves touch the x axis at points corresponding to the repeated roots.

$f(x) = (x-1)(x-3)^2$

$f(x) = x^2(x-4)^2$

Figure 3.6

Sketch the following curves by hand, marking clearly the values of x and y where they cross the co-ordinate axes. You can use a graphic calculator or computer graphics package to check your results.

1 $y = x(x-3)(x+4)$

2 $y = (x+1)(2x-5)(x-4)$

3 $y = (5-x)(x-1)(x+3)$

4 $y = x^2(x-3)$

5 $y = (x+1)^2(2-x)$

6 $y = (3x-4)(4x-3)^2$

7 $y = (x+2)^2(x-4)^2$

8 $y = (x-3)^2(4+x)^2$

9 Suggest an equation for this curve.

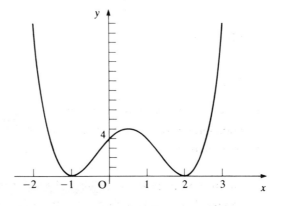

? What happens to the curve of a polynomial if it has a factor of the form $(x-a)^3$? Or $(x-a)^4$?

Polynomial equations

You have already met the formula

$$x = \frac{-b \pm \sqrt{b^2 - 4ac}}{2a}$$

for the solution of the quadratic equation $ax^2 + bx + c = 0$.

Unfortunately there is no such simple formula for the solution of a cubic equation, or indeed for any higher power polynomial equation. So you have to use one (or more) of three possible methods.

- Spotting one or more roots.
- Finding where the graph of the expression cuts the x axis.
- A numerical method.

EXAMPLE 3.6

Solve the equation $4x^3 - 8x^2 - x + 2 = 0$.

SOLUTION

Start by plotting the curve whose equation is $y = 4x^3 - 8x^2 - x + 2$. (You will also find it helpful at this stage to display it on a graphic calculator or computer.)

x	−1	0	1	2	3
y	−9	+2	−3	0	35

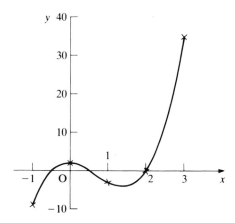

Figure 3.7

Figure 3.7 shows that one root is $x = 2$ and that there are two others. One is between $x = -1$ and $x = 0$ and the other between $x = 0$ and $x = 1$.

Try $x = -\frac{1}{2}$.

Substituting $x = -\frac{1}{2}$ in $y = 4x^3 - 8x^2 - x + 2$ gives

$$y = 4 \times \left(-\frac{1}{8}\right) - 8 \times \frac{1}{4} - \left(-\frac{1}{2}\right) + 2$$

$$y = 0.$$

So in fact the graph crosses the x axis at $x = -\frac{1}{2}$ and this is a root also.

Similarly, substituting $x = +\frac{1}{2}$ in $y = 4x^3 - 8x^2 - x + 2$ gives

$$y = 4 \times \tfrac{1}{8} - 8 \times \tfrac{1}{4} - \tfrac{1}{2} + 2$$
$$y = 0,$$

and so the third root is $x = \frac{1}{2}$.

The solution is $x = -\frac{1}{2}, \frac{1}{2}$ or 2.

This example worked out nicely, but many equations do not have roots which are whole numbers or simple fractions. In those cases you can find an approximate answer by drawing a graph. To be more accurate, you will need to use a *numerical* method, which will allow you to get progressively closer to the answer, homing in on it. Such methods are beyond the scope of this book but are covered in the next book in this series and in greater detail in *Numerical Methods*, also in this series.

The factor theorem

The equation $4x^3 - 8x^2 - x + 2 = 0$ has roots that are whole numbers or fractions. This means that it could, in fact, have been factorised

$$4x^3 - 8x^2 - x + 2 = (2x + 1)(2x - 1)(x - 2) = 0.$$

Few polynomial equations can be factorised, but when one can, the solution follows immediately.

Since $(2x + 1)(2x - 1)(x - 2) = 0$

it follows that either $2x + 1 = 0 \implies x = -\frac{1}{2}$

or $2x - 1 = 0 \implies x = \frac{1}{2}$

or $x - 2 = 0 \implies x = 2$

and so $x = -\frac{1}{2}, \frac{1}{2}$ or 2.

This illustrates an important result, known as the *factor theorem*, which may be stated as follows.

If $(x - a)$ is a factor of $f(x)$, then $f(a) = 0$ and $x = a$ is a root of the equation $f(x) = 0$. Conversely if $f(a) = 0$, then $(x - a)$ is a factor of $f(x)$.

EXAMPLE 3.7

Given that $f(x) = x^3 - 6x^2 + 11x - 6$:

(i) find $f(0)$, $f(1)$, $f(2)$, $f(3)$ and $f(4)$
(ii) factorise $x^3 - 6x^2 + 11x - 6$
(iii) solve the equation $x^3 - 6x^2 + 11x - 6 = 0$
(iv) sketch the curve whose equation is $f(x) = x^3 - 6x^2 + 11x - 6$.

SOLUTION

(i) $f(0) = 0^3 - 6 \times 0^2 + 11 \times 0 - 6 = -6$
$f(1) = 1^3 - 6 \times 1^2 + 11 \times 1 - 6 = 0$
$f(2) = 2^3 - 6 \times 2^2 + 11 \times 2 - 6 = 0$
$f(3) = 3^3 - 6 \times 3^2 + 11 \times 3 - 6 = 0$
$f(4) = 4^3 - 6 \times 4^2 + 11 \times 4 - 6 = 6$

(ii) Since f(1), f(2) and f(3) all equal 0, it follows that $(x-1)$, $(x-2)$ and $(x-3)$ are all factors. This tells you that

$$x^3 - 6x^2 + 11x - 6 = (x-1)(x-2)(x-3) \times \text{constant.}$$

By checking the coefficient of the term in x^3, you can see that the constant must be 1, and so

$$x^3 - 6x^2 + 11x - 6 = (x-1)(x-2)(x-3).$$

(iii) $x = 1, 2$ or 3.

(iv)

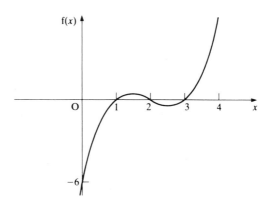

Figure 3.8

In the previous example, all three factors came out of the working, but this will not always happen. If not, it is often possible to find one factor (or more) by 'spotting' it, or by sketching the curve. You can then make the job of searching for further factors much easier by dividing the polynomial by the factor(s) you have found: you will then be dealing with a lower order polynomial.

EXAMPLE 3.8

Given that $f(x) = x^3 - x^2 - 3x + 2$:

(i) show that $(x-2)$ is a factor
(ii) solve the equation $f(x) = 0$.

SOLUTION

(i) To show that $(x-2)$ is a factor, it is necessary to show that $f(2) = 0$:

$$f(2) = 2^3 - 2^2 - 3 \times 2 + 2$$
$$= 8 - 4 - 6 + 2$$
$$= 0.$$

Therefore $(x - 2)$ is a factor of $x^3 - x^2 - 3x + 2$.

(ii) Since $(x - 2)$ is a factor you divide f(x) by $(x - 2)$

$$\begin{array}{r} x^2 + x - 1 \\ x - 2 \overline{\smash{\big)}\ x^3 - x^2 - 3x + 2} \\ \underline{x^3 - 2x^2} \\ x^2 - 3x \\ \underline{x^2 - 2x} \\ -x + 2 \\ \underline{-x + 2} \\ 0 \end{array}$$

so f$(x) = 0$ becomes $(x - 2)(x^2 + x - 1) = 0$,

$\Rightarrow$ either $x - 2 = 0$ or $x^2 + x - 1 = 0$.

Using the quadratic formula on $x^2 + x - 1 = 0$ gives

$$x = \frac{-1 \pm \sqrt{1 - 4 \times 1 \times (-1)}}{2}$$
$$= \frac{-1 \pm \sqrt{5}}{2}$$
$$= -1.618 \quad \text{or} \quad 0.618 \quad \text{(to 3 d.p.)}.$$

So the complete solution is $x = -1.618, 0.618$ or 2.

Spotting a root of a polynomial equation

Most polynomial equations do not have integer (or fraction) solutions. It is only a few special cases that work out nicely.

To check whether an integer root exists for any equation, look at the constant term. Decide what whole numbers divide into it, and test them.

EXAMPLE 3.9

Spot an integer root of the equation $x^3 - 3x^2 + 2x - 6 = 0$.

SOLUTION

The constant term is -6, and this is divisible by $-1, +1, -2, +2, -3, +3, -6$ and $+6$. So the only possible factors are $(x \pm 1), (x \pm 2), (x \pm 3)$ and $(x \pm 6)$. This limits the search somewhat.

f$(1) = -6$	No;		f$(-1) = -12$	No;
f$(2) = -6$	No;		f$(-2) = -30$	No;
f$(3) = 0$	Yes;		f$(-3) = -66$	No;
f$(6) = 114$	No;		f$(-6) = -342$	No.

$x = 3$ is an integer root of the equation.

EXAMPLE 3.10 Is there an integer root of the equation $x^3 - 3x^2 + 2x - 5 = 0$?

SOLUTION

The only possible factors are $(x \pm 1)$, $(x \pm 5)$.

$f(1) = -5$ No; $f(-1) = -11$ No;
$f(5) = 55$ No; $f(-5) = -215$ No.

There is no integer root.

The remainder theorem

Using the long division method, any polynomial can be divided by another polynomial of lesser order, but sometimes there will be a remainder. Look at $(x^3 + 2x^2 - 3x - 7) \div (x - 2)$.

$$
\begin{array}{r}
x^2 + 4x + 5 \\
x - 2 \overline{)\, x^3 + 2x^2 - 3x - 7} \\
\underline{x^3 - 2x^2} \\
4x^2 - 3x \\
\underline{4x^2 - 8x} \\
5x - 7 \\
\underline{5x - 10} \\
3
\end{array}
$$

The remainder

You can write this as

$$x^3 + 2x^2 - 3x - 7 = (x - 2)(x^2 + 4x + 5) + 3.$$

At this point it is convenient to call the polynomial $x^3 + 2x^2 - 3x - 7 = f(x)$.

So $f(x) = (x - 2)(x^2 + 4x + 5) + 3.$ ①

Substituting $x = 2$ into both sides of ① gives $f(2) = 3$.

So $f(2)$ is the remainder when $f(x)$ is divided by $(x - 2)$.

This result can be generalised to give the *remainder theorem*. It states that for a polynomial, $f(x)$,

$f(a)$ is the remainder when $f(x)$ is divided by $(x - a)$.

$f(x) = (x - a)g(x) + f(a)$ (the remainder theorem).

EXAMPLE 3.11

Find the remainder when $2x^3 - 3x + 5$ is divided by $x + 1$.

SOLUTION

The remainder is found by substituting $x = -1$ in $2x^3 - 3x + 5$.

$$2 \times (-1)^3 - 3 \times (-1) + 5$$
$$= -2 + 3 + 5$$
$$= 6$$

$\Rightarrow$ The remainder is 6.

EXAMPLE 3.12

When $x^2 - 6x + a$ is divided by $x - 3$, the remainder is 2. Find the value of a.

SOLUTION

The remainder is found by substituting $x = 3$ in $x^2 - 6x + a$.

$\Rightarrow \quad 3^2 - 6 \times 3 + a = \ 2$
$\Rightarrow \quad\quad\ 9 - 18 + a = \ 2$
$\Rightarrow \quad\quad\quad\quad -9 + a = \ 2$
$\Rightarrow \quad\quad\quad\quad\quad\quad a = 11$

When you are dividing by a linear expression any remainder will be a constant; dividing by a quadratic expression may give a linear remainder.

? A polynomial is divided by another of degree n.
What can you say about the remainder?

When dividing by polynomials of order 2 or more, the remainder is usually found most easily by actually doing the long division.

EXAMPLE 3.13

Find the remainder when $2x^4 - 3x^3 + 4$ is divided by $x^2 + 1$.

SOLUTION

$$
\begin{array}{r}
2x^2 - 3x - 2 \\
x^2 + 1 \overline{\smash{)}\ 2x^4 - 3x^3 + 4} \\
\underline{2x^4 + 2x^2} \\
-3x^3 - 2x^2 \\
\underline{-3x^3 - 3x} \\
-2x^2 + 3x + 4 \\
\underline{-2x^2 - 2} \\
3x + 6
\end{array}
$$

The remainder is $3x + 6$.

In a division such as the one in Example 3.13, it is important to keep a separate column for each power of x and this means that sometimes it is necessary to leave gaps, as in the example above. In arithmetic, zeros are placed in the gaps. For example, 2 thousand and 3 is written 2003.

EXERCISE 3C

1 Given that $f(x) = x^3 + 2x^2 - 9x - 18$:

  (i) find $f(-3)$, $f(-2)$, $f(-1)$, $f(0)$, $f(1)$, $f(2)$ and $f(3)$

  (ii) factorise $f(x)$

  (iii) solve the equation $f(x) = 0$

  (iv) sketch the curve with the equation $y = f(x)$.

2 The polynomial $p(x)$ is given by $p(x) = x^3 - 4x$.

  (i) Find the values of $p(-3)$, $p(-2)$, $p(-1)$, $p(0)$, $p(1)$, $p(2)$, $p(3)$.

  (ii) Factorise $p(x)$.

  (iii) Solve the equation $p(x) = 0$.

  (iv) Sketch the curve with the equation $y = p(x)$.

3 You are given that $f(x) = x^3 - 19x + 30$.

  (i) Calculate $f(0)$ and $f(3)$. Hence write down a factor of $f(x)$.

  (ii) Find p and q such that $f(x) \equiv (x - 2)(x^2 + px + q)$.

  (iii) Solve the equation $x^3 - 19x + 30 = 0$.

  (iv) Without further calculation draw a sketch of $y = f(x)$.

[MEI]

4 **(i)** Show that $x - 3$ is a factor of $x^3 - 5x^2 - 2x + 24$.

  (ii) Solve the equation $x^3 - 5x^2 - 2x + 24 = 0$.

  (iii) Sketch the curve with the equation $y = x^3 - 5x^2 - 2x + 24$.

5 **(i)** Show that $x = 2$ is a root of the equation $x^4 - 5x^2 + 2x = 0$ and write down another integer root.

  (ii) Find the other two roots of the equation $x^4 - 5x^2 + 2x = 0$.

  (iii) Sketch the curve with the equation $y = x^4 - 5x^2 + 2x$.

6 **(i)** The polynomial $p(x) = x^3 - 6x^2 + 9x + k$ has a factor $x - 4$. Find the value of k.

  (ii) Find the other factors of the polynomial.

  (iii) Sketch the curve with the equation $y = p(x)$.

7 The diagram shows the curve with the equation

$$y = (x + a)(x - b)^2$$

where a and b are positive integers.

(i) Write down the values of a and b, and also of c, given that the curve crosses the y axis at $(0, c)$.

(ii) Solve the equation $(x + a)(x - b)^2 = c$ (using the values of a, b and c you found in part (i)).

8 The function $f(x)$ is given by $f(x) = x^4 - 3x^2 - 4$.

(i) By treating $f(x)$ as a quadratic in x^2, factorise it in the form $(x^2...)(x^2...)$.

(ii) Complete the factorisation to the extent that is possible.

(iii) How many real roots has the equation $f(x) = 0$? What are they?

9 (i) Show that $x - 2$ is not a factor of $2x^3 + 5x^2 - 7x - 3$.

(ii) Find the remainder when $2x^3 + 5x^2 - 7x - 3$ is divided by $x - 2$.

10 The equation $f(x) = x^3 - 4x^2 + x + 6 = 0$ has three integer roots.

(i) List the eight values of a for which it is sensible to check whether $f(a) = 0$, and check each of them.

(ii) Solve $f(x) = 0$.

11 Factorise, as far as possible, the following expressions.

(i) $x^3 - x^2 - 4x + 4$ given that $(x - 1)$ is a factor.

(ii) $x^3 + 1$ given that $(x + 1)$ is a factor.

(iii) $x^3 + x - 10$ given that $(x - 2)$ is a factor.

(iv) $x^3 + x^2 + x + 6$ given that $(x + 2)$ is a factor.

12 (i) Show that neither $x = 1$ nor $x = -1$ is a root of $x^4 - 2x^3 + 3x^2 - 8 = 0$.

(ii) Find the remainder when $x^4 - 2x^3 + 3x^2 - 8$ is divided by

(a) $(x - 1)$ (b) $(x + 1)$ (c) $(x^2 - 1)$.

13 When $2x^3 + 3x^2 + kx - 6$ is divided by $x + 1$ the remainder is 7. Find the value of k.

14 When $x^3 + px^2 + p^2x - 36$ is divided by $x - 3$ the remainder is 21. Find a possible value of p.

15 When $x^3 + ax^2 + bx + 8$ is divided by $x - 3$ the remainder is 2 and when it is divided by $x + 1$ the remainder is -2.
Find a and b and hence obtain the remainder on dividing by $x - 2$.

16 When $f(x) = 2x^3 + ax^2 + bx + 6$ is divided by $x - 1$ there is no remainder and when $f(x)$ is divided by $x + 1$ the remainder is 10.
Find a and b and hence solve the equation $f(x) = 0$.

17 The diagram shows an open rectangular tank with a square base of side x metres and with a volume of $8\,\text{m}^3$.

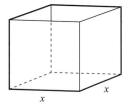

(i) Write down an expression in terms of x for the height of the tank.

(ii) Show that the surface area of the tank is

$$\left(x^2 + \frac{32}{x}\right)\text{m}^2.$$

(iii) Given that the surface area is $24\,\text{m}^2$ show that $x^3 - 24x + 32 = 0$.

(iv) Solve $x^3 - 24x + 32 = 0$ to find the possible values of x.

[MEI]

18 The sketch shows the graph of $y = f(x)$, where $f(x)$ is a cubic expression in x.

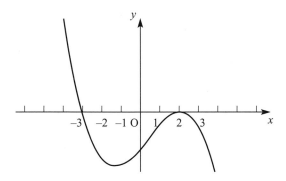

(i) Write down the values of x for which $f(x) = 0$.

(ii) The function $f(x)$ can be written in the form $a(x - p)(x - q)(x - r)$. Write down one set of possible values for p, q and r.

(iii) In fact $a = -2$. Find $f(0)$.

(iv) The expression can also be written as

$$f(x) = -2x^3 + bx^2 + cx + d.$$

Find the values of b, c and d.

[MEI]

19 The graph shows a curve drawn through a set of points which represent the results of several experiments. It is thought that the relationship between y and x may be modelled by a simple polynomial equation.

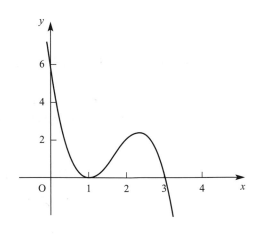

(i) Explain, with reference to the number of turning points, why the polynomial is not a quadratic.

(ii) A possible form of the equation is

$$y = a(x - b)^2 (x - c).$$

Write down the values of b and c. Substituting $x = 0$, calculate the value of a.

(iii) Find the values of the integers p, q, r and s when the equation is written in the form

$$y = px^3 + qx^2 + rx + s.$$

(iv) A further experiment produces the result that $y = 1.9$ when $x = 2$. State, with reasons, whether you think this supports the model.

[**MEI**]

20 The graph illustrates the results of an experiment. It is thought that the relationship between y and x may be modelled by a simple polynomial equation.

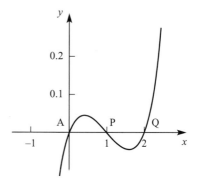

(i) Explain why the polynomial could be a cubic.

(ii) A cubic polynomial of the form $y = kx(x - c)(x - d)$ is suggested as a model. Use the information on the diagram to write down the values of c and d.

(iii) It is known that $y = 0.9$ when $x = 3$. Find the value of k.

(iv) After further experimentation it is found that $y = 5$ when $x = 4$. Comment on the suitability of the model.

(v) Following a theoretical discussion, a new model with the equation

$$y = 2^x - 1 - \tfrac{1}{2}x(x + 1)$$

is proposed. The graph of this equation also passes through A, P and Q. Calculate the values of y predicted when $x = 3$ and when $x = 4$. Comment.

[**MEI**]

The graphs of quadratic functions

Look at the curve in figure 3.9. It is the graph of $y = x^2 - 4x + 5$ and it has the characteristic shape of a quadratic; it is a parabola.

Notice that:

● it has a minimum point (or *vertex*) at $(2, 1)$

● it has a line of symmetry, $x = 2$.

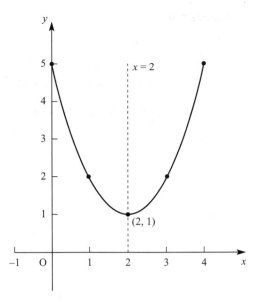

Figure 3.9

It is possible to find the vertex and the line of symmetry without plotting the points by using the technique of completing the square, which you met in Chapter 1.

Rewrite the expression with the constant term moved to the right

$$x^2 - 4x \qquad + 5.$$

Take the coefficient of x -4
divide it by 2 -2
square it $+4.$

Add this to the left-hand part and compensate by subtracting it from the constant term on the right

$$x^2 - 4x + 4 \qquad + 5 - 4.$$

This can now be written as $(x - 2)^2 + 1.$

This is the completed square form.

The minimum value is 1, so the vertex is $(2, 1)$.

The line of symmetry is $x - 2 = 0$ or $x = 2.$

EXAMPLE 3.14   Write $x^2 + 5x + 4$ in completed square form.

Hence state the equation of the line of symmetry and the co-ordinates of the vertex of the curve $y = x^2 + 5x + 4.$

SOLUTION

$x^2 + 5x \qquad + 4$

$x^2 + 5x + 6.25 \quad + 4 - 6.25$

$(x + 2.5)^2 - 2.25$ (This is the completed square form.)

$5 \div 2 = 2.5 \colon 2.5^2 = 6.25$

The line of symmetry is $x + 2.5 = 0$, or $x = -2.5$.

The vertex is $(-2.5, -2.25)$.

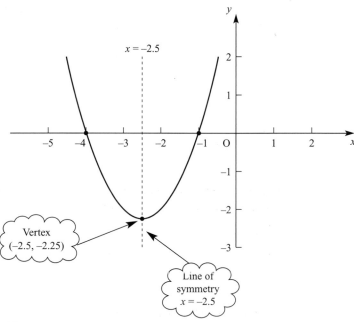

Vertex $(-2.5, -2.25)$

Line of symmetry $x = -2.5$

Figure 3.10

❓ The steps in this process ensure that you end up with an expression of the form $(x + p)^2 + q$. How does this work? How is it that the first three terms in the expanded form are always a perfect square?

⚠️ For this method, the coefficient of x^2 must be 1. To use it on, say, $2x^2 + 6x + 5$, you must write it as $2(x^2 + 3x + 2.5)$ and then work with $x^2 + 3x + 2.5$. In completed square form, it is $2(x + 1.5)^2 + 0.5$. Similarly treat $-x^2 + 6x + 5$ as $-1(x^2 - 6x - 5)$ and work with $x^2 - 6x - 5$. In completed square form it is $-1(x - 3)^2 + 14$.

Completing the square is an important technique. Knowing the symmetry and least (or greatest) value of a quadratic function will often give you valuable information about the situation it is modelling.

You may wish to use a graphic calculator or computer graphics package to check your answers to question 1.

1 For each of the following equations:

(a) write it in completed square form

(b) hence write down the equation of the line of symmetry and the co-ordinates of the vertex

(c) sketch the curve.

(i) $y = x^2 + 4x + 9$ (ii) $y = x^2 - 4x + 9$

(iii) $y = x^2 + 4x + 3$ (iv) $y = x^2 - 4x + 3$

(v) $y = x^2 + 6x - 1$ (vi) $y = x^2 - 10x$

(vii) $y = x^2 + x + 2$ (viii) $y = x^2 - 3x - 7$

(ix) $y = x^2 - \frac{1}{2}x + 1$ (x) $y = x^2 + 0.1x + 0.03$

2 Write the following as polynomials in descending powers of x.

(i) $(x + 2)^2 - 3$ (ii) $(x + 4)^2 - 4$

(iii) $(x - 1)^2 + 2$ (iv) $(x - 10)^2 + 12$

(v) $(x - \frac{1}{2})^2 + \frac{3}{4}$ (vi) $(x + 0.1)^2 + 0.99$

3 Write the following in completed square form.

(i) $2x^2 + 4x + 6$ (ii) $3x^2 - 18x - 27$

(iii) $-x^2 - 2x + 5$ (iv) $-2x^2 - 2x - 2$

(v) $5x^2 - 10x + 7$ (vi) $4x^2 - 4x - 4$

(vii) $-3x^2 - 12x$ (viii) $8x^2 + 24x - 2$

4 The curves below all have equations of the form $y = x^2 + bx + c$.
In each case find the values of b and c.

(i)

(3, 1)

(ii)

(−1, −1)

(iii)

(4, 0)

(iv)
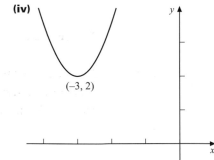
(−3, 2)

Using transformations to sketch the curves of functions

You now know how to sketch the curves of many functions. Frequently, curve sketching can be made easier by relating the equation of the function to that of a standard function of the same form. This allows you to map the points on the standard curve to equivalent points on the curve you need to draw.

The mappings you will use for curve sketching are called *transformations*. There are several types of transformation, each with different effects, and you will find that by using them singly or in combination you can sketch a large variety of curves much more quickly. In this chapter you will just use translations.

Translations

ACTIVITY 3.2

Using a graphic calculator or computer graphics package, draw the graphs of $y = x^2$, $y = x^2 + 3$, and $y = x^2 - 2$ on the same axes.

What do you notice?

Can you see how the second and third graphs could be obtained from the first one?

How could your findings be generalised?

Repeat the procedure using the graphs of $y = x^2$, $y = (x - 2)^2$ and $y = (x + 3)^2$. What happens now?

Figure 3.11 shows the graphs of $y = x^2$ and $y = x^2 + 3$. For any given value of x, the y co-ordinate for the second curve is 3 units more than the y co-ordinate for the first curve.

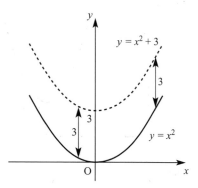

Figure 3.11

Although the curves appear to get closer together as you move away from the line of symmetry, their vertical separation is, in fact, constant. Each of the vertical arrows is 3 units long.

You can see that the graphs of $y = x^2 + 3$ and $y = x^2$ are exactly the same shape, but $y = x^2$ has been translated through 3 units in the positive y direction to obtain $y = x^2 + 3$.

Similarly, $y = x^2 - 2$ could be obtained by translating $y = x^2$ through 2 units in the negative y direction (i.e. -2 units in the positive y direction).

In general, for any function $f(x)$, the curve $y = f(x) + s$ can be obtained from that of $y = f(x)$ by translating it through s units in the positive y direction.

What about the relationship between the graphs of $y = x^2$ and $y = (x-2)^2$? Figure 3.12 shows the graphs of these two functions. Again, these curves have exactly the same shape, but as you can see, this time they are separated by a constant 2 units in the x direction.

You may find it surprising that $y = x^2$ moves in the positive x direction when 2 is subtracted from x. It happens because x must be correspondingly larger if $(x-2)$ is to give the same output that x did in the first mapping.

Notice that the axis of symmetry of the curve $y = (x-2)^2$ is the line $x = 2$.

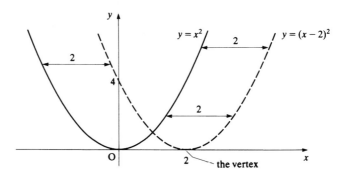

Figure 3.12

In general, the curve with equation $y = f(x - t)$ can be obtained from the curve with equation $y = f(x)$ by a translation of t units in the positive x direction.

Combining these results, $y = f(x - t) + s$ is obtained from $y = f(x)$ by a translation of s units in the positive y direction and t units in the positive x direction.

This translation is represented by the vector $\begin{pmatrix} t \\ s \end{pmatrix}$.

Note

The last result may be written as:

the graph of $y = f(x)$ when translated by $\begin{pmatrix} t \\ s \end{pmatrix}$ results in the graph $y - s = f(x - t)$.

Writing the result in this form shows the symmetry of the results. Translating $y = f(x)$ by t in the positive x direction is equivalent to replacing x with $x - t$. Translating $y = f(x)$ by s in the positive y direction is equivalent to replacing y with $y - s$.

EXAMPLE 3.15

Figure 3.13 shows the graph of $y = x^3$ translated by $\begin{pmatrix} -1 \\ 4 \end{pmatrix}$. Show that the resulting graph has the equation $y = x^3 + 3x^2 + 3x + 5$.

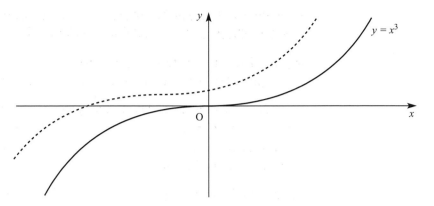

Figure 3.13

SOLUTION

After a translation of $\begin{pmatrix} -1 \\ 4 \end{pmatrix}$, the resulting graph has the equation

$$y = (x - (-1))^3 + 4 \quad \longleftarrow \quad \boxed{\text{This is } y - 4 = (x - (-1))^3.}$$

$\Rightarrow \quad y = (x + 1)^3 + 4$

$\Rightarrow \quad y = (x + 1)(x^2 + 2x + 1) + 4$

$\Rightarrow \quad y = (x^3 + 2x^2 + x + x^2 + 2x + 1) + 4$

$\Rightarrow \quad y = (x^3 + 3x^2 + 3x + 1) + 4$

$\Rightarrow \quad y = x^3 + 3x^2 + 3x + 5$, as required.

Using the technique of completeting the square, any quadratic expression of the form $y = x^2 + bx + c$ can be written as $y = (x - t)^2 + s$, so its graph can be sketched by relating it to the graph of $y = x^2$. It is the graph of $y = x^2$ translated by $\begin{pmatrix} t \\ s \end{pmatrix}$.

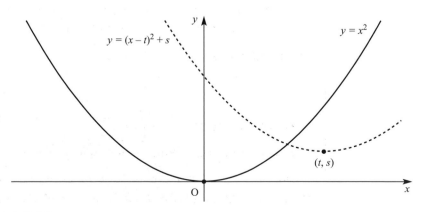

Figure 3.14

? In this chapter you have met two ways of looking at the graph of a quadratic function, completing the square and using translations.
What are the advantages and disadvantages of each way?

EXAMPLE 3.16

(i) Find values of s and t such that $x^2 - 2x + 5 \equiv (x - t)^2 + s$.

(ii) Sketch the graph of $y = x^2 - 2x + 5$ and state the position of its vertex and the equation of its axis of symmetry.

SOLUTION

Since the form of the right-hand side is given, it is easiest to expand this and then compare coefficients:

$$x^2 - 2x + 5 \equiv (x - t)^2 + s$$

$$\Rightarrow \quad x^2 - 2x + 5 \equiv x^2 - 2xt + t^2 + s.$$

Comparing coefficients gives $t = 1$ and $s = 4$.

Rewriting the equation as $y = (x - 1)^2 + 4$ or $(y - 4) = (x - 1)^2$ shows that the curve can be obtained from the graph of $y = x^2$ by a translation of 1 unit in the positive x direction, and 4 units in the positive y direction, i.e. a translation $\begin{pmatrix} 1 \\ 4 \end{pmatrix}$.

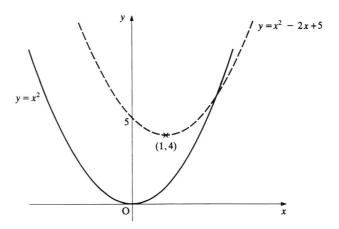

Figure 3.15

The vertex is $(1, 4)$ and the axis of symmetry is the line $x = 1$ (see figure 3.15).

? Would you be justified in finding the values of s and t by substituting, for example, $x = 0$ and $x = 1$ in the identity $x^2 - 2x + 5 \equiv (x - t)^2 + s$?

ACTIVITY 3.3

Draw the line $y = 2x + 3$. Find the equation obtained when the line is translated through $\binom{4}{1}$:

(i) by a graphical method

(ii) by transforming the equation.

EXAMPLE 3.17

Figure 3.16 shows part of the scalloped bottom of a roller blind.

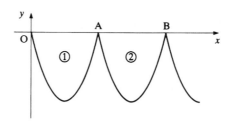

Figure 3.16

The equation of curve ① with respect to the x and y axes shown is $y = x^2 - 4x$ for $0 \leqslant x \leqslant 4$.

Find the equation of curve ②.

SOLUTION

The equation of curve ① can be factorised to give $y = x(x - 4)$, so when $y = 0$, $x = 0$ or 4.

Clearly, O is $(0, 0)$ and A is $(4, 0)$.

Curve ② is therefore obtained from curve ① by a translation of 4 units in the positive x direction.

To find the equation of curve ②, you replace x by $(x - 4)$ in the equation of curve ①.

Using the factorised form, the equation of curve ② is

$$y = (x - 4)[(x - 4) - 4] \quad \text{for } 0 \leqslant x - 4 \leqslant 4$$
$$\Rightarrow \quad y = (x - 4)(x - 8) \quad \text{for } 4 \leqslant x \leqslant 8.$$

EXERCISE 3E

1 Starting with the graph of $y = x^2$, give the vectors for the translations which can be used to sketch the following curves.
State also the equation of the line of symmetry of each of these curves.

(i) $y = x^2 + 3$ **(ii)** $y = (x + 4)^2$

(iii) $y = x^2 - 7$ **(iv)** $y = (x - 1)^2$

(v) $y = (x - 2)^2 + 10$ **(vi)** $y = (x + 5)^2 + 6$

(vii) $y = x^2 - 2x$ **(viii)** $y = x^2 - 4x + 3$

2 Starting with the graph of $y = x^3$, find the equation of the graph resulting from the following translations. (You do not need to multiply out any brackets.)

(i) $\begin{pmatrix} 0 \\ 4 \end{pmatrix}$ (ii) $\begin{pmatrix} 4 \\ 0 \end{pmatrix}$ (iii) $\begin{pmatrix} -3 \\ 0 \end{pmatrix}$

(iv) $\begin{pmatrix} 0 \\ -20 \end{pmatrix}$ (v) $\begin{pmatrix} 5 \\ 6 \end{pmatrix}$ (vi) $\begin{pmatrix} -7 \\ 1 \end{pmatrix}$

3 A cubic graph has the equation $y = 3(x-1)(x+2)(x+5)$.

Write in similar form the equation of the graph after a translation of $\begin{pmatrix} 3 \\ 0 \end{pmatrix}$.

4 (i) On the same diagram, sketch the lines $y = 3x$ and $y = 3x - 3$.

(ii) $y = 3x$ can be transformed to $y = 3x - 3$ by a translation of $\begin{pmatrix} 0 \\ a \end{pmatrix}$.
What is the value of a?

(iii) $y = 3x$ can be transformed to $y = 3x - 3$ by a translation of $\begin{pmatrix} b \\ 0 \end{pmatrix}$.
What is the value of b?

5 Find, in the form $y = mx + c$, the equation of the resulting straight line when the graph of $y = 2x$ is translated by the following vectors.

(i) $\begin{pmatrix} 0 \\ 6 \end{pmatrix}$ (ii) $\begin{pmatrix} -8 \\ 0 \end{pmatrix}$ (iii) $\begin{pmatrix} -5 \\ -10 \end{pmatrix}$

6 (i) Show that $x^2 + 6x + 5$ can be written in the form $(x + 3)^2 + a$ where a is a constant to be determined.

(ii) Sketch the graph of $y = x^2 + 6x + 5$, giving the equation of the axis of symmetry and the co-ordinates of the vertex.

7 Given that $f(x) = x^2 - 6x + 11$, find values of p and q such that
$$f(x) = (x - p)^2 + q.$$

On the same set of axes, sketch and label the following curves.

(i) $y = f(x)$ (ii) $y = f(x + 4)$

8 The graph of $y = x^2 + 8x + 3$ is translated by $\begin{pmatrix} -6 \\ 4 \end{pmatrix}$.

Find, in the form $y = ax^2 + bx + c$, the equation of the resulting graph.

9 The diagram shows the graph of $y = g(x)$.

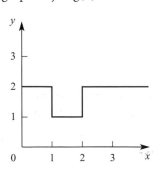

(i) Write down the equation of the graph given by each of the following diagrams.

(a)

(b)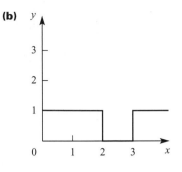

(ii) Sketch the graph of $y = g(x + 2) + 3$.

10 The sketch shows the graph of $y = h(x)$.

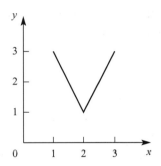

Sketch the graphs of the following, using a separate set of axes for each graph.

(i) $y = h(x) - 1$ (ii) $y = h(x - 2)$ (iii) $y = h(x + 2) - 3$

11 The diagram shows the graph of $y = f(x)$ which has a maximum point at $(-2, 2)$, a minimum point at $(2, -2)$, and passes through the origin.

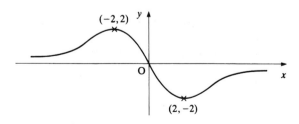

Sketch the following graphs, using a separate set of axes for each graph, and indicating the co-ordinates of the turning points.

(i) $y = f(x - 2)$ (ii) $y = f(x) + 2$ (iii) $y = f(x + 2) - 2$

12 The table gives some values of y for the function $y = f(x)$.

x	0	1	2	3	4	5	6
$y = f(x)$	0.5	1	3	6	10	12	13

Find the value of y when $x = 3$, when the graph is translated by the following vectors.

(i) $\begin{pmatrix} 0 \\ 3 \end{pmatrix}$ **(ii)** $\begin{pmatrix} 0 \\ -1 \end{pmatrix}$ **(iii)** $\begin{pmatrix} 2 \\ 0 \end{pmatrix}$

(iv) $\begin{pmatrix} -3 \\ 0 \end{pmatrix}$ **(v)** $\begin{pmatrix} -1 \\ 5 \end{pmatrix}$ **(vi)** $\begin{pmatrix} 3 \\ 3 \end{pmatrix}$

Binomial expansions

A special type of polynomial is produced when a binomial (i.e. two-part) expression like $(x + 1)$ is raised to a power. The resulting polynomial is often called a *binomial expansion*.

The simplest binomial expansion is $(x + 1)$ itself. This and other powers of $(x + 1)$ are given below.

$$
\begin{array}{rcccccccccc}
(x + 1)^1 = & & & & & 1x & + & 1 \\
(x + 1)^2 = & & & & 1x^2 & + & 2x & + & 1 \\
(x + 1)^3 = & & & 1x^3 & + & 3x^2 & + & 3x & + & 1 \\
(x + 1)^4 = & & 1x^4 & + & 4x^3 & + & 6x^2 & + & 4x & + & 1 \\
(x + 1)^5 = & 1x^5 & + & 5x^4 & + & 10x^3 & + & 10x^2 & + & 5x & + & 1
\end{array}
$$

If you look at the coefficients on the right-hand side above you will see that they form a pattern.

$$
\begin{array}{ccccccccccc}
& & & & & (1) \\
& & & & 1 & & 1 \\
& & & 1 & & 2 & & 1 \\
& & 1 & & 3 & & 3 & & 1 \\
& 1 & & 4 & & 6 & & 4 & & 1 \\
1 & & 5 & & 10 & & 10 & & 5 & & 1
\end{array}
$$

> These numbers are called *binomial* coefficients.

This is called *Pascal's triangle*, or the *Chinese triangle*. Each number is obtained by adding the two above it, for example

$$
\begin{array}{ccc}
4 & + & 6 \\
\text{gives} & 10
\end{array}
$$

This pattern of coefficients is very useful. It enables you to write down the expansions of other binomial expressions. For example,

$$
\begin{array}{rccccccc}
(x + y) = & & & 1x & + & 1y \\
(x + y)^2 = & & 1x^2 & + & 2xy & + & 1y^2 \\
(x + y)^3 = & 1x^3 & + & 3x^2y & + & 3xy^2 & + & 1y^3
\end{array}
$$

> Notice how in each term the sum of the powers of x and y is the same as the power of $(x + y)$.

> This is a binomial expression.

> These numbers are called binomial coefficients.

EXAMPLE 3.18

Write out the binomial expansion of $(x + 2)^4$.

SOLUTION

The binomial coefficients for power 4 are   1   4   6   4   1.

In each term, the sum of the powers of x and 2 must equal 4.

So the expansion is

$$1 \times x^4 \quad + \quad 4 \times x^3 \times 2 \quad + \quad 6 \times x^2 \times 2^2 \quad + \quad 4 \times x \times 2^3 \quad + \quad 1 \times 2^4$$

i.e. $x^4 \quad + \quad 8x^3 \quad + \quad 24x^2 \quad + \quad 32x \quad + \quad 16.$

EXAMPLE 3.19

Write out the binomial expansion of $(2a - 3b)^5$.

SOLUTION

The binomial coefficients for power 5 are   1   5   10   10   5   1.

The expression $(2a - 3b)$ is treated as $(2a + (-3b))$.

So the expansion is

$$1 \times (2a)^5 + 5 \times (2a)^4 \times (-3b) + 10 \times (2a)^3 \times (-3b)^2 + 10 \times (2a)^2 \times (-3b)^3$$
$$+ 5 \times (2a) \times (-3b)^4 + 1 \times (-3b)^5$$

i.e. $32a^5 - 240a^4b + 720a^3b^2 - 1080a^2b^3 + 810ab^4 - 243b^5.$

Historical note

Blaise Pascal has been described as the greatest might-have-been in the history of mathematics. Born in France in 1623, he was making discoveries in geometry by the age of 16 and had developed the first computing machine before he was 20.

Pascal suffered from poor health and religious anxiety, so that for periods of his life he gave up mathematics in favour of religious contemplation. The second of these periods was brought on when he was riding in his carriage: his runaway horses dashed over the parapet of a bridge, and he was only saved by the miraculous breaking of the traces. He took this to be a sign of God's disapproval of his mathematical work. A few years later a toothache subsided when he was thinking about geometry and this, he decided, was God's way of telling him to return to mathematics.

Pascal's triangle (and the binomial theorem) had actually been discovered by Chinese mathematicians several centuries earlier, and can be found in the works of Yang Hui (around 1270 A.D.) and Chu Shi-kie (in 1303 A.D.). Pascal is remembered for his application of the triangle to elementary probability, and for his study of the relationships between binomial coefficients.

Pascal died at the early age of 39.

Tables of binomial coefficients

Values of binomial coefficients can be found in books of tables. It is helpful to use these when the power becomes large, since writing out Pascal's triangle becomes progressively longer and more tedious, row by row.

EXAMPLE 3.20

Write out the full expansion of $(x + y)^{10}$.

SOLUTION

The binomial coefficients for the power 10 can be found from tables to be

$$1 \quad 10 \quad 45 \quad 120 \quad 210 \quad 252 \quad 210 \quad 120 \quad 45 \quad 10 \quad 1$$

and so the expansion is

$$x^{10} + 10x^9y + 45x^8y^2 + 120x^7y^3 + 210x^6y^4 + 252x^5y^5 + 210x^4y^6 + 120x^3y^7$$
$$+ 45x^2y^8 + 10xy^9 + y^{10}.$$

There are $10 + 1 = 11$ terms.

 As the numbers are symmetrical about the middle number, tables do not always give the complete row of numbers.

The formula for a binomial coefficient

There will be times when you need to find binomial coefficients that are outside the range of your tables. The tables may, for example, list the binomial coefficients for powers up to 20. What happens if you need to find the coefficient of x^{17} in the expansion of $(x + 2)^{25}$? Clearly you need a formula that gives binomial coefficients.

The first thing you need is a notation for identifying binomial coefficients. It is usual to denote the power of the binomial expression by n, and the position in the row of binomial coefficients by r, where r can take any value from 0 to n. So for row 5 of Pascal's triangle

$$n = 5: \qquad 1 \qquad 5 \qquad 10 \qquad 10 \qquad 5 \qquad 1$$
$$r = 0 \quad r = 1 \quad r = 2 \quad r = 3 \quad r = 4 \quad r = 5$$

The general binomial coefficient corresponding to values of n and r is written as ^nC_r and said as 'N C R'.

An alternative notation is $\binom{n}{r}$. Thus $^5C_3 = \binom{5}{3} = 10$.

The next step is to find a formula for the general binomial coefficient ^nC_r. However, to do this you must be familiar with the term *factorial*.

The quantity '8 factorial', written 8!, is

$$8! = 8 \times 7 \times 6 \times 5 \times 4 \times 3 \times 2 \times 1 = 40\,320.$$

Similarly, $12! = 12 \times 11 \times 10 \times 9 \times 8 \times 7 \times 6 \times 5 \times 4 \times 3 \times 2 \times 1 = 479\,001\,600$,

and $n! = n \times (n - 1) \times (n - 2) \times \ldots \times 1$, where n is a positive integer.

⚠ Note that 0! is defined to be 1. You will see the need for this when you use the formula for ^nC_r.

ACTIVITY 3.4

The table shows an alternative way of laying out Pascal's triangle.

		Column (r)								
		0	1	2	3	4	5	6	...	r
	1	1	1							
	2	1	2	1						
Row (n)	3	1	3	3	1					
	4	1	4	6	4	1				
	5	1	5	10	10	5	1			
	6	1	6	15	20	15	6	1		
	...	...	...	...	...	...	...	...	...	
	...	...	...	...	...	...	...	...	...	...
	n	1	n	?	?	?	?	?	?	?

Show that $^nC_r = \dfrac{n!}{r!(n-r)!}$, by following the procedure below.

The numbers in column 0 are all 1.

To find each number in column 1 you multiply the 1 in column 0 by the row number, n.

(i) Find, in terms of n, what you must multiply each number in column 1 by to find the corresponding number in column 2.

(ii) Repeat the process to find the relationship between each number in column 2 and the corresponding one in column 3.

(iii) Show that repeating the process leads to

$$^nC_r = \frac{n(n-1)(n-2)\ldots(n-r+1)}{1\times2\times3\times\ldots\times r} \text{ for } r \geqslant 1.$$

(iv) Show that this can also be written as

$$^nC_r = \frac{n!}{r!(n-r)!}$$

and that it is also true for $r = 0$.

EXAMPLE 3.21

Use the formula $^nC_r = \dfrac{n!}{r!\,(n-r)!}$ to calculate:

(i) $^5C_0$ **(ii)** $^5C_1$ **(iii)** $^5C_2$ **(iv)** $^5C_3$ **(v)** $^5C_4$ **(vi)** $^5C_5$.

SOLUTION

(i) $^5C_0 = \dfrac{5!}{0!\,(5-0)!} = \dfrac{120}{1 \times 120} = 1$

(ii) $^5C_1 = \dfrac{5!}{1!\,4!} = \dfrac{120}{1 \times 24} = 5$

(iii) $^5C_2 = \dfrac{5!}{2!\,3!} = \dfrac{120}{2 \times 6} = 10$

(iv) $^5C_3 = \dfrac{5!}{3!\,2!} = \dfrac{120}{6 \times 2} = 10$

(v) $^5C_4 = \dfrac{5!}{4!\,1!} = \dfrac{120}{24 \times 1} = 5$

(vi) $^5C_5 = \dfrac{5!}{5!\,0!} = \dfrac{120}{120 \times 1} = 1$

Note

You can see that these numbers, 1, 5, 10, 10, 5, 1, are row 5 of Pascal's triangle.

 Most scientific calculators have factorial buttons, e.g. $\boxed{x!}$. Many also have $\boxed{^nC_r}$ buttons. Find out how best to use your calculator to find binomial coefficients, as well as practising non-calculator methods.

EXAMPLE 3.22

Find the coefficient of x^{17} in the expansion of $(x+2)^{25}$.

SOLUTION

$(x+2)^{25} = {}^{25}C_0\, x^{25} + {}^{25}C_1\, x^{24}\, 2^1 + {}^{25}C_2\, x^{23}\, 2^2 + \ldots + {}^{25}C_8\, x^{17}\, 2^8 + \ldots\, {}^{25}C_{25}\, 2^{25}$

So the required term is $^{25}C_8 \times 2^8 \times x^{17}$

$$^{25}C_8 = \frac{25!}{8!\,17!} = \frac{25 \times 24 \times 23 \times 22 \times 21 \times 20 \times 19 \times 18 \times \cancel{17!}}{8! \times \cancel{17!}}$$

$$= 1\,081\,575.$$

So the coefficient of x^{17} is $1\,081\,575 \times 2^8 = 276\,883\,200$.

Note

Notice how 17! was cancelled in working out $^{25}C_8$. Factorials become large numbers very quickly and you should keep a look-out for such opportunities to simplify calculations.

The expansion of $(1 + x)^n$

When deriving the result for ^nC_r you found the binomial coefficients in the form

$$1 \qquad n \qquad \frac{n(n-1)}{2!} \qquad \frac{n(n-1)(n-2)}{3!} \qquad \frac{n(n-1)(n-2)(n-3)}{4!} \qquad \dots$$

This form is commonly used in the expansion of expressions of the type $(1 + x)^n$.

$$(1 + x)^n = 1 + nx + \frac{n(n-1)x^2}{1 \times 2} + \frac{n(n-1)(n-2)x^3}{1 \times 2 \times 3} + \frac{n(n-1)(n-2)(n-3)x^4}{1 \times 2 \times 3 \times 4} + \dots$$

$$+ \frac{n(n-1)}{1 \times 2} x^{n-2} + nx^{n-1} + 1x^n$$

EXAMPLE 3.23

Use the binomial expansion to write down the first four terms of $(1 + x)^9$.

SOLUTION

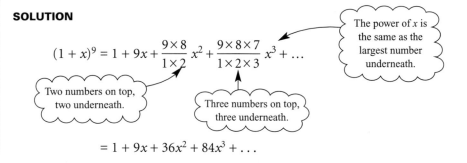

The power of x is the same as the largest number underneath.

$$(1 + x)^9 = 1 + 9x + \frac{9 \times 8}{1 \times 2}x^2 + \frac{9 \times 8 \times 7}{1 \times 2 \times 3}x^3 + \dots$$

Two numbers on top, two underneath.

Three numbers on top, three underneath.

$$= 1 + 9x + 36x^2 + 84x^3 + \dots$$

EXAMPLE 3.24

Use the binomial expansion to write down the first four terms of $(1 - 3x)^7$. Simplify the terms.

SOLUTION

Think of $(1 - 3x)^7$ as $(1 + (-3x))^7$. Keep the brackets while you write out the terms.

$$(1 + (-3x))^7 = 1 + 7(-3x) + \frac{7 \times 6}{1 \times 2}(-3x)^2 + \frac{7 \times 6 \times 5}{1 \times 2 \times 3}(-3x)^3 + \dots$$

$$= 1 - 21x + 189x^2 - 945x^3 + \dots \quad \longleftarrow \quad \text{Note how the signs alternate.}$$

EXAMPLE 3.25

(i) Write down the binomial expansion of $(1 - x)^4$.

(ii) Using $x = 0.03$ and the first three terms of the expansion find an approximate value for $(0.97)^4$.

(iii) Use your calculator to find the percentage error in your answer.

SOLUTION

(i) $(1 - x)^4 = (1 + (-x))^4$

$\qquad = 1 + 4(-x) + 6(-x)^2 + 4(-x)^3 + (-x)^4$

$\qquad = 1 - 4x + 6x^2 - 4x^3 + x^4$

(ii) $(0.97)^4 \approx 1 - 4(0.03) + 6(0.03)^2$
$$= 0.8854$$

(iii) $(0.97)^4 = 0.885\,292\,81$
Error $= 0.8854 - 0.885\,292\,81$
$$= 0.000\,107\,19$$

Percentage error $= \dfrac{\text{error}}{\text{true value}} \times 100$
$$= \dfrac{0.000\,107\,19}{0.885\,292\,81} \times 100$$
$$= 0.0121\%$$

❷ A Pascal puzzle

$1.1^2 = 1.21 \qquad 1.1^3 = 1.331 \qquad 1.1^4 = 1.4641$

What is 1.1^5?

What is the connection between your results and the coefficients in Pascal's triangle?

Relationships between binomial coefficients

There are several useful relationships between binomial coefficients.

Symmetry

Because Pascal's triangle is symmetrical about its middle, it follows that

$$^nC_r = {}^nC_{n-r}.$$

Adding terms

You have seen that each term in Pascal's triangle is formed by adding the two above it. This is written formally as

$$^nC_r + {}^nC_{r+1} = {}^{n+1}C_{r+1}.$$

Sum of terms

You have seen that

$$(x + y)^n = {}^nC_0 x^n + {}^nC_1 x^{n-1}y + {}^nC_2 x^{n-2} y^2 + \ldots + {}^nC_n y^n$$

Substituting $x = y = 1$ gives

$$2^n = {}^nC_0 + {}^nC_1 + {}^nC_2 + \ldots + {}^nC_n.$$

Thus the sum of the binomial coefficients for power n is 2^n.

The binomial theorem and its applications

The binomial expansions covered in the last few pages can be stated formally as the binomial theorem for positive integer powers:

$$(a + b)^n = \sum_{r=0}^{n} {}^nC_r a^{n-r}b^r \qquad \text{for } n \in \mathbb{Z}^+, \qquad \text{where } {}^nC_r = \frac{n!}{r!(n-r)!} \qquad \text{and } 0! = 1.$$

Note

Notice the use of the summation symbol, $\sum$. The right-hand side of the statement reads 'the sum of ${}^nC_r \, a^{n-r}b^r$ for values of r from 0 to n'.
It therefore means

$$\underset{r=0}{{}^nC_0 a^n} + \underset{r=1}{{}^nC_1 a^{n-1}b} + \underset{r=2}{{}^nC_2 a^{n-2}b^2} + \dots + \underset{r=k}{{}^nC_k a^{n-k}b^k} + \dots + \underset{r=n}{{}^nC_n b^n}.$$

The binomial theorem is used on other types of expansion and these are covered later in this series. It has applications in many areas of mathematics, some of which are covered by other books in this series.

Binomial approximations

The binomial theorem is used to write expressions in approximate form so that they will be easier to work with. This is covered later in this series.

The binomial distribution

In some situations involving repetitions of trials with two possible outcomes, the probabilities of the various possible results are given by the terms of a binomial expansion. This is covered in *Statistics 1*.

Selections

The number of ways of selecting r objects from n (all different) is given by ${}^nC_r$. This is also covered in *Statistics 1*.

EXERCISE 3F

1 Write out the following binomial expansions.

   (i) $(x + 1)^4$ (ii) $(1 + x)^7$ (iii) $(x + 2)^5$
   (iv) $(2x + 1)^6$ (v) $(2x - 3)^4$ (vi) $(2x + 3y)^3$

2 Use a non-calculator method to calculate the following binomial coefficients. Check your answers using your calculator's shortest method.

   (i) ${}^4C_2$ (ii) ${}^6C_2$ (iii) ${}^6C_3$
   (iv) ${}^6C_4$ (v) ${}^6C_0$ (vi) ${}^{12}C_9$
   (vii) ${}^{12}C_3$ (viii) ${}^{15}C_{11}$ (ix) ${}^8C_8$

3 Find:

   (i) the coefficient of x^5 in the expansion of $(1 + x)^8$

   (ii) the coefficient of x^4 in the expansion of $(1 - x)^{10}$

   (iii) the coefficient of x^6 in the expansion of $(1 + 3x)^{12}$

   (iv) the coefficient of x^7 in the expansion of $(1 - 2x)^{15}$

   (v) the value of the term in the expansion of $\left(x - \frac{1}{x}\right)^8$ which is independent of x.

4 **(i)** Write down the binomial expansion of $(1 + x)^4$.

   (ii) Use the first two terms of the expansion to find an approximate value for $(1.002)^4$, substituting $x = 0.002$.

   (iii) Find, using your calculator, the percentage error in making this approximation.

5 **(i)** Simplify $(1 + x)^3 - (1 - x)^3$.

   (ii) Show that $a^3 - b^3 = (a - b)(a^2 + ab + b^2)$.

   (iii) Substitute $a = 1 + x$ and $b = 1 - x$ in the result in part (ii) and show that your answer is the same as that for part (i).

6 **(i)** Write down the binomial expansion of $(2 - x)^5$.

   (ii) By substituting $x = 0.01$ in the first three terms of your expansion, obtain an approximate value for 1.99^5.

   (ii) Use your calculator to find the percentage error in your answer.

7 **(i)** On the same axes for $0 \leqslant x \leqslant 1$ and $0 \leqslant y \leqslant 1$ plot the curves with equations:

     (a) $y = 1$ **(b)** $y = 1 - 3x$

     (c) $y = 1 - 3x + 3x^2$ **(d)** $y = (1 - x)^3$.

   (ii) On your curves mark points A, B, C and D corresponding to the values of y when $x = 0.2$.

   (iii) State the lengths on your graph which represent the errors in estimating the values of $(0.8)^3$ by using the following numbers of terms of the binomial expansion of $(1 - x)^3$ with $x = 0.2$.

     (a) 1   **(b)** 2   **(c)** 3

8 A sum of money, £P, is invested such that compound interest is earned at a rate of $r\%$ per year. The amount, £A, in the account n years later is given by

$$A = P\left(1 + \frac{r}{100}\right)^n.$$

   (i) Write down the first four terms in this expansion when $P = 1000$, $r = 10$, $n = 10$ and add them to get an approximate value for A.

   (ii) Compare your result with what you get using your calculator for 1000×1.1^{10}.

   (iii) Find the error in using the sum of these four terms instead of the true value.

9 **(i)** Show that $(2 + x)^4 = 16 + 32x + 24x^2 + 8x^3 + x^4$ for all x.

   (ii) Find the values of x for which $(2 + x)^4 = 16 + 16x + x^4$.

                                                                  [MEI]

10 The diagram shows sketches of the graphs of $y = f(x)$ and $y = g(x)$, where $f(x) = x^3 - 6x^2 - 13x + 42$ and $g(x) = (2 - x)^4$.

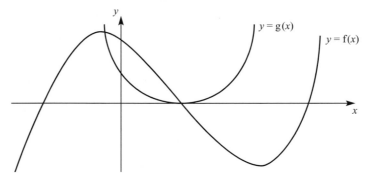

(i) Use the factor theorem to find a linear factor of $f(x)$.
Express $f(x)$ as the product of this linear factor and a quadratic factor.
(ii) Find the co-ordinates of the points where the graph of $y = f(x)$ cuts the x axis.
(iii) Expand $g(x)$ in ascending powers of x, simplifying the coefficients.
(iv) The first *two* terms of the expansion in part (iii) may be used to give an aproximation to $g(x)$ when x is small.
Use your calculator to find the error in using this approximation when $x = 0.1$.

[**MEI**]

INVESTIGATIONS

Cubes

A cube is painted red. It is then cut up into a number of identical cubes, as in figure 3.17.

How many of the cubes have the following numbers of faces painted red?

(i) 3   **(ii)** 2   **(iii)** 1   **(iv)** 0

In figure 3.17 there are 125 cubes but your answer should cover all possible cases.

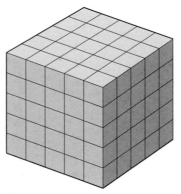

Figure 3.17

Routes to victory

In a recent soccer match, Blackburn Rovers beat Newcastle United 2–1. What could the half-time score have been?

(i) How many different possible half-time scores are there if the final score is 2–1? How many if the final score is 4–3?
(ii) How many different 'routes' are there to any final score? For example, for the above match, putting Blackburn's score first, the sequence could be:

$$0{-}0 \rightarrow 0{-}1 \rightarrow 1{-}1 \rightarrow 2{-}1$$
$$\text{or} \quad 0{-}0 \rightarrow 1{-}0 \rightarrow 1{-}1 \rightarrow 2{-}1$$
$$\text{or} \quad 0{-}0 \rightarrow 1{-}0 \rightarrow 2{-}0 \rightarrow 2{-}1.$$

So in this case there are three routes.

Investigate the number of routes that exist to any final score (up to a maximum of five goals for either team).
Draw up a table of your results. Is there a pattern?

1 A polynomial in x has terms in positive integer powers of x, and may also have a constant term.

2 The order of a polynomial in x is the highest power of x which appears in the polynomial.

3 The factor theorem states that if $(x - a)$ is a factor of a polynomial $f(x)$ then $f(a) = 0$ and $x = a$ is a root of the equation $f(x) = 0$.
Conversely if $f(a) = 0$, then $x - a$ is a factor of $f(x)$.

4 The remainder theorem states that $f(a)$ is the remainder when $f(x)$ is divided by $(x - a)$.

5 The curve of a polynomial function of order n has up to $(n - 1)$ turning points.

6 The behaviour of the curve of a polynomial of order n, for large positive and negative values of n, depends on whether n is even or odd, and whether the coefficient of the term in x^n is positive or negative.

7 The vertex and line of symmetry of a quadratic may be found by completing the square.

8 Translations of the graph of the function $y = f(x)$:

Translation	Resulting function
$\begin{pmatrix} t \\ 0 \end{pmatrix}$	$y = f(x - t)$
$\begin{pmatrix} 0 \\ s \end{pmatrix}$	$y = f(x) + s$
$\begin{pmatrix} t \\ s \end{pmatrix}$	$y = f(x - t) + s$

9 Binomial coefficients, denoted by ^nC_r or $\begin{pmatrix} n \\ r \end{pmatrix}$, can be found
   • using Pascal's triangle
   • using tables
   • using the formula $^nC_r = \dfrac{n!}{r!(n-r)!}$.

10 The binomial expansion of $(1 + x)^n$ may also be written

$$(1 + x)^n = 1 + nx + \frac{n(n-1)}{2!}x^2 + \frac{n(n-1)(n-2)}{3!}x^3 + \ldots + nx^{n-1} + x^n.$$

4

Uncertainty

When the learned man errs, he errs in a learned way.

Arabic proverb

The Avonford Star

New bypass to cost £23,642,186.94

At last we are able to reveal to our readers the cost, down to the very last penny, of the Avonford bypass.

Work is due to start the year after next and is expected to take 57 weeks and 3 days.

? Are you convinced by the costing 'down to the very last penny'? Between what limits do you think the final cost might actually fall? What about the length of time the work will take?

Mathematics is often described as a precise subject and so it is. But there are times when the most precise statement you can make is to say that you cannot know the exact answer. However, you will often be able to say that it will lie within certain limits.

This chapter looks at techniques for dealing with such situations.

Errors and inequalities

? Sarah and her brother Stephen walk from home to school each morning. One day they time themselves on what turns out to be a typical journey. As a result Stephen tells his friends 'It takes me 6 minutes 28 seconds to walk to school', whereas Sarah says 'It takes me between 6 and 7 minutes to walk to school'.

Whose statement is more likely to be true?

Variability

Virtually every real situation involves variability. It is important to build this into the solution to any problem, as in the next example.

EXAMPLE 4.1

A car's petrol tank holds 50 litres of petrol. The manufacturers claim that the car will travel 12 km on a litre of petrol. In fact, according to circumstances (such as how well the car's engine is tuned and how fast it is driven) the car may travel as little as 10 km on a litre of petrol or as much as 12.5 km. Is it safe to set out with only one full tank of petrol on a journey across a 550 km stretch of desert where no petrol is available?

SOLUTION

If the manufacturer's claim is accepted, the car can travel $50 \times 12 = 600$ km on a full tank, and so the journey is quite safe.

In practice, however, the car may travel anything between $50 \times 10 = 500$ km and $50 \times 12.5 = 625$ km, so it is possible that it will run out of petrol. It would be unwise to set out without a spare can of petrol.

The distance, d km, that could be travelled on a full tank by the car in the example is given by the inequalities

$$d \geqslant 500 \quad \text{and} \quad d \leqslant 625.$$

These two conditions would usually be written together in the form

$$500 \leqslant d \leqslant 625.$$

We say that 500 and 625 are the *lower* and *upper bounds* for d.

 When an answer contains two inequalities, they must both be in the same direction: $625 \geqslant d \geqslant 500$ is also correct.

ⓔ The accuracy of given or stored information

It is important to realise that the way in which a number is stated gives you information about the bounds within which it lies. The statement 'This piece of wood is 5 metres long', is actually telling you that its length ℓ metres is subject to the inequality

$$4.5 \leqslant \ell < 5.5.$$

If the statement had been 'This piece of wood is 5.0 metres long', the corresponding inequality would have been

$$4.95 \leqslant \ell < 5.05.$$

If the statement had been 'This piece of wood is 5.23 metres long', then the appropriate inequality would be

$$5.225 \leqslant \ell < 5.235.$$

In other words, you can take the final digit to be rounded and all the others to be accurate.

 There are various conventions about when a number ending in a 5 is rounded up or down. The common convention that '5 rounds up' is used here.

Whenever a number is given in rounded form you can write down an inequality which applies to its true value.

- $x = 12$ to the nearest whole number $\Leftrightarrow 11.5 \leqslant x < 12.5$.

- $y = 4.67$ to 3 significant figures $\Leftrightarrow 4.665 \leqslant y < 4.675$.

- $z = 0.1872$ to 4 decimal places $\Leftrightarrow 0.18715 \leqslant z < 0.18725$.

 It is quite wrong to give figures to a higher level of accuracy than you can justify. When presenting any figures or experimental data you should consider all possible sources of error in the collection of the information, the conduct of the experiment or in the actual measuring processes. When a figure is retrieved from a computer or calculator, the final digit should always be treated as unreliable because of the limited memory space assigned to any number within the machine.

When carrying out a calculation you should always be aware of the possible effect of errors on your answer and be prepared to establish bounds within which it lies.

 In mathematics, the word 'error' is not usually used to mean 'mistake'. What does it mean?

The difference between a true value and that which is actually obtained is called the *absolute error*. The *relative error* or *percentage error* is the absolute error written as a proportion or as a percentage of the true value.

These terms are illustrated in the following example.

EXAMPLE 4.2

A rectangular lawn is stated to be 22 m long and 12 m wide.

(i) Between what bounds does its area, A m², lie?

In fact the true area is 272.55 m². The lawn's owner states that it is $22 \times 12 = 264$ m². Find:

(ii) the absolute error
(iii) the percentage error in the owner's statement.

SOLUTION

(i) The smallest possible area is clearly the product of the least possible values of the length and width, 21.5×11.5. Similarly for the greatest possible area you multiply the greatest values of length and width, so

$$21.5 \times 11.5 \leqslant A < 22.5 \times 12.5$$
$$247.25 \leqslant A < 281.25.$$

(ii) The absolute error is the difference between the true value and that calculated.

$$\text{Absolute error} = 272.55 - 264$$
$$= 8.55 \text{ m}^2$$

(iii) The percentage error is the absolute error written as a percentage of the true value.

$$\text{Percentage error} = \frac{\text{absolute error}}{\text{true value}} \times 100\ \%$$
$$= \frac{8.55}{272.55} \times 100\ \%$$
$$= 3.1\%$$

> The relative error can be given as 0.031 or $\frac{31}{1000}$ or 3.1%.

 Large errors can occur when a calculation involves subtracting one number from another that is almost the same size, particularly when you are dividing by this answer.

ACTIVITY 4.1 In this activity you should take the value of π on your calculator to be accurate.

(i) Find, as a percentage, the relative error when π is given the following approximate values. (In each case, state whether the error is positive or negative.)

(a) 3   **(b)** $\frac{22}{7}$ **(c)** 3.14   **(d)** $\sqrt{10}$

(ii) The value of π can be calculated to any required level of accuracy from Gregory's series

$$\pi \approx 4 \times \left(1 - \tfrac{1}{3} + \tfrac{1}{5} - \tfrac{1}{7} + \tfrac{1}{9} - \tfrac{1}{11} + \dots \right).$$

Find, as a percentage, the relative error when the calculation is done using:

(a) 1 term: i.e. $\pi = 4 \times (1)$
(b) 2 terms: i.e. $\pi = 4 \times \left(1 - \tfrac{1}{3}\right)$
(c) 3 terms
(d) 4 terms
(e) 5 terms
(f) 6 terms.

Note

You have to take a very large number of terms to find π at all accurately by this method.

The algebra of inequalities

In the examples above, no algebra was involved in the calculations. That will not always be the case and it is just as important to be able to handle algebraic inequalities as it is to solve algebraic equations. The solution to an inequality is a range of possible values, not specific value(s) as in the case of an equation.

Linear inequalities

 The methods for linear inequalities are much the same as those for equations but you must be careful when multiplying or dividing through an inequality by a negative number.

Take for example the following statement:

$$5 > 3 \text{ is true}$$

Multiply both sides by -1 $-5 > -3$ is false.

 It is actually the case that multiplying or dividing by a negative number reverses the inequality, but you may prefer to avoid the difficulty, as shown in the example below.

EXAMPLE 4.3

Solve $5x - 3 \leqslant 2x - 15$.

SOLUTION

Add 3 to, and subtract $2x$ from, both sides $\Rightarrow 5x - 2x \leqslant -15 + 3$

Tidy up $\Rightarrow 3x \leqslant -12$

Divide both sides by 3 $\Rightarrow x \leqslant -4$

Note

Since there was no need to multiply or divide both sides by a negative number, no problems arose in this example.

EXAMPLE 4.4

Solve $2y + 6 > 7y + 11$.

SOLUTION

Subtract 6 and $7y$ from both sides $\Rightarrow$ $2y - 7y > 11 - 6$

Tidy up $\Rightarrow$ $-5y > +5$

> **Beware:** do not divide both sides by -5.

Add $5y$ to both sides and subtract 5 $\Rightarrow$ $-5 > +5y$

> This now allows you to divide both sides by $+5$.

Divide both sides by $+5$ $\Rightarrow$ $-1 > y$

Note that logically $-1 > y$ is the same as $y < -1$, so the solution is $y < -1$.

Quadratic inequalities

When dealing with a quadratic inequality the easiest method is to sketch the associated graph. You could use a graphic calculator or a computer graphics package.

EXAMPLE 4.5

Solve **(i)** $x^2 - 4x + 3 > 0$ **(ii)** $x^2 - 4x + 3 \leqslant 0$.

SOLUTION

The graph of $y = x^2 - 4x + 3$ is shown in figure 4.1 with the thick parts of the x axis corresponding to the solutions to the two parts of the question.

(i) You want the values of x for which $y > 0$, which that is where the curve is above the x axis.

(ii) You want the values of x for $y \leqslant 0$, that is where the curve crosses or is below the x axis.

> Here the end points *are not* included in the inequality so you draw open circles: ○

> Here the end points *are* included in the inequality so you draw solid circles: ●

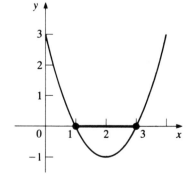

Figure 4.1

The solution is:

$x < 1$ or $x > 3$.

The solution is:

$x \geqslant 1$ and $x \leqslant 3$,

usually written $1 \leqslant x \leqslant 3$.

? What is the best method to use for sketching a quadratic graph by hand when you want to know the intersections with the x axis, as in Example 4.5?

! Notice that, in part (i), for two separate intervals it is impossible to combine the inequalities.

Notice the logic in the use of the words *or* and *and* in the solutions to Example 4.5. In part (i) the value x could be in either one or other of two regions, so *or* was the appropriate word. In part (ii) there was only one region, bounded on both sides. For the value x to be in the region, both inequalities must hold, so *and* was the correct word.

In part (i) the question involved the strict inequality, $>$, and not $\geqslant$. This was followed through into the answer which was also given in terms of strict inequalities. In part (ii) the inequality sign in the question was *less than or equal to*, $\leqslant$, and so the answer also involved such inequalities, $\leqslant$ and $\geqslant$.

Quadratic inequalities can also be solved by algebraic rather than graphical methods.

For example, you can solve $x^2 - 4x + 3 > 0$ from Example 4.5 part (i), algebraically like this.

$$x^2 - 4x + 3 > 0$$
$$\Rightarrow \quad (x-1)(x-3) > 0$$

For the product of two numbers to be positive, both must be positive or both must be negative

$\Rightarrow \quad x - 1 > 0$ and $x - 3 > 0 \quad$ or $\quad x - 1 < 0$ and $x - 3 < 0$
$\Rightarrow \quad\quad x > 1$ and $x > 3 \quad\quad$ or $\quad\quad x < 1$ and $x < 3$
$\Rightarrow \quad\quad\quad x > 3 \quad\quad\quad\quad$ or $\quad\quad\quad x < 1.$

? How can you solve $x^2 - 4x + 3 \leqslant 0$ using a similar argument?

? What are the advantages of using a graphical method to solve quadratic inequalities?

EXERCISE 4A

1 Solve the following inequalities.

(i) $5a + 6 > 2a + 24$ **(ii)** $3b - 5 \leqslant b - 1$

(iii) $4(c - 1) > 3(c - 2)$ **(iv)** $d - 3(d + 2) \geqslant 2(1 + 2d)$

(v) $\frac{1}{2}e + 3\frac{1}{2} < e$ **(vi)** $-f - 2f - 3 < 4(1 + f)$

(vii) $5(2 - 3g) + g \geqslant 8(2g - 4)$ **(viii)** $3(h + 2) - 2(h - 4) > 7(h + 2)$

2 Solve the following inequalities by sketching by hand the curves of the functions involved. You could check your sketches using a graphic calculator or computer graphics package.

(i) $p^2 - 5p + 4 < 0$ **(ii)** $p^2 - 5p + 4 \geqslant 0$

(iii) $x^2 + 3x + 2 \leqslant 0$ **(iv)** $x^2 + 3x > -2$

(v) $y^2 - 2y - 3 > 0$ **(vi)** $z(z - 1) \leqslant 20$

(vii) $q^2 - 4q + 4 > 0$ **(viii)** $y(y - 2) > 8$

(ix) $3x^2 + 5x - 2 < 0$ **(x)** $2y^2 - 11y - 6 \geqslant 0$

(xi) $4x - 3 \geqslant x^2$ **(xii)** $10y^2 > y + 3$

KEY POINTS

1 Linear inequalities are dealt with like equations *but* if you multiply or divide by a negative number, you must reverse the inequality sign.

2 When solving a quadratic inequality it is advisable to sketch the graph.

e Absolute error = value obtained − true value

$$\text{Relative error} = \frac{\text{absolute error}}{\text{true value}}$$

Percentage error = relative error × 100.

5

Indices

'A good notation has a subtlety and suggestiveness which at times makes it seem almost like a live teacher.'

Bertrand Russell

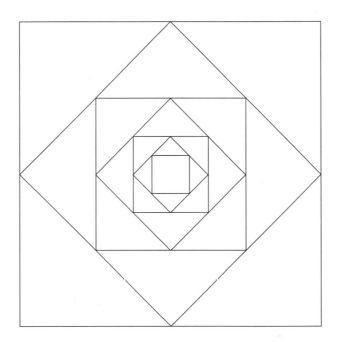

❓ The sides of the large square in this diagram are 8 cm long. The total length of all the lines is $(a + b\sqrt{2})$ cm. The numbers a and b are rational. What are their values?

Working with square roots

You often meet square roots while doing mathematics, and there are times when it is helpful to be able to manipulate them, rather than just find their values from your calculator. This ensures that you are working with the exact value of the square root, rather than a rounded-off version. It may also keep your work tidier, without long numbers appearing at every line. Sometimes you find that the square roots cancel out, and this may indicate a relationship that you would otherwise have missed.

A number which is partly rational and partly square root, like $(\frac{1}{2} + \sqrt{5})$, is an example of a *surd*. Surds may also involve cube roots, etc.

The basic fact about the square root of a number is that when multiplied by itself, it gives the original number: $\sqrt{5} \times \sqrt{5} = 5$.

This can be rearranged to give

$$\sqrt{5} = \frac{5}{\sqrt{5}} \qquad \text{and} \qquad \frac{1}{\sqrt{5}} = \frac{\sqrt{5}}{5}.$$

Both of these are useful results.

Surds may be added or subtracted just like algebraic expressions, keeping the rational numbers and the square roots separate.

The symbol $\sqrt{}$ means 'the positive square root of'. Thus $\sqrt{8} = +2.828...$ and the solution of $x^2 = 8$ is $x = +\sqrt{8}$ or $x = -\sqrt{8}$, often written as $x = \pm\sqrt{8}$.

EXAMPLE 5.1

Add $(2 + 3\sqrt{5})$ to $(3 - \sqrt{5})$.

SOLUTION

$$(2 + 3\sqrt{5}) + (3 - \sqrt{5}) = 2 + 3 + 3\sqrt{5} - \sqrt{5}$$
$$= 5 + 2\sqrt{5}$$

EXAMPLE 5.2

Simplify $4(\sqrt{7} - 2\sqrt{2}) + 3(2\sqrt{7} + \sqrt{2})$.

SOLUTION

$$4(\sqrt{7} - 2\sqrt{2}) + 3(2\sqrt{7} + \sqrt{2}) = 4\sqrt{7} - 8\sqrt{2} + 6\sqrt{7} + 3\sqrt{2}$$
$$= 10\sqrt{7} - 5\sqrt{2}$$

When multiplying two surds, do so term by term, as in the following examples.

EXAMPLE 5.3

Simplify $(2 + \sqrt{3})^2$.

SOLUTION

$$(2 + \sqrt{3})^2 = (2 + \sqrt{3}) \times (2 + \sqrt{3})$$
$$= (2 \times 2) + (2 \times \sqrt{3}) + (\sqrt{3} \times 2) + (\sqrt{3} \times \sqrt{3})$$
$$= 4 + 2\sqrt{3} + 2\sqrt{3} + 3$$
$$= 7 + 4\sqrt{3}$$

EXAMPLE 5.4   Simplify $(\sqrt{2} + \sqrt{3})(\sqrt{2} + 2\sqrt{3})$.

SOLUTION

$$(\sqrt{2} + \sqrt{3})(\sqrt{2} + 2\sqrt{3}) = (\sqrt{2} \times \sqrt{2}) + (\sqrt{2} \times 2\sqrt{3}) + (\sqrt{3} \times \sqrt{2}) + (\sqrt{3} \times 2\sqrt{3})$$
$$= 2 + 2\sqrt{6} + \sqrt{6} + 2 \times 3$$
$$= 8 + 3\sqrt{6}$$

Notice that in the last example you use the fact that $\sqrt{2} \times \sqrt{3} = \sqrt{2 \times 3} = \sqrt{6}$.

EXAMPLE 5.5   Simplify $(2 + \sqrt{3}) \times (2 - \sqrt{3})$.

SOLUTION

$$(2 + \sqrt{3}) \times (2 - \sqrt{3}) = (2 \times 2) - (2 \times \sqrt{3}) + (\sqrt{3} \times 2) - (\sqrt{3} \times \sqrt{3})$$
$$= 4 - 2\sqrt{3} + 2\sqrt{3} - 3$$
$$= 1$$

You will notice that in the last example the terms involving square roots disappear, leaving an answer that is a rational number. This is because the two expressions to be multiplied together are the factors of the difference of two squares:

$$(a + b)(a - b) = a^2 - b^2.$$

In this case $a = 2$ and $b = \sqrt{3}$, so that

$$(2 + \sqrt{3})(2 - \sqrt{3}) = 2^2 - (\sqrt{3})^2$$
$$= 4 - 3 = 1.$$

This is the basis of a useful technique for simplifying a fraction whose bottom line is a surd. The technique, called *rationalising the denominator*, is illustrated in the next example.

EXAMPLE 5.6   Simplify by rationalising the denominator $\dfrac{(4 + \sqrt{5})}{(3 + \sqrt{5})}$.

SOLUTION

Multiply both the top line and the bottom line by $(3 - \sqrt{5})$. You can see that this will make the bottom line into an expression of the form $(a + b)(a - b)$, which is $(a^2 - b^2)$, and is a rational number.

$$\frac{(4 + \sqrt{5})}{(3 + \sqrt{5})} = \frac{(4 + \sqrt{5}) \times (3 - \sqrt{5})}{(3 + \sqrt{5}) \times (3 - \sqrt{5})}$$

$$= \frac{12 - 4\sqrt{5} + 3\sqrt{5} - 5}{9 - 3\sqrt{5} + 3\sqrt{5} - 5}$$

$$\frac{7 - \sqrt{5}}{4} \quad = \quad 1\tfrac{3}{4} - \tfrac{1}{4}\sqrt{5}$$

Note

This technique involves multiplying the top line and the bottom line of a fraction by the same amount. This does not change the value of the fraction: it is equivalent to multiplying the fraction by 1.

Leave all answers in this exercise in surd form, where appropriate.

1 Simplify the following.

(i) $\dfrac{7}{\sqrt{7}}$ (ii) $\dfrac{9}{3\sqrt{3}}$ (iii) $\dfrac{(2+\sqrt{2})}{\sqrt{2}}$ (iv) $\dfrac{5\sqrt{5}}{\sqrt{125}}$ (v) $\dfrac{6}{\sqrt{3}}-\dfrac{8}{2\sqrt{2}}$

2 Simplify the following.

(i) $(3+\sqrt{2})+(5+2\sqrt{2})$ (ii) $(5+3\sqrt{2})-(5-2\sqrt{2})$

(iii) $4(1+\sqrt{5})+3(5+4\sqrt{5})$ (iv) $3(\sqrt{2}-\sqrt{5})+5(\sqrt{2}+\sqrt{5})$

(v) $3(\sqrt{2}-1)+3(\sqrt{2}+1)$

3 Simplify the following.

(i) $(3+\sqrt{2})(4-\sqrt{2})$ (ii) $(2-\sqrt{3})^2$

(iii) $(3-\sqrt{5})(\sqrt{5}+5)$ (iv) $(1+\sqrt{5})(1-\sqrt{5})$

(v) $(\tfrac{1}{2}+\tfrac{1}{2}\sqrt{3})^2$ (vi) $(2-\sqrt{7})(\sqrt{7}-1)$

(vii) $(4+\sqrt{2})(4-\sqrt{2})$ (viii) $(5+\sqrt{30})(6-\sqrt{30})$

(ix) $(\sqrt{7}+\sqrt{5})(\sqrt{7}-\sqrt{5})$

4 Simplify the following by rationalising the denominator.

(i) $\dfrac{(3+\sqrt{2})}{(4-\sqrt{2})}$ (ii) $\dfrac{(2-\sqrt{3})}{(1+\sqrt{3})}$ (iii) $\dfrac{(3-\sqrt{5})}{(\sqrt{5}+5)}$ (iv) $\dfrac{1}{(1-\sqrt{5})}$

(v) $\dfrac{\sqrt{3}}{(\tfrac{1}{2}-\tfrac{1}{2}\sqrt{3})}$ (vi) $\dfrac{2}{(\sqrt{7}-1)}$ (vii) $\dfrac{(4+\sqrt{2})}{(4-\sqrt{2})}$ (viii) $\dfrac{(6+\sqrt{30})}{(6-\sqrt{30})}$

Negative and fractional indices

Figure 5.1 refers to the moons of the planet Jupiter. For six of its moons, the time, T, that each one takes to orbit Jupiter is plotted against the average radius, r, of its orbit. (The remaining ten moons of Jupiter would be either far off the scale or bunched together near the origin.)

The curves $T = kr^1$ and $T = kr^2$ (using suitable units and constant k) are also drawn on figure 5.1. You will see that the curve defined by Jupiter's moons lies somewhere between the two.

? How could you express the equation of the curve defined by Jupiter's moons?

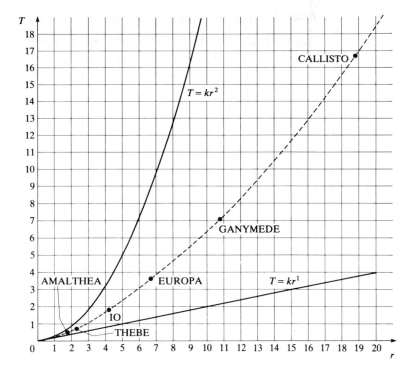

Figure 5.1

You may have suggested that the equation of the curve defined by Jupiter's moons could be written as $T = kr^{1\frac{1}{2}}$. If so, well done! This is correct, but what would a power, or index, of $1\frac{1}{2}$ mean?

Before answering this question it is helpful to review the language and laws relating to positive whole number indices.

Terminology

In the expression a^m the number represented by a is called the *base* of the expression; m is the *index*, or the *power* to which the base is raised. (The plural of index is indices.)

Multiplication

Multiplying 3^6 by 3^4 gives

$$3^6 \times 3^4 = (3 \times 3 \times 3 \times 3 \times 3 \times 3) \times (3 \times 3 \times 3 \times 3)$$
$$= 3^{10}.$$

Clearly it is not necessary to write down all the 3s like that. All you need to do is to add the powers: $6 + 4 = 10$

and so $\quad 3^6 \times 3^4 = 3^{6+4} = 3^{10}$.

This can be written in general form as

$$a^m \times a^n = a^{m+n}.$$

Another important multiplication rule arises when a base is successively raised to one power and then another, as for example in $(3^4)^2$:

$$(3^4)^2 = (3^4) \times (3^4)$$
$$= (3 \times 3 \times 3 \times 3) \times (3 \times 3 \times 3 \times 3)$$
$$= 3^8.$$

In this case the powers to which 3 is raised are multiplied: $4 \times 2 = 8$. Written in general form this becomes:

$$(a^m)^n = a^{mn}.$$

Division

In the same way, dividing 3^6 by 3^4 gives

$$3^6 \div 3^4 = \frac{(3 \times 3 \times 3 \times 3 \times 3 \times 3)}{(3 \times 3 \times 3 \times 3)}$$
$$= 3^2.$$

In this case you subtract the powers: $6 - 4 = 2$

and so
$$3^6 \div 3^4 = 3^{6-4} = 3^2.$$

This can be written in general form as

$$a^m \div a^n = a^{m-n}.$$

Extending the use of indices

Using these rules you can now go on to give meanings to indices which are not positive whole numbers.

Index zero

If you divide 3^4 by 3^4 the answer is 1, since this is a number divided by itself. However you can also carry out the division using the rules of indices to get

$$3^4 \div 3^4 = 3^{4-4}$$
$$= 3^0$$

and so it follows that $3^0 = 1$.

The same argument applies to 5^0, 2.9^0 or any other (non-zero) number raised to the power zero; they are all equal to 1.

In general $a^0 = 1$.

Negative indices

Dividing 3^4 by 3^6 gives

$$3^4 \div 3^6 = \frac{3 \times 3 \times 3 \times 3}{3 \times 3 \times 3 \times 3 \times 3 \times 3}$$

$$3^{4-6} = \frac{1}{3 \times 3}$$

and so $\qquad 3^{-2} = \frac{1}{3^2}.$

This can be generalised to $a^{-m} = \frac{1}{a^m}$.

Fractional indices

What number multiplied by itself gives the answer 3? The answer, as you will know, is the square root of 3, usually written $\sqrt{3}$. Suppose instead that the square root of 3 is written 3^p; what then is the value of p?

Since $\qquad\qquad 3^p \times 3^p = 3^1$

it follows that $\qquad p + p = 1$

and so $\qquad\qquad p = \frac{1}{2}.$

In other words, the square root of a number can be written as that number raised to the power $\frac{1}{2}$: $\sqrt{a} = a^{\frac{1}{2}}$.

The same argument may be extended to other roots, so that the cube root of a number may be written as that number raised to the power $\frac{1}{3}$, the fourth root corresponds to power $\frac{1}{4}$ and so on.

This can be generalised to: $\sqrt[n]{a} = a^{\frac{1}{n}}$.

In the example of Jupiter's moons, or indeed the moons or planets of any system, the relationship between T and r is of the form

$$T = kr^{1\frac{1}{2}}.$$

Squaring both sides gives

$$T \times T = kr^{1\frac{1}{2}} \times kr^{1\frac{1}{2}}$$

which may be written as $T^2 = cr^3$ (where the constant $c = k^2$).

This is one of Kepler's laws of planetary motion, first stated in 1619.

The use of indices not only allows certain expressions to be written more simply, but also, and this is more important, it makes it possible to carry out arithmetical and algebraic operations (like multiplication and division) on them. These processes are shown in the following examples.

EXAMPLE 5.7

Write the following numbers as the base 5 raised to a power.

(i) 625   **(ii)** 1   **(iii)** $\dfrac{1}{125}$ **(iv)** $5\sqrt{5}$

SOLUTION

Notice that $5^1 = 5$, $5^2 = 25$, $5^3 = 125$, $5^4 = 625$, ...

(i) $625 = 5^4$ **(ii)** $1 = 5^0$ **(iii)** $\dfrac{1}{125} = \dfrac{1}{5^3} = 5^{-3}$ **(iv)** $5\sqrt{5} = 5^1 \times 5^{\frac{1}{2}} = 5^{1\frac{1}{2}}$

EXAMPLE 5.8

Simplify

(i) $(2^3)^4$ **(ii)** $27^{\frac{1}{3}}$ **(iii)** $4^{-2\frac{1}{2}}$.

SOLUTION

(i) $(2^3)^4 = 2^{12} = 4096$

(ii) $27^{\frac{1}{3}} = \sqrt[3]{27} = 3$

(iii) $4^{-2\frac{1}{2}} = (2^2)^{-\frac{5}{2}} = 2^{2\times(-\frac{5}{2})} = 2^{-5} = \dfrac{1}{32}$

EXAMPLE 5.9

Simplify $8^{\frac{2}{3}}$.

SOLUTION

There are two ways to approach this.

(i) $8^{\frac{2}{3}} = (8^2)^{\frac{1}{3}} = (64)^{\frac{1}{3}} = 4$

(ii) $8^{\frac{2}{3}} = (8^{\frac{1}{3}})^2 = (2)^2 = 4$

Both give the same answer, and both are correct.

❓ Which of these methods do you prefer? Why?

EXAMPLE 5.10

Simplify $\left(4\sqrt{2} \times \dfrac{1}{16} \times \sqrt[5]{32}\right)^2$.

SOLUTION

$$
\begin{aligned}
\left(4\sqrt{2} \times \frac{1}{16} \times \sqrt[5]{32}\right)^2 &= (2^2 \times 2^{\frac{1}{2}} \times 2^{-4} \times (2^5)^{\frac{1}{5}})^2 \\
&= (2^{2\frac{1}{2}} \times 2^{-4} \times 2^1)^2 \\
&= (2^{2\frac{1}{2}-4+1})^2 \\
&= (2^{-\frac{1}{2}})^2 \\
&= 2^{-1} \\
&= \tfrac{1}{2}
\end{aligned}
$$

Note

In Example 5.10 all the terms are expressed as a power of the base 2. When using the laws of indices you should always make sure that all the terms you are multiplying or dividing are written to the same base.

Mixed bases

If a problem involves a combination of different bases, you may well need to split them, using the rule

$$(a \times b)^n = a^n \times b^n$$

before going on to work with each base in turn.

For example, $6^3 = (2 \times 3)^3$
$$= 2^3 \times 3^3$$

which is another way of saying $216 = 8 \times 27$.

Simplifying sums and differences of fractional powers

The next two examples illustrate a type of simplification which you will often find you need to do.

EXAMPLE 5.11 Simplify $5^{\frac{1}{2}} - 5^{\frac{3}{2}} + 5^{\frac{5}{2}}$.

SOLUTION

This can be written as

$$\sqrt{5} - 5\sqrt{5} + 5^2\sqrt{5}$$
$$= (1 - 5 + 25)\sqrt{5}$$
$$= 21\sqrt{5}.$$

$$5^{\frac{5}{2}} = 5^{2\frac{1}{2}}$$
$$= 5^2 5^{\frac{1}{2}}$$
$$= 5^2 \sqrt{5}$$

EXAMPLE 5.12 Simplify $3(x + 7)^{\frac{1}{2}} - \frac{2}{3}(x + 7)^{\frac{3}{2}}$.

SOLUTION

The expression is $3(x + 7)^{\frac{1}{2}} - \frac{2}{3}(x + 7)(x + 7)^{\frac{1}{2}}$

$$= (3 - \frac{2}{3}(x + 7))(x + 7)^{\frac{1}{2}}$$

$$= \frac{(9 - 2x - 14)}{3}(x + 7)^{\frac{1}{2}}$$

$$= -\frac{(5 + 2x)}{3}(x + 7)^{\frac{1}{2}}.$$

... or

$$-\frac{(5 + 2x)}{3}\sqrt{x + 7}$$

EXERCISE 5B

Answer these questions without using your calculator, but do use it to check your answers.

1 Write the following numbers as powers of 3.

   (i) 81   **(ii)** 1   **(iii)** 27

   (iv) $\dfrac{1}{27}$ **(v)** $\sqrt{3}$ **(vi)** 3

2 Write the following numbers as powers of 4.

   (i) 16   **(ii)** 2   **(iii)** $\dfrac{1}{4}$

   (iv) $\dfrac{1}{2}$ **(v)** 8   **(vi)** $\dfrac{1}{8}$

3 Write the following numbers as powers of 10.

   (i) 1000   **(ii)** 0.0001   **(iii)** $\dfrac{1}{1000}$

   (iv) $\sqrt{1000}$ **(v)** $\dfrac{1}{\sqrt{10}}$ **(vi)** one millionth

4 Write the following as whole numbers or fractions.

   (i) 2^{-5} **(ii)** $27^{\frac{1}{3}}$ **(iii)** $27^{-\frac{1}{3}}$

   (iv) $625^{\frac{1}{4}}$ **(v)** $625^{-\frac{1}{4}}$ **(vi)** 19^{0}

5 Simplify the following, writing your answer in the form x^{n}.

   (i) $(x^{3})^{6}$ **(ii)** $x^{2} \times x^{8}$ **(iii)** $x^{10} \div x^{12}$

   (iv) $\sqrt{x^{16}}$ **(v)** $\sqrt{x^{-3}}$ **(vi)** $(x^{-4})^{3}$

   (vii) $x^{\frac{1}{2}} \times x^{1\frac{1}{2}}$ **(viii)** $\sqrt[3]{x^{6}}$ **(ix)** $\sqrt[5]{x^{2\frac{1}{2}}}$

   (x) $(x^{-3})^{4} \times (x^{\frac{1}{3}})^{6}$

6 Simplify the following, writing your answers in the form $ax^{m}y^{n}$.

   (i) $3x^{2}y \times 4x^{6}y^{2}$ **(ii)** $\sqrt{16x^{8}y^{-2}}$ **(iii)** $(2x^{4}y^{\frac{3}{2}})^{6}$

   (iv) $\dfrac{12x^{8}y^{\frac{3}{2}}}{6x^{10}y^{\frac{5}{2}}}$ **(v)** $\sqrt{x^{6}y^{4}} \times \sqrt[3]{x^{3}y^{-6}}$

7 Simplify the following.

   (i) $3\sqrt{3} \times 3^{\frac{1}{2}}$ **(ii)** 1000×10^{-2} **(iii)** $\sqrt{25} \times 5^{-2}$

   (iv) $7^{\frac{1}{2}} \times 7^{-\frac{1}{2}}$ **(v)** $\sqrt{5^{4} \times 5^{6}}$ **(vi)** $\sqrt[3]{243 \times 81}$

8 Simplify the following.

   (i) $\dfrac{7^{-2}}{7^{-4}}$ **(ii)** $(3^{\frac{1}{2}})^{2}$ **(iii)** $(3^{2})^{\frac{1}{2}}$

   (iv) $(\sqrt{27})^{4}$ **(v)** $\sqrt[4]{16^{3}}$ **(vi)** $(4^{-\frac{1}{2}})^{-2}$

9 Simplify the following.

  (i) $64^{\frac{1}{2}} - 64^{\frac{1}{3}}$

  (ii) $(11^2)^3 - (11^3)^2$

  (iii) $25^{\frac{1}{2}} - \dfrac{5^{-4}}{5^{-5}}$

  (iv) $2^0 + 2^{-1} + 2^{-2} + 2^{-3} + 2^{-4}$

  (v) $(3^{\frac{1}{2}})^2 - (3^2)^{\frac{1}{2}}$

  (vi) $3^1 - 3^{-1}$

10 Simplify the following.

  (i) $2^{\frac{1}{2}} + 2^{\frac{3}{2}}$

  (ii) $4^{\frac{1}{3}} - 4^{\frac{4}{3}}$

  (iii) $7^{\frac{1}{2}} - 7^{\frac{3}{2}} + 7^{\frac{5}{2}}$

11 Simplify the following.

  ☆☆

  (i) $(1 + x)^{\frac{1}{2}} + (1 + x)^{\frac{3}{2}}$

  (ii) $4(2 + 3x)^{\frac{1}{2}} + 3(2 + 3x)^{\frac{3}{2}}$

  (iii) $6(x + y)^{\frac{1}{2}} - 5(x + y)^{\frac{3}{2}}$

  (iv) $x^{\frac{1}{2}} + x^{-\frac{1}{2}}$

  (v) $(x^2 - 2x + 3)^{\frac{1}{2}} - (x^2 - 2x + 3)^{\frac{3}{2}}$

KEY POINTS

1 Multiplication: $\qquad a^m \times a^n = a^{m+n}$.

2 Division: $\qquad a^m \div a^n = a^{m-n}$.

3 Power zero: $\qquad a^0 = 1$.

4 Negative indices: $\qquad a^{-m} = \dfrac{1}{a^m}$.

5 Fractional indices: $\qquad a^{\frac{1}{n}} = \sqrt[n]{a}$.

6 Power of a power: $\qquad (a^m)^n = a^{mn}$.

6 The language of mathematics

Where there are problems, there is life.

A.A. Zinoviev

Problem solving

 A diagram such as the one above is called a mystic rose. How many lines are there in this one?

What real situations might it be representing?

Problem solving is an essential part of mathematics. In order to solve problems you need to know how to approach them and to have the language with which to express the work you are doing.

There are several ways in which you might approach the problem of finding how many lines there are in the mystic rose.

You could try counting them, but you would almost certainly get lost somewhere in the middle; even if you came out with an answer, you would still need to check it by counting again. Clearly a more subtle approach is called for.

Some people will sit and think, and come up with the answer. Others may sit and think and get nowhere. If this happens to you, you should start by simplifying the problem. The mystic rose in the picture has 18 points, but start by taking the simplest mystic rose you can. Figure 6.1 shows some diagrams that you could use to get yourself started.

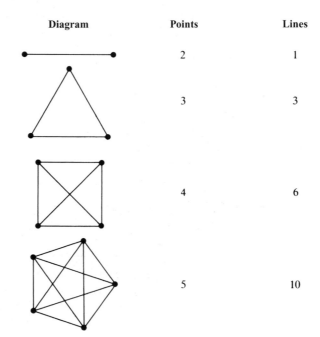

Diagram	Points	Lines
	2	1
	3	3
	4	6
	5	10

Figure 6.1

You can see a pattern building up.

Points	Lines
2	1
3	3
4	6
5	10

You have probably noticed that the numbers on the right-hand side are increasing in steps which are themselves increasing by 1 each time: 2, 3, 4, ... The next step should be 5, the one after that 6. So you can predict the next two rows to be

6   15 $(10 + 5)$

7   21 $(15 + 6)$.

?   If you draw these mystic roses, do you find that the predictions are indeed correct?

So, is the problem now solved? Not yet. There is still quite a long way to go.

You have an idea, or theory, about how you might be able to work out the answer for the 18-point mystic rose. Such an idea is called a *conjecture*. Now you need to do two things:

- to express your conjecture neatly, preferably using algebra, and

- to prove it.

You have a method which is a lot better than counting lines in a diagram, but it is still quite clumsy.

What you want is a *rule* (or *formula*) relating the number of lines directly to the number of points. You may manage to see such a rule just by looking at the numbers, but even if you find one, you must still be able to prove it. Otherwise you have no guarantee that it will not break down when you use it with larger numbers.

The best approach is to look at how the numbers you have found arise in the actual mystic rose. Take the case of 5 points giving 10 lines. The number 10 arises because

$$10 = 4 + 3 + 2 + 1$$

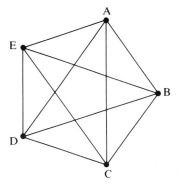

Figure 6.2

In figure 6.2, point A is connected to four other points: B, C, D and E.

Point B is also connected to four other points: A, C, D and E, but one of these lines, AB, has already been counted. So there are three new lines from B.

Similarly there are two new lines from C: CD and CE. Finally, there is only one from D: DE.

By the time you get to E, all the lines to it have already been drawn.

$$4 + 3 + 2 + 1 = 10$$

It may help you to think about the situation in another way: saying that there are four lines through each of the five points, A, B, C, D and E, giving $5 \times 4 = 20$ lines. However each of these is being counted twice, once at each end, so the actual number of lines is $\frac{1}{2} \times 5 \times 4 = 10$.

Applying this argument to the 18-point rose gives the number of lines to be $\frac{1}{2} \times 18 \times 17 = 153$.

This is clearly much neater than counting lines, or adding $1 + 2 + 3 \dots$ up to 17. But it is much more than that. It gives an answer that can be *generalised*, that is it can be applied to any mystic rose, not just one with 18 points. But how are you going to communicate your general solution to other people?

You could say 'Take the number of points, multiply it by one less than itself and then divide the answer by two', but this is quite a mouthful, and not worthy of such a neat solution. A much better method involves the use of letters to represent the numbers of lines and points, say N and p.

The result is now written $N = \frac{1}{2} \times p \times (p - 1)$

or $N = \dfrac{p(p - 1)}{2}$.

> The result is now in a *general* form. It has been *generalised*.

Looking at the original problem has also allowed you to prove the result. The argument:

'There are p points. Each is joined to $(p - 1)$ other points, giving $p(p - 1)$ lines. However each line is counted twice, so there are $\frac{1}{2}p(p - 1)$ lines'

is a proof.

However you have still not quite finished.

Imagine that you show the result to someone who wants to find fault with it. Such a person might ask 'What happens when $p = 3.9$? Or 0?' You know that this is a silly question because the number of points must be a whole number, and at least 1. (Note that for $p = 1$, $N = 0$; there are no lines joining a single point to itself.) However, that information has not been included in the answer so far, and it must be if the answer is to be foolproof.

You might rewrite the answer as

$N = \dfrac{p(p - 1)}{2}$ where p is a positive whole number.

The last part of the statement is still a little clumsy. It would be nice to be able to say *p is a positive whole number* more concisely, and this is dealt with later in the chapter.

Conclusion

There are several important lessons to be learnt from the example of the mystic rose. It shows that an approach to problem solving involves the following steps.

- Solve similar but simplified versions of the same problem.

- Look for any patterns in your results.

- Form a conjecture so that you can predict what will happen in more complicated cases.

- Check that your predictions are correct.

- Generalise your conjecture to deal with all similar problems.

- Express your result concisely, in a form that can be understood by other people.

- Seek an explanation for what you have found in terms of the problem, so that you can prove your conjecture.

The modelling cycle

Another approach to problem-solving is described as *modelling*. You use it when you are trying to get at the mathematics underlying real-life situations. Here is a simple example to show you the process (often, the problem is more complicated).

Katie is planning to walk from Land's End to John O'Groats to raise money for charity. She wants to know how long it will take her. The distance is 874 miles.

This is the first stage of her planning calculation.

> I can walk at 4 mph.
>
> Distance = Speed × Time
>
> $\qquad 874 = 4 \times$ Time
>
> $\qquad$ Time = 219 hours
>
> $\qquad \dfrac{219}{24} = 9.1\ldots$

So it will take 10 days.

Katie knows that 10 days is unrealistic. She changes the last part of the calculation to

$$\frac{219}{8} = 27.3\ldots$$

So it will take 28 days.

❓ Explain the reasoning behind this change. What is her plan now?

Katie finds out the times some other people have taken on the same walk:

45 days   51 days   70 days   84 days.

Seeing these figures, she decides her plan is still unrealistic.

❓ In what ways could she change her plan so that her calculations give a more reasonable answer, such as 60 days?

❓ Look at the flow chart showing the modelling process (figure 6.3). Identify on the chart the different stages of Katie's work.

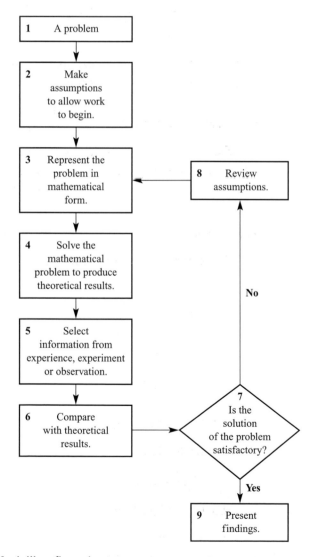

Figure 6.3 *Modelling flow chart*

Types of numbers

The first numbers which a child meets are the *counting numbers*, 1, 2, 3, …, and before too long the number zero. When this is included, the resulting set is called the *natural numbers* and is denoted by $\mathbb{N}$.

A little later the child learns about negative whole numbers like −1 and −5; when these are included, the set of numbers is called the *integers* and is denoted by $\mathbb{Z}$. Thus the integers are all the whole numbers, positive, negative or zero. The counting numbers are often denoted by $\mathbb{Z}^+$.

Another step up is to include the fractions like $\frac{3}{4}$ and $-\frac{17}{9}$. The complete set is then called the *rational numbers* and is denoted by $\mathbb{Q}$. A rational number is an integer divided by a non-zero integer; if the resulting fraction cancels down to an integer, like $\frac{18}{9} = 2$, it is still a rational number.

There are still some numbers which have not been included, like π and $\sqrt{2}$. These cannot be written as fractions and so are called *irrational numbers*. The combined set of all the rational numbers and all the irrational numbers is called the set of *real numbers*, and is denoted by $\mathbb{R}$.

This information is summarised in the table and the Venn diagram (figure 6.4).

Name	Symbol	Description
Counting numbers	$\mathbb{Z}^+$	Positive whole numbers: 1, 2, 3, …
Natural numbers	$\mathbb{N}$	Counting numbers and zero: 0, 1, 2, 3, …
Integers	$\mathbb{Z}$	All whole numbers: …, −2, −1, 0, 1, 2, …
Rational numbers	$\mathbb{Q}$	$\frac{m}{n}$ where m and n are integers $(n \neq 0)$, e.g. $\frac{2}{3}, -\frac{15}{7}, 17$
Real numbers	$\mathbb{R}$	Rational and irrational numbers, e.g. $\pi, (\sqrt{3} + 6), -\frac{5}{7}, 6$

The symbol $\in$ (the Greek letter epsilon) is used to mean *belongs to the set of* … . So the statement *p is a positive whole number* at the end of the mystic rose example can now be written

$$p \in \{\text{counting numbers}\} \qquad \text{or as} \qquad p \in \mathbb{Z}^+$$

Figure 6.4

 The term natural number is also sometimes used to denote the set of counting numbers, $\{1, 2, 3, 4, ...\}$, without the number 0.

EXERCISE 6A

1 A snooker table is l feet long and w feet wide.

  (i) Write down expressions for the perimeter, p feet, and the area, A square feet, of the table.

  (ii) Find the values of p and A in the cases when:
    (a) $l = 6$ and $w = 3$ (a children's table)
    (b) $l = 12$ and $w = 6$ (a full size table).

A manufacturer makes tables in a variety of sizes. The length is always exactly twice the width and is always a whole number of feet; the smallest table is 3 feet long, the largest 12 feet.

  (iii) Write down expressions for p and A in terms of l, giving all of the information as precisely as possible.

2 First class stamps cost f pence each, second class stamps s pence each.

  (i) Write down an expression for the change, c pence, which you would have from £5 after buying 8 first class stamps and 6 second class stamps.

  (ii) What would be the significance of a negative value for c?

The Post Office sets the values of f and s from time to time.

  (iii) State in precise mathematical terms what you can say about the numbers f and s.

3 The height h metres of the gas in a gasometer at time t hours after midnight on a typical day is given by

$$h = \frac{(t - 12)^2}{6} + 6.$$

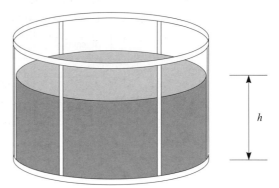

(i) Find the value of h at three-hourly intervals throughout one day, starting at midnight.

(ii) Draw the graph of h (vertical axis) against t (horizontal axis) for this period.

(iii) Do you think that the height of gas in a gasometer might really vary in this way during a day? Give your reasons.

4 The lengths of the two shorter sides of a right-angled triangle are a cm and b cm and the length of the hypotenuse is h cm.

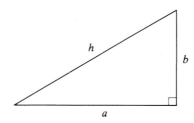

(i) Write down an expression for h in terms of a and b.

(ii) Find the value of h in the cases when:

(a) $a = 3$, $b = 4$

(b) $a = 8$, $b = 15$

(c) $a = 20$, $b = 21$

(d) $a = 1$, $b = 1$.

(iii) If a and b are natural numbers, does it follow that h must also be a natural number?

5 The scheduling department of a railway estimates that the time t minutes for a journey of k km involving s stops on the way is given by

$$t = 3 + 5s + \tfrac{1}{2}k.$$

   (i) Find the time for a journey of 200 km with two stops on the way.
   (ii) A train sets out at 13:45 and arrives at its destination 240 km away at 16:23. How many stops does it make on the way?

6 The diagram shows a rectangular piece of card with a square cut away from each corner. The card is then folded up to make an open box of volume $V\,\text{cm}^3$, as shown. The original piece of card had length l cm and width w cm. The cut-away squares are each of side x cm.

   (i) Write down expressions for A, the area of card remaining in cm^2, and V in cm^3.
   (ii) Find the values of A and V in the case $l = 40$, $w = 20$ and $x = 5$.
   (iii) Investigate, for the case $l = 10$ and $w = 6$, to find the value of x that makes V greatest.

7 A printer quotes the cost £C of printing n Christmas cards as

$$C = 25 + 0.05n.$$

   (i) Find the cost of printing:
      (a) 100 cards
      (b) 1000 cards.
   (ii) Find the cost per card of printing:
      (a) 100 cards
      (b) 1000 cards.
   (iii) Find the cost per card of printing n cards.
   (iv) The cost £C is made up of a fixed cost for setting up the press and a 'run-on' cost per card printed. State the amount of each of these costs.
   (v) What can you say about the number n?

8 The diagram shows 1-, 2-, 3- and 4-section girder bridges, each made up of equilateral triangles of side 8 m.

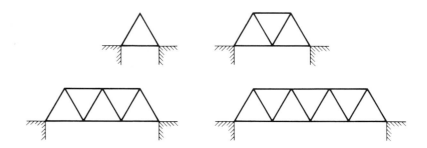

(i) Find the relationship between n, the number of sections in a bridge, and g, the total length of the girders.

(ii) Show that your answer to part (i) gives the correct answer for a bridge with six sections.

(iii) Find the number of sections in the largest bridge that can be made when the following lengths of girder are available.

    (a) nineteen 8 m lengths

    (b) twenty-two 8 m lengths

(iv) Given that a number m of 8 m lengths of girder are available, what is the horizontal span, s m, of the largest bridge that can be made from them?

9 A motor salesman is negotiating the price of a fleet of n identical new cars to a car hire company, and offers a total price £C, given by

$$C = 12\,000n - 100n^2.$$

(i) Find the total cost of an order for:

    (a) 1 car   **(b)** 5 cars   **(c)** 10 cars.

(ii) Find the average cost per car when the number of cars ordered is:

    (a) 1   **(b)** 5   **(c)** 10.

(iii) Find an expression for the average cost per car when n cars are ordered.

(iv) Explain why this offer would not be appropriate for large values of n.

10 Jasmine is inventing a new game in which you move counters round the squares on a board. To make the game more interesting, she decides not to have standard dice but instead to have a red die with faces numbered −2, −1, 0, 0, 1, and 6, and a green die with faces marked −2, −1, 0, 0, 2, and 4.

In one trial version of the game the score, s, from throwing the two dice is the sum of the score r on the red die and the score g on the green die.

In another trial version the score, p, is the product of the scores r and g on the two dice.

(i) Write down expressions for s and p in terms of r and g.

(ii) What are the greatest and least possible values of: **(a)** s **(b)** p?

(iii) List the possible scores under each of the two versions of the game.

Writing mathematics

Using the symbols ⇒, ⇐, and ⇔.

We have often used the symbol ⇒ in this book. It means 'leads to' or 'implies' and is very helpful when you want to present an argument logically, step by step.

Look at figure 6.5.

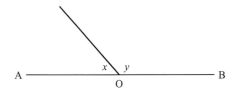

Figure 6.5

You can say

> AOB is a straight line
> ⇒ $\angle x + \angle y = 180°$.

Another way of expressing the same idea is to use the word *therefore* (often denoted by the symbol ∴).

> AOB is a straight line
> ∴ $\angle x + \angle y - 180°$.

A third way of writing the same thing is to use the words *if … then …* .

If AOB is a straight line, *then* $\angle x + \angle y = 180°$.

You can write the symbol ⇒ the other way round, as ⇐. In that case it means 'is implied by' or 'follows from'.

In the example above you can write

> AOB is a straight line ⇐ $\angle x + \angle y = 180°$

and in this case it is still true.

Note

In situations like this where both the symbols ⇒ and ⇐ give true statements, the two symbols are written together as ⇔. You can read this as 'implies and is implied by' or 'is equivalent to'. Thus

> AOB is a straight line ⇔ $\angle x + \angle y = 180°$.

 Is the statement   AOB is a straight line ⇐ $\angle x + \angle y = 180°$
logically the same as $\angle x + \angle y = 180° ⇒$ AOB is a straight line?

In the next two examples, the implication is true in one direction but not in the other.

EXAMPLE 6.1

Write one of the symbols ⇒, ⇐ or ⇔ between the two statements A and B.

A: Nimrod is a cat.
B: Nimrod has whiskers.

SOLUTION

You can write A ⇒ B. Since all cats have whiskers and Nimrod is a cat, it must be true that Nimrod has whiskers.

However you cannot write A ⇐ B. That is saying 'Nimrod has whiskers', implies 'Nimrod is a cat'. However there are other sorts of animals that have whiskers, so you cannot conclude that Nimrod is a cat.

Nor can you write A ⇔ B because that is saying that *both* A ⇒ B and A ⇐ B are true; in fact only the first is true.

EXAMPLE 6.2

Write one of the symbols ⇒, ⇐ or ⇔ between the two statements A and B.

A: The hands of the clock are at right angles.
B: The clock is showing 3 o'clock.

SOLUTION

You can write A ⇐ B because it is true that at 3 o'clock the hands are at right angles.

However you cannot write A ⇒ B because there are other times, for example 9 o'clock, when the hands are at right angles.

Nor can you write A ⇔ B because that is saying that *both* A ⇒ B and A ⇐ B are true; in fact only the second is true.

Figure 6.6

❓ Which symbol would you use to connect the statements P and Q?

P: The three sides of triangle T are equal.
Q: The three angles of triangle T are equal.

The words 'necessary' and 'sufficient'

Two other words which you will sometimes find useful are *necessary* and *sufficient*.

- *Necessary* is often used (or implied) when giving the conditions under which a statement is true. Thus a necessary condition for a living being to be a spider is that it has eight legs. However this is not a *sufficient* condition because there are other creatures with eight legs, for example scorpions.

- The word *sufficient* is also used when giving conditions under which you can be certain that a statement is true. Thus being a spider is a *sufficient* condition for a creature to have eight legs (but not a *necessary* one).

? **1** To show that an integer n is divisible by 5, is it
(i) necessary **(ii)** sufficient
to show that it ends in zero?

2 For the equation $ax^2 + bx + c = 0$ to have two distinct real roots is the condition that the discriminant, $b^2 - 4ac$, is greater than zero
(i) necessary **(ii)** sufficient?

With a little thought you will see that if A is a *sufficient* condition for B, then A $\Rightarrow$ B. Similarly if A is a *necessary* condition for B, then A $\Leftarrow$ B. The investigation at the end of Exercise 6B may help you to see this.

? If A is both a necessary and sufficient condition for B, what symbol should connect A and B?

In each case write one of the symbols $\Rightarrow$, $\Leftarrow$ or $\Leftrightarrow$ between the two statements A and B.

1 A: The object is a cube. B: The object has six faces.

2 A: Jasmine has spots. B: Jasmine is a leopard.

3 A: The polygon has four sides. B: The polygon is a quadrilateral.

4 A: Today is 1 January. B: Today is New Year's Day.

5 A: $x = 29$. B: $x > 10$.

6 A: This month has exactly 28 days. B: This month is February and it is not a leap year.

7 A: $x^3 = x$. B: $x = -1$.

8 A: $xy = 0$. B: $x = 0$ and $y = 0$.

9 A: PQRS is a rectangle.   B: PQRS is a parallelogram.

10 A: $\dfrac{p}{q} = \dfrac{q}{p}$.   B: $p = q$.

11 A: $x = 3$.   B: $x^2 = 9$.

12 A: $6 < x < 8$.   B: $x = 7$.

13 The number n is a positive integer greater than 1.
     A: n has exactly two factors.   B: n is a prime number.

14 A: m and n are odd integers.   B: $m + n$ is an even integer.

15 O and P are points.
     A: $0\text{ cm} \leqslant OP < 5\text{ cm}$.   B: P lies inside the sphere with centre O and radius 5 cm.

INVESTIGATION

By looking at your answers to questions 1 to 15 above, complete each of the spaces in the right-hand column of a copy of this table with one of the following statements.

- A is a necessary condition for B.

- A is a sufficient condition for B.

- A is a necessary and sufficient condition for B.

$A \Rightarrow B$	
$A \Leftarrow B$	
$A \Leftrightarrow B$	

The converse of a theorem

When theorems, or general results, are involved it is quite common to use the word *converse* to express the idea behind the $\Leftarrow$ symbol.

Thus, for the triangle ABC (see figure 6.7), Pythagoras' theorem states

     Angle $BCA = 90° \Rightarrow AB^2 = BC^2 + CA^2$

and its converse is

     Angle $BCA = 90° \Leftarrow AB^2 = BC^2 + CA^2$.

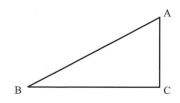

Figure 6.7

Note

It would be more usual to write the converse the other way round, as

$AB^2 = BC^2 + CA^2 \Rightarrow$ Angle BCA = 90°.

Since in this case both the theorem and its converse are true, you would be correct to use the $\Leftrightarrow$ symbol.

Angle BCA = 90° $\Leftrightarrow AB^2 = BC^2 + CA^2$.

You may find it easier to think in terms of *If … then …*, when deciding just what the converse of a result or theorem says. For example, if you had to write down the converse of the theorem that the angle in a semi-circle is 90°. This can be stated as:

If AB is a diameter of the circle through points A, B and C, *then* $\angle$ACB = 90° (see figure 6.8).

To find the converse, change over the *If* and the *then*, and write the statement so that it reads sensibly. In this case it becomes:

If $\angle$ACB = 90°, *then* AB is a diameter of the circle through points A, B and C.

Figure 6.8

---

 1 Is the converse of this theorem true?

2 State a theorem for which the converse is not true.

EXERCISE 6C

For each of the following statements:

(i) *state the converse*
(ii) *state whether the converse is true.*

1 If a triangle has two sides equal, then it has two angles equal.

2 If Fred murdered Alf, then Alf is dead.

3 If a number is an integer, then the square of the number is an integer.

4 ABCD is a square $\Rightarrow$ Each of the angles of ABCD is 90°.

5 If $x = y$, then $x^2 = y^2$.

6 For a quadrilateral PQRS:

If P, Q, R and S all lie on a circle, then $\angle$PQR + $\angle$PSR = 180°.

7 If it is sunny, then Struan goes swimming.

8 In the diagram:

lines l and m are parallel $\Rightarrow \angle x = \angle y$.

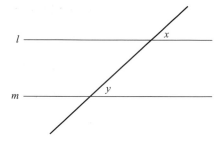

9 n is an odd prime number $\Rightarrow n > 2$.

10 A cubic equation has at least one root.

11 A triangle with three equal sides has three equal angles.

12 The curve of a quadratic function has one turning point.

Proof

This chapter began with an investigation into the number of lines in a mystic rose. The approach was to start by looking at simple cases and then, systematically, to go on to more complicated ones. This built up a sequence of answers.

Points, p	Lines, N
2	1
3	3
4	6
5	10
⋮	⋮

These figures led to a conjecture, in the form of the the general formula

$$N = \frac{p(p-1)}{2}$$

and a proof was given showing that this result must indeed be correct because of the geometry of the situation.

It is very important to realise that just making a conjecture, or finding a formula that fits your figures, is not enough. You must either prove that your conjecture is correct or you must disprove it, i.e. prove that it is wrong.

Disproving a conjecture

To disprove a conjecture all you need is a single *counter-example*. Look at this conjecture.

$n^2 + n + 1$ is a prime number.

- $n = 1 \Rightarrow n^2 + n + 1 = 3$ and 3 is prime
- $n = 2 \Rightarrow n^2 + n + 1 = 7$ and 7 is prime
- $n = 3 \Rightarrow n^2 + n + 1 = 13$ and 13 is prime.

So far so good, but when you come to $n = 4$

- $n = 4 \Rightarrow n^2 + n + 1 = 21$ and $21 = 3 \times 7$ is not prime.

Nothing more needs to be said. The case of $n = 4$ provides a counter-example and one counter-example is all that is needed to disprove a conjecture. The conjecture is false.

However, sometimes it is easier to disprove a conjecture by exposing a fault in the argument that led to its being proposed.

Proof by exhaustion

With some conjectures you can test all the possible cases. An example is

> 97 is a prime number.

If you show that none of the whole numbers between 2 and 96 is a factor of 97, then it must indeed be a prime number. However a moment's thought shows that you do not need to try all of them, only those that are less than $\sqrt{97}$, i.e. from 2 up to 9.

$97 \div 2 = 48\frac{1}{2}$ No	$97 \div 3 = 32\frac{1}{3}$ No	$97 \div 4 = 24\frac{1}{4}$ No
$97 \div 5 = 19\frac{2}{5}$ No	$97 \div 6 = 16\frac{1}{6}$ No	$97 \div 7 = 13\frac{6}{7}$ No
$97 \div 8 = 12\frac{1}{8}$ No	$97 \div 9 = 10\frac{7}{9}$ No	

Since none of the numbers divides into it, 97 must be prime.

?   It was not strictly necessary to test all the numbers from 2 up to 9 above. Which numbers were necessary and which were not?

This method of proof, by trying out all the possibilities, is called *proof by exhaustion*. In theory, it is the possibilities that get exhausted, not you!

Proof by deduction

In the example above with $n^2 + n + 1$, there are an infinite number of possible values of n. In such a situation, you may be able to find a thousand, or a million, or a billion, values for which the conjecture holds, but you have still not proved it. There will always be other values that you have not tried.

In these cases, you must use proof by deduction, providing a logical argument as to why the conjecture must be true. This will often require you to use algebra, as in the next example.

EXAMPLE 6.3

There is a trick for squaring numbers which, like $5\frac{1}{2}$, are [a whole number $+ \frac{1}{2}$].

Take the whole number and multiply it by one more than itself and then add $\frac{1}{4}$.

Thus

$$\begin{aligned}
\left(5\frac{1}{2}\right)^2 &= 5 \times (5 + 1) + \frac{1}{4} \\
&= 5 \times 6 + \frac{1}{4} \\
&= 30\frac{1}{4}.
\end{aligned}$$

Prove this trick will work whatever the value of the whole number.

SOLUTION

Start by letting the whole number part be n.

Then the number is $\left(n + \frac{1}{2}\right)$

$$\begin{aligned}
\left(n + \frac{1}{2}\right)^2 &= n^2 + n + \frac{1}{4} \\
&= n(n + 1) + \frac{1}{4} \\
&= \text{the whole number} \times \text{one more than itself} + \frac{1}{4}.
\end{aligned}$$

$\Rightarrow$ The method will work whatever the value of n.

Proof by contradiction

Another method of proof involves showing that if a conjecture is not true, then an impossible conclusion follows.

EXAMPLE 6.4

e *This example is enrichment material.*

Four people A, B, C and D, share an amount of £1000.

Prove that at least one of them receives £250 or more.

SOLUTION

Denote the amounts they receive by £a, £b, £c and £d.

Assume that no one receives £250 or more.

i.e. that what you are asked to prove is false.

$$\begin{aligned}
a &< 250 \\
b &< 250 \\
c &< 250 \\
d &< 250
\end{aligned}$$

Adding these four inequalities gives

$$a + b + c + d < 1000.$$

But this contradicts the known fact that $a + b + c + d = 1000$.

Therefore the assumption that 'no one receives £250 or more' is false.

Therefore at least one of A, B, C and D receives £250 or more.

EXERCISE 6D

In each question a conjecture is given. Decide whether it is true or false.
If it is true, prove it using a suitable method (and naming the method).
If it is false give a counter-example.

1 The sum of any three consecutive integers is divisible by 6.

2 An easy way to remember 7 times 8 is that $56 = 7 \times 8$, and the numbers 5, 6, 7 and 8 are consecutive. There is exactly one other multiplication of two single-digit numbers with the same pattern.

3 $x^2 > x \Rightarrow x > 1$.

4 ABCD is a parallelogram. Sides AB and DC are parallel; sides AD and BC are parallel. AC = BD.

5 A triangle with sides $(x^2 + 1)$, $(x^2 - 1)$, $2x$ is right-angled.

6 The circle with equation $x^2 + y^2 = 36$ passes through exactly four points for which both the x and y co-ordinates are integers.

7 The value of $(n^2 + n + 41)$ is a prime number for all positive integer values of n.

8 A number is divisible by 9 if the sum of its digits is divisible by 9.

9 There is no real number x such that $x^2 = -4$.

10 An octagon is formed by joining the points (7, 0), (5, 5), (0, 7), (−5, 5), (−7, 0), (−5, −5), (0, −7), (5, −5) and (7, 0). The octagon is regular.

11 ABC is a three-digit number.

(i) ABC is divisible by 3 $\Leftrightarrow$ CBA is divisible by 3.
(ii) ABC is divisible by 5 $\Leftrightarrow$ CBA is divisible by 5.

12 No square number ends in a 2.

13 n is prime $\Rightarrow n^2 + n + 1$ is prime.

14 The sum of n consecutive integers is divisible by n, where n is a positive integer.

15 The interior angle of a regular polygon with n sides is $\frac{(2n - 4)}{n}$ right angles.

16 Given that $5 \geqslant m > n \geqslant 0$ and that m and n are integers, the equation $m^n = n^m$ has exactly one solution.

17 Given that p and q are odd numbers $p^2 + q^2$ cannot be divisible by 4.

18 (i) One cannot logically say 'I always tell lies'.

(ii) It is impossible to draw any conclusion when someone tells you 'I always tell the truth'.

19 The smallest value of n (>1) for which $1^2 + 2^2 + 3^2 + \ldots + n^2$ is a perfect square is 24.

INVESTIGATION

Call the prime numbers, in order, p_1, p_2, p_3, and so on. Thus $p_1 = 2$, $p_2 = 3$, $p_3 = 5$, ...

(i) Show that $p_1 + 1$, $p_1 p_2 + 1$, $p_1 p_2 p_3 + 1$, $p_1 p_2 p_3 p_4 + 1$ are all prime numbers.

(ii) Explain why $p_1 p_2 p_3 \ldots p_n + 1$ is either prime or has a prime factor greater than p_n for all positive integer values of n.

(iii) How does this allow you to prove that there is an infinite number of prime numbers?

KEY POINTS

1 When solving a problem it is often helpful to follow these steps.
- Solve similar but simplified versions of the same problem.
- Look for patterns in your results.
- Form a conjecture so that you can predict what would happen in more complicated cases.
- Check that your predictions are correct.
- Express your conjecture in general form, using algebra if appropriate.
- Prove your conjecture.

2 Types of numbers

Counting numbers	$\mathbb{Z}^+$	1, 2, 3, ...
Natural numbers	$\mathbb{N}$	0, 1, 2, 3, ...
Integers	$\mathbb{Z}$	... −2, −1, 0, 1, 2, ...
Rational numbers	$\mathbb{Q}$	where m and n are integers and $n \neq 0$
Real numbers	$\mathbb{R}$	Rational and irrational (e.g. $\sqrt{2}$, π) numbers

3 $\Rightarrow$ means 'implies', 'if ... then ...', 'therefore'.
$\Leftarrow$ means 'is implied by', 'follows from'.
$\Leftrightarrow$ means 'implies and is implied by', 'is equivalent to'.

The converse of A $\Rightarrow$ B is A $\Leftarrow$ B.
If A $\Leftarrow$ B, A is a *necessary* condition for B.
If A $\Rightarrow$ B, A is a *sufficient* condition for B.

4 Methods of proof
- deduction
- exhaustion
- contradiction

5 Methods of disproof
- contradiction
- deduction

Concepts for Advanced Mathematics

C2

7 Sequences and series

Population, when unchecked, increases in a geometrical ratio.
Subsistence increases only in an arithmetical ratio. A slight
acquaintance with numbers will show the immensity of the first
power in comparison with the second.

Thomas Malthus (1798)

? Each of the following sequences is related to one of the pictures above.

(i)   5000, 10 000, 20 000, 40 000, … .

(ii) 8, 0, 10, 10, 10, 10, 12, 8, 0, … .

(iii) 5, 3.5, 0, −3.5, −5, −3.5, 0, 3.5, 5, 3.5, … .

(iv) 20, 40, 60, 80, 100, … .

(a) Identify which sequence goes with which picture.

(b) Give the next few numbers in each sequence.

(c) Describe the pattern of the numbers in each case.

(d) Decide whether the sequence will go on for ever, or come to a stop.

Definitions and notation

A *sequence* is a set of numbers in a given order, like

$$\frac{1}{2}, \frac{1}{4}, \frac{1}{8}, \frac{1}{16}, \dots .$$

Each of these numbers is called a *term* of the sequence. When writing the terms of a sequence algebraically, it is usual to denote the position of any term in the sequence by a subscript, so that a general sequence might be written:

$$a_1, a_2, a_3, \dots, \text{ with general term } a_k.$$

For the sequence above, the first term is $a_1 = \frac{1}{2}$, the second term is $a_2 = \frac{1}{4}$, and so on.

When the terms of a sequence are added together, like

$$\frac{1}{2} + \frac{1}{4} + \frac{1}{8} + \frac{1}{16} + \dots$$

the resulting sum is called a *series*. The process of adding the terms together is called *summation* and indicated by the symbol $\sum$ (the Greek letter sigma), with the position of the first and last terms involved given as *limits*.

So $a_1 + a_2 + a_3 + a_4 + a_5$ is written $\sum_{k=1}^{k=5} a_k$ or $\sum_{k=1}^{5} a_k$.

In cases like this one, where there is no possibility of confusion, the sum would normally be written more simply as $\sum_{1}^{5} a_k$.

If all the terms were to be summed, it would usually be denoted even more simply, as $\sum_{k} a_k$, or even $\sum a_k$.

A sequence may have an infinite number of terms, in which case it is called an *infinite sequence*. The corresponding series is called an *infinite series*.

In mathematics, although the word *series* can describe the sum of the terms of any sequence, it is usually used only when summing the sequence provides some useful or interesting overall result.
For example:

> This series has a finite number of terms (6).

$$(1 + x)^5 = 1 + 5x + 10x^2 + 10x^3 + 5x^4 + x^5$$

> Both of these series have an infinite number of terms.

$$\pi = 2\sqrt{3}\left[1 + \frac{1}{3}\left(\frac{-1}{3}\right) + \frac{1}{5}\left(\frac{-1}{3}\right)^2 + \frac{1}{7}\left(\frac{-1}{3}\right)^3 + \dots\right]$$

$$\sin x = x - \frac{x^3}{3!} + \frac{x^5}{5!} - \dots \text{ (where } x \text{ is measured in radians).}$$

The phrase 'sum of a sequence' is often used to mean the sum of the terms of a sequence (i.e. the series).

Patterns in sequences

SCORECARD · J.GREEN

OUT	4	4	5	10	3	2	4	8	6
HOME	3	5	7	1	4	5	4	5	7

Figure 7.1

Any ordered set of numbers, like the scores of this golfer on an 18-hole round (see figure 7.1) form a sequence. In mathematics, we are particularly interested in those which have a well-defined pattern, often in the form of an algebraic formula linking the terms. The sequences you met at the start of this chapter show various types of pattern.

Arithmetic sequences

A sequence in which the terms increase by the addition of a fixed amount (or decrease by subtraction of a fixed amount), is described as *arithmetic*. The increase from one term to the next is called the *common difference*.

Thus the sequence 5 8 11 14... is arithmetic with

+3 +3 +3

common difference 3.

This sequence can be written algebraically in two quite different ways.

(i) $a_k = 2 + 3k$ for $k = 1, 2, 3, \ldots$

When $k = 1$, $a_1 = 2 + 3 = 5$

$k = 2$, $a_2 = 2 + 6 = 8$

$k = 3$, $a_3 = 2 + 9 = 11$

> This version has the advantage that the right-hand side begins with the first term of the sequence.

and so on.

(An equivalent way of writing this is $a_k = 5 + 3(k - 1)$ for $k = 1, 2, 3, \ldots$.)

(ii) $a_1 = 5$

$a_{k+1} = a_k + 3$ for $k = 1, 2, 3, \ldots$

Substituting $k = 1 \implies a_2 = a_1 + 3 = 5 + 3 = 8$

$k = 2 \implies a_3 = a_2 + 3 = 8 + 3 = 11$

$k = 3 \implies a_4 = a_3 + 3 = 11 + 3 = 14$

and so on.

The first form, which defines the value of a_k directly, is called a *deductive definition*. The second, which defines each term by relating it to the previous one, is described as *inductive*. You should be prepared to use either.

<table>
<tr><td>**EXAMPLE 7.1**</td></tr>
</table>

A sequence is defined deductively by $a_k = 3k - 1$ for $k = 1, 2, 3, \ldots$.

(i) Write down the first six terms of the sequence, and say what kind of sequence it is.

(ii) Find the value of the series $\sum_{k=1}^{k=6} a_k$.

SOLUTION

(i) Substituting $k = 1, 2, \ldots, 6$ in $a_k = 3k - 1$ gives

$a_1 = 3 - 1 = 2$ $\quad a_2 = 6 - 1 = 5$ $\quad a_3 = 9 - 1 = 8$
$a_4 = 12 - 1 = 11$ $\quad a_5 = 15 - 1 = 14$ $\quad a_6 = 18 - 1 = 17,$

so the sequence is   2, 5, 8, 11, 14, 17, ...

This is an arithmetic sequence with common difference 3.

(ii) $\sum_{k=1}^{k=6} a_k = a_1 + a_2 + a_3 + a_4 + a_5 + a_6$

$= 2 + 5 + 8 + 11 + 14 + 17$

$= 57.$

Arithmetic sequences are dealt with in more detail later in this chapter.

Geometric sequences

A sequence in which you find each term by multiplying the previous one by a fixed number is described as *geometric*; the fixed number is the *common ratio*.

Thus $\underbrace{10 \quad 20 \quad 40 \quad 80}_{\times 2 \ \times 2 \ \times 2}\ldots$ is a geometric sequence with common ratio 2.

It may be written algebraically as

$$a_k = 5 \times 2^k \text{ for } k = 1, 2, 3, \ldots \qquad \text{(deductive definition)}$$

or as $\quad a_1 = 10$

$$a_{k+1} = 2a_k \quad \text{for } k = 1, 2, 3, \ldots \qquad \text{(inductive definition)}.$$

Geometric sequences are also dealt with in more detail later in this chapter.

Periodic sequences

A sequence which repeats itself at regular intervals is called *periodic*. In the case of the fish bar at the start of this chapter, the number of hours it is open each day forms the sequence

$$\begin{array}{ccccccc} a_1 = 8, & a_2 = 0, & a_3 = 10, & a_4 = 10, & a_5 = 10, & a_6 = 10, & a_7 = 12, \\ \text{(Sun)} & \text{(Mon)} & \text{(Tues)} & \text{(Wed)} & \text{(Thurs)} & \text{(Fri)} & \text{(Sat)} \end{array}$$

$$\begin{array}{cc} a_8 = 8, & a_9 = 0, \ldots . \\ \text{(Sun)} & \text{(Mon)} \end{array}$$

There is no neat algebraic formula for the terms of this sequence but you can see that $a_8 = a_1$, $a_9 = a_2$, and so on.

In general,

$$a_{k+7} = a_k \text{ for } k = 1, 2, 3, \ldots .$$

This sequence is periodic, with period 7. Each term is repeated after seven terms.

A sequence for which

$$a_{k+p} = a_k \text{ for } k = 1, 2, 3, \ldots \text{ (for a fixed integer, } p)$$

is periodic. The period is the smallest positive value of p for which this is true.

Oscillating sequences

The terms of an oscillating sequence, like

$$5, 6, 5, 4, 5, 6, 5, 4, \ldots$$

lie above and below a middle number, in this case 5 (see figure 7.2).

Figure 7.2

In this example, the sequence is also periodic, with period 4. However, some oscillating sequences, like

$$8, -4, 2, -1, \tfrac{1}{2}, \dots$$

are non-periodic. You will notice that the middle value, 0, is not itself a term in this sequence.

EXAMPLE 7.2

A sequence is defined by $a_k = (-1)^k$ for $k = 1, 2, 3, \dots$.

(i) Write down the first six terms of this sequence and describe its pattern.

(ii) Find the value of the series $\displaystyle\sum_{2}^{5} a_k$.

(iii) Describe the sequence defined by $b_k = 5 + (-1)^k \times 2$ for $k = 1, 2, 3, \dots$.

SOLUTION

(i) $a_1 = (-1)^1 = -1 \qquad a_2 = (-1)^2 = +1 \qquad a_3 = (-1)^3 = -1$
$a_4 = (-1)^4 = +1 \qquad a_5 = (-1)^5 = -1 \qquad a_6 = (-1)^6 = +1$

The sequence is $-1, +1, -1, +1, -1, +1, \dots$.

It is oscillating, and periodic with period 2. It is also geometric, with common ratio -1.

(ii) $\displaystyle\sum_{2}^{5} a_k = a_2 + a_3 + a_4 + a_5$
$\qquad\qquad = (+1) + (-1) + (+1) + (-1)$
$\qquad\qquad = 0.$

(iii) $b_1 = 5 + (-1) \times 2 = 3 \qquad\qquad b_2 = 5 + (-1)^2 \times 2 = 7$
$\qquad b_3 = 5 + (-1)^3 \times 2 = 3 \qquad\qquad b_4 = 5 + (-1)^4 \times 2 = 7$

and so on, giving the sequence $3, 7, 3, 7, \dots$, which is oscillating and periodic with period 2.

❓ Identify some more examples of each of the types of sequence, arthmetic, geometric, periodic and oscillating.
For each of your sequences, define a_k.

Sequences with other patterns

There are many other possible patterns in sequences. Figure 7.3 shows a well-known children's toy in which squares are stacked to make a tower. The smallest square has sides 1 cm long, and the length of the sides increases in steps of 1 cm.

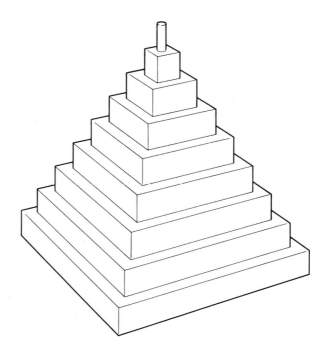

Figure 7.3

The areas of these squares, in cm^2, form the sequence

$$1^2, 2^2, 3^2, 4^2, 5^2, \ldots \quad \text{or} \quad 1, 4, 9, 16, 25, \ldots .$$

This sequence does not fit any of the patterns described so far. If you subtract each term from the next, however, you will find that the differences form a pattern.

Sequence 1 4 9 16 25 ...
Difference   3 5 7 9 ...

These differences form an arithmetic sequence with common difference 2. The next difference in the sequence is $9 + 2 = 11$, and so the next term in the areas sequence is $25 + 11 = 36$, which is indeed 6^2.

Looking at the differences between the terms often helps you to spot the pattern within a sequence. Sometimes you may need to look at the differences of the differences, or go even further.

EXERCISE 7A

1 For each of the following sequences, write down the next four terms (assuming the same pattern continues) and describe its pattern as fully as you can.

(i) 7, 10, 13, 16, …   **(ii)** 8, 7, 6, 5, …
(iii) 10, 30, 90, 270, …   **(iv)** 64, 32, 16, 8, …
(v) 2, 2, 2, 5, 2, 2, 2, 5, 2, 2, 2, 5, …   **(vi)** 4, 6, 7, 6, 4, 2, 1, 2, 4, 6, 7, 6, …
(vii) 1, −2, 4, −8, 16, …   **(viii)** 2, 4, 6, 8, 2, 4, 6, 8, 2, …
(ix) 4.1, 3.9, 3.7, 3.5, …   **(x)** 1, 1.1, 1.21, 1.331, …

2 Write down the first four terms of the sequences defined below.
In each case, k takes the values 1, 2, 3, … .

(i) $a_k = 2k + 1$ **(ii)** $a_k = 3 \times 2^k$
(iii) $a_k = 2k + 2^k$ **(iv)** $a_k = \frac{1}{k}$
(v) $a_{k+1} = a_k + 3, a_1 = 12$ **(vi)** $a_{k+1} = -a_k, a_1 = -5$
(vii) $a_{k+1} = \frac{1}{2}a_k, a_1 = 72$ **(viii)** $a_{k+2} = a_k, a_1 = 4, a_2 = 6$
(ix) $a_k = 5 + (-1)^k$ **(x)** $a_{k+1} = a_k + 2k + 1, a_1 = 1$

3 Find the value of the series $\sum_{1}^{4} a_k$ in each of the following cases.

(i) $a_k = 2 + 5k$ **(ii)** $a_k = 3 \times 2^k$
(iii) $a_k = \frac{12}{k}$ **(iv)** $a_{k+1} = 3a_k, a_1 = 1$
(v) $a_k = 2 + (-1)^k$

4 Express each of the following series in the form $\sum_{1}^{n} a_k$, where n is an integer and a_k is an algebraic expression for the kth term of the series.

(i) $1 + 2 + 3 + … + 10$ **(ii)** $21 + 22 + 23 + … + 30$
(iii) $210 + 220 + 230 + … + 300$ **(iv)** $211 + 222 + 233 + … + 310$
(v) $190 + 180 + 170 + … + 100$

5 Find the values of the following.

(i) $\sum_{1}^{5} k$ **(ii)** $\sum_{1}^{20} k^2 - \sum_{1}^{19} k^2$ **(iii)** $\sum_{0}^{5} (k^2 - 5k)$

6 The Fibonacci sequence is given by 1, 1, 2, 3, 5, 8, … .

(i) Write down the sequence of the differences between the terms in this sequence, and comment on what you find.
(ii) Write down the next three terms of the Fibonacci sequence.
(iii) Write down the sequence formed by the ratio of one term to the next, $\frac{a_{k+1}}{a_k}$, using decimals. What do you notice about it?

167

7 The terms of a sequence are defined by

$$a_k = 4 + (-1)^k \times 2$$

(i) Write down the first six terms of this sequence.

(ii) Describe the sequence.

(iii) What would be the effect of changing the sequence to

    (a) $a_k = 4 + (-2)^k$

    (b) $a_k = 4 + \left(-\frac{1}{2}\right)^k$?

8 A sequence of numbers $t_1, t_2, t_3, t_4, \ldots$ is formed by taking a starting value of t_1 and using the rule

$$t_{k+1} = t_k^2 - 2, \qquad \text{for } k = 1, 2, 3, \ldots.$$

(i) If $t_1 = \sqrt{2}$, calculate t_2, t_3 and t_4.

Show that $t_5 = 2$, and write down the value of t_{100}.

(ii) If $t_1 = 2$, show that all terms of the sequence are the same.

Find the other value of t_1 for which all the terms of the sequence are the same.

(iii) Determine whether the sequence converges, diverges or is periodic in the cases when

    (a) $t_1 = 3$ **(b)** $t_1 = 1$ **(c)** $t_1 = \dfrac{\sqrt{5} - 1}{2}$.

[MEI]

9 The number π may be calculated using Gregory's series

$$\frac{\pi}{4} = 1 - \frac{1}{3} + \frac{1}{5} - \frac{1}{7} + \cdots$$

(This series was discovered by James Gregory, a Scottish mathematician, in 1671.)

(i) Calculate estimates of π using 1, 2, 3, 4, 5, 6, 7 and 8 terms of this series.

(ii) Comment upon your answers to (i).

10 The harmonic series is given by S in

$$S = 1 + \frac{1}{2} + \frac{1}{3} + \frac{1}{4} + \frac{1}{5} + \frac{1}{6} + \frac{1}{7} + \frac{1}{8} + \cdots.$$

(i) Explain why grouping the terms in the form

$$S = 1 + \frac{1}{2} + \left(\frac{1}{3} + \frac{1}{4}\right) + \left(\frac{1}{5} + \frac{1}{6} + \frac{1}{7} + \frac{1}{8}\right) + \left(\cdots\right.$$

allows you to conclude that $S > 1 + \frac{1}{2} + \frac{1}{2} + \frac{1}{2} + \cdots.$

(ii) Explain how this method can be used to show that S is infinite.

e *The product of a sequence*

The terms of a sequence may be multiplied together to obtain their product, denoted by Π, (rather than Σ for their sum). Investigate the following products.

(i) $\displaystyle\prod_{k=1}^{n} \frac{k}{k+1}$ where n is a positive integer greater than 1.

(ii) Wallis' product: $\dfrac{\pi}{2} = \left(\dfrac{2}{1} \times \dfrac{2}{3}\right) \times \left(\dfrac{4}{3} \times \dfrac{4}{5}\right) \times \left(\dfrac{6}{5} \times \dfrac{6}{7}\right) \times \dots$.

(This expression was discovered by John Wallis, an English mathematician, in 1650.)

Does Wallis' product provide an easier way of finding π than Gregory's series (see question 9)?

Arithmetic sequences and series

Earlier in this chapter, you learned that successive terms of an arithmetic sequence increase (or decrease) by a fixed amount called the common difference, d. So:

$$a_{k+1} = a_k + d.$$

When the terms of an arithmetic sequence are added together, the sum is called an arithmetic series. An alternative name is an *arithmetic progression*, often abbreviated to A.P.

Notation

When describing arithmetic series and sequences in this book, the following conventions will be used:

- first term, $a_1 = a$

- number of terms $= n$

- last term, $a_n = l$

- common difference $= d$

- the general term, a_k, is that in position k (i.e. the kth term).

Thus in the arithmetic sequence 5, 7, 9, 11, 13, 15, 17,

$a = 5$, $l = 17$, $d = 2$ and $n = 7$.

The terms are formed as follows.

$$a_1 = a \qquad\quad = 5$$
$$a_2 = a + d \quad = 5 + 2 \qquad = 7$$
$$a_3 = a + 2d = 5 + 2 \times 2 = 9$$
$$a_4 = a + 3d = 5 + 3 \times 2 = 11$$
$$a_5 = a + 4d = 5 + 4 \times 2 = 13$$
$$a_6 = a + 5d = 5 + 5 \times 2 = 15$$
$$a_7 = a + 6d = 5 + 6 \times 2 = 17$$

The 7th term is the 1st term (5) plus six times the common difference (2).

You can see that any term is given by the first term plus a number of differences. The number of differences is, in each case, one less than the number of the term. You can express this mathematically as

$$a_k = a + (k - 1)d.$$

For the last term, this becomes

$$l = a + (n - 1)d.$$

These are both general formulae which apply to any arithmetic sequence.

EXAMPLE 7.3

Find the 17th term in the arithmetic sequence 12, 9, 6, … .

SOLUTION

In this case $a = 12$ and $d = -3$.

Using $a_k = a + (k - 1)d$, you obtain
$$a_{17} = 12 + (17 - 1) \times (-3)$$
$$= 12 - 48$$
$$= -36.$$

The 17th term is -36.

EXAMPLE 7.4

How many terms are there in the sequence 11, 15, 19, …, 643?

SOLUTION

This is an arithmetic sequence with first term, $a = 11$, last term, $l = 643$ and common difference, $d = 4$.

Using the result $l = a + (n - 1)d$, you have
$$643 = 11 + 4(n - 1)$$
$$\Rightarrow \quad 4n = 643 - 11 + 4$$
$$\Rightarrow \quad n = 159.$$

There are 159 terms.

Note

The relationship $l = a + (n - 1)d$ may be rearranged to give

$$n = \frac{l - a}{d} + 1.$$

This gives the number of terms in an A.P. directly if you know the first term, the last term and the common difference.

The sum of the terms of an arithmetic sequence

When Carl Friederich Gauss (1777–1855) was at school he was always quick to answer mathematics questions. One day his teacher, hoping for half an hour of peace and quiet, told his class to add up all the whole numbers from 1 to 100. Almost at once the 10-year-old Gauss announced that he had done it and that the answer was 5050.

Gauss had not of course added the terms one by one. Instead he wrote the series down twice, once in the given order and once backwards, and added the two together:

$$S = \quad 1 + \quad 2 + \quad 3 + \ldots + \quad 98 + \quad 99 + 100$$
$$S = 100 + \quad 99 + \quad 98 + \ldots + \quad 3 + \quad 2 + \quad 1.$$

Adding, $2S = 101 + 101 + 101 + \ldots + 101 + 101 + 101$.

Since there are 100 terms in the series,

$$2S = 101 \times 100$$
$$S = 5050.$$

The numbers 1, 2, 3, … , 100 form an arithmetic sequence with common difference 1. Gauss' method can be used for finding the sum of any arithmetic series.

It is common to use the letter S to denote the sum of a series. When there is any doubt as to the number of terms that are being summed, this is indicated by a subscript: S_5 indicates five terms, S_n indicates n terms.

EXAMPLE 7.5

Find the value of $8 + 6 + 4 + \ldots + (-32)$.

SOLUTION

This is an arithmetic series, with common difference -2. The number of terms, n, may be calculated using

$$n = \frac{l - a}{d} + 1$$

$$n = \frac{-32 - 8}{-2} + 1$$

$$= 21.$$

The sum S of the series is then found as follows.

$$S = \quad 8 + \quad 6 + \dots - 30 - 32$$
$$S = -32 - 30 - \dots + \quad 6 + \quad 8$$
$$\overline{2S = -24 - 24 - \dots - 24 - 24}$$

Since there are 21 terms, this gives $2S = -24 \times 21$, so $S = -12 \times 21 = -252$.

Generalising this method by writing the series in the conventional notation gives:

$$S = \quad [a] \quad + \quad [a+d] \quad + \dots + [a+(n-2)d] + [a+(n-1)d]$$
$$S = [a+(n-1)d] + [a+(n-2)d] + \dots + \quad [a+d] \quad + \quad [a]$$
$$\overline{2S = [2a+(n-1)d] + [2a+(n-1)d] + \dots + [2a+(n-1)d] + [2a+(n-1)d]}$$

Since there are n terms, it follows that

$$S = \tfrac{1}{2}n[2a+(n-1)d].$$

This result may also be written

$$S = \tfrac{1}{2}n(a+l).$$

EXAMPLE 7.6

Find the sum of the first 100 terms of the sequence

$$1, 1\tfrac{1}{4}, 1\tfrac{1}{2}, 1\tfrac{3}{4}, \dots .$$

SOLUTION

In this arithmetic sequence

$a = 1$, $d = \tfrac{1}{4}$ and $n = 100$.

Using $S = \tfrac{1}{2}n[2a+(n-1)d]$, you have

$$S = \tfrac{1}{2} \times 100\left(2 + 99 \times \tfrac{1}{4}\right)$$

$$= 1337\tfrac{1}{2}.$$

EXAMPLE 7.7

Jamila starts a job on a salary of £9000 per year, and this increases by an annual increment of £1000. Assuming that apart from the increment, Jamila's salary does not increase, find

(i) her salary in the 12th year
(ii) the length of time she has been working when her total earnings are £100 000.

SOLUTION

Jamila's annual salaries (in pounds) form the arithmetic sequence

$$9000, 10\,000, 11\,000, \dots .$$

The first term, $a = 9000$, and the common difference, $d = 1000$.

(i) Her salary in the 12th year is calculated using:

$$a_k = a + (k - 1)d$$
$$\Rightarrow \quad a_{12} = 9000 + (12 - 1) \times 1000$$
$$= 20\,000.$$

(ii) The number of years that have elapsed when her total earnings are £100 000 is given by:

$$S = \tfrac{1}{2}n[2a + (n - 1)d]$$

where $S = 100\,000$, $a = 9000$ and $d = 1000$.

This gives $\quad 100\,000 = \tfrac{1}{2}n[2 \times 9000 + 1000(n - 1)]$.

This simplifies to the quadratic equation:

$$n^2 + 17n - 200 = 0.$$

Factorising,

$$(n - 8)(n + 25) = 0$$
$$\Rightarrow n = 8 \text{ or } -25.$$

The root $n = -25$ is irrelevant, so the answer is $n = 8$.

Jamila has earned a total of £100 000 after eight years.

EXERCISE 7B

1 Are the following sequences arithmetic?
If so, state the common difference and the seventh term.

(i) 27, 29, 31, 33, …   (ii) 1, 2, 3, 5, 8, …   (iii) 2, 4, 8, 16, …
(iv) 3, 7, 11, 15, …   (v) 8, 6, 4, 2, …

2 The first term of an arithmetic sequence is –8 and the common difference is 3.

(i) Find the seventh term of the sequence.
(ii) The last term of the sequence is 100.
     How many terms are there in the sequence?

3 The first term of an arithmetic sequence is 12, the seventh term is 36 and the last term is 144.

(i) Find the common difference.
(ii) Find how many terms there are in the sequence.

4 There are 20 terms in an arithmetic sequence.
The first term is –5 and the last term is 90.

(i) Find the common difference.
(ii) Find the sum of the terms in the sequence.

5 The kth term of an arithmetic sequence is given by

$$a_k = 14 + 2k.$$

(i) Write down the first three terms of the sequence.

(ii) Calculate the sum of the first 12 terms of this sequence.

6 Below is an arithmetic sequence.

$$120, 114, \ldots, 36$$

(i) How many terms are there in the sequence?

(ii) What is the sum of the terms in the sequence?

7 The fifth term of an arithmetic sequence is 28 and the tenth term is 58.

(i) Find the first term and the common difference.

(ii) The sum of all the terms in this sequence is 444.
How many terms are there?

8 The sixth term of an arithmetic sequence is twice the third term, and the first term is 3. The sequence has ten terms.

(i) Find the common difference.

(ii) Find the sum of all the terms in the sequence.

9 A set of 12 new stamps is to be issued; the denominations increase in steps of 2p, starting with 1p:

$$1p, 3p, 5p, 7p, \ldots .$$

(i) What is the highest denomination of stamp in the set?

(ii) What is the total cost of the complete set?

10 (i) Find the sum of all the odd numbers between 50 and 150.

(ii) Find the sum of all the even numbers from 50 to 150, inclusive.

(iii) Find the sum of the terms of the arithmetic sequence with first term 50, common difference 1 and 101 terms.

(iv) Explain the relationship between your answers to parts (i), (ii) and (iii).

11 The first term of an arithmetic sequence is 3000 and the tenth term is 1200.

(i) Find the sum of the first 20 terms of the sequence.

(ii) After how many terms does the sum of the sequence become negative?

12 An arithmetic progression has first term 7 and common difference 3.

(i) Write down a formula for the kth term of the progression.
Which term of the progression equals 73?

(ii) Write down a formula for the sum of the first n terms of the progression.
How many terms of the progression are required to give a sum equal to 6300?

[MEI]

13 (i) The kth term of an arithmetic progression is given by $t_k = 3 + 7k$. Write down the first term and the common difference of this progression.

Calculate also $\sum\limits_{k=1}^{100} t_k$.

(ii) The sum S_n of the first n terms of an arithmetic progression is given by $S_n = 3n + 2n^2$. Write down the first and second terms of the progression and find a formula for the kth term.

[**MEI**]

14 Paul's starting salary in a company is £14 000 and during the time he stays with the company it increases by £500 each year.

(i) What is his salary in his sixth year?
(ii) How many years has Paul been working for the company when his total earnings for all his years there are £126 000?

15 A jogger is training for a 10 km charity run. He starts with a run of 400 m; then he increases the distance he runs by 200 m each day.

(i) How many days does it take the jogger to reach a distance of 10 km in training?
(ii) What total distance will he have run in training by then?

16 A piece of string 10 m long is to be cut into pieces, so that the lengths of the pieces form an arithmetic sequence.

(i) The lengths of the longest and shortest pieces are 1 m and 25 cm respectively; how many pieces are there?
(ii) If the same string had been cut into 20 pieces with lengths that formed an arithmetic sequence, and if the length of the second longest had been 92.5 cm, how long would the shortest piece have been?

17 The training programme of a pilot requires him to fly 'circuits' of an airfield. Each day he flies 3 more circuits than the day before. On the fifth day he flew 14 circuits.

Calculate how many circuits he flew:
(i) on the first day
(ii) in total by the end of the fifth day
(iii) in total by the end of the nth day
(iv) in total from the end of the nth day to the end of the $2n$th day. Simplify your answer.

[**MEI**]

18 As part of a fund-raising campaign, I have been given some books of raffle tickets to sell. Each book has the same number of tickets and all the tickets I have been given are numbered in sequence. The number of the ticket on the front of the 5th book is 205 and that on the front of the 19th book is 373.

(i) By writing the number of the ticket on the front of the first book as *a* and the number of tickets in each book as *d*, write down two equations involving *a* and *d*.

(ii) From these two equations find how many tickets are in each book and the number on the front of the first book I have been given.

(iii) The last ticket I have been given is numbered 492. How many books have I been given?

[MEI]

Geometric sequences and series

Figure 7.4

A human being begins life as one cell, which divides into two, then four... .

The terms of a geometric sequence are formed by multiplying one term by a fixed number, the common ratio, to obtain the next. This can be written inductively as:

$$a_{k+1} = ra_k \text{ with first term } a_1.$$

The sum of the terms of a geometric sequence is called a *geometric series*. An alternative name is a *geometric progression*, shortened to G.P.

Notation

When describing geometric sequences in this book, the following conventions are used:

- first term $a_1 = a$

- common ratio $= r$

- number of terms $= n$

- the general term a_k is that in position k (i.e. the kth term).

Thus in the geometric sequence   3, 6, 12, 24, 48,

$$a = 3, r = 2 \text{ and } n = 5.$$

The terms of this sequence are formed as follows.

$$
\begin{aligned}
a_1 &= a &&= 3 \\
a_2 &= a \times r &&= 3 \times 2 &&= 6 \\
a_3 &= a \times r^2 &&= 3 \times 2^2 &&= 12 \\
a_4 &= a \times r^3 &&= 3 \times 2^3 &&= 24 \\
a_5 &= a \times r^4 &&= 3 \times 2^4 &&= 48
\end{aligned}
$$

You will see that in each case the power of r is one less than the number of the term: $a_5 = ar^4$ and 4 is one less than 5. This can be written deductively as

$$a_k = ar^{k-1},$$

and the last term is

$$a_n = ar^{n-1}.$$

These are both general formulae which apply to any geometric sequence.

Given two consecutive terms of a geometric sequence, you can always find the common ratio by dividing the later term by the earlier. For example, the geometric sequence … 5, 8, … has common ratio $r = \frac{8}{5}$.

EXAMPLE 7.8

Find the seventh term in the geometric sequence 8, 24, 72, 216, … .

SOLUTION

In the sequence, the first term, $a = 8$ and the common ratio, $r = 3$.

The kth term of a geometric sequence is given by $a_k = ar^{k-1}$,

and so $\quad a_7 = 8 \times 3^6$
$$= 5832.$$

EXAMPLE 7.9

How many terms are there in the geometric sequence 0.2, 1, 5, …, 390 625?

SOLUTION

The last (nth) term of a geometric sequence is given by $a_n = a \times r^{n-1}$.

In this case $a = 0.2$ and $r = 5$, so:

$$390\,625 = 0.2 \times 5^{n-1}.$$

You can solve this type of equation using logarithms, which you will meet in Chapter 11. This particular equation is solved there in Example 11.3. However, you can also use trial and improvement or a graphic calculator and these methods are shown here.

Method 1: Trial and improvement

When solving a problem by trial and improvement, remember to show your trials and their outcomes.

$$390\,625 = 0.2 \times 5^{n-1}$$

$$5^{n-1} = \frac{390\,625}{0.2} = 1\,953\,125$$

$n-1$	5^{n-1}	large/small
50	8.88×10^{34}	much too large
5	3 125	much too small
10	9 765 625	too large but 'near'
9	1 953 125	✓

$$\Rightarrow \quad n-1 = 9$$
$$\Rightarrow \quad n = 10$$

There are 10 terms.

In trial and improvement, the answer will often not work out to be a whole number, but it does here.

Method 2: On a graphic calculator or computer

To solve $390\,625 = 0.2 \times 5^{n-1}$,

draw $y = 0.2 \times 5^{n-1}$

and $y = 390\,625$.

Use an intersect function or zoom to find where the graphs intersect.

- - - Equation 1: $y = 0.2(5\wedge(x-1))$
— Equation 2: $y = 390\,625$

Figure 7.5

This gives $n = 10$.

When using a graphic calculator, remember to state the equations of the graphs you have drawn, and the functions you have used.

 How would you use a spreadsheet to solve the equation $390\,625 = 0.2 \times 5^{n-1}$?

The sum of the terms of a geometric sequence

The origins of chess are obscure, with several countries claiming the credit for its invention. One story is that it came from China. It is said that its inventor presented the game to the Emperor, who was so impressed that he asked the inventor what he would like as a reward.

'One grain of rice for the first square on the board, two for the second, four for the third, eight for the fourth, and so on up to the last square', came the answer.

The Emperor agreed, but it soon became clear that there was not enough rice in the whole of China to give the inventor his reward.

How many grains of rice was the inventor actually asking for?

The answer is the geometric series with 64 terms and common ratio 2:

$$1 + 2 + 4 + 8 + \ldots + 2^{63}.$$

This can be summed as follows.

Call the series S:

$$S = 1 + 2 + 4 + 8 + \ldots + 2^{63}. \qquad \text{①}$$

Now multiply it by the common ratio, 2:

$$2S = 2 + 4 + 8 + 16 + \ldots + 2^{64}. \qquad \text{②}$$

Then subtract ① from ②

$$\text{②} \quad 2S = \qquad 2 + 4 + 8 + 16 + \ldots + 2^{63} + 2^{64}$$

$$\text{①} \quad S = \quad 1 + 2 + 4 + 8 + \ldots \qquad + 2^{63}$$

subtracting: $\quad S = -1 + 0 + 0 + 0 + \ldots \qquad + 2^{64}.$

The total number of rice grains requested was therefore $2^{64} - 1$ (which is about 1.85×10^{19}).

? How many tonnes of rice is this, and how many tonnes would you expect there to be in China at any time?

(One hundred grains of rice weigh about 2 grammes. The world annual production of all cereals is about 1.8×10^9 tonnes.)

Note

The method shown above can be used to sum any geometric series.

EXAMPLE 7.10 Find the value of $0.2 + 1 + 5 + \ldots + 390\,625$.

SOLUTION

This is a geometric series with common ratio 5.

Let $\quad S = 0.2 + 1 + 5 + \ldots + 390\,625$. ①

Multiplying by the common ratio, 5 gives:

$$5S = 1 + 5 + 25 + \ldots + 390\,625 + 1\,953\,125.$$ ②

Subtracting ① from ②:

$$5S = \qquad 1 + 5 + 25 + \ldots + 390\,625 + 1\,953\,125$$
$$S = \quad 0.2 + 1 + 5 + 25 + \ldots + 390\,625$$

$$4S = -0.2 + 0 \ldots \qquad\qquad + 0 \qquad + 1\,953\,125.$$
This gives $\quad 4S = 1\,953\,124.8$
$\Rightarrow \qquad\qquad S = 488\,281.2.$

The same method can be applied to the general geometric series to give a formula for its value:

$$S = a + ar + ar^2 + \ldots + ar^{n-1}.$$ ①

Multiplying by the common ratio r gives:

$$rS = ar + ar^2 + ar^3 + \ldots + ar^n.$$ ②

Subtracting ① from ②, as before, gives:

$$(r-1)S = -a + ar^n$$
$$= a(r^n - 1)$$
so $\qquad S = \dfrac{a(r^n - 1)}{(r-1)}.$

The sum to n terms is often written as S_n, and that for an infinite series as S_∞ or S.

For values of r between -1 and 1, the sum to n terms is usually written as:

$$S_n = \frac{a(1 - r^n)}{(1 - r)}.$$

This ensures that you are working with positive numbers in the brackets.

Infinite geometric series

The series $1 + \frac{1}{2} + \frac{1}{4} + \frac{1}{8} + \frac{1}{16} + \ldots$ is geometric, with common ratio $\frac{1}{2}$.

Summing the terms one by one gives $1, 1\frac{1}{2}, 1\frac{3}{4}, 1\frac{7}{8}, 1\frac{15}{16}, \ldots$.

Clearly the more terms you take, the nearer the sum gets to 2. In the limit, as the number of terms tends to infinity, the sum tends to 2.

As $n \to \infty$, $S_n \to 2$.

This is an example of a *convergent* series. The sum to infinity is a finite number.

You can see this by substituting $a = 1$ and $r = \frac{1}{2}$ in the formula for the sum of the series:

$$S_n = \frac{a\left(1 - r^n\right)}{1 - r}$$

giving $S_n = \dfrac{1 \times \left(1 - \left(\frac{1}{2}\right)^n\right)}{\left(1 - \dfrac{1}{2}\right)}$

$$= 2 \times \left(1 - \left(\frac{1}{2}\right)^n\right).$$

The larger the number of terms, n, the smaller $\left(\frac{1}{2}\right)^n$ becomes and so the nearer S_n is to the limiting value of 2 (see figure 7.6). Notice that $\left(\frac{1}{2}\right)^n$ can never be negative, however large n becomes; so S_n can never exceed 2.

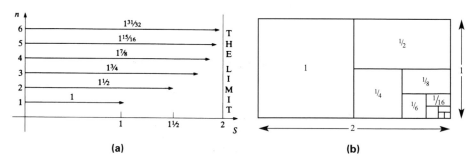

(a) (b)

Figure 7.6

In the general geometric series $a + ar + ar^2 + \ldots$ the terms become progressively smaller in size if the common ratio r is between -1 and 1. This was the case above: r had the value $\frac{1}{2}$. In such cases, the geometric series is *convergent*.

If, on the other hand, the value of r is greater than 1 (or less than -1) the terms in the series become larger and larger in size and so it is described as *divergent*.

A series corresponding to a value of r of exactly $+1$ consists of the first term a repeated over and over again. A sequence corresponding to a value of r of exactly -1 oscillates between $+a$ and $-a$. Neither of these is convergent.

It only makes sense to talk about the sum of an infinite series if it is convergent. Otherwise the sum is undefined.

The condition for a geometric series to converge, $-1 < r < 1$, ensures that as $n \to \infty$, $r^n \to 0$, and so the formula for the sum of a geometric series:

$$S_n = \frac{a(1 - r^n)}{(1 - r)}$$

may be rewritten for an infinite series as:

$$S = \frac{a}{1 - r} \quad \text{or} \quad S_\infty = \frac{a}{1 - r}.$$

EXAMPLE 7.11

Find the sum of the terms of the infinite sequence 0.2, 0.02, 0.002, … .

SOLUTION

This is a geometric sequence with $a = 0.2$ and $r = 0.1$.

Its sum is given by

$$S_\infty = \frac{a}{1 - r}$$

$$= \frac{0.2}{1 - 0.1}$$

$$= \frac{0.2}{0.9}$$

$$= \frac{2}{9}.$$

Note

You may have noticed that the sum of the series $0.2 + 0.02 + 0.002 + …$ is $0.\dot{2}$, and that this recurring decimal is indeed the same as $\frac{2}{9}$.

EXAMPLE 7.12

The first three terms of an infinite geometric sequence are 16, 12 and 9.

(i) Write down the common ratio.

(ii) Find the sum of the terms of the sequence.

SOLUTION

(i) The common ratio is $\frac{3}{4}$.

(ii) The sum of the terms of an infinite geometric series is given by:

$$S_\infty = \frac{a}{1-r}.$$

In this case $a = 16$ and $r = \frac{3}{4}$, so:

$$S_\infty = \frac{16}{1 - \frac{3}{4}} = 64.$$

❓ **A paradox**

Consider the following arguments.

(i) $S = 1 - 2 + 4 - 8 + 16 - 32 + 64 - \ldots$

$\Rightarrow \ S = 1 - 2(1 - 2 + 4 - 8 + 16 - 32 + \ldots)$

$\qquad = 1 - 2S$

$\Rightarrow 3S = 1$

$\Rightarrow \ S = \frac{1}{3}.$

(ii) $S = 1 + (-2 + 4) + (-8 + 16) + (-32 + 64) + \ldots$

$\Rightarrow \ S = 1 + 2 + 8 + 32 + \ldots$

So S diverges towards $+\infty$.

(iii) $S = (1 - 2) + (4 - 8) + (16 - 32) + \ldots$

$\Rightarrow \ S = -1 - 4 - 8 - 16 \ldots$

So S diverges towards $-\infty$.

What is the sum of the series: $\frac{1}{3}$, $+\infty$, $-\infty$, or something else?

EXERCISE 7C

1 Are the following sequences geometric?
If so, state the common ratio and calculate the seventh term.

(i)   5, 10, 20, 40, …   **(ii)** 2, 4, 6, 8, …

(iii) 1, −1, 1, −1, …   **(iv)** 5, 5, 5, 5, …

(v) 6, 3, 0, −3, …   **(vi)** 6, 3, $1\frac{1}{2}$, $\frac{3}{4}$, …

(vii) 1, 1.1, 1.11, 1.111, …

2 A geometric sequence has first term 3 and common ratio 2.
The sequence has eight terms.

(i) Find the last term.

(ii) Find the sum of the terms in the sequence.

3 The first term of a geometric sequence of positive terms is 5 and the fifth term is 1280.

(i) Find the common ratio of the sequence.

(ii) Find the eighth term of the sequence.

4 A geometric sequence has first term $\frac{1}{9}$ and common ratio 3.

(i) Find the fifth term.

(ii) Which is the first term of the sequence which exceeds 1000?

5 (i) Find how many terms there are in the geometric sequence 8, 16, …, 2048.

(ii) Find the sum of the terms in this sequence.

6 (i) Find how many terms there are in the geometric sequence
200, 50, …, 0.195 312 5.

(ii) Find the sum of the terms in this sequence.

7 The fifth term of a geometric sequence is 48 and the ninth term is 768. All the terms are positive.

(i) Find the common ratio.

(ii) Find the first term.

(iii) Find the sum of the first ten terms.

8 The first three terms of an infinite geometric sequence are 4, 2 and 1.

(i) State the common ratio of this sequence.

(ii) Calculate the sum to infinity of its terms.

9 The first three terms of an infinite geometric sequence are 0.7, 0.07, 0.007.

(i) Write down the common ratio for this sequence.

(ii) Find, as a fraction, the sum to infinity of the terms of this sequence.

(iii) Find the sum to infinity of the geometric series $0.7 - 0.07 + 0.007 - \ldots$, and hence show that $\frac{7}{11} = 0.6\dot{3}$.

10 The first three terms of a geometric sequence are 100, 90 and 81.

(i) Write down the common ratio of the sequence.

(ii) Which is the position of the first term in the sequence that has value less than 1?

(iii) Find the sum to infinity of the terms of this sequence.

(iv) After how many terms is the sum of the sequence greater than 99% of the sum to infinity?

11 A geometric series has first term 4 and its sum to infinity is 5.

(i) Find the common ratio.

(ii) Find the sum to infinity if the first term is excluded from the series.

12 (i) The third term of a geometric progression is 16 and the fourth term is 12.8. Find the common ratio and the first term.

(ii) The sum of the first n terms of a geometric progression is $2^{(2n+1)} - 2$. Find the first term and the common ratio.

[MEI]

13 (i) The first two terms of a geometric series are 3 and 4. Find the third term.

(ii) Given that x, 4, $x + 6$ are consecutive terms of a geometric series, find:

(a) the possible values of x

(b) the corresponding values of the common ratio of the geometric series.

(iii) Given that x, 4, $x + 6$ are the sixth, seventh and eighth terms of a geometric series and that the sum to infinity of the series exists, find:

(a) the first term

(b) the sum to infinity.

[MEI]

14 The first four terms in an infinite geometric series are 54, 18, 6, 2.

(i) What is the common ratio r?

(ii) Write down an expression for the nth term of the series.

(iii) Find the sum of the first n terms of the series.

(iv) Find the sum to infinity.

(v) How many terms are needed for the sum to be greater than 80.999?

15 A geometric progression has first term a and common ratio r.
The sum of the first three terms is 4.88 and the sum to infinity is 10.

(i) Write down two equations involving a and r.

Show that $1 - r^3 = 0.488$.

Hence find the values of a and r.

(ii) The kth term of the progression is u_k.

Calculate the value of $\sum_{k=1}^{\infty} (u_k)^2$.

[MEI]

16 A tank is filled with 20 litres of water. Half the water is removed and replaced with anti-freeze and thoroughly mixed. Half this mixture is then removed and replaced with anti-freeze. The process continues.

(i) Find the first five terms in the sequence of amounts of water in the tank at each stage.

(ii) Find the first five terms in the sequence of amounts of anti-freeze in the tank at each stage.

(iii) Is either of these sequences geometric? Explain.

17 A pendulum is set swinging. Its first oscillation is through an angle of 30°, and each succeeding oscillation is through 95% of the angle of the one before it.

(i) After how many swings is the angle through which it swings less than 1°?

(ii) What is the total angle it has swung through at the end of its tenth oscillation?

18 A ball is thrown vertically upwards from the ground. It rises to a height of 10 m and then falls and bounces. After each bounce it rises vertically to $\frac{2}{3}$ of the height from which it fell.

    (i) Find the height to which the ball bounces after the nth impact with the ground.

    (ii) Find the total distance travelled by the ball from the first throw to the tenth impact with the ground.

19 The first three terms of an arithmetic sequence, a, $a + d$ and $a + 2d$, are the same as the first three terms, a, ar, ar^2, of a geometric sequence ($a \neq 0$).

Show that this is only possible if $r = 1$ and $d = 0$.

20 A company offers a ten-year contract to an employee. This gives a starting salary of £15 000 a year with an annual increase of 8% of the previous year's salary.

    (i) Show that the amounts of annual salary form a geometric sequence and write down its common ratio.

    (ii) How much does the employee expect to earn in the tenth year?

    (iii) Show that the total amount earned over the 10 years is nearly £217 500.

After considering the offer, the employee asks for a different scheme of payment. This has the same starting salary of £15 000 but with a fixed annual pay rise £d.

    (iv) Find d if the total amount paid out over 10 years is to be the same under the two schemes.

[MEI]

21 A money-making venture ('pyramid selling') works as follows.

You are asked to send a completed questionnaire with details of your lifestyle, together with a cheque for £20, to the firm DOZIDATA. The information is fed into a computer. Many other people also participate and the databank is offered for sale to a market research company.

You are promised £200 from DOZIDATA after 6 months, provided that you have recruited three friends to join in the scheme.

Suppose that the process is modelled on a month-by-month basis so that, at the end of each month, each person has managed to recruit three others not already in the venture. Thus your pyramid looks like this.

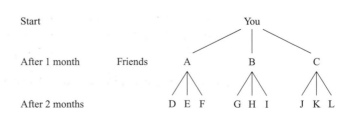

(i) How many people are involved in your pyramid after
    (a) 3 months
    (b) 6 months?

(ii) How much money has DOZIDATA taken from your pyramid after 6 months?

(iii) After 6 months how much profit has DOZIDATA made from your pyramid?
    How much profit have you made?

(iv) If the scheme continues to work, after how long would all 60 million UK residents be in your pyramid?

[**MEI**]

22 (i) An eccentric and rather unfit gardener needs to spread 4000 kg of sand over his garden. He spreads 5 kg during the first day then increases the amount he spreads each subsequent day by 2 kg, so that he spreads 7 kg during the second day, 9 kg during the third day, and so on.

Find an expression for the mass of sand he has spread by the end of n days. How many days will it take him to spread all 4000 kg?

(ii) His neighbour, who prides himself on his fitness, also needs to spread 4000 kg of sand over his garden. He decides to spread 200 kg each day but discovers that, after spreading 200 kg during the first day, during each subsequent day he can only spread 95% of the amount he spread during the previous day.

    (a) Show that, after n days, he has spread $4000(1 - 0.95^n)$ kg.
    (b) How many days will it take him to spread 3900 kg?
    (c) Explain why he will never spread all 4000 kg.

[**MEI**]

23 The first three terms of a geometric series are 6, 2.4, 0.96.

(i) (a) Write down an expression for the nth term.
    (b) Find the sum of the first eight terms.

A ball is dropped from a height of 15 m on to a concrete path and bounces repeatedly. After each impact it rebounds to a height 0.4 times the height from which it has just fallen.

(ii) To what height does it rebound after the nth impact? After how many impacts does it first rebound to a height of less than 1 cm?

(iii) Write down a series expression for the total distance travelled by the ball from the instant when it is dropped until the nth impact.
    Hence find the total distance travelled by the ball before it comes to rest.

(iv) Write an expression for this total distance using Σ notation.

[**MEI**]

24 Mr and Mrs Brown have found a house they wish to buy which is valued at £50 000. In order to buy it they borrow £50 000 from a bank, intending to pay back the loan over a period of 30 years. At the end of each year the bank charges interest of 8% on the amount still owing and the Browns then pay back a fixed amount £P, so that the amount in pounds owed after their first payment is $(50\,000 \times 1.08) - P$.

(i) Write down an expression for the amount owed after their second payment and show that the amount in pounds owed to the bank after their third payment is:

$$(50\,000 \times 1.08^3) - P(1 + 1.08 + 1.08^2).$$

(ii) Generalise your answers to part (i) to write down a formula for the amount owed to the bank after their nth payment ($n \leqslant 30$).
Use the formula for the sum of a geometric progression to simplify this formula.
Use this simplified formula with $n = 30$ to find the amount £P, giving your answer to the nearest penny.

(iii) The value of the Browns' house increases by $k\%$ each year, where k is constant. They discover that, after 30 years, the value of their house equals the total amount they paid to buy it.
Find the value of k, giving your answer to 3 significant figures.

[MEI]

INVESTIGATIONS

Mortgage

A householder takes out a 25-year mortgage of £40 000 from a building society at a time when the interest rate is 10%. Each year the householder's payments have to cover the interest on the outstanding mortgage, and an element of repayment.

Suppose, as an example, that the householder pays a fixed £5000 a year. In the first year, the interest is 10% of £40 000, i.e. £4000, so £1000 of the £5000 goes towards repayment, leaving £39 000 owing.

In the second year, the interest is 10% of £39 000, i.e. £3900, and so the repayment is £1100, leaving £37 900 owing at the start of the third year, and so on.

If the calculation is done correctly, the final payment at the end of year 25 should repay the last of the mortgage, as well as that year's interest. What is the correct annual payment for such a mortgage? (The figure of £5000 was only a working example.)

What is the total amount paid out to the building society?

Snowflakes

Draw an equilateral triangle with sides 9 cm long.

Trisect each side and construct equilateral triangles on the middle section of each side as shown in diagram (b).

Repeat the procedure for each of the small triangles as shown in (c) and (d) so that you have the first four stages in an infinite sequence.

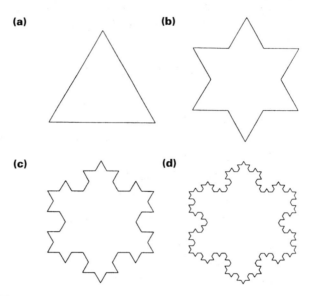

(a) **(b)** **(c)** **(d)**

Figure 7.7

Calculate the length of the perimeter of the figure for each of the first six steps, starting with the original equilateral triangle.

What happens to the length of the perimeter as the number of steps increases?

Does the area of the figure increase without limit?

Achilles and the tortoise

Achilles (it is said) once had a race with a tortoise. The tortoise started 100 m ahead of Achilles and moved at $\frac{1}{10}$ ms^{-1} compared to Achilles' speed of 10 ms^{-1}.

Achilles ran to where the tortoise started only to see that it had moved 1 m further on. So he ran on to that spot but again the tortoise had moved further on, this time by 0.01 m. This happened again and again: whenever Achilles got to the spot where the tortoise was, it had moved on. Did Achilles ever manage to catch the tortoise?

1 A sequence is an ordered set of numbers, $a_1, a_2, a_3, \ldots, a_k, \ldots a_n$, where a_k is the general term.

2 A series is the sum of the terms of a sequence:

$$a_1 + a_2 + a_3 + \ldots + a_n = \sum_{k=1}^{k=n} a_k.$$

3 In an arithmetic sequence, $a_{k+1} = a_k + d$ where d is a fixed number called the common difference.

4 In a geometric sequence, $a_{k+1} = ra_k$ where r is a fixed number called the common ratio.

5 In a periodic sequence, $a_{k+p} = a_k$ for a fixed integer, p, called the period.

6 In an oscillating sequence the terms rise above and fall below a middle value.

7 For an arithmetic sequence with first term a, common difference d and n terms:

- the kth term, $a_k = a + (k-1)d$
- the last term, $l = a + (n-1)d$
- the sum of the terms $= \frac{1}{2}n(a + l) = \frac{1}{2}n[2a + (n-1)d]$.

8 For a geometric sequence with first term a, common ratio r and n terms:

- the kth term, $a_k = ar^{k-1}$
- the last term, $a_n = ar^{n-1}$
- the sum of the terms $= \dfrac{a(r^n - 1)}{(r - 1)} = \dfrac{a(1 - r^n)}{(1 - r)}$.

9 For an infinite geometric series to converge, $-1 < r < 1$.

In this case the sum of all the terms is given by $\dfrac{a}{(1 - r)}$.

8

Differentiation

Hold infinity in the palm of your hand.

William Blake

This picture illustrates one of the more frightening rides at an amusement park. To ensure that the ride is absolutely safe, its designers need to know the gradient of the curve at any point. What do we mean by the gradient of a curve?

The gradient of a curve

To understand what this means, think of a log on a log-flume, as in figure 8.1. If you draw the straight line $y = mx + c$ passing along the bottom of the log, then this line is a tangent to the curve at the point of contact. The gradient m of the tangent is the gradient of the curve at the point of contact.

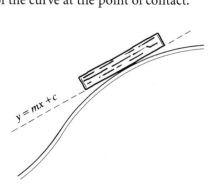

$y = mx + c$

Figure 8.1

One method of finding the gradient of a curve is shown for point A in figure 8.2.

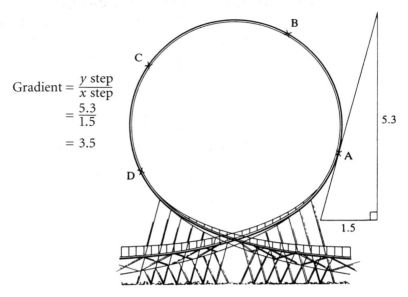

$$\text{Gradient} = \frac{y \text{ step}}{x \text{ step}}$$

$$= \frac{5.3}{1.5}$$

$$= 3.5$$

Figure 8.2

ACTIVITY 8.1   Find the gradient at the points B, C and D using the method shown in figure 8.2. (Use a piece of tracing paper to avoid drawing directly on the book!) Repeat the process for each point, using different triangles, and see whether you get the same answers.

You probably found that your answers were slightly different each time, because they depended on the accuracy of your drawing and measuring. Clearly you need a more accurate method of finding the gradient at a point. As you will see in this chapter, a method is available which can be used on many types of curve, and which does not involve any drawing at all.

Finding the gradient of a curve

Figure 8.3 shows the part of the graph $y = x^2$ which lies between $x = -1$ and $x = 3$. What is the value of the gradient at the point P(3, 9)?

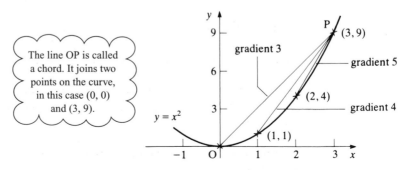

> The line OP is called a chord. It joins two points on the curve, in this case (0, 0) and (3, 9).

Figure 8.3

You have already seen that drawing the tangent at the point by hand provides only an approximate answer. A different approach is to calculate the gradients of chords to the curve. These will also give only approximate answers for the gradient of the curve, but they will be based entirely on calculation and not depend on your drawing skill. Three chords are marked on figure 8.3.

Chord $(0, 0)$ to $(3, 9)$:   gradient $= \dfrac{9-0}{3-0} = 3$

Chord $(1, 1)$ to $(3, 9)$:   gradient $= \dfrac{9-1}{3-1} = 4$

Chord $(2, 4)$ to $(3, 9)$:   gradient $= \dfrac{9-4}{3-2} = 5$

Clearly none of these three answers is exact, but which of them is the most accurate?

Of the three chords, the one closest to being a tangent is that joining $(2, 4)$ to $(3, 9)$, the two points that are closest together.

You can take this process further by 'zooming in' on the point $(3, 9)$ and using points which are much closer to it, as in figure 8.4.

Figure 8.4

The x co-ordinate of point A is 2.7, the y co-ordinate 2.7^2, or 7.29 (since the point lies on the curve $y = x^2$). Similarly B and C are $(2.8, 7.84)$ and $(2.9, 8.41)$. The gradients of the chords joining each point to $(3, 9)$ are as follows.

Chord $(2.7, 7.29)$ to $(3, 9)$:   gradient $= \dfrac{9-7.29}{3-2.7} = 5.7$

Chord $(2.8, 7.84)$ to $(3, 9)$:   gradient $= \dfrac{9-7.84}{3-2.8} = 5.8$

Chord $(2.9, 8.41)$ to $(3, 9)$:   gradient $= \dfrac{9-8.41}{3-2.9} = 5.9$

These results are getting closer to the gradient of the tangent. What happens if you take points much closer to $(3, 9)$, for example $(2.99, 8.9401)$ and $(2.999, 8.994\,001)$?

The gradients of the chords joining these to $(3, 9)$ work out to be 5.99 and 5.999 respectively.

ACTIVITY 8.2   Take points X, Y, Z on the curve $y = x^2$ with x co-ordinates 3.1, 3.01 and 3.001 respectively, and find the gradients of the chords joining each of these points to (3, 9).

It looks as if the gradients are approaching the value 6, and if so this is the gradient of the tangent at (3, 9).

Taking this method to its logical conclusion, you might try to calculate the gradient of the 'chord' from (3, 9) to (3, 9), but this is undefined because there is a zero in the denominator. So although you can find the gradient of a chord which is as close as you like to the tangent, it can never be exactly that of the tangent. What you need is a way of making that final step from a chord to a tangent.

The concept of a *limit* enables us to do this, as you will see in the next section. It allows us to confirm that in the limit as point Q tends to point P(3, 9), the chord QP tends to the tangent of the curve at P, and the gradient of QP tends to 6 (see figure 8.5).

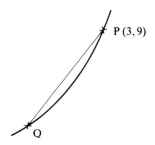

Figure 8.5

The idea of a limit is central to calculus, which is sometimes described as the study of limits.

Historical note

This method of using chords approaching the tangent at P to *calculate* the gradient of the tangent was first described clearly by Pierre de Fermat (c.1608–65). He spent his working life as a civil servant in Toulouse and produced an astonishing amount of original mathematics in his spare time.

Finding the gradient from first principles

Although the work in the previous section was more formal than the method of drawing a tangent and measuring its gradient, it was still somewhat experimental. The result that the gradient of $y = x^2$ at (3, 9) is 6 was a sensible conclusion, rather than a proved fact.

In this section the method is formalised and extended.

Take the point P(3, 9) and another point Q close to (3, 9) on the curve $y = x^2$. Let the x co-ordinate of Q be $3 + h$ where h is small. Since $y = x^2$ at Q, the y co-ordinate of Q will be $(3 + h)^2$.

⚠ Figure 8.6 shows Q in a position where h is positive, but negative values of h would put Q to the left of P.

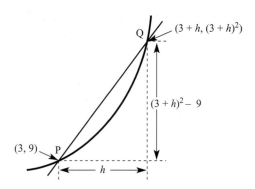

Figure 8.6

From figure 8.6, the gradient of PQ is $\dfrac{(3 + h)^2 - 9}{h}$

$$= \frac{9 + 6h + h^2 - 9}{h}$$

$$= \frac{6h + h^2}{h}$$

$$= \frac{h(6 + h)}{h}$$

$$= 6 + h.$$

For example, when $h = 0.001$, the gradient of PQ is 6.001, and when $h = -0.001$, the gradient of PQ is 5.999. The gradient of the tangent at P is between these two values. Similarly the gradient of the tangent would be between $6 - h$ and $6 + h$ for all small non-zero values of h.

For this to be true the gradient of the tangent at (3, 9) must be *exactly* 6.

ACTIVITY 8.3

Using a similar method, find the gradient of the tangent to the curve at
(i) (1, 1)   **(ii)** (−2, 4)   **(iii)** (4, 16).

What do you notice?

The gradient function

The work so far has involved finding the gradient of the curve $y = x^2$ at a particular point $(3, 9)$, but this is not the way in which you would normally find the gradient at a point. Rather you would consider the general point, (x, y), and then substitute the value(s) of x (and/or y) corresponding to the point of interest.

EXAMPLE 8.1

Find the gradient of the curve $y = x^3$ at the general point (x, y).

SOLUTION

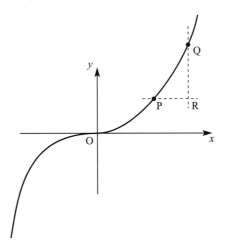

Figure 8.7

Let P have the general value x as its x co-ordinate, so P is the point (x, x^3) (since it is on the curve $y = x^3$). Let the x co-ordinate of Q be $(x + h)$ so Q is $((x + h), (x + h)^3)$. The gradient of the chord PQ is given by

$$\frac{QR}{PR} = \frac{(x + h)^3 - x^3}{(x + h) - x}$$

$$= \frac{x^3 + 3x^2h + 3xh^2 + h^3 - x^3}{h}$$

$$= \frac{3x^2h + 3xh^2 + h^3}{h}$$

$$= \frac{h(3x^2 + 3xh + h^2)}{h}$$

$$= 3x^2 + 3xh + h^2.$$

As Q takes values closer to P, h takes smaller and smaller values and the gradient approaches the value of $3x^2$ which is the gradient of the tangent at P. The gradient of the curve $y = x^3$ at the point (x, y) is equal to $3x^2$.

Note

If the equation of the curve is written as $y = f(x)$, then the *gradient function* (i.e. the gradient at the general point (x, y) is written as $f'(x)$. Using this notation the result above can be written as $f(x) = x^3 \Rightarrow f'(x) = 3x^2$.

EXERCISE 8A

1 Use the method in Example 8.1 to prove that the gradient of the curve $y = x^2$ at the point (x, y) is equal to $2x$.

2 Use the binomial theorem to expand $(x + h)^4$ and hence find the gradient of the curve $y = x^4$ at the point (x, y).

3 Copy the table below, enter your answer to question 2, and suggest how the gradient pattern should continue when $f(x) = x^5$, $f(x) = x^6$ and $f(x) = x^n$ (where n is a positive whole number).

$f(x)$	$f'(x)$ (gradient at (x, y))
x^2	$2x$
x^3	$3x^2$
x^4	
x^5	
x^6	
$\vdots$	
x^n	

4 Prove the result when $f(x) = x^5$.

Note

The result you should have obtained from question 3 is known as *Wallis's rule* and can be used as a formula.

 How can you use the binomial theorem to prove this general result for integer values of n?

An alternative notation

So far h has been used to denote the difference between the x co-ordinates of our points P and Q, where Q is close to P.

h is sometimes replaced by δx. The Greek letter δ is shorthand for 'a small change in' and so δx represents a small change in x and δy a corresponding small change in y.

In figure 8.8 the gradient of the chord PQ is $\frac{\delta y}{\delta x}$.

In the limit as $\delta x \to 0$, δx and δy both become infinitesimally small and the value obtained for $\frac{\delta y}{\delta x}$ approaches the gradient of the tangent at P.

Figure 8.8

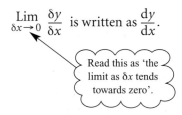

$$\underset{\delta x \to 0}{\text{Lim}} \frac{\delta y}{\delta x} \text{ is written as } \frac{dy}{dx}.$$

Read this as 'the limit as δx tends towards zero'.

Using this notation, Wallis's rule becomes

$$y = x^n \Rightarrow \frac{dy}{dx} = nx^{n-1}.$$

The gradient function, $\frac{dy}{dx}$ or $f'(x)$ is sometimes called the *derivative* of y with respect to x, and when you find it you have *differentiated* y with respect to x.

Note

There is nothing special about the letters x, y and f.

If, for example, your curve represented time (t) on the horizontal axis and velocity (v) on the vertical axis, then the relationship may be referred to as $v = g(t)$, i.e. v is a function of t, and the gradient function is given by $\frac{dv}{dt} = g'(t)$.

ACTIVITY 8.4

Plot the curve with equation $y = x^3 + 2$, for values of x from -2 to $+2$. On the same axes and for the same range of values of x, plot the curves $y = x^3 - 1$, $y = x^3$ and $y = x^3 + 1$.

What do you notice about the gradients of this family of curves when $x = 0$?

What about when $x = 1$ or $x = -1$?

ACTIVITY 8.5 Differentiate the equation $y = x^3 + c$, where c is a constant.

How does this result help you to explain your findings in Activity 8.4?

Historical note

The notation $\frac{dy}{dx}$ was first used by the German mathematician and philosopher Gottfried Leibniz (1646–1716) in 1675. Leibniz was a child prodigy and a self-taught mathematician. The terms 'function' and 'co-ordinates' are due to him and, because of his influence, the sign '=' is used for equality and '×' for multiplication. In 1684 he published his work on calculus (which deals with the way in which quantities change) in a six-page article in the periodical *Acta Eruditorum*.

Sir Isaac Newton (1642–1727) worked independently on calculus but Leibniz published his work first. Newton always hesitated to publish his discoveries. Newton used different notation (introducing 'fluxions' and 'moments of fluxions') and his expressions were thought to be rather vague. Over the years the best aspects of the two approaches have been combined, but at the time the dispute as to who 'discovered' calculus first was the subject of many articles and reports, and indeed nearly caused a war between England and Germany.

Differentiating by using standard results

The method of differentiation from first principles will always give the gradient function, but it is rather tedious and, in practice, it is hardly ever used. Its value is in establishing a formal basis for differentiation rather than as a working tool.

If you look at the results of differentiating $y = x^n$ for different values of n a pattern is immediately apparent, particularly when you include the result that the line $y = x$ has constant gradient 1.

y	$\frac{dy}{dx}$
x^1	1
x^2	$2x^1$
x^3	$3x^2$

This pattern continues and, in general

$$y = x^n \quad \Rightarrow \quad \frac{dy}{dx} = nx^{n-1}.$$

This can be extended to functions of the type $y = kx^n$ for any constant k, to give

$$y = kx^n \quad \Rightarrow \quad \frac{dy}{dx} = knx^{n-1}.$$

Another important result is that

$$y = c \quad \Rightarrow \quad \frac{dy}{dx} = 0 \quad \text{where } c \text{ is any constant.}$$

This follows from the fact that the graph of $y = c$ is a horizontal line with gradient zero (see figure 8.9).

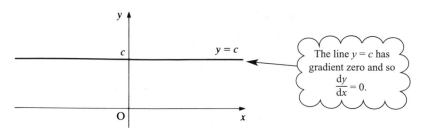

Figure 8.9

EXAMPLE 8.2

For each of these functions of x, find the gradient function.

(i) $y = x^5$ **(ii)** $z = 7x^6$ **(iii)** $p = 11$

SOLUTION

(i) $\dfrac{dy}{dx} = 5x^4$

(ii) $\dfrac{dz}{dx} = 6 \times 7x^5 = 42x^5$

(iii) $\dfrac{dp}{dx} = 0$

Sums and differences of functions

Many of the functions you will meet are sums or differences of simpler ones. For example, the function $(3x^2 + 4x^3)$ is the sum of the functions $3x^2$ and $4x^3$.

To differentiate a function such as this you differentiate each part separately and then add the results together.

EXAMPLE 8.3

Differentiate $y = 3x^2 + 4x^3$.

SOLUTION

$$\frac{dy}{dx} = 6x + 12x^2$$

Note

This may be written in general form as:

$$y = f(x) + g(x) \quad \Rightarrow \quad \frac{dy}{dx} = f'(x) + g'(x).$$

EXAMPLE 8.4

Given that $y = x^3 - 4x^2 + x - 1$

(i) find $\dfrac{dy}{dx}$

(ii) find the gradient of the curve at the point $(3, -7)$.

SOLUTION

(i) $\dfrac{dy}{dx} = 3x^2 - 8x + 1$.

(ii) At $(3, -7)$, $x = 3$.

Substituting $x = 3$ in the expression for $\dfrac{dy}{dx}$ gives

$$\dfrac{dy}{dx} = 3 \times 3^2 - 8 \times 3 + 1$$
$$= 4.$$

EXERCISE 8B

1 Differentiate the following functions using the rules

$$y = kx^n \quad \Longrightarrow \quad \dfrac{dy}{dx} = knx^{n-1}$$

and $y = f(x) + g(x) \quad \Longrightarrow \quad \dfrac{dy}{dx} = f'(x) + g'(x)$.

(i) $y = x^5$

(ii) $y = 4x^2$

(iii) $y = 2x^3$

(iv) $y = x^{11}$

(v) $y = 4x^{10}$

(vi) $y = 3x^5$

(vii) $y = 7$

(viii) $y = 7x$

(ix) $y = 2x^3 + 3x^5$

(x) $y = x^7 - x^4$

(xi) $y = x^2 + 1$

(xii) $y = x^3 + 3x^2 + 3x + 1$

(xiii) $y = x^3 - 9$

(xiv) $y = \frac{1}{2}x^2 + x + 1$

(xv) $y = 3x^2 + 6x + 6$

(xvi) $A = 4\pi r^2$

(xvii) $A - \frac{4}{3}\pi r^3$

(xviii) $d = \frac{1}{4}t^2$

(xix) $C = 2\pi r$

(xx) $V = \ell^3$

EXAMPLE 8.5

Figure 8.10 shows the graph of

$$y = x^2(x - 6) = x^3 - 6x^2.$$

Find the gradient of the curve at the points A and B where it meets the x axis.

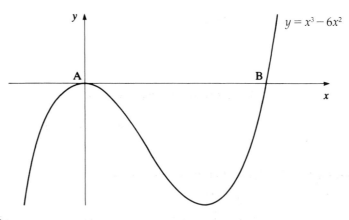

Figure 8.10

SOLUTION

The curve cuts the x axis when $y = 0$, and so at these points

$$x^2(x - 6) = 0$$
$$\Rightarrow \qquad x = 0 \text{ (twice) or } 6.$$

Differentiating $y = x^3 - 6x^2$ gives

$$\frac{dy}{dx} = 3x^2 - 12x.$$

At the point $(0, 0)$, $\dfrac{dy}{dx} = 0$

and at $(6, 0)$, $\qquad \dfrac{dy}{dx} = 3 \times 6^2 - 12 \times 6 = 36.$

At $A(0, 0)$ the gradient of the curve is 0 and at $B(6, 0)$ the gradient of the curve is 36.

Note

This curve goes through the origin. You can see from the graph and from the value of $\dfrac{dy}{dx}$ that the x axis is a tangent to the curve at this point. You could also have deduced this from the fact that $x = 0$ is a repeated root of the equation $x^3 - 6x^2 = 0$.

EXAMPLE 8.6

Find the points on the curve with equation $y = x^3 + 6x^2 + 5$ where the value of the gradient is -9.

SOLUTION

The gradient at any point on the curve is given by

$$\frac{dy}{dx} = 3x^2 + 12x.$$

Therefore you need to find points at which $\dfrac{dy}{dx} = -9$, i.e.

$$3x^2 + 12x = -9$$
$$3x^2 + 12x + 9 = 0$$
$$3(x^2 + 4x + 3) = 0$$
$$3(x + 1)(x + 3) = 0$$
$$\Rightarrow \qquad x = -1 \text{ or } -3.$$

When $x = -1$, $y = (-1)^3 + 6(-1)^2 + 5 = 10.$

When $x = -3$, $y = (-3)^3 + 6(-3)^2 + 5 = 32.$

Therefore the gradient is -9 at the points $(-1, 10)$ and $(-3, 32)$ (see figure 8.11).

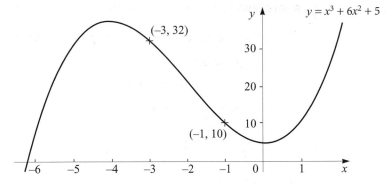

Figure 8.11

1 (i) Sketch the curve $y = x^2 - 4$.

(ii) Write down the co-ordinates of the points where the curve crosses the x axis.

(iii) Differentiate $y = x^2 - 4$.

(iv) Find the gradient of the curve at the points where it crosses the x axis.

2 (i) Sketch the curve $y = x^2 - 6x$.

(ii) Differentiate $y = x^2 - 6x$.

(iii) Show that the point $(3, -9)$ lies on the curve $y = x^2 - 6x$ and find the gradient of the curve at this point.

(iv) Relate your answer to the shape of the curve.

3 (i) Plot, on the same axes, the graphs with equations

$$y = 2x + 5 \quad \text{and} \quad y = 4 - x^2 \quad \text{for } -3 \leqslant x \leqslant 3.$$

(ii) Show that the point $(-1, 3)$ lies on both graphs.

(iii) Differentiate $y = 4 - x^2$ and so find its gradient at $(-1, 3)$.

(iv) Do you have sufficient evidence to decide whether the line $y = 2x + 5$ is a tangent to the curve $y = 4 - x^2$?

(v) Is the line joining $(2\frac{1}{2}, 0)$ to $(0, 5)$ a tangent to the curve $y = 4 - x^2$?

4 (i) Sketch the curve $y = x^3 - 6x^2 + 11x - 6$.

(ii) Where does this curve cut the x axis?

(iii) Differentiate $y = x^3 - 6x^2 + 11x - 6$.

(iv) Show that the tangents to the curve at two of the points at which it cuts the x axis are parallel.

5 (i) Sketch the curve $y = x^2 + 3x - 1$.

(ii) Differentiate $y = x^2 + 3x - 1$.

(iii) Find the co-ordinates of the point on the curve $y = x^2 + 3x - 1$ at which it is parallel to the line $y = 5x - 1$.

(iv) Is the line $y = 5x - 1$ a tangent to the curve $y = x^2 + 3x - 1$? Give reasons for your answer.

6 (i) Sketch, on the same axes, the curves with equations

$$y = x^2 - 9 \quad \text{and} \quad y = 9 - x^2 \quad \text{for } -4 \leqslant x \leqslant 4.$$

(ii) Differentiate $y = x^2 - 9$.

(iii) Find the gradient of $y = x^2 - 9$ at the points $(2, -5)$ and $(-2, -5)$.

(iv) Find the gradient of the curve $y = 9 - x^2$ at the points $(2, 5)$ and $(-2, 5)$.

(v) The tangents to $y = x^2 - 9$ at $(2, -5)$ and $(-2, -5)$, and those to $y = 9 - x^2$ at $(2, 5)$ and $(-2, 5)$ are drawn to form a quadrilateral.
Describe this quadrilateral and give reasons for your answer.

7 (i) Sketch, on the same axes, the curves with equations

$$y = x^2 - 1 \quad \text{and} \quad y = x^2 + 3 \quad \text{for } -3 \leqslant x \leqslant 3.$$

(ii) Find the gradient of the curve $y = x^2 - 1$ at the point $(2, 3)$.

(iii) Give two explanations, one involving geometry and the other involving calculus, as to why the gradient at the point $(2, 7)$ on the curve $y = x^2 + 3$ should have the same value as your answer to part (ii).

(iv) Give the equation of another curve with the same gradient function as $y = x^2 - 1$.

8 The function $f(x) = ax^3 + bx + 4$, where a and b are constants, goes through the point $(2, 14)$ with gradient 21.

(i) Using the fact that $(2, 14)$ lies on the curve, find an equation involving a and b.

(ii) Differentiate $f(x)$ and, using the fact that the gradient is 21 when $x = 2$, form another equation involving a and b.

(iii) By solving these two equations simultaneously find the values of a and b.

9 In his book *Mathematician's Delight*, W.W. Sawyer observes that the arch of Victoria Falls Bridge appears to agree with the curve

$$y = \frac{116 - 21x^2}{120}$$

taking the origin as the point mid-way between the feet of the arch, and taking the distance between its feet as 4.7 units.

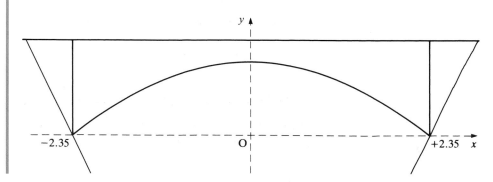

(i) Find $\frac{dy}{dx}$.

(ii) Evaluate $\frac{dy}{dx}$ when $x = -2.35$ and when $x = 2.35$.

(iii) Find the value of x for which $\frac{dy}{dx} = -0.5$.

10 The diagram shows part of the graph of $y = f(x)$. The co-ordinates of A and B are respectively $(a, f(a))$ and $(b, f(b))$.

(i) In the case when $f(x) = x^2$, $a = 4$, $b = 4.01$, calculate the exact value of the expression

$$\frac{f(b) - f(a)}{b - a}.$$

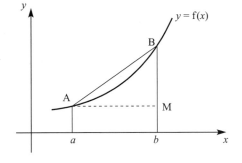

(ii) State what is represented in the diagram by the expression

$$\frac{f(b) - f(a)}{b - a}.$$

(iii) Interpret the meaning of this expression in the limit as b tends to a.

[**MEI**]

11 The graph of $y = f(x) = 3x^2 + 1$ is shown below.

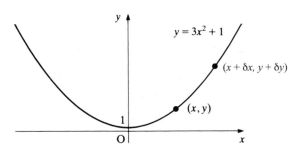

(i) Write down and expand the expression for the y co-ordinate, $f(x + \delta x)$, when x is replaced by $x + \delta x$. Call this expression $y + \delta y$.

(ii) Find $\frac{\delta y}{\delta x}$ by substituting your answer from (i) in

$$\frac{\delta y}{\delta x} = \frac{f(x + \delta x) - f(x)}{(x + \delta x) - x},$$

i.e. find the gradient of the chord joining (x, y) to $(x + \delta x, y + \delta y)$.

(iii) Now let δx tend to zero, and show that your answer from (ii) gives $6x$ as the gradient function $\frac{dy}{dx}$.

12 A curve is given by $y = 2x - x^2$.

  (i) Find an expression for the y co-ordinate, $y + \delta y$, of the point on the curve with x co-ordinate $x + \delta x$, in terms of x and δx.

  (ii) Hence write down an expression for $\frac{\delta y}{\delta x}$ in terms of x and δx, and simplify it.

  (iii) By considering the limit as δx tends to zero, obtain an expression for the gradient function $\frac{dy}{dx}$ for $y = 2x - x^2$.

Tangents and normals

Now that you know how to find the gradient of a curve at any point you can use this to find the equation of the tangent at any specified point on the curve.

EXAMPLE 8.7

Find the equation of the tangent to the curve $y = x^2 + 3x + 2$ at the point $(2, 12)$.

SOLUTION

Calculating $\frac{dy}{dx}$: $\frac{dy}{dx} = 2x + 3$.

Substituting $x = 2$ into the expression $\frac{dy}{dx}$ to find the gradient m of the tangent at that point:

$$m = 2 \times 2 + 3$$
$$= 7.$$

The equation of the tangent is given by

$$y - y_1 = m(x - x_1).$$

In this case $x_1 = 2$, $y_1 = 12$ so

$$y - 12 = 7(x - 2)$$
$$\Rightarrow \qquad y = 7x - 2.$$

This is the equation of the tangent.

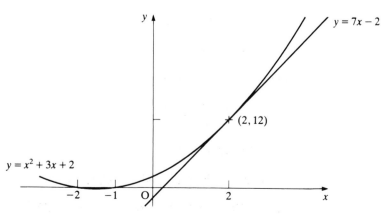

Figure 8.12

The *normal* to a curve at a particular point is the straight line which is at right angles to the tangent at that point (see figure 8.13). Remember that for perpendicular lines, $m_1 m_2 = -1$.

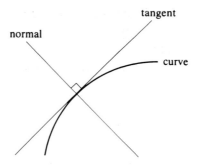

tangent

normal

curve

Figure 8.13

If the gradient of the tangent is m_1, the gradient, m_2, of the normal is clearly given by

$$m_2 = -\frac{1}{m_1}.$$

This enables you to find the equation of the normal at any specified point on a curve.

EXAMPLE 8.8

Find the equation of the normal to the curve $y = x^3 - 2x + 1$ at the point (2, 5).

SOLUTION

$$y = x^3 - 2x + 1 \quad \Rightarrow \quad \frac{dy}{dx} = 3x^2 - 2.$$

Substituting $x = 2$ to find the gradient m_1 of the tangent at the point (2, 5):

$$m_1 = 3 \times 2^2 - 2 = 10.$$

The gradient m_2 of the normal to the curve at this point is given by

$$m_2 = -\frac{1}{m_1} = -\frac{1}{10}.$$

The equation of the normal is given by

$$y - y_1 = m_2(x - x_1)$$

and in this case $x_1 = 2$, $y_1 = 5$ so

$$y - 5 = -\frac{1}{10}(x - 2)$$

$$y = -\frac{1}{10}x + \frac{26}{5}.$$

Tidying this up by multiplying both sides by 10:

$$10y = -x + 52 \quad \text{or} \quad x + 10y = 52.$$

1 The graph of $y = 6x - x^2$ is shown below.

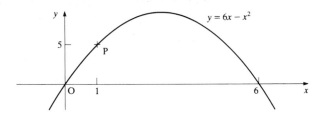

The marked point, P, is $(1, 5)$.

   (i) Find the gradient function $\dfrac{dy}{dx}$.

   (ii) Find the gradient of the curve at P.

   (iii) Find the equation of the tangent at P.

2 **(i)** Sketch the curve $y = 4x - x^2$.

   (ii) Differentiate $y = 4x - x^2$.

   (iii) Find the gradient of $y = 4x - x^2$ at the point $(1, 3)$.

   (iv) Find the equation of the tangent to the curve $y = 4x - x^2$ at the point $(1, 3)$.

3 **(i)** Sketch the curve $y = x^3 - 4x^2$.

   (ii) Differentiate $y = x^3 - 4x^2$.

   (iii) Find the gradient of $y = x^3 - 4x^2$ at the point $(2, -8)$.

   (iv) Find the equation of the tangent to the curve $y = x^3 - 4x^2$ at the point $(2, -8)$.

   (v) Find the co-ordinates of the other point at which this tangent meets the curve.

4 **(i)** Sketch the curve $y = 6 - x^2$.

   (ii) Find the gradient of the curve at the points $(-1, 5)$ and $(1, 5)$.

   (iii) Find the equations of the tangents to the curve at these points.

   (iv) Find the co-ordinates of the point of intersection of these two tangents.

5 **(i)** Sketch the curve $y = x^4 - 4x^2$.

   (ii) What are the co-ordinates of the three points where this curve crosses or touches the x axis?

   (iii) Differentiate $y = x^4 - 4x^2$ and hence find the gradients at the three points you found in (ii).

   (iv) Find the equations of the tangents to the curve at the three points you found in (ii).

   (v) The points of intersection of the three tangents are the vertices of a triangle. What is the area of the triangle?

6 **(i)** Sketch the curve $y = x^2 + 4$, and the straight line $y = 4x$, on the same axes.

   (ii) Show that both $y = x^2 + 4$ and $y = 4x$ pass through the point $(2, 8)$.

   (iii) Show that $y = x^2 + 4$ and $y = 4x$ have the same gradient at $(2, 8)$, and state what you conclude from this result and that in (ii).

7 **(i)** Sketch the curve $y = x^2 - 5$.

(ii) Find the gradient of the curve $y = x^2 - 5$ at the points $(-2, -1)$ and $(2, -1)$.

(iii) Find the equations of the normals to the curve $y = x^2 - 5$ at the points $(-2, -1)$ and $(2, -1)$.

(iv) Find the co-ordinates of the point of intersection of the two normals you found in (iii).

8 Given that $f(x) = x^3 + 3x^2 + 2x$:

(i) factorise $f(x)$ and hence find where the curve of $f(x)$ cuts the x axis

(ii) find $\dfrac{dy}{dx}$

(iii) find the equation of the normal to the curve at each of the three points found in (i)

(iv) state whether the three normals all intersect in one point. If they do, state the co-ordinates of the point. If not, describe how they do intersect.

9 **(i)** Find the equation of the tangent to the curve $y = 2x^3 - 15x^2 + 42x$ at $(2, 40)$.

(ii) Using your expression for $\dfrac{dy}{dx}$, find the co-ordinates of another point on the curve at which the tangent is parallel to the one at $(2, 40)$.

(iii) Find the equation of the normal at this point.

10 **(i)** Given that $y = x^3 - 4x^2 + 5x - 2$, find $\dfrac{dy}{dx}$.

The point P is on the curve and its x co-ordinate is 3.

(ii) Calculate the y co-ordinate of P.

(iii) Calculate the gradient at P.

(iv) Find the equation of the tangent at P.

(v) Find the equation of the normal at P.

(vi) Find the values of x for which the curve has a gradient of 5.

[MEI]

11 **(i)** Sketch the curve whose equation is $y = x^2 - 3x + 2$ and state the co-ordinates of the points A and B where it crosses the x axis.

(ii) Find the gradient of the curve at A and at B.

(iii) Find the equations of the tangent and normal to the curve at both A and B.

(iv) The tangent at A meets the tangent at B at the point P. The normal at A meets the normal at B at the point Q. What shape is the figure APBQ?

12 **(i)** Find the points of intersection of $y = 2x^2 - 9x$ and $y = x - 8$.

(ii) Find $\dfrac{dy}{dx}$ for the curve and hence find the equation of the tangent to the curve at each of the points in (i).

(iii) Find the point of intersection of the two tangents.

(iv) The two tangents from a point to a circle are always equal in length. Are the two tangents to the curve $y = 2x^2 - 9x$ (a parabola) from the point you found in (iii) equal in length?

13 Given that $y = x^3 - x + 6$:

(i) find $\dfrac{dy}{dx}$.

On the curve representing y, P is the point where $x = -1$.

(ii) Calculate the y co-ordinate of the point P.

(iii) Calculate the value of $\dfrac{dy}{dx}$ at P.

(iv) Find the equation of the tangent at P.

The tangent at the point Q is parallel to the tangent at P.

(v) Find the co-ordinates of Q.

(vi) Find the equation of the normal to the curve at Q.

[MEI]

Maximum and minimum points

ACTIVITY 8.6

Plot the graph of $y = x^4 - x^3 - 2x^2$, taking values of x from -2.5 to $+2.5$ in steps of 0.5, and answer these questions.

(i) How many turning points has the graph?

(ii) What is the gradient at a turning point?

(iii) One of the turning points is a maximum and the others are minima. Which are of each type?

(iv) Is the maximum the highest point of the graph?

(v) Do the two minima occur exactly at the points you plotted?

(vi) Estimate the lowest value that y takes.

Gradient at a turning point

Figure 8.14 shows the graph of $y = -x^2 + 16$. It has a *maximum point* at (0,16).

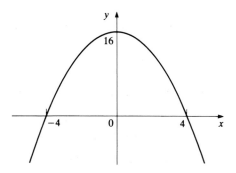

Figure 8.14

You will see that

- at the maximum point the gradient $\frac{dy}{dx}$ is zero
- the gradient is positive to the left of the maximum and negative to the right of it.

This is true for any maximum point (see figure 8.15).

Figure 8.15

In the same way, for any minimum point (see figure 8.16):

- the gradient is zero at the minimum
- the gradient goes from negative to zero to positive.

Figure 8.16

EXAMPLE 8.9

Find the turning points on the curve of $y = x^3 - 3x + 1$, and sketch the curve.

SOLUTION

The gradient function for this curve is

$$\frac{dy}{dx} = 3x^2 - 3.$$

The x values for which $\frac{dy}{dx} = 0$ are given by

$$3x^2 - 3 = 0$$
$$3(x^2 - 1) = 0$$
$$3(x + 1)(x - 1) = 0$$
$$\Rightarrow \qquad x = -1 \text{ or } 1.$$

The signs of the gradient function just either side of these values tell you the nature of each turning point.

For $x = -1$: $x = -2 \Rightarrow \dfrac{\mathrm{d}y}{\mathrm{d}x} = 3(-2)^2 - 3 = +9$

$x = 0 \Rightarrow \dfrac{\mathrm{d}y}{\mathrm{d}x} = 3(0)^2 - 3 = -3.$

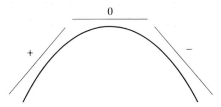

Figure 8.17

For $x = 1$: $x = 0 \Rightarrow \dfrac{\mathrm{d}y}{\mathrm{d}x} = -3$

$x = 2 \Rightarrow \dfrac{\mathrm{d}y}{\mathrm{d}x} = 3(2)^2 - 3 = +9.$

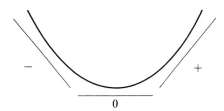

Figure 8.18

Thus the turning point at $x = -1$ is a maximum and the one at $x = 1$ is a minimum.

Substituting the x values of the turning points into the original equation, $y = x^3 - 3x + 1$, gives

when $x = -1$, $y = (-1)^3 - 3(-1) + 1 = 3$

when $x = 1$, $y = (1)^3 - 3(1) + 1 = -1.$

There is a maximum at $(-1, 3)$ and a minimum at $(1, -1)$. The sketch can now be drawn (see figure 8.19).

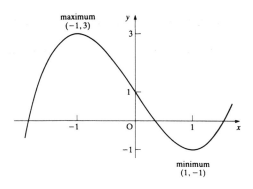

Figure 8.19

In this case you knew the general shape of the cubic curve and the positions of all of the turning points, so it was easy to select values of x for which to test the sign of $\frac{dy}{dx}$. The curve of a more complicated function may have several maxima and minima close together, and even some points at which the gradient is undefined. To decide in such cases whether a particular turning point is a maximum or a minimum, you must look at points which are *just* either side of it.

EXAMPLE 8.10

Find all the turning points on the curve of $y = 2t^4 - t^2 + 1$ and sketch the curve.

SOLUTION

$$\frac{dy}{dt} = 8t^3 - 2t$$

At a turning point, $\frac{dy}{dt} = 0$, so

$$8t^3 - 2t = 0$$
$$2t(4t^2 - 1) = 0$$
$$2t(2t - 1)(2t + 1) = 0$$
$$\Rightarrow \quad \frac{dy}{dt} = 0 \text{ when } t = -0.5, 0 \text{ or } 0.5.$$

You may find it helpful to summarise your working in a table like the one below. You can find the various signs, + or −, by taking a test point in each interval, for example $t = 0.25$ in the interval $0 < t < 0.5$.

	$t < -0.5$	-0.5	$-0.5 < t < 0$	0	$0 < t < 0.5$	0.5	$t > 0.5$
Sign of $\frac{dy}{dt}$	−	0	+	0	−	0	+
Turning point		min		max		min	

There is a maximum point when $t = 0$ and there are minimum points when $t = -0.5$ and $+0.5$.

When $t = 0$: $\quad y = 2(0)^4 - (0)^2 + 1 = 1.$
When $t = -0.5$: $\quad y = 2(-0.5)^4 - (-0.5)^2 + 1 = 0.875.$
When $t = 0.5$: $\quad y = 2(0.5)^4 - (0.5)^2 + 1 = 0.875.$

Therefore $(0, 1)$ is a maximum point and $(-0.5, 0.875)$ and $(0.5, 0.875)$ are minima.

The graph of this function is shown in figure 8.20.

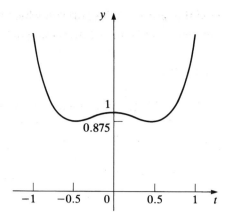

Figure 8.20

Increasing and decreasing functions

When the gradient is positive, the function is described as an increasing function. Similarly, when the gradient is negative, it is a decreasing function. These terms are often used for functions that are increasing or decreasing for all values of x.

EXAMPLE 8.11

Show that $y = x^3 + x$ is an increasing function.

SOLUTION

$y = x^3 + x \Rightarrow \dfrac{dy}{dx} = 3x^2 + 1.$

Since $x^2 \geq 0$ for all real values of x, $\dfrac{dy}{dx} \geq 1$

$\Rightarrow y = x^3 + x$ is an increasing function.

Figure 8.21 shows its graph.

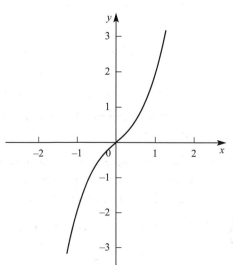

Figure 8.21

EXAMPLE 8.12

Find the range of values of x for which the function $y = x^2 - 6x$ is a decreasing function.

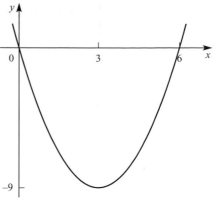

SOLUTION

$y = x^2 - 6x \Rightarrow \dfrac{dy}{dx} = 2x - 6.$

y decreasing $\Rightarrow \dfrac{dy}{dx} < 0$

$\Rightarrow \quad 2x - 6 < 0$

$\Rightarrow \quad\quad x < 3.$

Figure 8.22 shows the graph of $y = x^2 - 6x$. **Figure 8.22**

EXERCISE 8E

Most of the questions in this exercise require you to find the turning points of a curve and then to use them as a guide for sketching it. You will find it helpful to use a graphic calculator to check your final answers.

1 Given that $y = x^2 + 8x + 13$:

   (i) find $\dfrac{dy}{dx}$, and the value of x for which $\dfrac{dy}{dx} = 0$

   (ii) showing your working clearly, decide whether the point corresponding to this x value is a maximum or a minimum by considering the gradient either side of it

   (iii) show that the corresponding y value is -3

   (iv) sketch the curve.

2 Given that $y = x^2 + 5x + 2$:

   (i) find $\dfrac{dy}{dx}$, and the value of x for which $\dfrac{dy}{dx} = 0$

   (ii) classify the point that corresponds to this x value as a maximum or a minimum

   (iii) find the corresponding y value

   (iv) sketch the curve.

3 Given that $y = x^3 - 12x + 2$:

   (i) find $\dfrac{dy}{dx}$, and the values of x for which $\dfrac{dy}{dx} = 0$

   (ii) classify the points that correspond to these x values

   (iii) find the corresponding y values

   (iv) sketch the curve.

4 (i) Find the co-ordinates of the turning points of the curve $y = x^3 - 6x^2$, and determine whether each one is a maximum or a minimum.

   (ii) Use this information to sketch the graph of $y = x^3 - 6x^2$.

5 Find $\dfrac{dy}{dx}$ when $y = x^3 - x$ and show that $y = x^3 - x$ is an increasing function for $x < -\dfrac{1}{\sqrt{3}}$ and $x > \dfrac{1}{\sqrt{3}}$.

6 Given that $y = x^3 + 4x$:

   (i) find $\dfrac{dy}{dx}$

   (ii) show that $y = x^3 + 4x$ is an increasing function for all values of x.

7 Given that $y = x^3 + 3x^2 - 9x + 6$:

   (i) find $\dfrac{dy}{dx}$ and factorise the quadratic expression you obtain

   (ii) write down the values of x for which $\dfrac{dy}{dx} = 0$

   (iii) show that one of the points corresponding to these x values is a minimum and the other a maximum

   (iv) show that the corresponding y values are 1 and 33 respectively

   (v) sketch the curve.

8 Given that $y = 9x + 3x^2 - x^3$:

   (i) find $\dfrac{dy}{dx}$ and factorise the quadratic expression you obtain

   (ii) find the values of x for which the curve has turning points, and classify these turning points

   (iii) find the corresponding y values

   (iv) sketch the curve.

9 **(i)** Find the co-ordinates and nature of each of the turning points of $y = x^3 - 2x^2 - 4x + 3$.

   (ii) Sketch the curve.

10 **(i)** Find the co-ordinates and nature of each of the turning points of the curve with equation $y = x^4 + 4x^3 - 36x^2 + 300$.

   (ii) Sketch the curve.

11 **(i)** Differentiate $y = x^3 + 3x$.

   (ii) What does this tell you about the number of turning points of the curve with equation $y = x^3 + 3x$?

   (iii) Find the values of y corresponding to $x = -3, -2, -1, 0, 1, 2$ and 3.

   (iv) Hence sketch the curve and explain your answer to (ii).

12 A curve has equation $y = x^4 - 8x^2 + 16$.

   (i) Find $\dfrac{dy}{dx}$.

   (ii) Find the co-ordinates of any turning points and determine their nature.

   (iii) Sketch the curve.

   (iv) Factorise $z^2 - 8z + 16$, and hence factorise $x^4 - 8x^2 + 16$.

   (v) Explain how knowing the factors of $x^4 - 8x^2 + 16$, and the value of y when $x = 0$ could have enabled you to sketch the curve without using calculus.

13 You are given that $y = 2x^3 + 3x^2 - 72x + 130$.

   (i) Find $\dfrac{dy}{dx}$.

P is the point on the curve where $x = 4$.

(ii) Calculate the y co-ordinate of P.

(iii) Calculate the gradient at P and hence find the equation of the tangent to the curve at P.

(iv) There are two stationary points on the curve. Find their co-ordinates.

[MEI]

14 You are given that $y = x^3 - 12x + 5$.

(i) Find $\dfrac{dy}{dx}$.

The curve with equation $y = x^3 - 12x + 5$ has two stationary points.

(ii) Find the co-ordinates of these two stationary points.

The co-ordinates of the stationary points give the impression that the left-hand point is a maximum and the right-hand point is a mimimum.

(iii) State how you would decide whether this is the case.

(iv) Draw a sketch of the curve with equation $y = x^3 - 12x + 5$.

(v) Find the equation of the tangent to this curve at the point where $x = 0$.

[MEI]

15 A curve has the equation $y = 2x^3 - 3x^2 - 36x + 120$.

(i) Calculate the values of y when x is 3 and when x is -2.

(ii) Find $\dfrac{dy}{dx}$.

(iii) Use your expression for $\dfrac{dy}{dx}$ to find the co-ordinates of the two stationary points on the curve.

(iv) By considering the values of $\dfrac{dy}{dx}$ near the stationary points, decide which type of stationary point each is.

(v) Sketch the curve. Deduce the range of values of k for which the equation $2x^3 - 3x^2 - 36x + 120 = k$ has three real roots.

[MEI]

Stationary points

It is possible for the value of $\dfrac{dy}{dx}$ to be zero at a point on a curve without it being a maximum or minimum. This is the case with the curve $y = x^3$, at the point $(0, 0)$ (see figure 8.23).

$$y = x^3 \quad \Rightarrow \quad \frac{dy}{dx} = 3x^2$$

and when $x = 0$, $\dfrac{dy}{dx} = 0$.

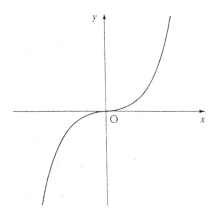

Figure 8.23

This is an example of a *point of inflection*. In general, a point of inflection occurs where the tangent to a curve crosses the curve. This can happen also when $\frac{dy}{dx} \neq 0$, as shown in figure 8.24.

Figure 8.24

If you are a driver you may find it helpful to think of a point of inflection as the point at which you change from left lock to right lock, or vice versa. Another way of thinking about a point of inflection is to view the curve from one side and see it as the point where the curve changes from being concave to convex.

At present you are considering only *stationary* points of inflection, those at which $\frac{dy}{dx} = 0$. Either side of such points the gradient has the same sign, so that it goes through the sequence $+ \quad 0 \quad +$ or $- \quad 0 \quad -$, as in figure 8.25.

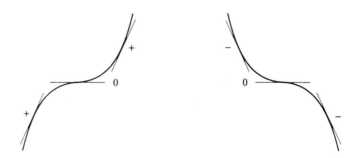

Figure 8.25

A stationary point of inflection is not a turning point, but in common with a maximum and a minimum, it is called a *stationary point*.

? The map shows the motor-racing circuit at Brands Hatch.
At what points of the circuit are there points of inflection, and how can the drivers know when they are at one?

Figure 8.26

EXAMPLE 8.13

Find and classify all the stationary points on the curve $y = 3x^5 - 5x^3$, then use the information to sketch the curve.

SOLUTION

$$\frac{dy}{dx} = 15x^4 - 15x^2$$
$$= 15x^2(x^2 - 1)$$
$$= 15x^2(x - 1)(x + 1).$$

At a stationary point, $\frac{dy}{dx} = 0$; stationary points occur at $x = -1, 0$ and 1.

	$x < -1$	-1	$-1 < x < 0$	0	$0 < x < 1$	1	$x > 1$
Sign of $\frac{dy}{dx}$	$+$	0	$-$	0	$-$	0	$+$
Turning point		max		inflection		min	

There is a maximum when $x = -1$, a stationary point of inflection when $x = 0$ and a minimum when $x = 1$.

When $x = -1$, $y = 3(-1)^5 - 5(-1)^3 = 2$: maximum at $(-1, 2)$.
When $x = 0$, $y = 0$: stationary point of inflection at $(0, 0)$.
When $x = 1$, $y = 3(1)^5 - 5(1)^3 = -2$: minimum at $(1, -2)$.

To draw a sketch of the graph you also need to know where the curve cuts the x axis. This is at the point where $y = 0$, given by

$$3x^5 - 5x^3 = x^3(3x^2 - 5) = 0$$

$$\therefore x = 0 \quad \text{or} \quad 3x^2 - 5 = 0 \quad \Rightarrow \quad x = \pm \sqrt{\tfrac{5}{3}} = \pm 1.29.$$

The curve is shown in figure 8.27.

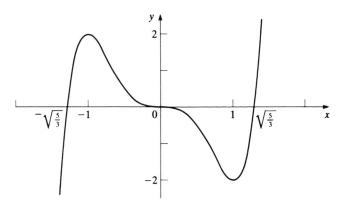

Figure 8.27

EXERCISE 8F

1 Given that $y = x^3 - x^2 - x + 4$:

  (i) find $\dfrac{dy}{dx}$ and factorise the quadratic expression you obtain

  (ii) write down the values of x for which $\dfrac{dy}{dx} = 0$

  (iii) classify the stationary points as maxima, minima, or stationary points of inflection by considering the gradient of the curve either side of them

  (iv) find the corresponding y values

  (v) sketch the curve.

2 Given that $y = 3x^4 - 4x^3$:

  (i) find $\dfrac{dy}{dx}$ and factorise the expression you obtain

  (ii) write down the values of x for which $\dfrac{dy}{dx} = 0$

  (iii) by considering the nature of the gradient near these two points, show that one is a minimum point and the other a point of inflection

  (iv) find the corresponding y values

  (v) find the co-ordinates of A, B and C in the diagram.

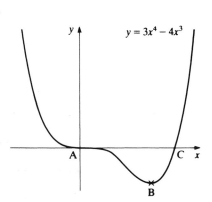

3 Given that $y = 3x^4 - 8x^3 + 6x^2 + 2$:

(i) find $\dfrac{dy}{dx}$

(ii) find the co-ordinates of any stationary points and determine their nature

(iii) sketch the curve.

Higher derivatives

Figure 8.28 shows a sketch of a function $y = f(x)$, and beneath it a sketch of the corresponding gradient function $\dfrac{dy}{dx} = f'(x)$.

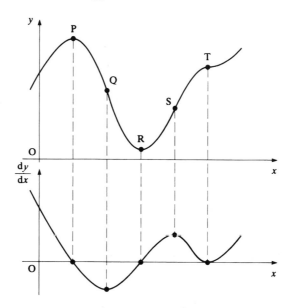

Figure 8.28

ACTIVITY 8.7 Sketch the graph of the gradient of $\dfrac{dy}{dx}$ against x for the function illustrated in figure 8.28. Do this by tracing the two graphs shown in figure 8.28, and extending the dashed lines downwards on to a third set of axes.

You can see that P is a maximum point, R is a minimum point and T is a stationary point of inflection. Q and S are called non-stationary points of inflection. What can you say about the gradient of $\dfrac{dy}{dx}$ at these points: is it positive, negative or zero?

The gradient of any point on the curve of $\dfrac{dy}{dx}$ is given by $\dfrac{d}{dx}\left(\dfrac{dy}{dx}\right)$. This is written as $\dfrac{d^2y}{dx^2}$ or $f''(x)$, and is called the *second derivative*. It is found by differentiating the function a second time.

⚠ The second derivative, $\dfrac{d^2y}{dx^2}$, is not the same as $\left(\dfrac{dy}{dx}\right)^2$.

EXAMPLE 8.14

Given that $y = x^5 + 2x$, find $\dfrac{d^2y}{dx^2}$.

SOLUTION

$$\frac{dy}{dx} = 5x^4 + 2$$

$$\frac{d^2y}{dx^2} = 20x^3.$$

Using the second derivative

You can use the second derivative to identify the nature of a stationary point, instead of looking at the sign of $\dfrac{dy}{dx}$ just either side of it.

Turning points

Notice that at P, $\dfrac{dy}{dx} = 0$ and $\dfrac{d^2y}{dx^2} < 0$. This tells you that the gradient, $\dfrac{dy}{dx}$, is zero and decreasing. It must be going from positive to negative, so P is a maximum point (see figure 8.29).

At R, $\dfrac{dy}{dx} = 0$ and $\dfrac{d^2y}{dx^2} > 0$. This tells you that the gradient, $\dfrac{dy}{dx}$, is zero and increasing. It must be going from negative to positive, so R is a minimum point (see figure 8.30)

Figure 8.29

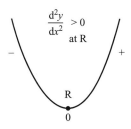

Figure 8.30

The next example illustrates the use of the second derivative to identify the nature of stationary points.

EXAMPLE 8.15

Given that $y = 2x^3 + 3x^2 - 12x$:

(i) find $\dfrac{dy}{dx}$, and find the values of x for which $\dfrac{dy}{dx} = 0$

(ii) find the value of $\dfrac{d^2y}{dx^2}$ at each stationary point and hence determine its nature

(iii) find the y values of each of the stationary points

(iv) sketch the curve given by $y = 2x^3 + 3x^2 - 12x$.

SOLUTION

(i) $\dfrac{dy}{dx} = 6x^2 + 6x - 12$

$\qquad = 6(x^2 + x - 2)$

$\qquad = 6(x + 2)(x - 1)$

$\dfrac{dy}{dx} = 0$ when $x = -2$ or 1.

(ii) $\dfrac{d^2y}{dx^2} = 12x + 6$.

When $x = -2$, $\qquad \dfrac{d^2y}{dx^2} = 12 \times (-2) + 6 = -18$.

$\qquad\qquad\qquad\qquad \dfrac{d^2y}{dx^2} < 0 \Rightarrow$ a maximum.

When $x = 1$, $\qquad \dfrac{d^2y}{dx^2} = 6(2 \times 1 + 1) = 18$.

$\qquad\qquad\qquad\qquad \dfrac{d^2y}{dx^2} > 0 \Rightarrow$ a minimum.

(iii) When $x = -2$, $\qquad y = 2(-2)^3 + 3(-2)^2 - 12(-2)$

$\qquad\qquad\qquad\qquad = 20$,

so $(-2, 20)$ is a maximum point.

When $x = 1$, $\qquad y = 2 + 3 - 12$

$\qquad\qquad\qquad\qquad = -7$,

so $(1, -7)$ is a minimum point.

(iv)

Figure 8.31

 Remember that you are looking for the value of $\dfrac{d^2y}{dx^2}$ at the turning point.

Note

On occasions when it is difficult or laborious to find $\dfrac{d^2y}{dx^2}$, remember that you can always classify the nature of a stationary point by looking at the sign of $\dfrac{dy}{dx}$ for points just either side of it.

Points of inflection

When a curve is drawn on Cartesian axes, the points of inflection may be divided into two categories: non-stationary and stationary.

At a non-stationary point of inflection, $\frac{d^2y}{dx^2} = 0$ but $\frac{dy}{dx} \neq 0$ as shown in figure 8.32.

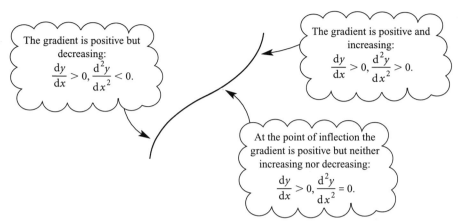

The gradient is positive but decreasing:
$$\frac{dy}{dx} > 0, \frac{d^2y}{dx^2} < 0.$$

The gradient is positive and increasing:
$$\frac{dy}{dx} > 0, \frac{d^2y}{dx^2} > 0.$$

At the point of inflection the gradient is positive but neither increasing nor decreasing:
$$\frac{dy}{dx} > 0, \frac{d^2y}{dx^2} = 0.$$

Figure 8.32

ACTIVITY 8.8

Draw a diagram like that in figure 8.33 to illustrate a non-stationary point of inflection on a decreasing curve, commenting on the gradient and how it is changing before, at and after the point of inflection.

At a stationary point of inflection, both $\frac{dy}{dx}$ and $\frac{d^2y}{dx^2}$ equal zero, as in the case of $y = x^3$ at the origin (see figure 8.33).

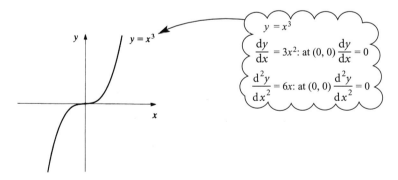

$$y = x^3$$

$$\frac{dy}{dx} = 3x^2: \text{ at } (0, 0) \frac{dy}{dx} = 0$$

$$\frac{d^2y}{dx^2} = 6x: \text{ at } (0, 0) \frac{d^2y}{dx^2} = 0$$

Figure 8.33

⚠ While it is true for all stationary points of inflection that $\dfrac{\mathrm{d}y}{\mathrm{d}x}$ and $\dfrac{\mathrm{d}^2y}{\mathrm{d}x^2} = 0$, it is also true for some turning points. For example, the curve $y = x^4$ has a minimum point at the origin (see figure 8.34).

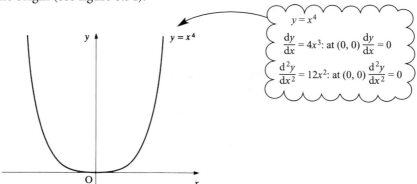

$$y = x^4$$

$$\frac{\mathrm{d}y}{\mathrm{d}x} = 4x^3 \text{: at } (0, 0) \frac{\mathrm{d}y}{\mathrm{d}x} = 0$$

$$\frac{\mathrm{d}^2y}{\mathrm{d}x^2} = 12x^2 \text{: at } (0, 0) \frac{\mathrm{d}^2y}{\mathrm{d}x^2} = 0$$

Figure 8.34

Consequently, if both $\dfrac{\mathrm{d}y}{\mathrm{d}x}$ and $\dfrac{\mathrm{d}^2y}{\mathrm{d}x^2}$ are zero at a point, you still need to check the values of $\dfrac{\mathrm{d}y}{\mathrm{d}x}$ either side of the point in order to determine its nature.

EXAMPLE 8.16

(i) Find the stationary points on the curve $y = x^4 + x^3$.

(ii) Classify the stationary points.

(iii) Sketch the curve $y = x^4 + x^3$.

SOLUTION

(i) $\dfrac{\mathrm{d}y}{\mathrm{d}x} = 4x^3 + 3x^2$

$\qquad = x^2(4x + 3)$.

For a stationary point, $\quad \dfrac{\mathrm{d}y}{\mathrm{d}x} = 0 \Rightarrow x = 0 \text{ or } -\tfrac{3}{4}$.

$x = 0 \Rightarrow y = 0$; $x = -\tfrac{3}{4} \Rightarrow y = -\tfrac{27}{256}$

The stationary points are at $(0, 0)$ and $(-\tfrac{3}{4}, -\tfrac{27}{256})$.

(ii) $\dfrac{\mathrm{d}^2y}{\mathrm{d}x^2} = 12x^2 + 6x$.

When $x = -\tfrac{3}{4}$, $\dfrac{\mathrm{d}^2y}{\mathrm{d}x^2} > 0$, $\quad \Rightarrow \quad (-\tfrac{3}{4}, -\tfrac{27}{256})$ is a minimum point.

When $x = 0$, $\dfrac{\mathrm{d}^2y}{\mathrm{d}x^2} = 0$, so you need to investigate further.

$\qquad x$ is just less than $0 \Rightarrow \dfrac{\mathrm{d}y}{\mathrm{d}x} > 0$.

$\qquad x$ is just greater than $0 \Rightarrow \dfrac{\mathrm{d}y}{\mathrm{d}x} > 0$.

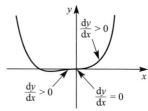

Figure 8.35

Conclusion: there is a stationary point of inflection at $(0, 0)$.

(iii)

Figure 8.36

EXERCISE 8G

Many of the questions in this exercise require you to find the stationary points of a curve and then use them as a guide for sketching it. You will find it helpful to use a graphic calculator to check your final answers.

1 For each of the following functions, find $\dfrac{dy}{dx}$ and $\dfrac{d^2y}{dx^2}$.

(i) $y = x^3$ (ii) $y = x^5$ (iii) $y = 4x^2$

2 Find any stationary points on the curves of the following functions and identify their nature. You do not need to sketch the curves but you should check your answers, if possible, using a graphic calculator.

(i) $y = x^2 + 2x + 4$ (ii) $y = 6x - x^2$

(iii) $y = x^3 - 3x$ (iv) $y = 4x^5 - 5x^4$

(v) $y = x^4 + x^3 - 2x^2 - 3x + 1$

3 You are given that $y = x^4 - 8x^2$.

(i)   Find $\dfrac{dy}{dx}$.

(ii) Find $\dfrac{d^2y}{dx^2}$.

(iii) Find any stationary points and identify their nature.

(iv) Hence sketch the curve.

4 Given that $y = x^5 - 3$:

(i)   find $\dfrac{dy}{dx}$

(ii) find the co-ordinates of any stationary points and determine their nature

(iii) sketch the curve.

5 Given that $y = -x^4 + 4x^3 - 8$:

   (i) find the co-ordinates of any stationary points and determine their nature

   (ii) sketch the curve.

6 (i) Find the position and nature of the stationary points of the curve
$y = 3x^5 - 10x^3 + 15x$.

   (ii) Sketch the curve.

7 Given that $y = (x - 1)^2 (x - 3)$:

   (i) multiply out the right-hand side and find $\dfrac{dy}{dx}$

   (ii) find the position and nature of any stationary points

   (iii) sketch the curve.

8 Given that $y = x^2(x - 2)^2$:

   (i) multiply out the right-hand side and find $\dfrac{dy}{dx}$

   (ii) find the position and nature of any stationary points

   (iii) sketch the curve.

9 The function $y = px^3 + qx^2$, where p and q are constants, has a stationary point at $(1, -1)$.

   (i) Using the fact that $(1, -1)$ lies on the curve, form an equation involving p and q.

   (ii) Differentiate y and, using the fact that $(1, -1)$ is a stationary point, form another equation involving p and q.

   (iii) Solve these two equations simultaneously to find the values of p and q.

10 Given the function $y = 3x^4 + 4x^3$:

   (i) find $\dfrac{dy}{dx}$

   (ii) show that the graph of the function y has stationary points at $x = 0$ and $x = -1$ and find their co-ordinates

   (iii) determine whether each of the stationary points is a maximum, minimum or point of inflection, giving reasons for your answers

   (iv) sketch the graph of the function y, giving the co-ordinates of the stationary points and the points where the curve cuts the axes.

[MEI]

Applications

There are many situations in which you need to find the maximum or minimum value of an expression. The examples which follow, and those in Exercise 8H, illustrate a few of these.

EXAMPLE 8.17

Judith's father has agreed to let her have part of his garden as a vegetable plot. He says that she can have a rectangular plot with one side against an old wall. He hands her a piece of rope 5 m long, and invites her to mark out the part she wants. Judith wants to enclose the largest area possible.

What dimensions would you advise her to use?

SOLUTION

Let the dimensions of the bed be x m × y m as shown in figure 8.37.

Figure 8.37

The area, A m^2, to be enclosed is given by A = xy.

Since the rope is 5 m long $2x + y = 5$ or $y = 5 - 2x$.

Writing A in terms of x only A = $x(5 - 2x) = 5x - 2x^2$.

To maximise A, which is now written as a function of x, you differentiate A with respect to x

$$\frac{dA}{dx} = 5 - 4x.$$

At a turning point, $\frac{dA}{dx} = 0$, so

$$5 - 4x = 0$$

$$x = \tfrac{5}{4} = 1.25.$$

$$\frac{d^2A}{dx^2} = -4 \Rightarrow \text{ the turning point is a maximum.}$$

The corresponding value of y is $5 - 2(1.25) = 2.5$. Judith should mark out a rectangle 1.25 m wide and 2.5 m long.

EXAMPLE 8.18

A stone is projected vertically upwards with a speed of $30\,\text{ms}^{-1}$. Its height, $h\,\text{m}$, above the ground after t seconds ($t < 6$) is given by:

$$h = 30t - 5t^2.$$

(i) Find $\dfrac{dh}{dt}$ and $\dfrac{d^2h}{dt^2}$.

(ii) Find the maximum height reached.

(iii) Sketch the graph of h against t.

SOLUTION

(i)　$\dfrac{dh}{dt} = 30 - 10t.$

$\dfrac{d^2h}{dt^2} = -10.$

(ii) For a turning point, $\quad\dfrac{dh}{dt} = 0$

$$30 - 10t = 0$$

$\Rightarrow \qquad\qquad\qquad 10(3 - t) = 0$

$\Rightarrow \qquad\qquad\qquad\qquad t = 3.$

$\dfrac{d^2h}{dt^2} < 0 \Rightarrow$ the turning point is a maximum.

The maximum height is
$$h = 30(3) - 5(3)^2 = 45\,\text{m}.$$

(iii)

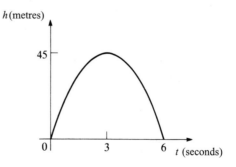

Figure 8.38

Note

For a position–time graph, such as this one, the gradient, $\dfrac{dh}{dt}$, is the velocity and $\dfrac{d^2h}{dt^2}$ is the acceleration.

1 A farmer wants to construct a temporary rectangular enclosure of length x m and width y m for his prize bull while he works in the field. He has 120 m of fencing and wants to give the bull as much room to graze as possible.

    (i) Write down an expression for y in terms of x.

    (ii) Write down an expression in terms of x for the area, A, to be enclosed.

    (iii) Find $\dfrac{dA}{dx}$ and $\dfrac{d^2A}{dx^2}$, and so find the dimensions of the enclosure that give the bull the maximum area in which to graze. State this maximum area.

2 A square sheet of card of side 12 cm has four equal squares of side x cm cut from the corners. The sides are then turned up to make an open rectangular box to hold drawing pins as shown in the diagram.

    (i) Form an expression for the volume, V, of the box in terms of x.

    (ii) Find $\dfrac{dV}{dx}$ and $\dfrac{d^2V}{dx^2}$, and show that the volume is a maximum when the depth is 2 cm.

3 The sum of two numbers, x and y, is 8.

    (i) Write down an expression for y in terms of x.

    (ii) Write down an expression for S, the sum of the squares of these two numbers, in terms of x.

    (iii) By considering $\dfrac{dS}{dx}$ and $\dfrac{d^2S}{dx^2}$, find the least value of the sum of their squares.

4 A new children's slide is to be built with a cross-section as shown in the diagram. A long strip of metal 80 cm wide is available for the shute and will be bent to form the base and two sides.

The designer thinks that for maximum safety the area of the cross-section should be as large as possible.

(i) Write down an equation linking x and y.

(ii) Using your answer to (i), form an expression for the cross-sectional area, A, in terms of x.

(iii) By considering $\dfrac{\mathrm{d}A}{\mathrm{d}x}$ and $\dfrac{\mathrm{d}^2A}{\mathrm{d}x^2}$, find the dimensions which make the slide as safe as possible.

5   A carpenter wants to make a box to hold toys. The box is to be made so that its volume is as large as possible. A rectangular sheet of thin plywood measuring 1.5 m by 1 m is available to cut into pieces as shown.

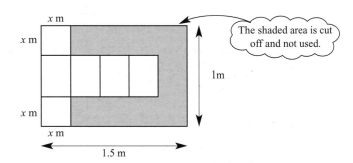

The shaded area is cut off and not used.

(i) Write down the dimensions of one of the four rectangular faces in terms of x.

(ii) Form an expression for the volume, V, of the made-up box, in terms of x.

(iii) Find $\dfrac{\mathrm{d}V}{\mathrm{d}x}$ and $\dfrac{\mathrm{d}^2V}{\mathrm{d}x^2}$.

(iv) Hence find the dimensions of a box with maximum volume, and the corresponding volume.

6   A piece of wire 16 cm long is cut into two pieces. One piece is $8x$ cm long and is bent to form a rectangle measuring $3x$ cm by x cm. The other piece is bent to form a square.

(i) Find in terms of x:
   (a) the length of a side of the square
   (b) the area of the square.

(ii) Show that the combined area of the rectangle and the square is A cm^2 where $A = 7x^2 - 16x + 16$.

(iii) Find the value of x for which A has its minimum value.

(iv) Find the minimum value of A.

[MEI]

7 A piece of wire 30 cm long is going to be made into two frames for blowing bubbles. The wire is to be cut into two parts. One part is bent into a circle of radius r cm and the other part is bent into a square of side x cm.

(i) Write down an expression for the perimeter of the circle in terms of r, and hence write down an expression for r in terms of x.

(ii) Show that the combined area, A, of the two shapes can be written as

$$A = \frac{(4 + \pi)x^2 - 60x + 225}{\pi}.$$

(iii) Find the lengths that must be cut if the area is to be a minimum.

8 Johannes Kepler was one of the founders of modern astronomy. A less well-known fact is that he published a book in 1615 on the geometry of wine barrels. It looked at ways of estimating the volumes of various barrel shapes. He was prompted to make this study when he bought wine for his wedding. The wine merchant measured the capacity of a barrel by inserting a rod into the taphole, T, until it reached the lid, L. He then noted the length ℓ of the rod that was inside the barrel.

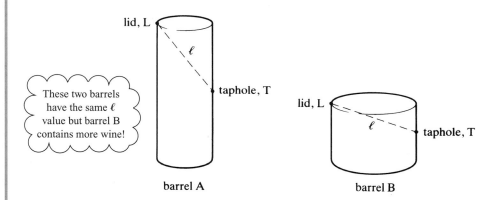

barrel A   barrel B

Think of the barrel as a cylinder of height h, with T half-way up.

(i) Find an expression for the square of the radius in terms of ℓ and h.

(ii) Hence find an expression for the volume V.

(iii) If ℓ is fixed and h is varied, what value of h gives the greatest volume?

(In fact Kepler found that the barrels he had bought were very close to this shape!)

9 A cylindrical can with a lid is to be made from a thin sheet of metal. Its height is to be h cm and its radius r cm. The surface area is to be 250π cm².

(i) Find h in terms of r.

(ii) Write down an expression for the volume, V, of the can in terms of r.

(iii) Find $\dfrac{\mathrm{d}V}{\mathrm{d}r}$ and $\dfrac{\mathrm{d}^2V}{\mathrm{d}r^2}$.

(iv) Use your answers to (iii) to show that the can's maximum possible volume is 1690 cm³ (to 3 significant figures), and find the corresponding dimensions of the can.

1. $y = kx^n \implies \dfrac{dy}{dx} = knx^{n-1}$

   $y = c \implies \dfrac{dy}{dx} = 0$

   } Where n is a positive integer and k and c are constants.

2. $y = f(x) + g(x) \implies \dfrac{dy}{dx} = f'(x) + g'(x).$

3. Tangent and normal at (x_1, y_1)

   Gradient of tangent, $m_1 = $ value of $\dfrac{dy}{dx}$.

   Gradient of normal, $m_2 = -\dfrac{1}{m_1}$.

   Equation of tangent is

   $$y - y_1 = m_1(x - x_1).$$

   Equation of normal is

   $$y - y_1 = m_2(x - x_1).$$

4. Stationary points

   At a stationary point, $\dfrac{dy}{dx} = 0$.

   The nature of a stationary point can be determined by looking at the sign of the gradient just either side of it.

5. The nature of a stationary point can also be determined by considering the sign of $\dfrac{d^2y}{dx^2}$.

   - If $\dfrac{d^2y}{dx^2} < 0$, the point is a maximum.

   - If $\dfrac{d^2y}{dx^2} > 0$, the point is a minimum.

6. If $\dfrac{d^2y}{dx^2} = 0$, the point could be a maximum, a minimum or a point of inflection.

   Check the values of $\dfrac{dy}{dx}$ on either side of the point to determine its nature.

9 Integration

Many small make a great.

Chaucer

 In what way can you say
that these four curves are
all parallel to each other?

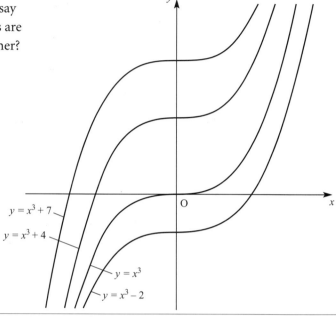

$y = x^3 + 7$

$y = x^3 + 4$

$y = x^3$

$y = x^3 - 2$

Reversing differentiation

In some situations you know the gradient function, $\frac{dy}{dx}$, and want to find the
function itself, y. For example, you might know that $\frac{dy}{dx} = 2x$ and want to find y.
You know from the previous chapter that if $y = x^2$ then $\frac{dy}{dx} = 2x$, but
$y = x^2 + 1$, $y = x^2 - 2$ and many other functions also give $\frac{dy}{dx} = 2x$.

Suppose that $f(x)$ is a function with $f'(x) = 2x$. Let $g(x) = f(x) - x^2$.
Then $g'(x) = f'(x) - 2x = 2x - 2x = 0$ for all x. So the graph of $y = g(x)$ has zero
gradient everywhere, i.e. the graph is a horizontal straight line.
Thus $g(x) = c$ (a constant). Therefore $f(x) = x^2 + c$.

All that you can say at this point is that if $\frac{dy}{dx} = 2x$ then $y = x^2 + c$ where c is
described as an *arbitrary constant*. An arbitrary constant may take any value.

The equation $\frac{dy}{dx} = 2x$ is an example of a *differential equation* and the process of
solving this equation to find y is called *integration*.

So the solution of the differential equation $\frac{dy}{dx} = 2x$ is $y = x^2 + c$.

Such a solution is often referred to as the *general solution* of the differential equation. It may be drawn as a family of curves as in figure 9.1. Each curve corresponds to a particular value of c.

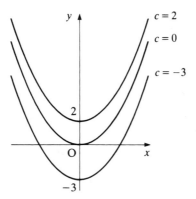

Recall from Activity 8.4 on page 198 that for each member of a family of curves, the gradient is the same for any particular value of x.

Figure 9.1 $y = x^2 + c$ for different values of c

Particular solutions

Sometimes you are given more information about a problem and this enables you to find just one solution, called the *particular solution*.

Suppose that in the previous example, in which

$$\frac{dy}{dx} = 2x \quad \Rightarrow \quad y = x^2 + c,$$

you were also told that when $x = 2$, $y = 1$.

Substituting these values in $y = x^2 + c$ gives

$$1 = 2^2 + c$$
$$c = -3$$

and so the particular solution is

$$y = x^2 - 3.$$

This is one of the curves shown in figure 9.1.

The rule for integrating x^n (n a positive integer)

Recall the rule for differentiation:

$$y = x^n \quad \Rightarrow \quad \frac{dy}{dx} = nx^{n-1}.$$

Similarly $\quad y = x^{n+1} \quad \Rightarrow \quad \frac{dy}{dx} = (n+1)x^n$

or $\quad y = \frac{1}{(n+1)}x^{n+1} \Rightarrow \quad \frac{dy}{dx} = x^n.$

Reversing this, integrating x^n gives $\dfrac{x^{n+1}}{n+1}$.

Note

In words: to integrate a power of x, add 1 to the power and divide by the new power.

⚠ Differentiating x gives 1, so integrating 1 gives x. This follows the pattern if you remember that $1 = x^0$.

EXAMPLE 9.1

Given that $\frac{dy}{dx} = 3x^2 + 4x + 3$:

(i) find the general solution of this differential equation

(ii) find the equation of the curve with this gradient function which passes through $(1, 10)$.

SOLUTION

(i) By integration, $y = \frac{3x^3}{3} + \frac{4x^2}{2} + 3x + c$

$\qquad\qquad\qquad = x^3 + 2x^2 + 3x + c$, where c is a constant.

(ii) Since the curve passes through $(1, 10)$,

$$10 = 1^3 + 2(1)^2 + 3(1) + c$$
$$c = 4$$
$$\Rightarrow \qquad y = x^3 + 2x^2 + 3x + 4.$$

EXAMPLE 9.2

The gradient function of a curve is $\frac{dy}{dx} = 4x - 12$.

(i) The minimum y value is 16. By considering the gradient function, find the corresponding x value.

(ii) Use the gradient function and your answer from (i) to find the equation of the curve.

SOLUTION

(i) At the minimum, the gradient of the curve must be zero,

$$4x - 12 = 0 \qquad \Rightarrow \qquad x = 3.$$

(ii) $\frac{dy}{dx} = 4x - 12$

$\qquad \Rightarrow y = 2x^2 - 12x + c.$

At the minimum point, $x = 3$ and $y = 16$

$$\Rightarrow 16 = 2 \times 3^2 - 12 \times 3 + c$$
$$\Rightarrow \quad c = 34$$
$$\Rightarrow \quad y = 2x^2 - 12x + 34.$$

1 Given that $\dfrac{dy}{dx} = 6x^2 + 5$:

    (i) find the general solution of the differential equation

    (ii) find the equation of the curve with gradient function $\dfrac{dy}{dx}$ and which passes through $(1, 9)$

    (iii) hence show that $(-1, -5)$ also lies on the curve.

2 The gradient function of a curve is $\dfrac{dy}{dx} = 4x$ and the curve passes through the point $(1, 5)$.

    (i) Find the equation of the curve.

    (ii) Find the value of y when $x = -1$.

3 The curve C passes through the point $(2, 10)$ and its gradient at any point is given by $\dfrac{dy}{dx} = 6x^2$.

    (i) Find the equation of the curve C.

    (ii) Show that the point $(1, -4)$ lies on the curve.

4 A stone is thrown upwards out of a window, and the rate of change of its height (h metres) is given by

$$\frac{dh}{dt} = 15 - 10t$$

where t is the time (in seconds). When $t = 0$, $h = 20$.

    (i) Show that the solution of the differential equation, under the given conditions, is

$$h = 20 + 15t - 5t^2.$$

    (ii) For what value of t does $h = 0$? (Assume $t \geqslant 0$.)

5 **(i)** Find the general solution of the differential equation

$$\frac{dy}{dx} = 5.$$

    (ii) Find the particular solution which passes through the point $(1, 8)$.

    (iii) Sketch the graph of this particular solution.

6 The gradient function of a curve is $3x^2 - 3$. The curve has two stationary points. One is a maximum with a y value of 5 and the other is a minimum with a y value of 1.

    (i) Find the value of x at each stationary point. Make it clear in your solution how you know which corresponds to the maximum and which to the minimum.

    (ii) Use the gradient function and one of your points from (i) to find the equation of the curve.

    (iii) Sketch the curve.

7 A curve passes through the point $(4, 1)$ and its gradient at any point is given by

$$\frac{dy}{dx} = 2x - 6.$$

(i) Find the equation of the curve.

(ii) Draw a sketch of the curve and state whether it passes under, over or through the point $(1, 4)$.

8 The slope of a children's slide is given by

$$\frac{dy}{dx} = \frac{9}{32}(x^2 - 4x) \qquad \text{for } 0 \leqslant x \leqslant 4$$

where the origin is taken to be at ground level beneath the highest point of the slide, which is 3 m above the ground. All units are metres.

(i) Find the equation of the curve described by the slide.

(ii) Sketch the curve of the slide, marking in the turning points.

(iii) Describe the slide's shape briefly, in simple English.

(iv) Does the slope of the slide ever exceed $45°$?

9 A curve passes through the point $(2, 3)$. The gradient of the curve is given by

$$\frac{dy}{dx} = 3x^2 - 2x - 1.$$

(i) Find y in terms of x.

(ii) Find the co-ordinates of any stationary points of the graph of y.

(iii) Sketch the graph of y against x, marking the co-ordinates of any stationary points and the point where the curve cuts the y axis.

[MEI]

10 The gradient of a curve is given by

$$\frac{dy}{dx} = 3x^2 - 8x + 5.$$

The curve passes through the point $(0, 3)$.

(i) Find the equation of the curve.

(ii) Find the co-ordinates of the two stationary points on the curve. State, with a reason, the nature of each stationary point.

(iii) State the range of values of k for which the curve has three distinct intersections with the line $y = k$.

(iv) State the range of values of x for which the curve has a negative gradient. Find the x co-ordinate of the point within this range where the curve is steepest.

[MEI]

Finding the area under a curve

Figure 9.2 shows a curve $y = f(x)$ and the area required is shaded.

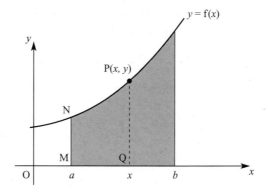

Figure 9.2

P is a point on the curve with an x co-ordinate between a and b. Let A denote the area bounded by MNPQ. As P moves, the values of A and x change, so you can see that the area A depends on the value of x. Figure 9.3 enlarges part of figure 9.2 and introduces T to the right of P.

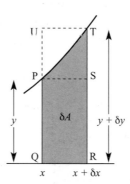

Figure 9.3

If T is close to P it is appropriate to use the notation δx (a small change in x) for the difference in their x co-ordinates and δy for the difference in their y co-ordinates. The area shaded in figure 9.3 is then referred to as δA (a small change in A).

This area δA will lie between the areas of the rectangles PQRS and UQRT

$$y\delta x < \delta A < (y + \delta y)\delta x.$$

Dividing by δx

$$y < \frac{\delta A}{\delta x} < y + \delta y.$$

In the limit as $\delta x \to 0$, δy also approaches zero so δA is sandwiched between y and something which tends to y.

But $\displaystyle \lim_{\delta x \to 0} \frac{\delta A}{\delta x} = \frac{dA}{dx}$.

This gives $\displaystyle \frac{dA}{dx} = y$.

Note

This important result is known as the fundamental theorem of calculus: the rate of change of the area under a curve is equal to the length of the moving boundary.

EXAMPLE 9.3

Find the area under the curve $y = 6x^5 + 6$ between $x = -1$ and $x = 2$.

SOLUTION

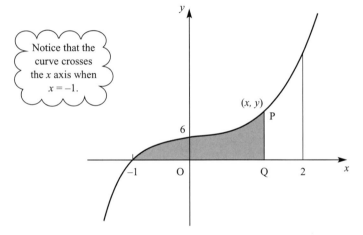

Notice that the curve crosses the x axis when $x = -1$.

Figure 9.4

Let A be the shaded area which is bounded by the curve, the x axis, and the moving boundary PQ (see figure 9.4).

Then $\displaystyle \frac{dA}{dx} = y = 6x^5 + 6$.

Integrating, $A = x^6 + 6x + c$.

When $x = -1$, the line PQ coincides with the left-hand boundary so $A = 0$

$\Rightarrow \quad 0 = 1 - 6 + c$

$\Rightarrow \quad c = 5$.

So $A = x^6 + 6x + 5$.

The required area is found by substituting $x = 2$

$A = 64 + 12 + 5$

$\quad = 81$ square units.

Note

The term 'square units' is used since area is a square measure and the units are unknown.

Standardising the procedure

Suppose that you want to find the area between the curve $y = f(x)$, the x axis, and the lines $x = a$ and $x = b$. This is shown shaded in figure 9.5.

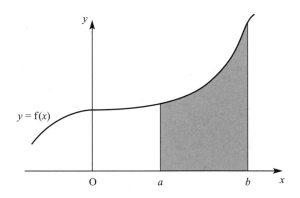

Figure 9.5

- $\dfrac{dA}{dx} = y = f(x)$.

- Integrate $f(x)$ to give $A = F(x) + c$.

- $A = 0$ when $x = a \Rightarrow \quad 0 = F(a) + c$
  $$\Rightarrow \quad c = -F(a)$$
  $$\Rightarrow \quad A = F(x) - F(a).$$

- The value of A when $x = b$ is $F(b) - F(a)$.

Notation

$F(b) - F(a)$ is written as $\left[F(x)\right]_a^b$.

EXAMPLE 9.4

Find the area between the curve $y = 20 - 3x^2$, the x axis and the lines $x = 1$ and $x = 2$.

SOLUTION

$f(x) = 20 - 3x^2 \Rightarrow F(x) = 20x - x^3$

$a = 1$ and $b = 2$

$$\Rightarrow \quad \text{Area} = \left[20x - x^3\right]_1^2$$
$$= (40 - 8) - (20 - 1)$$
$$= 13 \text{ square units.}$$

Area as the limit of a sum

Suppose you want to find the area between the curve $y = x^2 + 1$, the x axis and the lines $x = 1$ and $x = 5$. This area is shaded in figure 9.6.

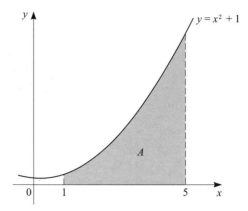

Figure 9.6

You can find an estimate of the shaded area, A, by considering the area of four rectangles of equal width, as shown in figure 9.7.

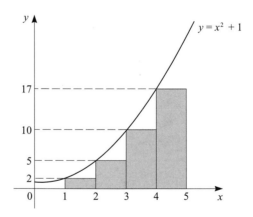

Figure 9.7

The estimated value of A is

$2 + 5 + 10 + 17 = 34$ square units.

This is an underestimate.

To get an overestimate, you take the four rectangles in figure 9.8.

The corresponding estimate for A is

$5 + 10 + 17 + 26 = 58$ square units.

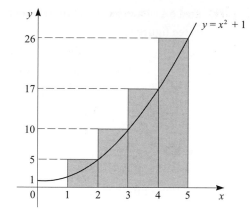

Figure 9.8

This means that the true value of A satisfies the inequality

$$34 < A < 58.$$

If you increase the number of rectangles, your bounds for A close in. The equivalent calculation using eight rectangles gives

$$1 + \frac{13}{8} + \frac{5}{2} + \frac{29}{8} + 5 + \frac{53}{8} + \frac{17}{2} + \frac{85}{8} < A < \frac{13}{8} + \frac{5}{2} + \frac{29}{8} + 5 + \frac{53}{8} + \frac{17}{2} + \frac{85}{8} + 13$$

$$39.5 < A < 51.5.$$

Similarly with 16 rectangles

$$42.375 < A < 48.375$$

and so on. With enough rectangles, the bounds for A can be brought as close together as you wish.

ACTIVITY 9.1

Use ICT to get the bounds closer.

Notation

This process can be expressed more formally. Suppose you have n rectangles, each of width δx. Notice that n and δx are related by

$$n\delta x = \text{width of required area.}$$

So in the example above,

$$n\delta x = 5 - 1 = 4.$$

In the limit, as $n \to \infty$, $\delta x \to 0$, the lower estimate $\to A$ and the higher estimate $\to A$.

The area δA of a typical rectangle may be written $y_i \delta x$ where y_i is the appropriate y value (see figure 9.9).

$$\delta A_i = y_i \delta x$$

Figure 9.9

So for a finite number of strips, n, as shown in figure 9.10, the area A is given approximately by

$$A \approx \delta A_1 + \delta A_2 + \ldots + \delta A_n$$

or $\quad A \approx y_1 \delta x + y_2 \delta x + \ldots + y_n \delta x.$

This can be written as $A \approx \sum_{i=1}^{i=n} \delta A_i$

or $\qquad A \approx \sum_{i=1}^{i=n} y_i \delta x.$

$\sum$ means 'the sum of' so all the δA_i are added from δA_1 (given by $i=1$) to δA_n (when $i=n$).

Figure 9.10

In the limit, as $n \to \infty$ and $\delta x \to 0$, the result is no longer an approximation; it is exact. At this point, $A \approx \sum y_i \delta x$ is written $A = \int y \, dx$, which you read as 'the integral of y with respect to x'. In this case $y = x^2 + 1$, and you require the area for values of x from 1 to 5, so you can write

$$A = \int_1^5 (x^2 + 1) \, dx.$$

Notice that in the limit:

- $\approx$ is replaced by $=$

- δx is replaced by dx

- $\sum$ is replaced by $\int$, the integral sign (the symbol is the Old English letter S)

● instead of summing for $i = 1$ to n the process is now carried out over a range of values of x (in this case 1 to 5), and these are called the *limits* of the integral. (Note that this is a different meaning of the word limit.)

This method must give the same results as the previous one which used $\frac{dA}{dx} = y$, and at this stage the notation $\left[F(x) \right]_{a}^{b}$ is used again.

In this case $\int_{1}^{5} (x^2 + 1) \, dx = \left[\frac{x^3}{3} + x \right]_{1}^{5}$.

> The limits have now moved to the right of the square brackets.

Recall that this notation means: find the value of $\frac{x^3}{3} + x$ when $x = 5$ (the upper limit) and subtract the value of $\frac{x^3}{3} + x$ when $x = 1$ (the lower limit).

$$\left[\frac{x^3}{3} + x \right]_{1}^{5} = \left(\frac{5^3}{3} + 5 \right) - \left(\frac{1^3}{3} + 1 \right)$$
$$= 45\tfrac{1}{3}.$$

So the area A is $45\tfrac{1}{3}$ square units.

EXAMPLE 9.5

Find the area under the curve $y = 4x^3 + 4$ between $x = -1$ and $x = 2$.

SOLUTION

The graph looks like that shown in figure 9.11.

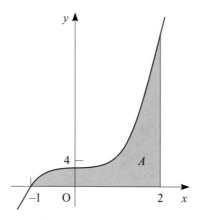

Figure 9.11

The shaded part is

$$A = \int_{-1}^{2} (4x^3 + 4) \, dx$$
$$= \left[x^4 + 4x \right]_{-1}^{2}$$
$$= \left(2^4 + 4(2) \right) - \left((-1)^4 + 4(-1) \right)$$
$$= 27 \text{ square units.}$$

Definite integrals

An expression like $\int_{-1}^{2}(4x^3 + 4)dx$ in the last example is called a *definite integral*. A definite integral has an upper limit and a lower limit and can be evaluated as a number, in this case 27.

Note

Interchanging the limits of definite integral has the effect of reversing the sign of the answer. In this case $\int_{2}^{-1}(4x^3 + 4)dx = -27$ and in general $\int_{a}^{b} f(x)dx = -\int_{b}^{a} f(x)dx.$

ACTIVITY 9.2

Figure 9.12 shows the region bounded by the graph of $y = x + 3$, the x axis and the lines $x = a$ and $x = b$.

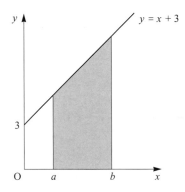

Figure 9.12

(i) Find the shaded area, A, by considering it as the difference between the two trapezia shown in figure 9.13.

(ii) Show that the expression for A you obtained in (i) may be written as

$$\left[\frac{x^2}{2} + 3x\right]_{a}^{b}.$$

(iii) Show that you obtain the same answer for A by integration.

 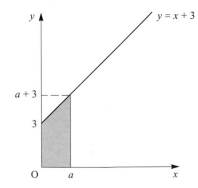

Figure 9.13

Indefinite integrals

The integral symbol can be used without the limits to denote that a function is to be integrated. Earlier in the chapter, you saw $\frac{dy}{dx} = 2x \Rightarrow y = x^2 + c$.

An alternative way of expressing this is

$$\int 2x \, dx = x^2 + c.$$

> Read as 'the integral of $2x$ with respect to x'.

EXAMPLE 9.6

Find $\int (2x^3 - 3x + 4) \, dx$.

SOLUTION

$$\int (2x^3 - 3x + 4) \, dx = 2\frac{x^4}{4} - 3\frac{x^2}{2} + 4x + c$$
$$= \frac{x^4}{2} - \frac{3x^2}{2} + 4x + c.$$

EXERCISE 9B

1 Find the following indefinite integrals.

(i) $\int 3x^2 \, dx$ **(ii)** $\int (5x^4 + 7x^6) \, dx$

(iii) $\int (6x^2 + 5) \, dx$ **(iv)** $\int (x^3 + x^2 + x + 1) \, dx$

(v) $\int (11x^{10} + 10x^9) \, dx$ **(vi)** $\int (3x^2 + 2x + 1) \, dx$

(vii) $\int (x^2 + 5) \, dx$ **(viii)** $\int 5 \, dx$

(ix) $\int (6x^2 + 4x) \, dx$ **(x)** $\int (x^4 + 3x^2 + 2x + 1) \, dx$

2 Evaluate the following definite integrals.

(i) $\int_1^2 2x \, dx$ **(ii)** $\int_0^3 2x \, dx$ **(iii)** $\int_0^3 3x^2 \, dx$

(iv) $\int_1^5 x \, dx$ **(v)** $\int_5^6 (2x+1) \, dx$ **(vi)** $\int_{-1}^2 (2x+4) \, dx$

(vii) $\int_3^5 (3x^2 + 2x) \, dx$ **(viii)** $\int_0^1 x^5 \, dx$ **(ix)** $\int_{-2}^{-1} (x^4 + x^3) \, dx$

(x) $\int_{-1}^1 x^3 \, dx$ **(xi)** $\int_{-5}^4 (x^3 + 3x) \, dx$ **(xii)** $\int_{-3}^{-2} 5 \, dx$

3 The graph of $y = 2x$ is shown below.

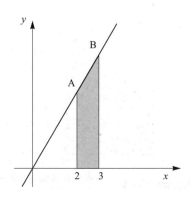

The shaded region is bounded by $y = 2x$, the x axis and the lines $x = 2$ and $x = 3$.

(i) Find the co-ordinates of the points A and B in the diagram.

(ii) Use the formula for the area of a trapezium to find the area of the shaded region.

(iii) Find the area of the shaded region as $\int_2^3 2x\,dx$, and confirm that your answer is the same as that for (ii).

(iv) The method of (ii) cannot be used to find the area under the curve $y = x^2$ bounded by the lines $x = 2$ and $x = 3$. Why?

4 (i) Sketch the curve $y = x^2$ for $-1 \leqslant x \leqslant 3$ and shade the area bounded by the curve, the lines $x = 1$ and $x = 2$ and the x axis.

(ii) Find, by integration, the area of the region you have shaded.

5 (i) Sketch the curve $y = 4 - x^2$ for $-3 \leqslant x \leqslant 3$.

(ii) For what values of x is the curve above the x axis?

(iii) Find the area between the curve and the x axis when the curve is above the x axis.

6 (i) Sketch the graph of $y = (x - 2)^2$ for values of x between $x = -1$ and $x = +5$. Shade the area under the curve, between $x = 0$ and $x = 2$.

(ii) Calculate the area you have shaded.

[MEI]

7 (i) Sketch the graph of $y = (x + 1)^2$ for values of x between $x = -1$ and $x = 4$.

(ii) Shade the area under the curve between $x = 1$, $x = 3$ and the x axis. Calculate this area.

[MEI]

8 (i) Sketch the curve $y = x^2$ and $y = x^3$ for $0 \leqslant x \leqslant 2$.

(ii) Which is the higher curve within the region $0 < x < 1$?

(iii) Find the area under each curve for $0 \leqslant x \leqslant 1$.

(iv) Which would you expect to be greater, $\int_1^2 x^2\,dx$ or $\int_1^2 x^3\,dx$?

Explain your answer in terms of your sketches, and confirm it by calculation.

9 (i) Sketch the curve $y = x^2 - 1$ for $-3 \leqslant x \leqslant 3$.

(ii) Find the area of the region bounded by $y = x^2 - 1$, the line $x = 2$ and the x axis.

(iii) Sketch the curve $y = x^2 - 2x$ for $-2 \leqslant x \leqslant 4$.

(iv) Find the area of the region bounded by $y = x^2 - 2x$, the line $x = 3$ and the x axis.

(v) Comment on your answers to (ii) and (iv).

10 (i) Shade, on a suitable sketch, the region with an area given by

$$\int_{-1}^2 (9 - x^2)\,dx.$$

(ii) Find the area of the shaded region.

11 (i) Sketch the curve with equation $y = x^2 + 1$ for $-3 \leqslant x \leqslant 3$.

(ii) Find the area of the region bounded by the curve, the lines $x = 2$ and $x = 3$, and the x axis.

(iii) Predict, with reasons, the value of $\int_{-3}^{-2}(x^2 + 1)\,dx$.

(iv) Evaluate $\int_{-3}^{-2}(x^2 + 1)\,dx$.

12 (i) Sketch the curve with equation $y = x^2 - 2x + 1$ for $-1 \leqslant x \leqslant 4$.

(ii) State, with reasons, which area you would expect from your sketch to be larger:

$$\int_{-1}^{3}(x^2 - 2x + 1)\,dx \quad \text{or} \quad \int_{0}^{4}(x^2 - 2x + 1)\,dx.$$

(iii) Calculate the values of the two integrals. Was your answer to (ii) correct?

13 (i) Sketch the curve with equation $y = x^3 - 6x^2 + 11x - 6$ for $0 \leqslant x \leqslant 4$.

(ii) Shade the regions with areas given by

(a) $\int_{1}^{2}(x^3 - 6x^2 + 11x - 6)\,dx$

(b) $\int_{3}^{4}(x^3 - 6x^2 + 11x - 6)\,dx.$

(iii) Find the values of these two areas.

(iv) Find the value of $\int_{1}^{1.5}(x^3 - 6x^2 + 11x - 6)\,dx.$

What does this, taken together with one of your answers to (iii), indicate to you about the position of the maximum point between $x = 1$ and $x = 2$?

14 (i) Differentiate $y = -x^2 + 2x + 3$.

(ii) Find the maximum value of y.

A gardener is considering a new design for his garden. He has a rectangular lawn measuring 5 m by 3 m, and wants to dig up part of it to include a flower bed. He draws a plan of the lawn and flower bed on graph paper, taking the bottom and left-hand edges as the axes, and chooses the scale so that 1 unit along each axis represents 1 metre on the ground.

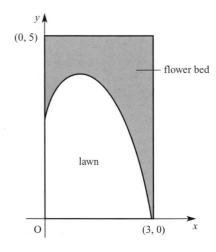

(iii) The equation of the curved edge of the flower bed is

$$y = -x^2 + 2x + 3.$$

Calculate the area of the flower bed.

[MEI]

15 The area under a velocity–time graph is the distance travelled. The graph below shows the relationship $v = t^2$ for the first 3 seconds of motion for a body moving from rest.

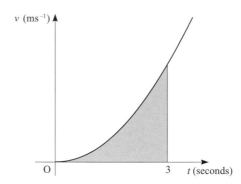

(i) Find the shaded area, and hence the distance travelled (in metres), during the first 3 seconds of motion.

(ii) Did the body travel further in the third second than it did in the first 2 seconds together?

16 The students in a university mathematics department have decided that their department building is an ugly concrete block. They have commissioned one of their number to paint a mural. Her design is shown in the diagram, where one unit on either axis represents 1 m. She wishes to estimate how much paint to buy. Given that one can of paint will cover $5\,m^2$, advise her on how many cans of each colour to buy.

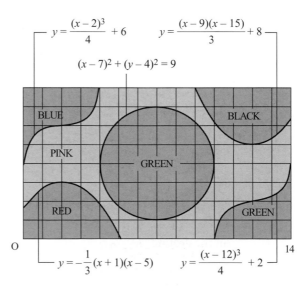

$y = \dfrac{(x-2)^3}{4} + 6$ $y = \dfrac{(x-9)(x-15)}{3} + 8$

$(x-7)^2 + (y-4)^2 = 9$

BLUE   BLACK

PINK   GREEN

RED   GREEN

$y = -\dfrac{1}{3}(x+1)(x-5)$ $y = \dfrac{(x-12)^3}{4} + 2$

Areas below the *x* axis

When a graph goes below the *x* axis, the corresponding *y* value is negative and so the value of *y* δ*x* is negative (see figure 9.14). So when an integral turns out to be negative you know that the area is below the *x* axis.

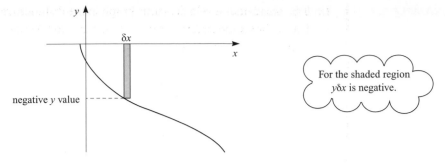

Figure 9.14

EXAMPLE 9.7

Find the area of the region bounded by the curve with equation $y = x^2 - 4x$, the lines $x = 1$ and $x = 2$, and the x axis.

SOLUTION

The region in question is shaded in figure 9.15.

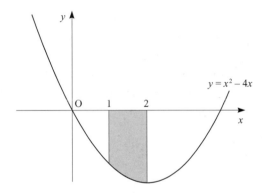

Figure 9.15

The shaded area is

$$I = \int_1^2 (x^2 - 4x)\,dx$$

$$= \left[\frac{x^3}{3} - 2x^2\right]_1^2$$

$$= \left(\frac{8}{3} - 8\right) - \left(\frac{1}{3} - 2\right)$$

$$= -\frac{11}{3}.$$

Therefore the shaded area is $\frac{11}{3}$ square units, and it is below the x axis.

EXAMPLE 9.8

Find the area between the curve and the x axis for the function $y = x^2 + 3x$ between $x = -1$ and $x = 2$.

SOLUTION

The first step is to draw a sketch of the function to see whether the curve goes below the x axis (see figure 9.16).

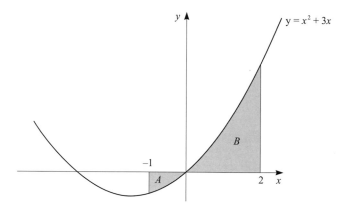

Figure 9.16

This shows that the y values are positive for $0 < x < 2$ and negative for $-1 < x < 0$. You therefore need to calculate the area in two parts.

$$\text{Area } A = \int_{-1}^{0} (x^2 + 3x)\,dx$$

$$= \left[\frac{x^3}{3} + \frac{3x^2}{2} \right]_{-1}^{0}$$

$$= 0 - \left(-\frac{1}{3} + \frac{3}{2} \right)$$

$$= -\frac{7}{6}.$$

$$\text{Area } B = \int_{0}^{2} (x^2 + 3x)\,dx$$

$$= \left[\frac{x^3}{3} + \frac{3x^2}{2} \right]_{0}^{2}$$

$$= \left(\frac{8}{3} + 6 \right) - 0$$

$$= \frac{26}{3}.$$

$$\text{Total area} = \frac{26}{3} + \frac{7}{6}$$

$$= \frac{59}{6} \text{ square units.}$$

1 Sketch each of these curves and find the area between the curve and the x axis between the given bounds.

(i) $y = x^3$ between $x = -3$ and $x = 0$.

(ii) $y = x^2 - 4$ between $x = -1$ and $x = 2$.

(iii) $y = x^5 - 2$ between $x = -1$ and $x = 0$.

(iv) $y = 3x^2 - 4x$ between $x = 0$ and $x = 1$.

(v) $y = x^4 - x^2$ between $x = -1$ and $x = 1$.

(vi) $y = 4x^3 - 3x^2$ between $x = -1$ and $x = 0.5$.

(vii) $y = x^5 - x^3$ between $x = -1$ and $x = 1$.

(viii) $y = x^2 - x - 2$ between $x = -2$ and $x = 3$.

(ix) $y = x^3 + x^2 - 2x$ between $x = -3$ and $x = 2$.

(x) $y = x^3 + x^2$ between $x = -2$ and $x = 2$.

2 The diagram shows a sketch of part of the curve with equation

$$y = 5x^4 - x^5.$$

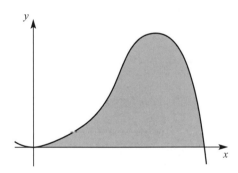

(i) Find $\dfrac{dy}{dx}$.

Calculate the co-ordinates of the stationary points.

(ii) Calculate the area of the shaded region enclosed by the curve and the x axis.

(iii) Evaluate $\int_0^6 x^4(5 - x)\,dx$ and comment on your result.

[MEI]

The area between two curves

EXAMPLE 9.9

Find the area enclosed by the line $y = x + 1$ and the curve $y = x^2 - 2x + 1$.

SOLUTION

First draw a sketch showing where these graphs intersect (see figure 9.17).

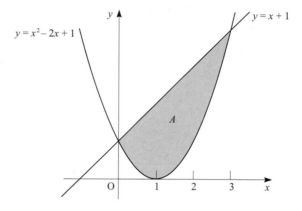

Figure 9.17

When they intersect

$$x^2 - 2x + 1 = x + 1$$
$$\Rightarrow \quad x^2 - 3x = 0$$
$$\Rightarrow \quad x(x - 3) = 0$$
$$\Rightarrow \quad x = 0 \text{ or } 3.$$

The shaded area can now be found in one of two ways.

Method 1

Area A can be treated as the difference between the two areas, B and C, shown in figure 9.18.

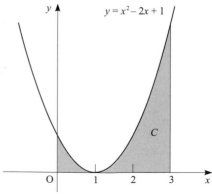

Figure 9.18

$A = B - C$

$= \int_0^3 (x+1)\,dx - \int_0^3 (x^2 - 2x + 1)\,dx$

$= \left[\dfrac{x^2}{2} + x\right]_0^3 - \left[\dfrac{x^3}{3} - x^2 + x\right]_0^3$

$= \left[\left(\dfrac{9}{2} + 3\right) - 0\right] - \left[\left(\dfrac{27}{3} - 9 + 3\right) - 0\right]$

$= \dfrac{9}{2}$ square units.

Method 2

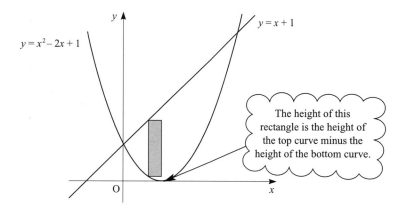

$y = x^2 - 2x + 1$

$y = x + 1$

The height of this rectangle is the height of the top curve minus the height of the bottom curve.

Figure 9.19

$A = \int_0^3 \{\text{top curve} - \text{bottom curve}\}\,dx$

$= \int_0^3 \Big((x+1) - (x^2 - 2x + 1)\Big)\,dx$

$= \int_0^3 (3x - x^2)\,dx$

$= \left[\dfrac{3x^2}{2} - \dfrac{x^3}{3}\right]_0^3$

$= \left[\dfrac{27}{2} - 9\right] - [0]$

$= \dfrac{9}{2}$ square units.

1 The diagram below shows the curve $y = x^2$ and the line $y = 9$. The enclosed region has been shaded.

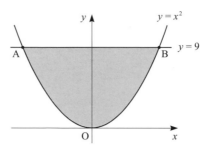

(i) Find the two points of intersection (labelled A and B).
(ii) Using integration, show that the area of the shaded region is 36 square units.

2 (i) Sketch the curves with equations $y = x^2 + 3$ and $y = 5 - x^2$ on the same axes, and shade the enclosed region.
(ii) Find the co-ordinates of the points of intersection of the curves.
(iii) Find the area of the shaded region.

3 (i) Sketch the curve $y = x^3$ and the line $y = 4x$ on the same axes.
(ii) Find the co-ordinates of the points of intersection of the curve $y = x^3$ and the line $y = 4x$.
(iii) Find the total area of the region bounded by $y = x^3$ and $y = 4x$.

4 (i) Sketch the curves with equations $y = x^2$ and $y = 4x - x^2$.
(ii) Find the co-ordinates of the points of intersection of the curves.
(iii) Find the area of the region enclosed by the curves.

5 (i) Sketch the curves $y = x^2$ and $y = 8 - x^2$ and the line $y = 4$ on the same axes.
(ii) Find the area of the region enclosed by the line $y = 4$ and the curve $y = x^2$.
(iii) Find the area of the region enclosed by the line $y = 4$ and the curve $y = 8 - x^2$.
(iv) Find the area enclosed by the curves $y = x^2$ and $y = 8 - x^2$.

6 (i) Sketch the curve $y = x^2 - 6x$ and the line $y = -5$.
(ii) Find the co-ordinates of the points of intersection of the line and the curve.
(iii) Find the area of the region enclosed by the line and the curve.

7 (i) Sketch the curve $y = x(4 - x)$ and the line $y = 2x - 3$.
(ii) Find the co-ordinates of the points of intersection of the line and the curve.
(iii) Find the area of the region enclosed by the line and the curve.

8 Find the area of the region enclosed by the curves with equations $y = x^2 - 16$ and $y = 4x - x^2$.

9 Find the area of the region enclosed by the curves with equations $y = -x^2 - 1$ and $y = -2x^2$.

10 **(i)** Sketch the curve with equation $y = x^3 + 1$ and the line $y = 4x + 1$.

(ii) Find the areas of the two regions enclosed by the line and the curve.

11 **(i)** On the same graph, sketch the line with equation $y = x + 1$ and the curve with equation $y = 5x - x^2 + 6$. Values of x should be taken from $x = -2$ to $x = +8$. Shade the region between the line and the curve.

(ii) Calculate the points of intersection of the line $y = x + 1$ and the curve $y = 5x - x^2 + 6$.

(iii) Use integration to calculate the area of the region which you have shaded in (i).

[MEI]

12 The diagram shows the curve with equation

$$y = x^2(3 - 2x - x^2).$$

P and Q are points on the curve with co-ordinates $(-2, 12)$ and $(1, 0)$ respectively.

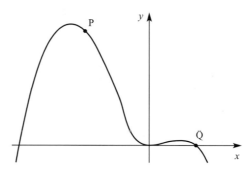

(i) Find $\dfrac{dy}{dx}$.

(ii) Find the equation of the line PQ.

(iii) Prove that the line PQ is a tangent to the curve at both P and Q.

(iv) Find the area of the region bounded by the line PQ and that part of the curve for which $-2 \leqslant x \leqslant 1$.

[MEI]

13 A shelf support is made of wood, with its cross-section in the shape shown. The top and bottom edges of the support are horizontal.

The shape of the curved edge of the shelf support is modelled by the equation

$$8y = (2x - 3)^3 \quad \text{for} \quad -1 \leqslant y \leqslant 1.$$

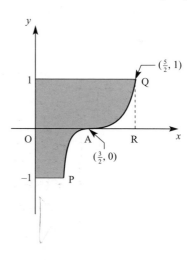

(i) Find the co-ordinates of the point P.

(ii) Using Pascal's triangle, or otherwise, write down the expansion of $(2x - 3)^3$.

(iii) Write down the integral which should be calculated in order to find the area AQR between the curve and the x axis.

(iv) Carry out the integration to find this area.

(v) Hence or otherwise calculate the area of cross-section of the self support.

[MEI]

14 The diagram shows the graph of $y = 4x - x^3$.
The point A has co-ordinates $(2, 0)$.

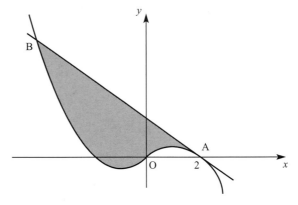

(i) Find $\frac{dy}{dx}$.
Then find the equation of the tangent to the curve at A.

(ii) The tangent at A meets the curve again at the point B.
Show that the x co-ordinate of B satisfies the equation

$$x^3 - 12x + 16 = 0.$$

Find the co-ordinates of B.

(iii) Calculate the area of the shaded region between the straight line AB and the curve.

[MEI]

The area between a curve and the *y* axis

So far you have calculated areas between curves and the x axis. You can also use integration to calculate the area between a curve and the y axis. In such cases, the integral involves dy and not dx. It is therefore necessary to write x in terms of y wherever it appears. The integration is then said to be carried out *with respect to y* instead of x.

EXAMPLE 9.10

Find the area between the curve $y = x - 1$ and the y axis between $y = 0$ and $y = 4$.

SOLUTION

Instead of strips of width δx and height y, you now sum strips of width δy and length x (see figure 9.20).

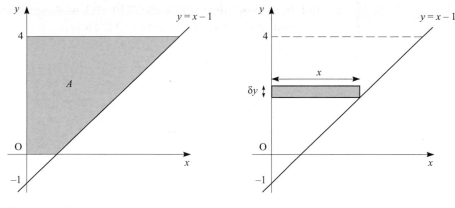

Figure 9.20

You write

$$A = \lim_{\delta y \to 0} \sum_{\substack{\text{over all} \\ \text{rectangles}}} x\,\delta y$$

> To integrate x with respect to y, write x in terms of y. For this graph $y = x - 1$ so $x = y + 1$.

$$= \int_0^4 x\,dy$$

$$= \int_0^4 (y + 1)\,dy$$

$$= \left[\frac{y^2}{2} + y\right]_0^4$$

$$= 12 \text{ square units.}$$

EXAMPLE 9.11

Find the area between the curve $y = \sqrt{x}$ and the y axis between $y = 0$ and $y = 3$.

SOLUTION

$$A = \int_0^3 x\,dy$$

$$= \int_0^3 y^2\,dy$$

> Since $y = \sqrt{x}$, $x = y^2$

$$= \left[\frac{y^3}{3}\right]_0^3$$

$$= 9 \text{ square units.}$$

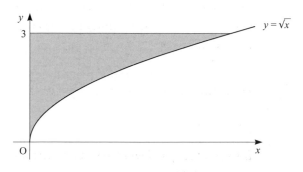

Figure 9.21

1 Find the area of the region bounded by each of these curves, the y axis and the lines $y = a$ and $y = b$.

(i) $y = 3x + 1$, $a = 1$, $b = 7$.

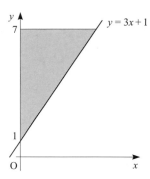

(ii) $y = \sqrt{x - 2}$, $a = 0$, $b = 2$.

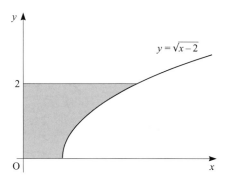

(iii) $y = \sqrt[3]{x}$, $a = 0$, $b = 2$.

(iv) $y = \sqrt{x} - 1$, $a = 0$, $b = 2$.

(v) $y = \sqrt[4]{x}$, $a = 1$, $b = 2$.

(vi) $y = \sqrt[3]{x} - 2$, $a = -1$, $b = 1$.

[MEI]

Numerical integration

There are times when you need to find the area under a graph but cannot do this by the integration methods you have met so far in this chapter.

- The function may be one that cannot be integrated algebraically. (There are many such functions.)

- The function may be one that can be integrated algebraically but which requires a technique with which you are unfamiliar.

- It may be that you do not know the function in algebraic form, but just have a set of points (perhaps derived from an experiment).

In these circumstances you can always find an approximate answer using a numerical method, but you must:

(i) have a clear picture in your mind of the graph of the function, and how your method estimates the area beneath it

(ii) understand that a numerical answer without any estimate of its accuracy, or error bounds, is valueless.

The trapezium rule

In this chapter just one numerical method of integration is introduced, namely the *trapezium rule* (another possible method is the subject of an investigation at the end of the chapter). As an illustration of the rule, it is used to find the area under the curve $y = \sqrt{5x - x^2}$ for values of x between 0 and 4.

It is in fact possible to integrate this function algebraically, but not using the techniques that you have met so far.

> *Note*
>
> You should not use a numerical method when an algebraic (sometimes called analytic) technique is available to you. Numerical methods should be used only when other methods fail.

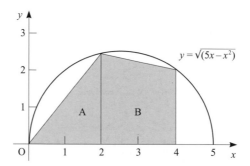

Figure 9.22

Figure 9.22 shows the area approximated by two trapezia of equal width.

Remember the formula for the area of a trapezium, Area $= \frac{1}{2}h(a + b)$, where a and b are the lengths of the parallel sides and h the distance between them.

In the cases of the trapezia A and B, the parallel sides are vertical. The left-hand side of trapezium A has zero height, and so the trapezium is also a triangle.

When $\quad x = 0 \quad \Rightarrow \quad y = \sqrt{0} = 0$

when $\quad x = 2 \quad \Rightarrow \quad y = \sqrt{6} = 2.4495$ (to 4 d.p.)

when $\quad x = 4, \quad \Rightarrow \quad y = \sqrt{4} = 2.$

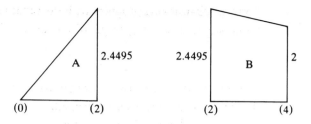

Figure 9.23

The area of trapezium A = $\frac{1}{2} \times 2 \times (0 + 2.4495)$ = 2.4495

The area of trapezium B = $\frac{1}{2} \times 2 \times (2.4495 + 2)$ = 4.4495

$$\text{\textit{Total}} \quad \underline{6.8990}$$

For greater accuracy you can use four trapezia, P, Q, R and S, each of width 1 unit as in figure 9.24. The area is estimated in just the same way.

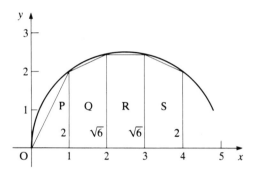

Figure 9.24

Trapezium P: $\frac{1}{2} \times 1 \times (0 + 2)$ = 1.0000

Trapezium Q : $\frac{1}{2} \times 1 \times (2 + 2.4495)$ = 2.2247

Trapezium R : $\frac{1}{2} \times 1 \times (2.4495 + 2.4495)$ = 2.4495

Trapezium S: $\frac{1}{2} \times 1 \times (2.4495 + 2)$ = 2.2247

$$\text{\textit{Total}} \quad \underline{7.8990}$$

These figures are given to 4 decimal places but the calculation has been done to more places on a calculator.

Accuracy

In this example, the first two estimates are 6.8989… and 7.8989… . You can see from figure 9.24 that the trapezia all lie underneath the curve, and so in this case the trapezium rule estimate of 7.8989… must be too small. You cannot, however, say by how much. To find that out you will need to take progressively more strips and see how the estimate homes in. Using 8 strips gives an estimate of 8.2407…, and 16 strips gives 8.3578… . The first figure, 8, looks reasonably certain but it is still not clear whether the second is 3, 4 or even 5. You need to take even more strips to be able to decide. In this example, the convergence is unusually slow because of the high curvature of the curve.

Use a graph-drawing program with the capability to calculate areas using trapezia. Calculate the area using progressively more strips and observe the convergence.

❓ If you have had your wits about you, you may have found a method of finding this area without using calculus at all.
How can this be done? How close is the 16-strip estimate?

The procedure

In the previous example, the answer of 7.8990 from four strips came from adding the areas of the four trapezia P, Q, R and S:

$$\tfrac{1}{2} \times 1 \times (0 + 2) + \tfrac{1}{2} \times 1 \times (2 + 2.4495) + \tfrac{1}{2} \times 1 \times (2.4495 + 2.4495) + \tfrac{1}{2} \times 1 \times (2.4495 + 2)$$

and this can be written as

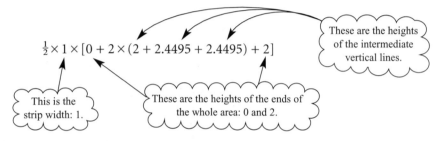

$$\tfrac{1}{2} \times 1 \times [0 + 2 \times (2 + 2.4495 + 2.4495) + 2]$$

These are the heights of the intermediate vertical lines.

This is the strip width: 1.

These are the heights of the ends of the whole area: 0 and 2.

This is often stated in words as Area $\approx \tfrac{1}{2} \times$ strip width $\times$ [ends + twice middles] or in symbols, for n strips of width h

$$A \approx \tfrac{1}{2} \times h \times [y_0 + y_n + 2(y_1 + y_2 + \ldots + y_{n-1})].$$

This is called the *trapezium rule* for width h (see figure 9.25).

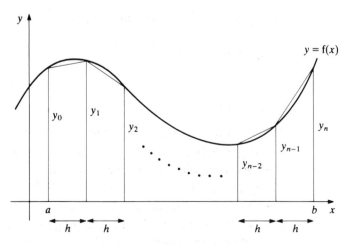

Figure 9.25

? Look at the three graphs in figure 9.26, and in each case state whether the trapezium rule would underestimate or overestimate the area, or whether you cannot tell.

(i)

(ii)

(iii)

Figure 9.26

 Some graphic calculators will work out the area under a curve. If you have such a calculator, use it to check your answers in the exercise.

1 Use the trapezium rule to estimate each of the areas shown.
Start with two strips, then four and then eight in each case.

State, with reasons, whether your final estimate is an overestimate or an underestimate, and to how many decimal places you believe it to be accurate.

(i) $y = \dfrac{3}{(x+1)}, x > -1$ **(ii)** $y = x + \dfrac{1}{x}$

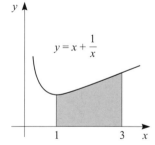

(iii) $y = \dfrac{1}{x^2}, x > 0$

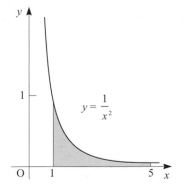

2 (i) Draw the graph of $y = \frac{1}{x}$ for values of x between 1 and 10.
Shade the region A bounded by the curve, the lines $x = 1$ and $x = 2$ and the x axis, and the region B bounded by the curve, the lines $x = 4$ and $x = 8$ and the x axis.

(ii) For each of the regions A and B, find estimates of the area using the trapezium rule with two, four and eight strips.

(iii) Which region has the greater area?

3 The speed v in ms^{-1} of a train is given at time t seconds in the following table.

t	0	10	20	30	40	50	60
v	0	5.0	6.7	8.2	9.5	10.6	11.6

The distance that the train has travelled is given by the area under the graph of the speed (vertical axis) against time (horizontal axis).

(i) Estimate the distance the train travels in this 1 minute period.

(ii) Give two reasons why your method cannot give a very accurate answer.

4 The definite integral $\int_0^1 \frac{1}{1+x^2} \, dx$ is known to equal $\frac{\pi}{4}$.

(i) Using the trapezium rule for four strips, find an approximation for π.

(ii) Repeat your calculation with 10 and 20 strips to obtain closer estimates.

(III) If you did not know the value of π, what value would you give it with confidence on the basis of your estimates in (i) and (ii)?

5 The table below gives the values of a function $f(x)$ for different values of x.

x	0	0.5	1.0	1.5	2.0	2.5	3.0
$f(x)$	1.000	1.225	1.732	2.345	3.000	3.674	4.359

(i) Apply the trapezium rule to the values in this table to obtain an approximation for $\int_0^3 f(x) dx$.

(ii) By considering the shape of the curve $y = f(x)$, explain whether the approximation calculated in (i) is likely to be an overestimate or an underestimate of the true area under the curve $y = f(x)$ between $x = 0$ and $x = 3$.

[MEI]

6 The graph of the function
$y = \sqrt{2 + x}$ is given in the
diagram.

The area of the shaded
region ABCD is to be found.

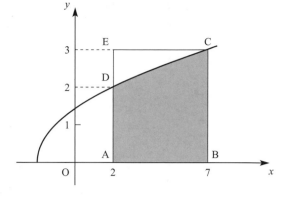

(i) Make a table of values for y, for integer values of x from $x = 2$ to $x = 7$,
giving each value of y correct to 4 decimal places.

(ii) Use the trapezium rule with five strips, each 1 unit wide, to calculate an
estimate for the area ABCD.
State, giving a reason, whether your estimate is too large or too small.

Another method is to consider the area ABCD as the area of the rectangle
ABCE minus the area of the region CDE.

(iii) Show that the area CDE is given by $\int_2^3 (y^2 - 4)\,dy$.
Calculate the exact value of this integral.

(iv) Find the exact value of the area ABCD.
Hence find, as a percentage, the relative error in using the trapezium rule.

[MEI]

7 (i) The table gives the values of the function
$(1 + x^2)^5$ for $x = 0, 0.2$ and 0.4.

Complete the table for $x = 0.1$ and 0.3.

Use the trapezium rule with four strips
to estimate the value of

$$\int_0^{0.4} (1 + x^2)^5\,dx.$$

x	$(1 + x^2)^5$
0	1.00000
0.1	
0.2	1.21665
0.3	
0.4	2.10034

(ii) Use the binomial theorem to expand $(1 + x^2)^5$ as a polynomial in
ascending powers of x.

The integral $\int_0^{0.4} (1 + 5x^2 + 10x^4)\,dx$ is to be used to estimate the integral
in (i).

Evaluate $\int_0^{0.4} (1 + 5x^2 + 10x^4)\,dx$.

(iii) The diagram overleaf shows a sketch of the graph of $y = (1 + x^2)^5$.
State whether the estimate in (i) is too high or too low and use the graph to
explain your answer.

State also whether the estimate in (ii) is too high or too low and explain
your answer.

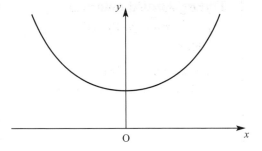

(iv) How could the methods for estimating $\int_0^{0.4} (1 + x^2)^5 dx$ used in (i) and (ii) be improved to give greater accuracy?

[MEI]

INVESTIGATIONS

Kopje

A new airport is being built in an African country. The site selected is a flat plain apart from a single *kopje*, a rock outcrop, which has to be removed. A contour map of the *kopje* is shown below, with contours in steps of 10 m above the surrounding plain.

Estimate the volume of rock and soil that has to be taken away. Your estimate should include bounds between which you are certain that the real answer lies.

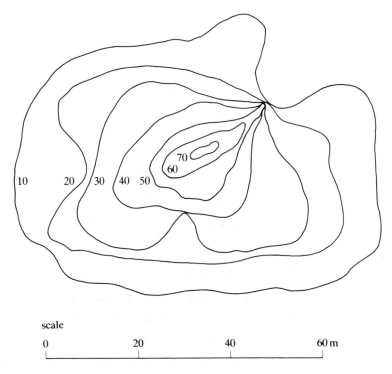

scale

| 0 | 20 | 40 | 60 m |

Figure 9.27

The mid-point rule

The trapezium rule is not the only numerical method for estimating the value of a definite integral. Another possible method is provided by the mid-point rule, in which the area under the curve is represented by a set of rectangular strips. The height of each rectangle is the same as the height of the curve in the middle of the strip. This is shown in the diagram below for

$$\int_0^4 \frac{1}{1+x^2}\,dx.$$

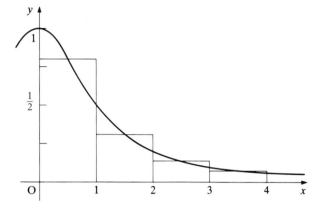

Figure 9.28

The accuracy of the estimates obtained using this method depends on the number of strips used, just as with the trapezium rule.

Use the mid-point rule with two strips, then four strips, then eight strips, and so on to estimate the value of

$$\int_0^4 \frac{1}{1+x^2}\,dx$$

to 2 decimal places.

Count the number of function evaluations $\left(\text{the number of times you needed to work out the value of } \frac{1}{1+x^2}\right)$ in order to find your answer.

Now use the trapezium rule to estimate the value of the same integral, using the same procedure with two, four and eight strips to ever-increasing accuracy.

How many function evaluations were required this time?
Which is the more efficient method?

1 $\dfrac{dy}{dx} = x^n \implies y = \dfrac{x^{n+1}}{n+1} + c$

2 $\displaystyle\int_a^b x^n \, dx = \left[\dfrac{x^{n+1}}{n+1} \right]_a^b = \dfrac{b^{n+1} - a^{n+1}}{n+1}$

3 Area A $= \displaystyle\int_a^b y \, dx$

$= \displaystyle\int_a^b f(x) \, dx$

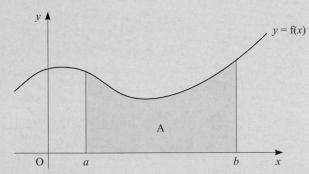

4 Area B $= \displaystyle\int_a^b (f(x) - g(x)) \, dx$

5 Area C $= \displaystyle\int_p^q x \, dy$

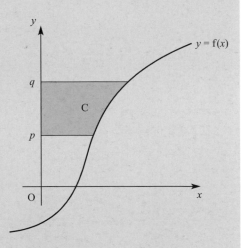

6 You can use the trapezium rule, with n strips of width h, to find an approximate value for a definite integral as

$$A = \dfrac{h}{2} \left[y_0 + 2(y_1 + y_2 + \ldots + y_{n-1}) + y_n \right].$$

10 Trigonometry

**I must go down to the seas again, to the lonely sea and the sky,
And all I ask is a tall ship and a star to steer her by.**

John Masefield

There are many situations in which you can measure *some* sides or angles of a triangle, but it is either impossible or impractical to measure them all.

❷ What information would you need to answer each of the questions below, and how would you obtain it?

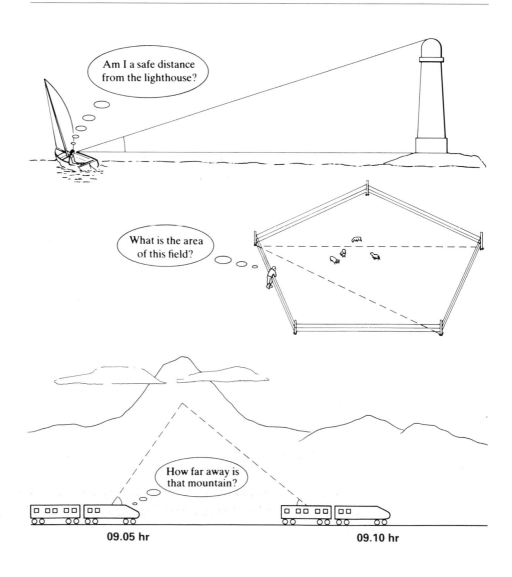

The questions on the previous page all involve the angles and the lengths of sides of triangles. The study of triangles is called trigonometry. This chapter starts with a review of some of the basic terms and ideas.

Angles of elevation and depression

The angle of elevation is the angle between the horizontal and a direction above the horizontal (see figure 10.1). The angle of depression is the angle between the horizontal and a direction below the horizontal (see figure 10.2).

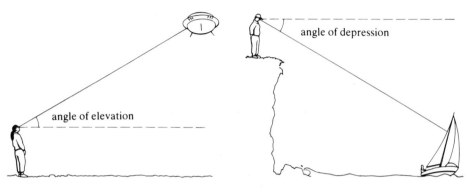

Figure 10.1　　　　　　　　**Figure 10.2**

Bearing

The bearing (or compass bearing) is the direction measured as an angle from north, clockwise (see figure 10.3).

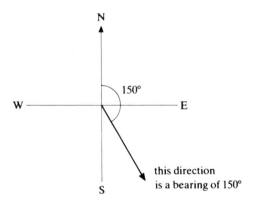

Figure 10.3

Trigonometrical functions

The simplest definitions of the trigonometrical functions are given in terms of the ratios of the sides of a right-angled triangle, for values of the angle θ between $0°$ and $90°$.

Figure 10.4

In figure 10.4

$$\sin \theta = \frac{\text{opposite}}{\text{hypotenuse}} \qquad \cos \theta = \frac{\text{adjacent}}{\text{hypotenuse}} \qquad \tan \theta = \frac{\text{opposite}}{\text{adjacent}}.$$

Sin is an abbreviation of sine, cos of cosine and tan of tangent. You will see from the triangle in figure 10.4 that

$$\sin \theta = \cos (90° - \theta) \text{ and } \cos \theta = \sin (90° - \theta).$$

Special cases

Certain angles occur frequently in mathematics and you will find it helpful to know the value of their trigonometrical functions.

(i) *The angles 30° and 60°*

In figure 10.5, triangle ABC is an equilateral triangle with side 2 units, and AD is a line of symmetry.

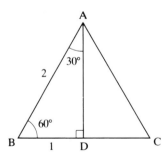

Figure 10.5

Using Pythagoras' theorem

$$AD^2 + 1^2 = 2^2, \implies AD = \sqrt{3}.$$

From triangle ABD,

$$\sin 60° = \frac{\sqrt{3}}{2}; \qquad \cos 60° = \frac{1}{2}; \qquad \tan 60° = \sqrt{3};$$

$$\sin 30° = \frac{1}{2}; \qquad \cos 30° = \frac{\sqrt{3}}{2}; \qquad \tan 30° = \frac{1}{\sqrt{3}}.$$

EXAMPLE 10.1

Without using a calculator, find the value of cos 60°sin 30° + cos²30°.
(Note that cos²30° means (cos 30°)².)

SOLUTION

$$\cos 60°\sin 30° + \cos^2 30° = \frac{1}{2} \times \frac{1}{2} + \left(\frac{\sqrt{3}}{2}\right)^2$$

$$= \frac{1}{4} + \frac{3}{4}$$

$$= 1.$$

(ii) *The angle 45°*

In figure 10.6, triangle PQR is a right-angled isosceles triangle with equal sides of length 1 unit.

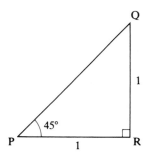

Figure 10.6

Using Pythagoras' theorem $PQ = \sqrt{2}$.

This gives

$$\sin 45° = \frac{1}{\sqrt{2}}; \qquad \cos 45° = \frac{1}{\sqrt{2}}; \qquad \tan 45° = 1.$$

(iii) *The angles 0° and 90°*

Although you cannot have an angle of 0° in a triangle (because one side would be lying on top of another), you can still imagine what it might look like. In figure 10.7, the hypotenuse has length 1 unit and the angle at X is very small.

Figure 10.7

If you imagine the angle at X becoming smaller and smaller until it is zero, you can deduce that

$$\sin 0° = \frac{0}{1} = 0; \qquad \cos 0° = \frac{1}{1} = 1; \qquad \tan 0° = \frac{0}{1} = 0.$$

If the angle at X is 0°, then the angle at Z is 90°, and so you can also deduce that

$$\sin 90° = \frac{1}{1} = 1; \qquad \cos 90° = \frac{0}{1} = 0.$$

However when you come to find tan 90°, there is a problem. The triangle suggests this has value $\frac{1}{0}$, but you cannot divide by zero.

If you look at the triangle XYZ, you will see that what we actually did was to draw it with angle X not zero but just very small, and to argue:

'We can see from this what will happen if the angle becomes smaller and smaller so that it is effectively zero.'

? Compare this argument with the ideas about limits which you met in Chapters 8 and 9 on differentiation and integration.

In this case we are looking at the limits of the values of sin θ, cos θ and tan θ as the angle θ approaches zero. The same approach can be used to look again at the problem of tan 90°.

If the angle X is not quite zero, then the side ZY is also not quite zero, and tan Z is 1 (XY is almost 1) divided by a very small number and so is large. The smaller the angle X, the smaller the side ZY and so the larger the value of tan Z. We conclude that in the limit when angle X becomes zero and angle Z becomes 90°, tan Z is infinitely large, and so we say

Read these arrows as 'tends to'.

as $Z \rightarrow 90°$ tan $Z \rightarrow \infty$ (infinity).

You can see this happening in the table of values below.

Z	tan Z
80°	5.67
89°	57.29
89.9°	572.96
89.99°	5729.6
89.999°	57296

When Z actually equals 90°, you say that tan Z is *undefined*.

Positive and negative angles

Unless given in the form of bearings, angles are measured from the x axis (see figure 10.8). Anti-clockwise is taken to be positive and clockwise to be negative.

an angle of $+135°$

an angle of $-30°$

Figure 10.8

Trigonometrical functions for angles of any size

Is it possible to extend the use of the trigonometrical functions to angles greater than 90°, like sin 120°, cos 275° or tan 692°? The answer is yes – provided you change the definition of sine, cosine and tangent to one that does not require the angle to be in a right-angled triangle. It is not difficult to extend the definitions, as follows.

First look at the right-angled triangle in figure 10.9 which has hypotenuse of unit length.

Figure 10.9

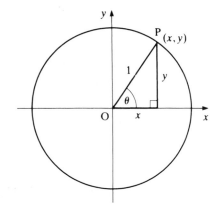

Figure 10.10

This gives rise to the definitions:

$$\sin \theta = \frac{y}{1} = y; \qquad \cos \theta = \frac{x}{1} = x; \qquad \tan \theta = \frac{y}{x}.$$

Now think of the angle θ being situated at the origin, as in figure 10.10, and allow θ to take any value. The vertex marked P has co-ordinates (x, y) and can now be anywhere on the unit circle.

You can now see that the definitions above can be applied to *any* angle θ, whether it is positive or negative, and whether it is less than or greater than 90°

$$\sin\theta = y, \qquad \cos\theta = x, \qquad \tan\theta = \frac{y}{x}.$$

For some angles, x or y (or both) will take a negative value, so the sign of $\sin\theta$, $\cos\theta$ and $\tan\theta$ will vary accordingly.

ACTIVITY 10.1 Draw x and y axes. For each of the four quadrants formed, work out the sign of $\sin\theta$, $\cos\theta$ and $\tan\theta$, from the definitions above.

Identities involving sin θ, cos θ and tan θ

Since $\tan\theta = \frac{y}{x}$ and $y = \sin\theta$ and $x = \cos\theta$ it follows that

$$\tan\theta = \frac{\sin\theta}{\cos\theta}.$$

It would be more accurate here to use the identity sign, $\equiv$, since the relationship is true for all values of θ

$$\tan\theta \equiv \frac{\sin\theta}{\cos\theta}.$$

An *identity* is different from an equation since an equation is only true for certain values of the variable, called the *solution* of the equation. For example, $\tan\theta = 1$ is an equation: it is true when $\theta = 45°$ or $225°$, but not when it takes any other value in the range $0° \leqslant \theta \leqslant 360°$.

By contrast, an *identity* is true for all values of the variable, for example

$$\tan 30° = \frac{\sin 30°}{\cos 30°}, \qquad \tan 72° = \frac{\sin 72°}{\cos 72°}, \qquad \tan(-339°) = \frac{\sin(-339°)}{\cos(-339°)},$$

and so on for all values of the angle.

In this book, as in mathematics generally, we often use an equals sign where it would be more correct to use an identity sign. The identity sign is kept for situations where we really want to emphasise that the relationship is an identity and not an equation.

Another useful identity can be found by applying Pythagoras' theorem to any point $P(x, y)$ on the unit circle

$$y^2 + x^2 \equiv OP^2$$

$$(\sin\theta)^2 + (\cos\theta)^2 \equiv 1.$$

This is written as

$$\sin^2\theta + \cos^2\theta \equiv 1.$$

The sine and cosine graphs

In figure 10.11, angles have been drawn at intervals of 30° in the unit circle, and the resulting *y* co-ordinates plotted relative to the axes on the right. They have been joined with a continuous curve to give the graph of $\sin \theta$ for $0° \leqslant \theta \leqslant 360°$.

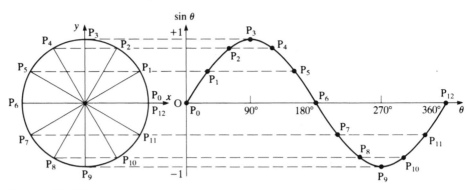

Figure 10.11

The angle 390° gives the same point P_1 on the circle as the angle 30°, the angle 420° gives point P_2 and so on. You can see that for angles from 360° to 720° the sine wave will simply repeat itself, as shown in figure 10.12. This is true also for angles from 720° to 1080° and so on.

Since the curve repeats itself every 360° the sine function is described as *periodic*, with *period* 360°.

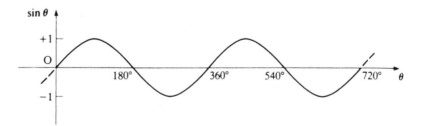

Figure 10.12

In a similar way you can transfer the *x* co-ordinates on to a set of axes to obtain the graph of $\cos \theta$. This is most easily illustrated if you first rotate the circle through 90° anticlockwise.

Figure 10.13 shows the circle in this new orientation, together with the resulting graph.

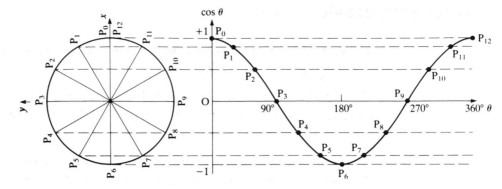

Figure 10.13

For angles in the interval $360° < \theta < 720°$, the cosine curve will repeat itself. You can see that the cosine function is also periodic with a period of 360°.

Notice that the graphs of $\sin \theta$ and $\cos \theta$ have exactly the same shape. The cosine graph can be obtained by translating the sine graph 90° to the left, as shown in figure 10.14.

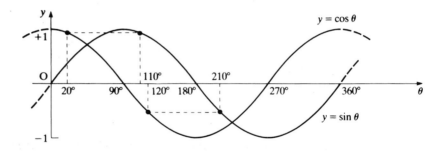

Figure 10.14

From the graphs it can be seen that, for example

$$\cos 20° = \sin 110°, \cos 90° = \sin 180°, \cos 120° = \sin 210°, \text{ etc.}$$

In general

$$\cos \theta \equiv \sin (\theta + 90°).$$

?　**1** What do the graphs of $\sin \theta$ and $\cos \theta$ look like for negative angles?

2 Draw the curve of $\sin \theta$ for $0° \leqslant \theta \leqslant 90°$.

Using only reflections, rotations and translations of this curve, how can you generate the curves of $\sin \theta$ and $\cos \theta$ for $0° \leqslant \theta \leqslant 360°$?

The tangent graph

The value of tan θ can be worked out from the definition tan $\theta = \frac{y}{x}$ or by using tan $\theta = \frac{\sin\theta}{\cos\theta}$.

You have already seen that tan θ is undefined for $\theta = 90°$. This is also the case for all other values of θ for which cos $\theta = 0$, namely 270°, 450°, …, and −90°, −270°, …

The graph of tan θ is shown in figure 10.15. The dotted lines $\theta = \pm 90°$ and $\theta = 270°$ are *asymptotes*. They are not actually part of the curve. Its branches get closer and closer to them without ever quite reaching them.

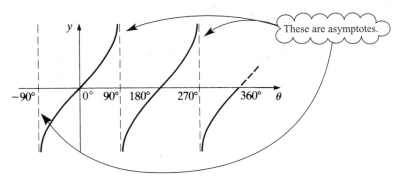

These are asymptotes.

Figure 10.15

> *Note*
>
> The graph of tan θ is periodic, like those for sin θ and cos θ, but in this case the period is 180°. Again, the curve for $0 \leqslant \theta < 90°$ can be used to generate the rest of the curve using rotations and translations.

ACTIVITY 10.2 Draw the graphs of $y = \sin\theta$, $y = \cos\theta$, and $y = \tan\theta$ for values of θ between −90° and 450°.

These graphs are very important. Keep them handy because they will be useful for solving trigonometrical equations.

> *Note*
>
> Some people use this diagram to help them remember when sin, cos and tan are positive, and when they are negative. A means all positive in this quadrant, S means sin positive, cos and tan negative, etc.

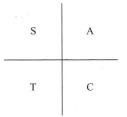

Figure 10.16

Solution of equations using graphs of trigonometrical functions

Suppose that you want to solve the equation cos θ = 0.5.

You press the calculator keys for arccos 0.5 (or cos⁻¹ 0.5 or invcos 0.5), and the answer comes up as 60°.

However, by looking at the graph of $y = \cos \theta$ (your own or figure 10.17) you can see that there are in fact infinitely many roots to this equation.

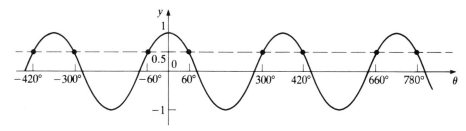

Figure 10.17

A calculator always gives the value of the solution in the range

$$0° \leqslant \theta \leqslant 180° \qquad (\cos)$$
$$-90° \leqslant \theta \leqslant 90° \qquad (\sin)$$
$$-90° < \theta < 90° \qquad (\tan).$$

e The solution in this range is called the *principal value* of the solution.

Other roots can be found by looking at the appropriate graph. Thus the roots for cos θ = 0.5 are seen (see figure 10.17) to be:

$$\theta = \dots, -420°, -300°, -60°, 60°, 300°, 420°, 660°, 780°, \dots .$$

EXAMPLE 10.2

Find values of θ in the interval −360° ⩽ θ ⩽ 360° for which sin θ = 0.5.

SOLUTION

sin θ = 0.5 ⟹ θ = 30° (calculator). Figure 10.18 shows the graph of sin θ.

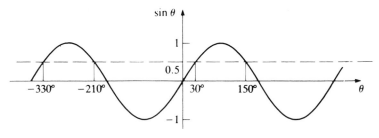

Figure 10.18

The values of θ for which sin θ = 0.5 are −330°, −210°, 30°, 150°.

EXAMPLE 10.3

Solve the equation $3\tan\theta = -1$ for $-180° \leq \theta \leq 180°$.

SOLUTION

$3\tan\theta = -1$

$\Rightarrow \quad \tan\theta = -\frac{1}{3}$

$\Rightarrow \quad \theta = -18.4°$ to 1 d.p. (calculator).

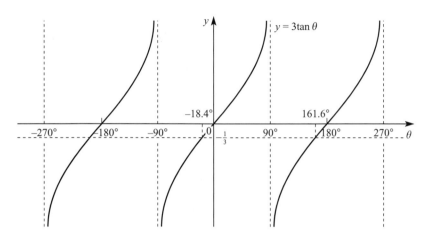

Figure 10.19

From figure 10.19, the other answer in the range is

$\theta = -18.4° + 180°$

$= 161.6°$

The values of θ are $-18.4°$ or $161.6°$ to 1 d.p.

❓ How can you find further roots of the equation $3\tan\theta = -1$, outside the range $-180° \leq \theta \leq 180°$?

EXAMPLE 10.4

Find values of θ in the interval $0° \leqslant \theta \leqslant 360°$ for which $\tan^2 \theta - \tan \theta = 2$.

SOLUTION

First rearrange the equation.

$$\tan^2 \theta - \tan \theta = 2$$

$$\Rightarrow \tan^2 \theta - \tan \theta - 2 = 0$$

This is a quadratic equation like $x^2 - x - 2 = 0$.

$$\Rightarrow (\tan \theta - 2)(\tan \theta + 1) = 0$$

$$\Rightarrow \tan \theta = 2 \text{ or } \tan \theta = -1.$$

$\tan \theta = 2 \Rightarrow \quad \theta = 63.4°$ (calculator)

$\qquad\qquad$ or $\theta = 63.4° + 180°$ (see figure 10.20)

$\qquad\qquad\qquad = 243.4°.$

$\tan \theta = -1 \Rightarrow \theta = -45°$ (calculator).

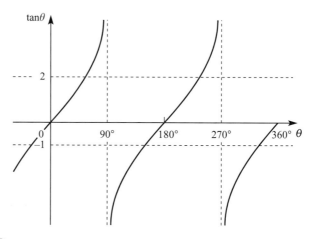

Figure 10.20

This is not in the range $0° \leqslant \theta \leqslant 360°$ so figure 10.20 is used to give

$$\theta = -45° + 180° = 135°$$

or $\qquad \theta = -45° + 360° = 315°.$

The values of θ are 63.4°, 135°, 243.4°, 315°.

| EXAMPLE 10.5 | Solve the equation $2\sin^2\theta = \cos\theta + 1$ for $0° \leqslant \theta \leqslant 360°$. |

SOLUTION

First use the identity $\sin^2\theta + \cos^2\theta = 1$ to obtain an equation containing only one trigonometrical function.

$$2\sin^2\theta = \cos\theta + 1$$

$$\Rightarrow \quad 2(1 - \cos^2\theta) = \cos\theta + 1$$

$$\Rightarrow \quad 2 - 2\cos^2\theta = \cos\theta + 1 \longleftarrow$$

$$\Rightarrow \quad 0 = 2\cos^2\theta + \cos\theta - 1$$

$$\Rightarrow \quad 0 = (2\cos\theta - 1)(\cos\theta + 1)$$

$$\Rightarrow \quad 2\cos\theta - 1 = 0 \text{ or } \cos\theta + 1 = 0$$

$$\Rightarrow \quad \cos\theta = \tfrac{1}{2} \text{ or } -1.$$

> This is a quadratic equation in $\cos\theta$. Rearrange it to equal zero and factorise it to solve the equation.

$\cos\theta = \tfrac{1}{2} \quad \Rightarrow \quad \theta = 60°$

or $\theta = 360° - 60° = 300°$ (see figure 10.21).

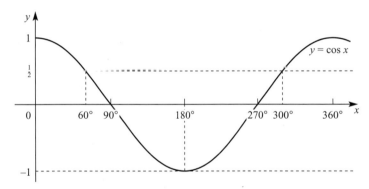

Figure 10.21

$\cos\theta = -1 \quad \Rightarrow \quad \theta = 180°$.

The values of θ are 60°, 180° or 300°.

| EXERCISE 10A | **1** In the triangle PQR, PQ = 17 cm, QR = 15 cm and PR = 8 cm. |

    (i) Show that the triangle is right-angled.

    (ii) Write down the values of $\sin Q$, $\cos Q$ and $\tan Q$, leaving your answers as fractions.

    (iii) Use your answers to part (ii) to show that

        (a) $\sin^2 Q + \cos^2 Q = 1$

        (b) $\tan Q = \dfrac{\sin Q}{\cos Q}$.

2 (i) Sketch the curve $y = \sin x$ for $0° \leqslant x \leqslant 360°$.

  (ii) Solve the equation $\sin x = 0.5$ for $0° \leqslant x \leqslant 360°$, and illustrate the two roots on your sketch.

  (iii) State the other roots for $\sin x = 0.5$, given that x is no longer restricted to values between $0°$ and $360°$.

  (iv) Write down, without using your calculator, the value of $\sin 330°$.

3 (i) Sketch the curve $y = \cos x$ for $-90° \leqslant x \leqslant 450°$.

  (ii) Solve the equation $\cos x = 0.6$ for $-90° \leqslant x \leqslant 450°$, and illustrate all the roots on your sketch.

  (iii) Sketch the curve $y = \sin x$ for $-90° \leqslant x \leqslant 450°$.

  (iv) Solve the equation $\sin x = 0.8$ for $-90° \leqslant x \leqslant 450°$, and illustrate all the roots on your sketch.

  (v) Explain why some of the roots of $\cos x = 0.6$ are the same as those for $\sin x = 0.8$, and why some are different.

4 Solve the following equations for $0° \leqslant x \leqslant 360°$.

  (i) $\tan x = 1$ **(ii)** $\cos x = 0.5$

  (iii) $\sin x = -\dfrac{\sqrt{3}}{2}$ **(iv)** $\tan x = -1$

  (v) $\cos x = -0.9$ **(vi)** $\cos x = 0.2$

  (vii) $\sin x = -0.25$ **(viii)** $\cos x = -1$

5 Write the following as fractions, or using square roots. You should not need your calculator.

  (i) $\sin 60°$ **(ii)** $\cos 45°$ **(iii)** $\tan 45°$

  (iv) $\sin 150°$ **(v)** $\cos 120°$ **(vi)** $\tan 180°$

  (vii) $\sin 390°$ **(viii)** $\cos (-30°)$ **(ix)** $\tan 315°$

6 Without using a calculator, show that:

  (i) $\sin 60°\cos 30° + \cos 60°\sin 30° = 1$

  (ii) $\sin^2 30° + \sin^2 45° = \sin^2 60°$

  (iii) $3\sin^2 30° = \cos^2 30°$.

7 In this question all the angles are in the interval $-180°$ to $180°$. Give all answers correct to 1 d.p.

  (i) Given that $\sin a < 0$ and $\cos a = 0.5$, find a.

  (ii) Given that $\tan \beta = 0.4463$ and $\cos \beta < 0$, find β.

  (iii) Given that $\sin \gamma = 0.8090$ and $\tan \gamma > 0$, find γ.

8 (i) Draw a sketch of the graph $y = \sin x$ and use it to demonstrate why $\sin x = \sin (180° - x)$.

  (ii) By referring to the graphs of $y = \cos x$ and $y = \tan x$, state whether the following are true or false.

  (a) $\cos x = \cos (180° - x)$ **(b)** $\cos x = -\cos (180° - x)$

  (c) $\tan x = \tan (180° - x)$ **(d)** $\tan x = -\tan (180° - x)$

9 (i) For what values of a are $\sin a$, $\cos a$ and $\tan a$ all positive?

(ii) Are there any values of a for which $\sin a$, $\cos a$ and $\tan a$ are all negative? Explain your answer.

(iii) Are there any values of a for which $\sin a$, $\cos a$ and $\tan a$ are all equal? Explain your answer.

10 Solve the following equations for $0° \leqslant x \leqslant 360°$

(i) $\sin x = 0.1$	**(ii)** $\cos x = 0.5$
(iii) $\tan x = -2$	**(iv)** $\sin x = -0.4$
(v) $\sin^2 x = 1 - \cos x$	**(vi)** $\sin^2 x = 1$
(vii) $1 - \cos^2 x = 2\sin x$	**(viii)** $\sin^2 x = 2\cos^2 x$
(ix) $2\sin^2 x = 3\cos x$	**(x)** $3\tan^2 x - 10\tan x + 3 = 0$

11 The diagram shows part of the curves $y = \cos x°$ and $y = \tan x°$ which intersect at the points A and B. Find the co-ordinates of A and B.

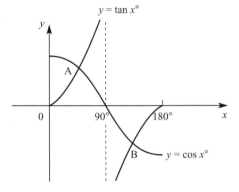

Triangles without right angles

Now that you have moved away from the simple trigonometrical definitions in terms of right-angled triangles, it is also time to look at other triangles, not just those with an angle of 90°.

There is a standard notation used for triangles. The vertices are labelled with capital letters, and the side opposite a vertex is labelled with the corresponding lower case letter, as in figure 10.22.

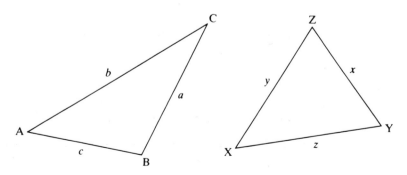

Figure 10.22

There are two rules which connect the values of the sides and angles of any triangle, the sine rule and the cosine rule.

The sine rule

For any triangle ABC: $\dfrac{a}{\sin A} = \dfrac{b}{\sin B} = \dfrac{c}{\sin C}$.

Proof

For the triangle ABC, CD is the perpendicular from C to AB (extended if necessary). There are two cases to consider, as shown in figure 10.23.

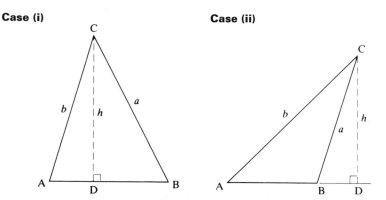

Case (i) **Case (ii)**

Figure 10.23

In $\triangle$ ACD, for each case, $\sin A = \dfrac{h}{b}$ therefore $h = b\sin A$.   ①

In $\triangle$ BCD, for case (i), $\sin B = \dfrac{h}{a}$, and for case (ii), $\sin(180° - B) = \dfrac{h}{a}$.

But $\sin(180° - B) = \sin B$, therefore in each case $h = a\sin B$.   ②

Combining ① and ② gives

$$a\sin B = b\sin A \qquad \text{or} \qquad \dfrac{a}{\sin A} = \dfrac{b}{\sin B}.$$

Similarly, starting with a perpendicular from A would give $\dfrac{b}{\sin B} = \dfrac{c}{\sin C}$.

EXAMPLE 10.6

Find the side AB in the triangle shown in figure 10.24.

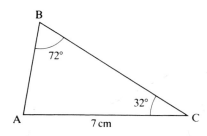

Figure 10.24

SOLUTION

Using the sine rule:

$$\frac{b}{\sin B} = \frac{c}{\sin C}$$

$$\Rightarrow \frac{7}{\sin 72°} = \frac{c}{\sin 32°}$$

$$\frac{7 \sin 32°}{\sin 72°} = c$$

$$c = 3.900.$$

> Do the calculation entirely on your calculator, and round only the final answer.

Side AB = 3.9 cm (to 1 d.p.)

Using the sine rule to find an angle

The sine rule may also be written as

$$\frac{\sin A}{a} = \frac{\sin B}{b} = \frac{\sin C}{c}$$

and this form is usually easier to use when you need to find an angle. You must however be careful because sometimes there are two possible answers, as in the next example.

EXAMPLE 10.7

Find the angle Z in the triangle XYZ, given that Y = 27°, $y = 4$ cm and $z = 5$ cm.

SOLUTION

The sine rule in $\triangle$ XYZ is $\dfrac{\sin X}{x} = \dfrac{\sin Y}{y} = \dfrac{\sin Z}{z}$

$$\Rightarrow \frac{\sin Z}{5} = \frac{\sin 27°}{4}$$

$$\sin Z = \frac{5 \sin 27°}{4} = 0.567\,488\,1.$$

$Z = 34.6°$ (to 1 d.p.)   or $Z = 180° - 34.6° = 145.4°$ (to 1 d.p.).

Both solutions are possible, as indicated in figure 10.25.

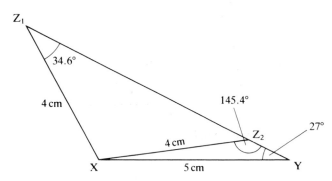

Figure 10.25

⚠ Sometimes only one solution is possible since the second would give a triangle with angle sum greater than 180°.

1 Find the length x in each of the following triangles.

(i)

(ii)

(iii)

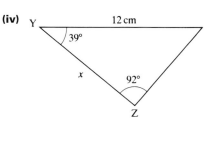

(iv)

2 Find the angle θ in each of the following triangles.

(i)

(ii)

(iii)

(iv)

3 Solve the triangle ABC (i.e. find the remaining angle and sides) given that $A = 37°$, $B = 78°$, $c = 8.2$ cm.

The cosine rule

Sometimes it is not possible to use the sine rule with the information you have about a triangle, for example when you know all three sides but none of the angles.

An alternative approach is to use the cosine rule, which can be written in two forms:

$$a^2 = b^2 + c^2 - 2bc \cos A \qquad \text{or} \qquad \cos A = \frac{b^2 + c^2 - a^2}{2bc}.$$

Like the sine rule, the cosine rule can be applied to any triangle.

Proof

For the triangle ABC, CD is the perpendicular from C to AB (extended if necessary). As with the sine rule, there are two cases to consider. Both are shown in figure 10.26.

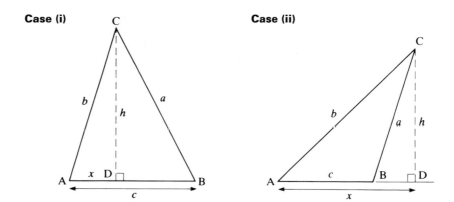

Figure 10.26

In $\triangle$ ACD $\quad b^2 = x^2 + h^2 \quad$ (Pythagoras' theorem) $\qquad$ ①

$\qquad\qquad \cos A = \frac{x}{b}$, therefore $x = b \cos A$. $\qquad$ ②

In $\triangle$ BCD, for case (i), $a^2 = (c - x)^2 + h^2$ (Pythagoras' theorem)

$\qquad\qquad$ for case (ii), $a^2 = (x - c)^2 + h^2$ (Pythagoras' theorem)

In both cases this expands to give

$$\begin{aligned}
a^2 &= c^2 - 2cx + x^2 + h^2 \\
&= c^2 - 2cx + b^2 \qquad \text{(using ①)} \\
&= c^2 - 2cb \cos A + b^2 \quad \text{(using ②)}
\end{aligned}$$

i.e. $\quad a^2 = b^2 + c^2 - 2bc \cos A$, as required.

Rearranging this

$$\begin{aligned}
2bc \cos A &= b^2 + c^2 - a^2 \\
\cos A &= \frac{b^2 + c^2 - a^2}{2bc} \text{ (the second form of the cosine rule).}
\end{aligned}$$

Starting with a perpendicular from a different vertex would give the following similar results.

$$b^2 = a^2 + c^2 - 2ac \cos B \qquad\qquad c^2 = a^2 + b^2 - 2ab \cos C$$

$$\cos B = \frac{a^2 + c^2 - b^2}{2ac} \qquad\qquad \cos C = \frac{a^2 + b^2 - c^2}{2ab}$$

EXAMPLE 10.8   Find the side AB in the triangle shown in figure 10.27.

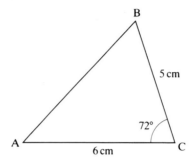

Figure 10.27

SOLUTION

$$c^2 = a^2 + b^2 - 2ab \cos C$$
$$\quad = 5^2 + 6^2 - 2 \times 5 \times 6 \cos 72°$$
$$AB = 6.5 \text{ cm (to 1 d.p.)}.$$

EXAMPLE 10.9   Find the angle Q in the triangle shown in figure 10.28.

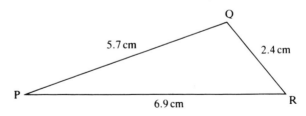

Figure 10.28

SOLUTION

The cosine rule for this triangle can be written as

$$\cos Q = \frac{p^2 + r^2 - q^2}{2pr}$$

$$\quad = \frac{2.4^2 + 5.7^2 - 6.9^2}{2 \times 2.4 \times 5.7}$$

$$Q = 110° \text{ (to nearest degree)}.$$

EXERCISE 10C

1 Find the length x in each of the following triangles.

(i)

(ii)

(iii)

(iv)

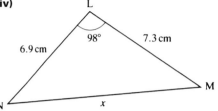

2 Find the angle θ in each of the following triangles.

(i)

(ii)

(iii)

(iv)

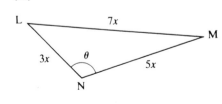

3 In the quadrilateral ABCD shown, find:

(i) AC

(ii) $\angle$ADC.

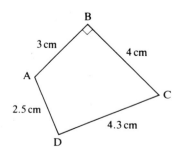

4 X, Y, and Z are three points on level ground. Point Y is 2 km from X on a bearing of 117°, and Z is 5 km from X on a bearing of 204°. Find:

(i) ∠YXZ

(ii) the distance YZ.

Using the sine and cosine rules together

In many situations it is necessary to choose between the sine and cosine rules, or possibly use both, as in the following example.

EXAMPLE 10.10

A ship S is 5 km from a lighthouse H on a bearing of 152°, and a tanker T is 7 km from the lighthouse on a bearing of 069°.
Find the distance and bearing of the ship from the tanker.

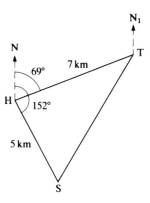

Figure 10.29

SOLUTION

$$\angle THS = 152° - 69° = 83°$$

Using the cosine rule

> The remaining decimal places are stored on the calculator: no rounding is done until the end.

$$h^2 = s^2 + t^2 - 2st\cos H$$
$$= 7^2 + 5^2 - 2 \times 7 \times 5 \times \cos 83°$$
$$= 49 + 25 - 8.530\ldots$$
$$= 65.469\ldots$$
$$h = 8.091\ldots$$

Therefore the distance of the ship from the tanker is 8.09 km (to 2 d.p.).

Using the sine rule

$$\frac{\sin T}{t} = \frac{\sin H}{h}$$

$$\frac{\sin T}{5} = \frac{\sin 83°}{8.0\ldots}$$

$$\sin T = 0.6\ldots$$

$$T = 37.8\ldots°$$

since

$$\angle N_1 TH = 180° - 69°$$

$$= 111°.$$

It follows that the bearing of the ship from the tanker (the reflex angle N_1TS) is

$$360° - 111° - 37.8\ldots° = 211° \text{ (to the nearest degree).}$$

EXERCISE 10D

1 A tower 60 m high stands on the top of a hill. From a point on the ground at sea level, the angles of elevation of the top and bottom of the tower are 49° and 37° respectively. Find the height of the hill.

2 Three points A, B and C lie in a straight line on level ground with B between A and C. A vertical mast BD stands at B and is supported by wires, two of which are along the lines AD and CD.

Given that $\angle DAB = 55°$, $\angle DCB = 42°$ and AB = 85 m, find the lengths of the wires AD and CD and the height of the mast.

3 Bradley is 4.5 km due south of Applegate, and Churchgate is 6.7 km from Applegate on a bearing 079°. How far is it from Bradley to Churchgate?

4 A ship travelling with a constant speed and direction is sighted from a lighthouse. At this time it is 2.7 km away, on a bearing of 042°. Half an hour later it is on a bearing of 115° at a distance of 7.6 km from the same lighthouse. Find its speed in kilometres per hour.

5 At midnight, a ship sailing due north passes two lightships, A and B, which are 10 km apart in a line due east from the ship. Lightship A is closer to the ship than B. At 2 am the bearings of the lightships are 149° and 142°.

(i) Draw a sketch to show A and B and the positions of the ship at midnight and 2 am.
(ii) Find the distance of the ship from A at 2 am.
(iii) Find the speed of the ship.

6 From a ship S, two other ships P and Q are on bearings of 315° and 075° respectively. The distance PS = 7.4 km and QS = 4.9 km. Find the distance PQ.

7 A yacht sets off from A and sails 3 km on a bearing of 045° to a point B. It then sails 1 km on a bearing of 322° to a point C. Find the distance AC.

8 From two points A and B on level ground, the angles of elevation of the top, P, of a lighthouse are found to be 27.6° and 46.2°. The distance between A and B is 34 m. Find:

(i) ∠APB

(ii) AP

(iii) the height of the tower.

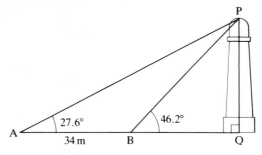

9 A helicopter leaves a point P and flies on a bearing of 162° for 3 km to a point Q, and then due west to a point R which is on a bearing of 220° from P.

(i) Find PR.

(ii) Find RQ.

The flight takes 4 minutes.

(iii) Find the speed of the helicopter in kilometres per hour.

10 A walker at point P can see the spires of St. Mary's (M) and St. George's (G) on bearings of 340° and 015° respectively. She then walks 500 m due north to a point Q and notes the bearings as 315° to St. Mary's and 030° to St. George's. Take the measurements as exact and assume they are all made in the same horizontal plane.

(i) Copy the diagram and fill in the information given.

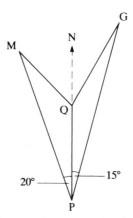

(ii) Calculate the distance PM to the nearest metre.

(iii) Given that the distance PG is 966 m, calculate MG, the distance between the spires, to the nearest metre.

11 The diagram shows three survey points, P, Q and R which are on a north–south line on level ground. From P, the bearing of the foot of a statue S is 104°, and from Q it is 081°. Point P is 400 m north of Q and Q is 300 m north of R.

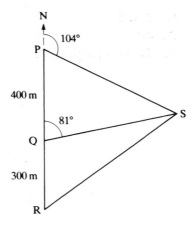

(i) Find the distance PS.

(ii) Find the distance RS.

(iii) Find the bearing of S from R.

12 In a gale, a tree started to lean and needed to be supported by struts which were wedged as shown below. There is also a simplified diagram of the struts with approximate dimensions.

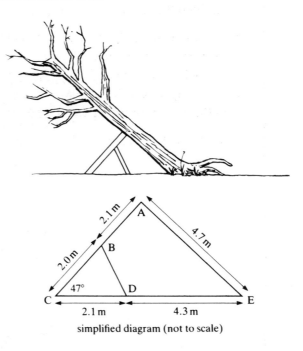

simplified diagram (not to scale)

Give all your answers correct to 2 significant figures.

(i) Use the cosine rule to calculate the length of BD.

(ii) Calculate the angle CAE.

[MEI]

The area of a triangle

As well as finding the unknown sides and angles of a triangle, if you are given enough information you can also find its area. A particularly useful rule is that for any triangle, using the same notation as before

$$\text{area} = \tfrac{1}{2}bc\sin A.$$

Proof

Figure 10.30 shows a triangle, ABC, the height of which is denoted by h.

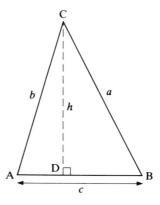

Figure 10.30

Using the fact that the area of a triangle is equal to half its base times it height

$$\text{area} = \tfrac{1}{2}ch. \qquad \textcircled{1}$$

In triangle ACD

$$\sin A = \frac{h}{b}$$

$$\Rightarrow \qquad h = b\sin A.$$

Substituting in ① gives

$$\text{area} = \tfrac{1}{2}bc\sin A.$$

Note

In this case point C was taken to be the top of the triangle, AB the base. Taking the other two points, in turn, to be the top give the equivalent results:

$$\text{area} = \tfrac{1}{2}ca\sin B \qquad \text{and} \qquad \text{area} = \tfrac{1}{2}ab\sin C.$$

EXAMPLE 10.11

Find the area of triangle ABC shown in figure 10.31.

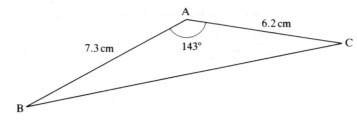

Figure 10.31

SOLUTION

$$\text{Area} = \frac{1}{2} bc \sin A$$

$$= \frac{1}{2} \times 7.3 \times 6.2 \times \sin 143°$$

$$= 13.6 \text{ cm}^2 \text{ (to 3 s.f.)}.$$

EXERCISE 10E

1 Find the area of each of the following triangles.

(i)

(ii)

(iii)

(iv)

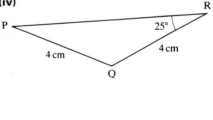

2 A triangular flower bed has two sides of length 3 m and the angle between them is 30°. Find

(i) the area of the bed

(ii) the amount of top soil (in m³) which would be needed to cover the bed evenly to a depth of 15 cm.

3 In the triangle XYZ, XY = 4.6 cm and YZ = 6.9 cm.
The area of the triangle is 7.3 cm².
Find two possible values for ∠XYZ.

4 An icosahedron is a solid with 20 faces, each of which is an equilateral triangle.
Find the surface area of an icosahedron whose edges are all 3 cm.

5 A field is in the shape of a regular pentagon of side 80 m, as in the diagram below.

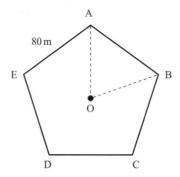

(i) Find ∠AOB where O is the centre of the pentagon.
(ii) Hence find the area of the field.

6 The diagram shows the end wall of a bungalow. The roof has one face inclined at 30° to the horizontal and the other inclined at 58° to the horizontal. The lengths are as shown in the diagram.

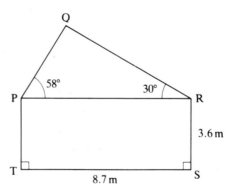

Find

(i) the length PQ
(ii) the length QR
(iii) the area of the end wall, TPQRS
(iv) the height of Q above TS.

7 The area of an irregularly shaped plot of land is often calculated by dividing it into triangles and taking appropriate measurements.

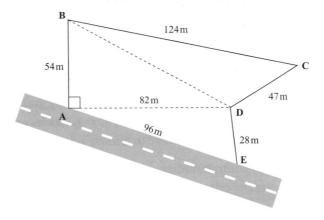

Using the information given in the diagram, calculate the area of the plot ABCDE.

Historical note

The word trigonometry is derived from three Greek words:

tria: *three*   gonia: *angle*   metron: *measure*
(τρια)   (γονια)   (μετρον)

and means the measuring (i.e. studying) of triangles.

Although its name has Greek origins, it is not possible to attribute the discovery of trigonometry to any one individual or nation. It may well have developed independently in a number of places, according to local needs and interests. The first known trigonometrical tables occur on a Babylonian clay tablet dated between 1900 and 1600 B.C. Hipparchus, working at Alexandria around 150 B.C., is credited with 12 books on the subject, work which was taken up subsequently by Ptolemy who produced in effect a book of sine tables in about 150 A.D. Much of this and later work in Greece, India and the Arab world was related to astronomy. There is also evidence on a papyrus that the ancient Egyptians used trigonometry in designing pyramids.

Circular measure

Have you ever wondered why angles are measured in degrees, and why there are 360° in one revolution?

There are various legends to support the choice of 360, most of them based in astronomy. One of these is that since the shepherd-astronomers of Sumeria thought that the solar year was 360 days long, this number was then used by the ancient Babylonian mathematicians to divide one revolution into 360 equal parts.

EXAMPLE 10.14

Solve $\tan^2 \theta = 2$ for $0 < \theta < \pi$.

SOLUTION

Here the range $0 < \theta < \pi$ indicates that radians are required.

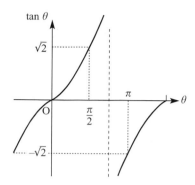

Figure 10.34

Since there is no request for multiples of π, set your calculator to radians.

$\tan^2 \theta = 2$

$\Rightarrow \tan \theta = \sqrt{2}$ or $\tan \theta = -\sqrt{2}$.

$\tan \theta = \sqrt{2}$ $\Rightarrow \theta = 0.955$ radians

$\tan \theta = -\sqrt{2}$ $\Rightarrow \theta = -0.955$ (not in range)

   or $\theta = -0.955 + \pi = 2.186$ radians.

The values of θ are 0.955 radians and 2.186 radians.

EXERCISE 10F

1 Express the following angles in radians, leaving your answers in terms of π where appropriate.

(i) 45°   (ii) 90°   (iii) 120°   (iv) 75°   (v) 300°

(vi) 23°   (vii) 450°   (viii) 209°   (ix) 150°   (x) 7.2°

2 Express the following angles in degrees, using a suitable approximation where necessary.

(i) $\dfrac{\pi}{10}$ (ii) $\dfrac{3\pi}{5}$

(iii) 2 radians   (iv) $\dfrac{4\pi}{9}$

(v) 3π (vi) $\dfrac{5\pi}{3}$

(vii) 0.4 radians   (viii) $\dfrac{3\pi}{4}$

(ix) $\dfrac{7\pi}{3}$ (x) $\dfrac{3\pi}{7}$

3 Write the following as fractions, or using square roots.

You should not need your calculator.

(i) $\sin \dfrac{\pi}{4}$ (ii) $\tan \dfrac{\pi}{3}$ (iii) $\cos \dfrac{\pi}{6}$ (iv) $\cos \pi$ (v) $\tan \dfrac{3\pi}{4}$

(vi) $\sin \dfrac{2\pi}{3}$ (vii) $\tan \dfrac{4\pi}{3}$ (viii) $\cos \dfrac{3\pi}{4}$ (ix) $\sin \dfrac{5\pi}{6}$ (x) $\cos \dfrac{5\pi}{3}$

4 Solve the following equation for $0 \leqslant \theta \leqslant 2\pi$, giving your answers as multiples of π.

(i) $\cos \theta = \dfrac{\sqrt{3}}{2}$ (ii) $\tan \theta = 1$ (iii) $\sin \theta = \dfrac{1}{\sqrt{2}}$

(iv) $\sin \theta = -\dfrac{1}{2}$ (v) $\cos \theta = -\dfrac{1}{\sqrt{2}}$ (vi) $\tan \theta = \sqrt{3}$

5 Solve the following equations for $-\pi < \theta < \pi$.

(i) $\sin \theta = 0.2$ (ii) $\cos \theta = 0.74$ (iii) $\tan \theta = 3$

(iv) $4 \sin \theta = -1$ (v) $\cos \theta = -0.4$ (vi) $2\tan \theta = -1$

6 Solve $3 \cos^2 \theta + 2 \sin \theta - 3 = 0$ for $0 \leqslant \theta \leqslant \pi$.

The length of an arc of a circle

From the definition of a radian, an angle of 1 radian at the centre of a circle corresponds to an arc of length r (the radius of the circle). Similarly, an angle of 2 radians corresponds to an arc length of $2r$ and, in general, an angle of θ radians corresponds to an arc length of θr, which is usually written $r\theta$ (figure 10.35).

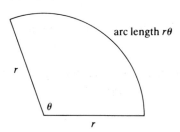

Figure 10.35

The area of a sector of a circle

A *sector* of a circle is the shape enclosed by an arc of the circle and two radii. It is the shape of a piece of cake. If the sector is smaller than a semi-circle it is called a *minor sector*; if it is larger than a semi-circle it is a *major sector*, see figure 10.36.

The area of a sector is a fraction of the area of the whole circle. The fraction is found by writing the angle θ as a fraction of one revolution, i.e. 2π (figure 10.37).

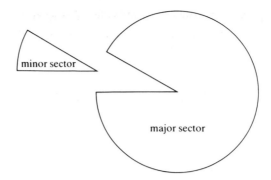

Figure 10.36

$$\text{Area} = \frac{\theta}{2\pi} \times \pi r^2$$
$$= \frac{1}{2}r^2\theta.$$

Figure 10.37

EXAMPLE 10.15   Calculate the arc length, perimeter, and area of a sector of angle $\frac{2\pi}{3}$ and radius 6 cm.

SOLUTION

Arc length $= r\theta$

$$= 6 \times \frac{2\pi}{3}$$

$$= 4\pi \text{ cm.}$$

Perimeter $= 4\pi + 6 + 6$

$$= 4\pi + 12.$$

Area $= \frac{1}{2}r^2\theta$

$$= \frac{1}{2}r \times 6^2 \times \frac{2\pi}{3}$$

$$= 12\pi \text{ cm}^2.$$

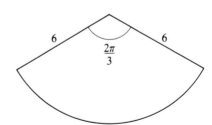

Figure 10.38

EXERCISE 10G

1 Each row of the table gives dimensions of a sector of a circle of radius r cm. The angle subtended at the centre of the circle is θ radians, the arc length of the sector is s cm and its area is A cm^2. Copy and complete the table.

r (cm)	θ (rad)	s (cm)	A (cm^2)
5	$\dfrac{\pi}{4}$		
8	1		
4		2	
	$\dfrac{\pi}{3}$	$\dfrac{\pi}{2}$	
5			10
	0.8	1.5	
	$\dfrac{2\pi}{3}$		4π

2 (i) (a) Find the area of the sector OAB in the diagram.

(b) Find the area of triangle OAB.

(c) Find the shaded area. (Note: this is called a *segment* of the circle.)

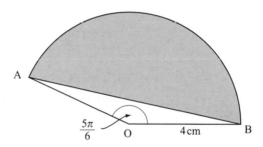

(ii) The diagram below shows two circles, each of radius 4 cm, with each one passing through the centre of the other.
Calculate the shaded area.
(Hint: Add the common chord AB to the sketch.)

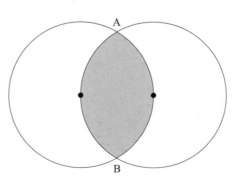

3 The diagram shows the cross-section of three pencils, each of radius 3.5 mm, held together by a stretched elastic band.
Find

 (i) the shaded area
 (ii) the stretched length of the band.

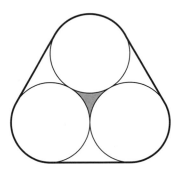

4 A circle, centre O, has two radii OA and OB. The line AB divides the circle into two regions with areas in the ratio 3:1.
If the angle AOB is θ (radians), show that

$$\theta - \sin\theta = \frac{\pi}{2}.$$

5 In a cricket match, a particular cricketer generally hits the ball anywhere in a sector of angle 100°. If the boundary (assumed circular) is 80 yards away, find

 (i) the length of boundary which the fielders should patrol
 (ii) the area of the ground which the fielders need to cover.

6 The silver brooch illustrated is in the shape of an ornamental cross.
The shaded areas represent where the metal is cut away. Each is part of a sector of a circle of angle $\frac{\pi}{4}$ and radius 1.8 cm.

The overall diameter of the brooch is 4.4 cm, and the diameter of the centre is 1 cm. The brooch is 1 mm thick.

Find the volume of silver in the brooch.

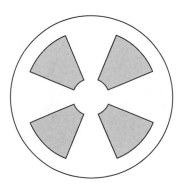

7 In the triangle OAB, OA = 3 m, OB = 8 m and angle AOB = $\frac{\pi}{12}$.
Calculate, correct to 2 decimal places

(i) the length of AB

(ii) the area of triangle OAB.

The plan of an ornamental garden below shows two circles, centre O, with radii 3 m and 8 m.

Paths of equal width are cut symmetrically across the circles.

The shaded areas represent flower beds.

BQ and AP are arcs of the circles.

Triangle OAB is the same triangle shown in the diagram above.

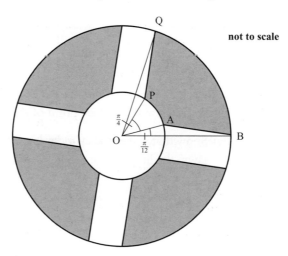

Given that angle POA = $\frac{\pi}{4}$, calculate the area of

(iii) sector OPA

(iv) sector OQB

(v) the flower bed PABQ.

8 The diagram below shows a simplified side view of a garden roller.
The radius of the cylinder is 30 cm.
The length of the handle is 130 cm.
The roller is leaning against a wall with the handle at an angle of 25° to the vertical.
The ground is horizontal.

(i) Calculate the height of the top of the handle above the ground.

Some time later, the top of the handle is found to have slipped down the wall so that it is now 80 cm above the ground.

(ii) Calculate the horizontal distance the cylinder has moved.

(iii) Calculate the angle through which the cylinder has turned, giving your answer both in radians and in degrees.

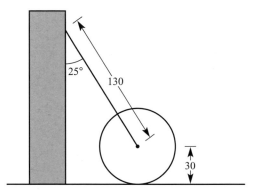

A gardener takes the roller on to a lawn. Just as he begins to roll he notices a small scratch at the highest point of the cylinder.

(iv) Show that, when the cylinder has been pushed a distance x cm on the lawn, the height of the scratch above the ground is

$$30\left\{1 + \cos\left(\frac{6x}{\pi}\right)^{\circ}\right\}\text{cm.}$$

[MEI]

9 A sports field is being designed. It consists of a cinder running track enclosing a grass games region, which is a rectangle PQRS with a semi-circle at each end, as shown in the diagram. The point M is the mid-point of QR.

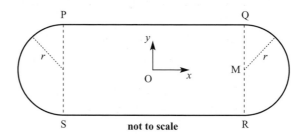

not to scale

(i) The length of the inside of the running track must be 400 m. The radius of the semi-circular ends is taken to be r metres.
Find an expression for the length PQ in terms of r.
Hence show that the area A m^2 of the rectangle PQRS is given by

$$A = 2r(200 - \pi r).$$

(ii) Draw the graph of A against r and show that A has maximum value when r is about 32. Show that the corresponding value of PQ is 100 m.

(iii) The diagram also shows an origin O at the centre of the rectangle with x and y axes parallel to the sides. Write down the equation of the circle with centre M passing through Q and R.

The designers want to mark out a rugby pitch on the grass region. This is to be a rectangle with its sides parallel to those of PQRS. Its length and breadth are to be in the ratio 2:1, so that the co-ordinates of the corner near Q can be written as $(2k, k)$, for some value of k.

(iv) Given that the rugby pitch must fit into the grass region, with its corners on the semi-circles, show that the value of k may be found from the equation

$$5k^2 - 200k + 1476 = 0.$$

Solve this equation and hence calculate the length and breadth of the pitch.

[MEI]

❓ A hunter leaves home and walks 5 km due south. He then finds the tracks of a bear which he follows due east for 5 km when he comes up on the bear and kills it. He is then 5 km from home.

What colour is the bear?

Lighthouses

(i) Investigate the distance from which a lighthouse of any particular height can be seen on a clear day at sea.

How does that distance vary with the height of the lighthouse?

(ii) When sailing, you measure the angle of elevation of the top of the lighthouse (with a sextant) and then calculate how far away it is.

What is your error if you do not allow for the curvature of the earth, and how will that error vary with your distance from the lighthouse?

(The radius of the earth is approximately 6370 km.)

Fuel gauge

Have you noticed that on some cars the fuel gauge reads less when the car is going uphill, and more when it is going downhill?

Assuming the fuel tank to be rectangular and the gauge to be recording the position of the liquid surface on the front wall of the tank (see figure 10.39), construct a mathematical model to explain this effect.

rear of car ←   → front of car

Figure 10.39

Draw a graph of the gauge reading against the angle of slope when the tank is

(i) $\frac{3}{4}$ full   (ii) $\frac{1}{2}$ full   (iii) $\frac{1}{4}$ full.

More trigonometrical graphs

Translations

You have already seen in figure 10.14 that translating the sine graph 90° to the left gives the cosine graph.

Using the result from Chapter 3 that a translation of $\begin{pmatrix} -90° \\ 0 \end{pmatrix}$ moves the graph of $y = f(\theta)$ to $y = f(\theta + 90°)$ gives

$$\cos \theta = \sin (\theta + 90°).$$

Results from translations can also be used in plotting graphs such as $y = \sin \theta + 1$. This is the graph of $y = \sin \theta$ translated by 1 unit upwards, as shown in figure 10.40.

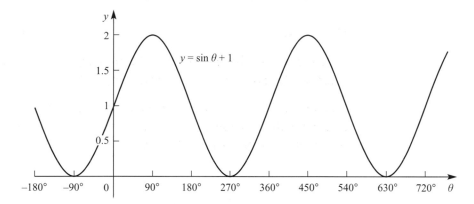

Figure 10.40

One-way stretches

Use a graphic calculator to draw the graphs of $y = \sin x$ and $y = 2\sin x$ on the same axes, for $0° \leqslant x \leqslant 180°$. Add $y = \frac{1}{2}\sin x$ and $y = 3\sin x$ to the display.

Describe what happens.

You will have noticed that for any value of x, the y co-ordinate of the point on the curve $y = 2\sin x$ is exactly double that on the curve $y = \sin x$, as shown in figure 10.41.

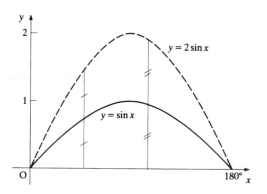

Figure 10.41

This is the equivalent of the curve being stretched parallel to the y axis. Since each y co-ordinate is doubled, this is called a *stretch of scale factor 2 parallel to the y axis.*

Note

The equation $y = 2\sin x$ could also be written as $\frac{y}{2} = \sin x$, so dividing y by 2 gives a stretch of scale factor 2 in the y direction.

In general, for any curve $y = f(x)$, and any value of a greater than zero, $y = af(x)$ is obtained from $y = f(x)$ by a stretch of scale factor a parallel to the y axis.

ACTIVITY 10.4

Use a graphic calculator to draw the graphs of $y = \sin x$ and $y = \sin 2x$ on the same axes, for $0° \leqslant x \leqslant 180°$.

Add $y = \sin 3x$ and $y = \sin \frac{1}{2}x$ to the display.

You will see that the graph of $y = \sin 2x$ is compressed parallel to the x axis, so that for any value of y, the x co-ordinate of the point on the curve $y = \sin 2x$ will be exactly half of that on the curve $y = \sin x$, as shown in figure 10.42.

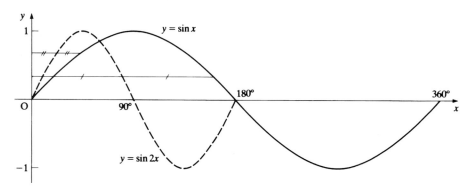

Figure 10.42

Since the curve is compressed to half its original size, this is referred to as a stretch of scale factor $\frac{1}{2}$ parallel to the x axis.

In general, for any curve $y = f(x)$ and any value of a greater than zero, $y = f(ax)$ is obtained from $y = f(x)$ by a stretch of scale factor $\frac{1}{a}$ parallel to the x axis. Similarly $y = f(\frac{x}{a})$ corresponds to a stretch of scale factor a parallel to the x axis.

Note

This is as you would expect: dividing x by a gives a stretch of scale factor a in the x direction, just as dividing y by a gives a stretch of scale factor a in the y direction.

EXAMPLE 10.16

Starting with the curve $y = \cos x$, show how transformations can be used to sketch these curves.

(i) $y = \cos 3x$ (ii) $y = 3 + \cos x$

(iii) $y = \cos (x - 60°)$ (iv) $y = 2\cos x$

SOLUTION

(i) The curve with equation $y = \cos 3x$ is obtained from the curve with equation $y = \cos x$ by a stretch of scale factor $\frac{1}{3}$ parallel to the x axis. There will therefore be one complete oscillation of the curve in 120° (instead of 360°). This is shown in figure 10.43.

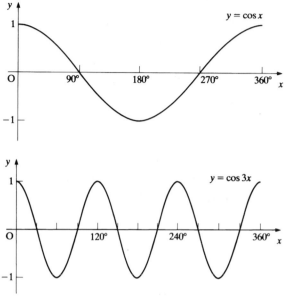

Figure 10.43

(ii) The curve of $y = 3 + \cos x$ is obtained from that of $y = \cos x$ by a translation $\binom{0}{3}$.

The curve therefore oscillates between $y = 4$ and $y = 2$ (see figure 10.44).

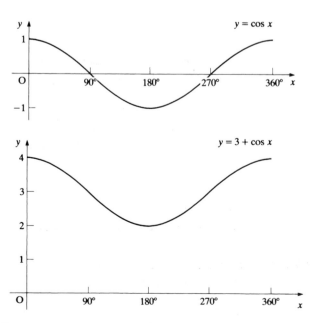

Figure 10.44

(iii) The curve of $y = \cos(x - 60°)$ is obtained from that of $y = \cos x$ by a translation of $\begin{pmatrix} 60° \\ 0 \end{pmatrix}$ (see figure 10.45).

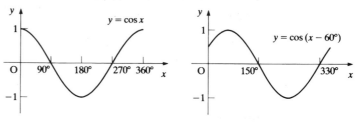

Figure 10.45

(iv) The curve of $y = 2\cos x$ is obtained from that of $y = \cos x$ by a stretch of scale factor 2 parallel to the y axis. The curve therefore oscillates between $y = 2$ and $y = -2$ (instead of between $y = 1$ and $y = -1$). This is shown in figure 10.46.

Figure 10.46

 It is always a good idea to check your results using a graphic calculator whenever possible.

As with translations, one-way stretches can be applied to other graphs as well as to trigonometrical graphs.

EXAMPLE 10.17

Figure 10.47 shows the graph of $y = f(x)$.

Sketch the graph of each of these functions.

(i) $y = f\left(\frac{1}{2}x\right)$ (ii) $y = 3f(x)$

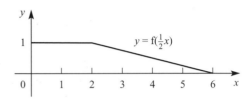

Figure 10.47

SOLUTION

(i) The graph of $y = f\left(\frac{1}{2}x\right)$ is a one-way stretch of the graph of $y = f(x)$ with scale factor 2 parallel to the x axis, as shown in figure 10.48.

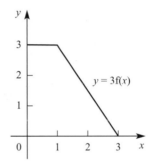

Figure 10.48

(ii) The graph of $y = 3f(x)$ is a one-way stretch of the graph of $y = f(x)$ with scale factor 3 parallel to the y axis, as shown in figure 10.49.

Figure 10.49

EXERCISE 10H

1 Starting with the graph of $y = \sin x$, state the transformations which can be used to sketch each of the following curves.

(i) $y = \sin(x - 90°)$ (ii) $y = \sin 3x$

(iii) $2y = \sin x$ (iv) $y = \sin \frac{x}{2}$

(v) $y = 2 + \sin x$

2 Starting with the graph of $y = \cos x$, state the transformations which can be used to sketch each of the following curves.

(i) $y = \cos(x + 60°)$ (ii) $3y = \cos x$

(iii) $y = \cos x + 1$ (iv) $y = \cos 2x$

3 For each of the following curves

(a) sketch the curve

(b) identify the curve as being the same as one of the following:

$$y = \pm \sin x, \qquad y = \pm \cos x, \qquad \text{or} \qquad y = \pm \tan x.$$

(i) $y = \sin (x + 360°)$ (ii) $y = \sin (x + 90°)$

(iii) $y = \tan (x - 180°)$ (iv) $y = \cos (x - 90°)$

(v) $y = \cos (x + 180°)$

4 Starting with the graph of $y = x^2$, state the transformations which can be used to sketch each of the following curves.
In each case there are two possible answers. Give both.

(i) $y = 4x^2$ (ii) $3y = x^2$

5 Starting with the graph of $y = x^3$, find the equation of the graph resulting from the following one-way stretches.

(i) Scale factor 2 parallel to the y axis

(ii) Scale factor 2 parallel to the x axis

(iii) Scale factor 3 parallel to the y axis

(iv) Scale factor $\frac{1}{2}$ parallel to the x axis

6 Starting with the graph of $y = \tan x$, find the equation of the graph and sketch the graph after the following transformations.

(i) Translation of $\begin{pmatrix} 0 \\ 4 \end{pmatrix}$

(ii) Translation of $\begin{pmatrix} -30° \\ 0 \end{pmatrix}$

(iii) One-way stretch with scale factor 2 parallel to the x axis

7 The graph of $y = \sin x$ is stretched with scale factor 4 parallel to the y axis.

(i) State the equation of the new graph.

(ii) Find the exact value of y on the new graph when $x = 240°$.

8 The diagram shows the graph of $y = f(x)$ which has a maximum point at $(-2, 2)$, a minimum point at $(2, -2)$, and passes through the origin.

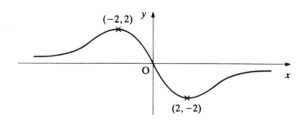

Sketch the following graphs, using a separate set of axes for each graph, and indicating the co-ordinates of the turning points.

(i) $y = 2f(x)$ (ii) $y = f(2x)$ (iii) $y = f\left(\frac{x}{2}\right)$

9 The diagram shows the graph of $y = g(x)$.

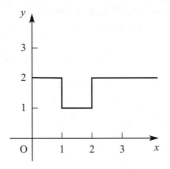

(i) Each of these graphs is a transformation of the graph of $y = g(x)$.
Write down the equation of each graph.

(a)

(b)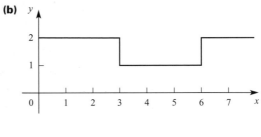

(ii) Sketch the graph of $y = g(2x)$.

10 The sketch shows the graph of $y = h(x)$.

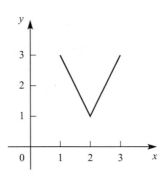

Sketch the graph of each of the following on a separate set of axes.

(i) $y = h(0.5x)$ (ii) $y = 2h(x)$ (iii) $y = h(3x)$

1 The point (x, y) at angle θ on the unit circle centre $(0, 0)$ has co-ordinates $(\cos \theta, \sin \theta)$ for all θ.

2 The graphs of $\sin \theta$, $\cos \theta$ and $\tan \theta$ are as shown below.

3 $\tan \theta = \dfrac{\sin \theta}{\cos \theta}$.

4 $\sin^2 \theta + \cos^2 \theta = 1$.

5 For a triangle ABC,

- area $= \dfrac{1}{2} ab \sin C$

- $\dfrac{a}{\sin A} = \dfrac{b}{\sin B} = \dfrac{c}{\sin C}$ (sine rule)

- $a^2 = b^2 + c^2 - 2bc \cos A$ (cosine rule)

6 Angles can be measured in radians. π radians $= 180°$.

7 For a circle of radius r, $\qquad$ arc length $= r\theta$

$\qquad\qquad\qquad\qquad\qquad$ area of sector $= \frac{1}{2}r^2\theta$ $\Bigg\}$ (θ in radians).

8 The graph of $y = \text{f}(ax)$ is a one-way stretch of the graph of $y = \text{f}(x)$ with scale factor $\dfrac{1}{a}$ parallel to the x axis.

9 The graph of $y = a\text{f}(x)$ is a one-way stretch of the graph of $y = \text{f}(x)$ with scale factor a parallel to the y axis.

11 Logarithms and exponentials

We have got so used to our existing mental software that we see no fault or limitation in it. We cannot see why it should ever need changing. And yet, in the last few decades, it has been shown that different thinking habits can be very much more powerful.

Edward de Bono

This cube has volume of $500\,\text{cm}^3$.

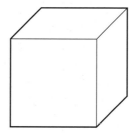

? How would you calculate the length of its side, correct to the nearest millimetre, without using the cube root button on your calculator?

Logarithms

You can think of multiplication in two ways. Look, for example, at 81×243, which is $3^4 \times 3^5$. You can work out the product using the numbers or you can work it out by adding the powers of a common base – in this case base 3.

Multiplying the numbers: $81 \times 243 = 19\,683$.

Adding the powers of the base 3: $4 + 5 = 9 : 3^9 = 19\,683$.

Another name for a power is a *logarithm*. Since $81 = 3^4$, you can say that the logarithm to the base 3 of 81 is 4. The word logarithm is often abbreviated to log and the statement would be written:

$$\log_3 81 = 4.$$

Notice that since $3^4 = 81$, $3^{\log_3 81} = 81$. This is an example of a general result:

$$a^{\log_a x} = x.$$

EXAMPLE 11.1

(i) Find the logarithm to the base 2 of each of these numbers.

(a) 64   (b) $\frac{1}{2}$ (c) 1   (d) $\sqrt{2}$

(ii) Show that $2^{\log_2 64} = 64$.

SOLUTION

(i) (a) $64 = 2^6$ and so $\log_2 64 = 6$

    (b) $\frac{1}{2} = 2^{-1}$ and so $\log_2 \frac{1}{2} = -1$

    (c) $1 = 2^0$ and so $\log_2 1 = 0$

    (d) $\sqrt{2} = 2^{\frac{1}{2}}$ and so $\log_2 \sqrt{2} = \frac{1}{2}$

(ii) $2^{\log_2 64} = 2^6 = 64$ as required

Logarithms to the base 10

Any positive number can be expressed as a power of 10. Before the days of calculators, logarithms to the base 10 were used extensively as an aid to calculation. There is no need for that nowadays but the logarithm function remains an important part of mathematics, particularly the natural logarithm which you will meet in the next book in this series. Base 10 logarithms continue to be a standard feature on calculators, and occur in some specialised contexts: the pH value of a liquid, for example, is a measure of its acidity or alkalinity and is given by $\log_{10}(1/\text{the concentration of } H^+ \text{ ions})$.

Since $1000 = 10^3$, $\log_{10} 1000 = 3$.

Similarly $\log_{10} 100 = 2$

$$\log_{10} 10 = 1$$

$$\log_{10} 1 = 0$$

$$\log_{10} \frac{1}{10} = \log_{10}(10^{-1}) = -1$$

$$\log_{10} \frac{1}{100} = \log_{10}(10^{-2}) = -2$$

and so on.

INVESTIGATION

There are several everyday situations in which quantities are measured on logarithmic scales.

What are the relationships between the following?

(i) An earthquake of intensity 7 on the Richter Scale, and one of intensity 8.

(ii) The frequency of the musical note middle C and that of the C above it.

(iii) The intensity of an 85 dB noise level and one of 86 dB.

The laws of logarithms

The laws of logarithms follow from those for indices, derived in Chapter 5.

Multiplication

Writing $xy = x \times y$ in the form of powers (or logarithms) to the base a and using the result that $x = a^{\log_a x}$ gives

$$a^{\log_a xy} = a^{\log_a x} \times a^{\log_a y}$$

and so $a^{\log_a xy} = a^{\log_a x + \log_a y}$.

Consequently $\log_a xy = \log_a x + \log_a y$.

Division

Similarly $\log_a \left(\dfrac{x}{y} \right) = \log_a x - \log_a y$.

Power zero

Since $a^0 = 1$, $\log_a 1 = 0$.

However, it is more usual to state such laws without reference to the base of the logarithms except where necessary, and this convention is adopted in the key points at the end of this chapter. As well as the laws given above, others may be derived from them, as follows.

Indices

Since $$x^n = x \times x \times x \times \ldots \times x \ (n \text{ times})$$

it follows that $$\log x^n = \log x + \log x + \log x + \ldots + \log x \ (n \text{ times}),$$

and so $$\log x^n = n \log x.$$

This result is also true for non-integer values of n and is particularly useful because it allows you to solve equations in which the unknown quantity is the power, as in the next example.

EXAMPLE 11.2

Solve the equation $2^n = 1000$.

SOLUTION

$$2^n = 1000.$$

Taking logarithms to the base 10 of both sides (since these can be found on a calculator),

$$\log_{10} (2^n) = \log_{10} 1000$$

$$n\log_{10} 2 = \log_{10} 1000$$

$$n = \frac{\log_{10} 1000}{\log_{10} 2} = 9.97 \text{ to 3 significant figures.}$$

Note

Most calculators just have 'log' and not 'log₁₀' on their keys.

EXAMPLE 11.3

How many terms are there in the geometric sequence 0.2, 1, 5, ..., 390 625?

SOLUTION

The last (nth) term of a geometric sequence is given by $a_n = a \times r^{n-1}$.

In this case $a = 0.2$ and $r = 5$, so:

$$390\,625 = 0.2 \times 5^{n-1}$$

$$5^{n-1} = \frac{390\,625}{0.2} = 1\,953\,125.$$

Taking logarithms to the base 10 of both sides:

$$(n-1)\log_{10} 5 = \log_{10} 1\,953\,125$$

$$n - 1 = \frac{\log_{10} 1\,953\,125}{\log_{10} 5}$$

$$n - 1 = 9$$

$$n = 10.$$

? In Example 7.9 you solved the equation

$$5^{n-1} = 1\,953\,125$$

by trial and improvement. Now that you can see how to solve it using logarithms, state the advantages of this method.

Roots

A similar line of reasoning leads to the conclusion that:

$$\log \sqrt[n]{x} = \frac{1}{n}\log x.$$

The logic runs as follows:

Since $\quad \sqrt[n]{x} \times \sqrt[n]{x} \times \sqrt[n]{x} \times \ldots \times \sqrt[n]{x} = x$

it follows that $\quad\quad\quad n\log \sqrt[n]{x} = \log x$

and so $\quad\quad\quad\quad \log \sqrt[n]{x} = \frac{1}{n}\log x.$

The logarithm of a number to its own base

Since $5^1 = 5$, it follows that $\log_5 5 = 1$.

Clearly the same is true for any number, and in general,

$$\log_a a = 1.$$

Reciprocals

Another useful result is that, for any base,

$$\log\left(\frac{1}{y}\right) = -\log y.$$

This is a direct consequence of the division law

$$\log_a\left(\frac{x}{y}\right) = \log_a x - \log_a y$$

with x set equal to 1:

$$\log\left(\frac{1}{y}\right) = \log 1 - \log y$$

$$= 0 - \log y$$

$$= -\log y.$$

If the number y is greater than 1, it follows that $\frac{1}{y}$ lies between 0 and 1 and $\log\left(\frac{1}{y}\right)$ is negative. So for any base (>1), the logarithm of a number between 0 and 1 is negative. You saw an example of this on page 320: $\log_{10}\left(\frac{1}{10}\right) = -1$.

The result $\log\left(\frac{1}{y}\right) = -\log y$ is often useful in simplifying expressions involving logarithms.

ACTIVITY 11.1   Draw the graph of $y = \log_2 x$, taking values of x like $\frac{1}{8}, \frac{1}{4}, \frac{1}{2}, 1, 2, 4, 8, 16$.

Use your graph to estimate the value of $\sqrt{2}$.

Graphs of logarithms

Whatever the value, a, of the base $(a > 1)$, the graph of $y = \log_a x$ has the same general shape (shown in figure 11.1).

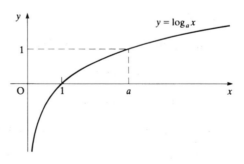

Figure 11.1

The graph has the following properties.

- The curve crosses the x axis at $(1, 0)$.

- The curve only exists for positive values of x.

- The line $x = 0$ is an asymptote, and for values of x between 0 and 1 the curve lies below the x axis.

- There is no limit to the height of the curve for large values of x, but its gradient progressively decreases.

- The curve passes through the point $(a, 1)$.

❓ Each of the points above can be justified by work that you have already covered. How?

Exponential functions

The relationship $y = \log_a x$ may be rewritten as $x = a^y$, and so the graph of $x = a^y$ is exactly the same as that of $y = \log_a x$. Interchanging x and y has the effect of reflecting the graph in the line $y = x$, and changing the relationship into $y = a^x$, as shown in figure 11.2.

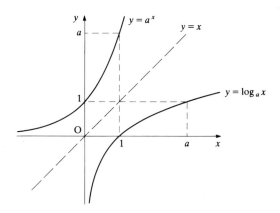

Figure 11.2

The function $y = a^x$ is called an *exponential function*. It is the *inverse* of the logarithm function. The effect of applying a function followed by its inverse is to bring you back to where you started.

Thus $\log_a (a^x) = x$, and $a^{(\log_a x)} = x$.

1 $2^x = 32 \iff x = \log_2 32$

Write similar logarithmic equivalents of these equations. In each case find also the value of x, using your knowledge of indices and not using your calculator.

(i) $3^x = 9$ **(ii)** $4^x = 64$ **(iii)** $2^x = \frac{1}{4}$

(iv) $5^x = \frac{1}{5}$ **(v)** $7^x = 1$ **(vi)** $16^x = 2$

2 Write the equivalent of these equations in exponential form. Without using your calculator, find also the value of y in each case.

(i) $y = \log_3 9$ **(ii)** $y = \log_5 125$ **(iii)** $y = \log_2 16$

(iv) $y = \log_6 1$ **(v)** $y = \log_{64} 8$ **(vi)** $y = \log_5 \frac{1}{25}$

3 Write down the values of the following without using a calculator. Use your calculator to check your answers for those questions which use base 10.

(i) $\log_{10} 10\,000$ **(ii)** $\log_{10}\left(\frac{1}{10\,000}\right)$

(iii) $\log_{10} \sqrt{10}$ **(iv)** $\log_{10} 1$

(v) $\log_3 81$ **(vi)** $\log_3\left(\frac{1}{81}\right)$

(vii) $\log_3 \sqrt{27}$ **(viii)** $\log_3 \sqrt[4]{3}$

(ix) $\log_4 2$ **(x)** $\log_5\left(\frac{1}{125}\right)$

4 Write the following expressions in the form $\log x$ where x is a number.

(i) $\log 5 + \log 2$ **(ii)** $\log 6 - \log 3$

(iii) $2\log 6$ **(iv)** $-\log 7$

(v) $\frac{1}{2}\log 9$ **(vi)** $\frac{1}{4}\log 16 + \log 2$

(vii) $\log 5 + 3\log 2 - \log 10$ **(viii)** $\log 12 - 2\log 2 - \log 9$

(ix) $\frac{1}{2}\log \sqrt{16} + 2\log\left(\frac{1}{2}\right)$ **(x)** $2\log 4 + \log 9 - \frac{1}{2}\log 144$

5 Express the following in terms of $\log x$.

(i) $\log x^2$ **(i)** $\log x^5 - 2\log x$

(iii) $\log \sqrt{x}$ **(iv)** $\log x^{\frac{3}{2}} + \log \sqrt[3]{x}$

(v) $3\log x + \log x^3$ **(vi)** $\log \left(\sqrt{x}\right)^5$

6 Express the following as a single logarithm.

$$2\log_{10} x - \log_{10} 7$$

Hence solve

$$2\log_{10} x - \log_{10} 7 = \log_{10} 63.$$

7 Use logarithms to the base 10 to solve the following equations.

(i) $2^x = 1\,000\,000$ **(ii)** $2^x = 0.001$

(iii) $1.08^x = 2$ **(iv)** $1.1^x = 100$

(v) $0.99^x = 0.000\,001$

8 A geometric series has first term 5 and common ratio 7.
The mth term is $28\,824\,005$.

Use logarithms to find the value of m.

9 Find how many terms there are in these geometric sequences.

(i) $-1, 2, -4, 8, \ldots, -16\,777\,216$

(ii) $0.1, 0.3, 0.9, 2.7, \ldots, 4\,304\,672.1$

10 In *A Man of Property* (the first book in the Forsyte Saga by John Galsworthy), Soames Forsyte states how many years it takes to double your money at 7% compound interest.

Given that interest is paid yearly, at the end of the year, what number of years does he say?

Modelling curves

When you obtain experimental data, you are often hoping to establish a mathematical relationship between the variables in question. Should the data fall on a straight line, you can do this easily because you know that a straight line with gradient m and intercept c has equation $y = mx + c$.

EXAMPLE 11.4

In an experiment the temperature θ (in °C) was measured at different times t (in seconds), in the early stages of a chemical reaction.
The results are shown in the table below.

t	20	40	60	80	100	120
θ	16.3	20.4	24.2	28.5	32.0	36.3

(i) Plot a graph of θ against t.

(ii) What is the relationship between θ and t?

SOLUTION

(i)

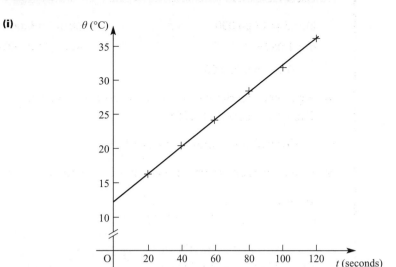

Figure 11.3

(ii) Figure 11.3 shows that the points lie reasonably close to a straight line and so it is possible to estimate its gradient and intercept.

Intercept: $\quad c = 12.3$

Gradient: $\quad m = \dfrac{36.3 - 16.3}{120 - 20}$

$\qquad\qquad\quad = 0.2$

In this case the equation is not $y = mx + c$ but $\theta = mt + c$, and so is given by

$\theta = 0.2t + 12.3$.

It is often the case, however, that your results do not end up lying on a straight line but on a curve, so that this straightforward technique cannot be applied. The appropriate use of logarithms can convert some curved graphs into straight lines. This is the case if the relationship has one of two forms, $y = kx^n$ or $y = ka^x$.

The techniques used in these two cases are illustrated in the following examples. In theory, logarithms to any base may be used, but in practice you would only use those available on your calculator: logarithms to the base 10 and natural logarithms. The base of natural logarithms is a number denoted by e, $2.718\,28\ldots$. In the next book in this series you will see how this apparently unnatural number arises naturally; for the moment what is important is that you can apply the techniques using base 10.

Relationships of the form $y = kx^n$

EXAMPLE 11.5

A water pipe is going to be laid between two points and an investigation is carried out as to how, for a given pressure difference, the rate of flow R litres per second varies with the diameter of the pipe d cm. The following data are collected.

d	1	2	3	5	10
R	0.02	0.32	1.62	12.53	199.80

It is suspected that the relationship between R and d may be of the form

$$R = kd^n$$

where k is a constant.

(i) Explain how a graph of log d against log R tells you whether this is a good model for the relationship.

(ii) Make out a table of values of $\log_{10} d$ against $\log_{10} R$ and plot these on a graph.

(iii) If appropriate, use your graph to estimate the values of n and k.

SOLUTION

(i) If the relationship is of the form $R = kd^n$, then taking logarithms gives

$$\log R = \log k + \log d^n$$

or $\quad \log R = n\log d + \log k.$

This equation is of the form $y = mx + c$, with log R replacing y, n replacing m, log d replacing x and log k replacing c. It is thus the equation of a straight line.

Consequently if the graph of log R against log d is a straight line, the model $R = kd^n$ is appropriate for the relationship and n is given by the gradient of the graph. The value of k is found from the intercept, log k, of the graph with the vertical axis.

$$\log_{10} k = \text{intercept} \Rightarrow k = 10^{\text{intercept}}.$$

(ii) Working to 2 decimal places (you would find it hard to draw the graph to greater accuracy) the logarithmic data are as follows.

$\log_{10} d$	0	0.30	0.48	0.70	1.00
$\log_{10} R$	−1.70	−0.49	0.21	1.10	2.30

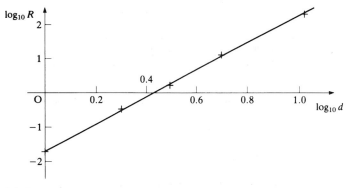

Figure 11.4

In this case the graph in figure 11.4 is indeed a straight line, with gradient 4 and intercept −1.70, so $n = 4$ and $c = 10^{-1.70} = 0.020$ (to 2 significant figures).

The proposed equation linking R and d is a good model for their relationship, and may be written as

$$R = 0.02d^4.$$

Exponential relationships

EXAMPLE 11.6

The temperature, θ in °C, of a cup of coffee at time t minutes after it is made is recorded as follows.

t	2	4	6	8	10	12
θ	81	70	61	52	45	38

(i) Plot the graph of θ against t.

(ii) Show how it is possible, by drawing a suitable graph, to test whether the relationship between θ and t is of the form $\theta = ka^t$, where k and a are constants.

(iii) Carry out the procedure.

SOLUTION

(i)

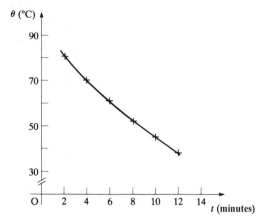

Figure 11.5

(ii) If the relationship is of the form $\theta = ka^t$, taking logarithms of both sides gives

$$\log \theta = \log k + \log a^t,$$

or $\quad \log \theta = t\log a + \log k.$

This is an equation of the form $y = mx + c$ with $\log \theta$ replacing y, t replacing x, $\log a$ replacing m and $\log k$ replacing c. It is thus the equation of a straight line.

Consequently if the graph of $\log \theta$ against t is a straight line, the model $\theta = ka^t$ is appropriate for the relationship, and $\log a$ is given by the gradient of the graph. The value of a is therefore found as $a = 10^{\text{gradient}}$. Similarly, the value of k is found from the intercept, $\log_{10} k$, of the line with the vertical axis: $k = 10^{\text{intercept}}$.

(iii) The table gives values of $\log_{10} \theta$ for the given values of t.

t	2	4	6	8	10	12
$\log_{10} \theta$	1.908	1.845	1.785	1.716	1.653	1.580

The graph of $\log_{10} \theta$ against t is as shown in figure 11.6.

The graph is indeed a straight line so the proposed model is appropriate.

The gradient is -0.029 and so $a = 10^{-0.029} = 0.935$.

The intercept is 1.978 and so $k = 10^{1.978} = 95.1$.

The relationship between θ and t is given by

$$\theta = 95.1 \times 0.935^t.$$

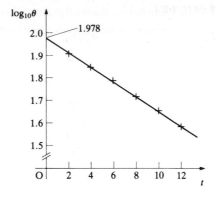

Figure 11.6

Note

Because the base of the exponential function, 0.935, is less than 1, the function's value decreases rather than increases with t.

1 The planet Saturn has many moons. The table below gives the mean radius of orbit and the time taken to complete one orbit, for five of the best-known of them.

Moon	Tethys	Dione	Rhea	Titan	Iapetus
Radius R ($\times 10^5$ km)	2.9	3.8	5.3	12.2	35.6
Period T (days)	1.9	2.7	4.5	15.9	79.3

It is believed that the relationship between R and T is of the form $R = kT^n$.

(i) How can this be tested by plotting log R against log T?

(ii) Make out a table of values of log R and log T and draw the graph.

(iii) Use your graph to estimate the values of k and n.

In 1980 a Voyager spacecraft photographed several previously unknown moons of Saturn. One of these, named 1980 S.27, has a mean orbital radius of 1.4×10^5 km.

(iv) Estimate how many days it takes this moon to orbit Saturn.

2 The table below shows the area, A cm^2, occupied by a patch of mould at time t days since measurements were started.

t	0	1	2	3	4	5
A	0.9	1.3	1.8	2.5	3.5	5.2

It is believed that A may be modelled by a relationship of the form $A = kb^t$.

(i) Show that the model may be written as $\log A = t\log b + \log k$.

(ii) What graph must be plotted to test this model?

(iii) Plot the graph and use it to estimate the values of b and k.

(iv) (a) Estimate the time when the area of mould was 2 cm^2.

    (b) Estimate the area of the mould after 3.5 days.

(v) How is this sort of growth pattern described?

3 The inhabitants of an island are worried about the rate of deforestation taking place. A research worker uses records over the last 200 years to estimate the number of trees at different dates. Her results are as follows.

Year	1800	1860	1910	1930	1950	1960	1970	1990
Trees (thousands)	3000	2900	3200	2450	1800	1340	1000	740

(i) Look at the figures and state when the deforestation may be taken to have begun, and the number of trees at that time.

It is suggested that the number of trees N has been decreasing exponentially with the number of years, t, since that time, so that N may be modelled by the equation.

$$N = ka^t$$

where k and a are constants.

(ii) Explain the meaning of the constant k in this situation, and also why you would expect the value of a to be less than 1.

(iii) Show that the model may be written as

$$\log N = t\log a + \log k.$$

(iv) Plot the graph of $\log N$ against t and use it to estimate the values of k and a.

(v) If this continues to be an appropriate model for the deforestation, in what year can the number of trees be expected to fall below 500 000?

4 The time after a train leaves a station is recorded in minutes as t and the distance that it has travelled in metres as s. The results are as follows.

t	0.5	1.0	1.5	2.0	2.5
s	420	1200	2200	3390	4740

It is suggested that the relationship between s and t is of the form $s = kt^n$ where k and n are constants.

(i) Draw the graph of log s against log t and explain why this tells you that this model is indeed appropriate.

(ii) Use your graph to estimate the values of k and n.

(iii) Estimate how far the train travelled in its first 100 seconds.

(iv) Explain why you would be wrong to use your results to estimate the distance the train has travelled after 10 minutes.

Note: This model is actually that of a train whose engine is working at constant power, with air resistance ignored.

5 All but one of the following pairs of readings satisfy, to 3 significant figures, a formula of the type $y = A \times x^B$:

x	1.51	2.13	3.50	4.62	5.07	7.21
y	2.09	2.75	4.09	5.10	6.21	7.28

Find the values of A and B, explaining your method.

If the values of x are correct, state which value of y appears to be wrong and estimate what the value should be.

[MEI]

6 An experimenter takes observations of a quantity y for various values of a variable x. He wishes to test whether these observations conform to a formula $y = A \times x^B$ and, if so, to find the values of the constants A and B.

Take logarithms of both sides of the formula. Use the result to explain what he should do, what will happen if there is no relationship, and if there is one, how to find A and B.

Carry this out accurately on squared paper for the observations in the table, and record clearly the resulting formula if there is one.

x	4	7	10	13	20
y	3	3.97	4.74	5.41	6.71

7 It is believed that the relationship between the variables x and y is of the form $y = Ax^n$. In an experiment the data in the table are obtained.

x	3	6	10	15	20
y	10.4	29.4	63.2	116.2	178.19

In order to estimate the constants A and n, $\log_{10} y$ is plotted against $\log_{10} x$.

(i) Draw the graph of $\log_{10} y$ against $\log_{10} x$.
(ii) Explain and justify how the shape of your graph enables you to decide whether the relationship is indeed of the form $y = Ax^n$.
(iii) Estimate the values of A and n.

[MEI]

8 For scuba diving, the maximum duration of a dive for an ascent without decompression stops is given by the table below.

Depth, d (metres)	Duration, T (minutes)
15	70
20	45
25	30
30	20
35	14
40	11
45	8
50	7

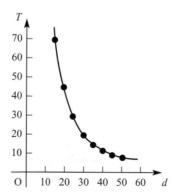

The graph of T against d suggests that the relationship might be modelled by an equation of the form $T = kd^n$ where T is the duration in minutes and d the depth in metres.

(i) Plot the graph of log T against log d.

(ii) Show how, by taking logarithms, $T = kd^n$ can be changed into a linear equation and explain how your graph confirms the suitability of the model.

(iii) Use your graph to estimate the values of n and k.

(iv) Explain whether you think it sensible to use this model to give the duration for diving to depths much greater than 50 metres.

[MEI]

9 A technical manual of ship designs contains the following information about the power needed to propel a 20 metre, round hulled craft of 127.5 tons displacement at different speeds.

Speed V in knots	6	7	8	9	10	11	12	15
Power P in brake horse power	36	78	142	240	497	906	1345	2126

Below is a sketch graph of P against V. This suggests that, for $6 \leqslant V \leqslant 12$, there may be a relationship between P and V which can be modelled by the equation $P = kV^n$ where k and n are as yet unknown.

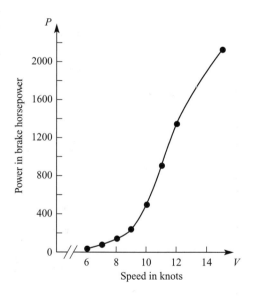

(i) Plot the values of log V against log P.

(ii) Comment on the location of the points and, where suitable, join them with a straight line.

(iii) Show how, by taking logarithms, the equation $P = kV^n$ can be changed into a linear equation.

(iv) Use the straight line which you have drawn in (ii) to find an estimate of n. Calculate an estimate for k explaining your method.

(v) Comment on the limitations of the equation $P = kV^n$ as a model for the power required to drive this craft at different speeds.

[MEI]

10 In a spectacular experiment on cell growth the following data were obtained, where N is the number of cells at a time t minutes after the start of the growth.

t	1.5	2.7	3.4	8.1	10
N	9	19	32	820	3100

At $t = 10$ a chemical was introduced which killed off the culture.

The relationship between N and t was thought to be modelled by $N = ab^t$, where a and b are constants.

(i) Show that the relationship is equivalent to $\log N = t\log b + \log a$.

(ii) Plot the values of $\log N$ against t and say how they confirm the supposition that the relationship is of the form $N = ab^t$.

(iii) Find the values of a and b.

(iv) If the growth had not been stopped at $t = 10$ and had continued according to your model, how many cells would there have been after 20 minutes?

[MEI]

11 It is believed that two quantities, z and d, are connected by a relationship of the form $z = kd^n$, where k and n are constants, provided that d does not exceed some fixed (but unknown) value, D.

An experiment produced the following data.

d	780	810	870	930	990	1050	1110	1170
z	2.1	2.6	3.2	4.0	4.8	5.6	5.9	6.1

(i) Explain why, if $z = kd^n$, then plotting $\log_{10} z$ against $\log_{10} d$ should produce a straight-line graph.

(ii) Draw up a table and plot the values of $\log_{10} z$ against $\log_{10} d$.

(iii) Use these points to suggest a value for D.

(iv) It is known that, for $d < D$, n is a whole number.
Use your graph to find the value of n.
Show also that $k \approx 5 \times 10^{-9}$.

(v) Use your value for n and the estimate $k = 5 \times 10^{-9}$ to find the value of d for which $z = 3.0$.

[MEI]

An experiment was conducted to discover how a certain type of heavy beam sagged with the loading upon it. The results are summarised in the table below, where w is the load in tonnes and y is the sag in mm.

w	1	2	3	4	5
y	18	27	39	56	82

A suggested model for these data is given by $y = a + bw^2$, where a and b are constants.

(i) Use the results for $w = 1$ and $w = 5$ to find estimates of a and b, correct to 1 decimal place.
Explain what a represents in the context of the model.

(ii) Calculate the sag predicted by this model when the beam supports a load of 3 tonnes.

A second model is given by $y = kc^w$, where k and c are constants.

(iii) Show that plotting $\log y$ against w should produce a straight line if this model is correct.

(iv) Plot the graph of $\log y$ against w and use your graph to estimate the values of k and c.

(v) Briefly compare the fit of the two models to the data.

[MEI]

1 A function of the form a^x is described as exponential.

2 $y = \log_a x \Leftrightarrow a^y = x.$

3 Logarithms to any base

Multiplication: $\qquad\qquad \log xy = \log x + \log y.$

Division: $\qquad\qquad\quad \log\left(\dfrac{x}{y}\right) = \log x - \log y.$

Logarithm of 1: $\qquad\quad \log 1 = 0.$

Powers: $\qquad\qquad\quad\; \log x^n = n \log x.$

Reciprocals: $\qquad\qquad \log\left(\dfrac{1}{y}\right) = -\log y.$

Roots: $\qquad\qquad\qquad \log \sqrt[n]{x} = \dfrac{1}{n} \log x.$

Logarithm to its own base: $\log_a a = 1.$

4 Logarithms may be used to discover the relationship between the variables in two types of situation.

$y = kx^n \Leftrightarrow \log y = \log k + n\log x$

Plot log y against log x: this relationship gives a straight line where n is the gradient and log k is the intercept.

$y = ka^x \Leftrightarrow \log y = \log k + x\log a$

Plot log y against x: this relationship gives a straight line where log a is the gradient and log k is the intercept.

12 Further differentiation and integration

To find the simple in the complex, the finite in the infinite – that is not a bad description of mathematics.

Jacob Schwartz

❓ How do you find the gradient at a point on curve A?
How would you find the gradient at a point on curve B?

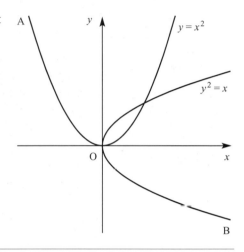

Differentiation

You have already seen how differentiating a function to find any stationary points helps you to sketch the curve of the function. However, the number of functions that you can differentiate at the moment is rather limited, since the only rule you have used is

$$y = kx^n \implies \frac{dy}{dx} = knx^{n-1} \text{ where } k \text{ is a constant and } n \text{ a positive integer.}$$

The work in this chapter enables you to differentiate some more functions.

Look at the function $f(x) = \frac{1}{x}$ (i.e. $y = x^{-1}$) where $x \neq 0$. Since n is negative in this case, we must start from first principles.

$$\frac{dy}{dx} = f'(x) = \lim_{h \to 0} \frac{f(x+h) - f(x)}{h}$$

Another way of writing this is to use δx for h throughout.

$\frac{dy}{dx}$ and $f'(x)$ are alternative ways of saying 'the derivative of $y = f(x)$ with respect to x'

For $y = f(x) = \dfrac{1}{x}$

$$f'(x) = \lim_{h \to 0} \frac{\dfrac{1}{x+h} - \dfrac{1}{x}}{h}$$

$$= \lim_{h \to 0} \frac{x - (x+h)}{x(x+h)h}$$

$$= \lim_{h \to 0} \frac{-h}{x(x+h)h}$$

$$= \lim_{h \to 0} \frac{-1}{x(x+h)}$$

$$= -\frac{1}{x^2}.$$

In the limit as $h \to 0$
$x + h \to x$.

So, $y = x^{-1} \Rightarrow \dfrac{dy}{dx} = -x^{-2}, \quad x \neq 0.$

Note

Notice that this is the result you would have obtained using the existing rule if you put $n = -1$, suggesting that the existing rule may be extended to other values of n. This is indeed true and the rule applies for all real values of n, including negative numbers and fractions.

EXAMPLE 12.1

Use the extended rule to differentiate the following functions.

(i) $y = \dfrac{1}{x^2}$

(ii) $y = \sqrt{x}$

SOLUTION

(i) $y = \dfrac{1}{x^2} = x^{-2}$

$$\frac{dy}{dx} = -2 \times x^{-2-1}$$

$$= -2x^{-3}$$

$$= -\frac{2}{x^3}.$$

(ii) $y = \sqrt{x} = x^{\frac{1}{2}}$

$$\frac{dy}{dx} = \frac{1}{2} \times x^{\frac{1}{2}-1}$$

$$= \frac{1}{2} x^{-\frac{1}{2}}$$

$$= \frac{1}{2\sqrt{x}}.$$

EXAMPLE 12.2

Given that $y = x\sqrt{x}$, find $\dfrac{dy}{dx}$ and evaluate $\dfrac{dy}{dx}$ at the point $(9, 27)$.

SOLUTION

$$y = x\sqrt{x} = x^{\frac{3}{2}}$$

$$\frac{dy}{dx} = \frac{3}{2} \times x^{\frac{3}{2}-1} = \frac{3}{2} x^{\frac{1}{2}}.$$

When $x = 9$, $\dfrac{dy}{dx} = \dfrac{3}{2} \times 9^{\frac{1}{2}}$

$\sqrt{x}$ or $x^{\frac{1}{2}}$ means the positive square root of x.

$$= \frac{3}{2} \times 3 = 4\frac{1}{2}.$$

In some of these questions you will find it useful to use a graphic calculator to check your answers.

1 Differentiate the following functions using the rules

$$y = kx^n \Rightarrow \frac{dy}{dx} = knx^{n-1} \quad \text{(for } k \text{ any constant, } n \text{ any real number)}$$

and $y = f(x) + g(x) \Rightarrow \frac{dy}{dx} = f'(x) + g'(x).$

(i) $y = \dfrac{1}{x^4}$

(ii) $y = 4x^{-5}$

(iii) $y = 7x^{-6}$

(iv) $y = \dfrac{3}{x^2}$

(v) $y = \dfrac{3}{x^5}$

(vi) $y = \dfrac{2}{x} + x^3$

(vii) $y = \dfrac{5}{x^3} - \dfrac{2}{x} + 1$

(viii) $y = x^{\frac{1}{4}}$

(ix) $y = 6x^{\frac{1}{3}}$

(x) $y = x^{\frac{3}{4}}$

(xi) $y = x^{-\frac{2}{3}}$

(xii) $y = \dfrac{1}{\sqrt{x}}$

(xiii) $y = \sqrt[5]{x}$

(xiv) $y = \sqrt{x} + \dfrac{1}{x^3} + 2x$

(xv) $y = \left(\sqrt[3]{x}\right)^4$

2 For each part of this question,

(a) find $\dfrac{dy}{dx}$

(b) find the gradient of the curve at the given point.

(i) $y = x^{-2}$; $(0.25, 16)$

(ii) $y = x^{-1} + x^{-4}$; $(-1, 0)$

(iii) $y = 4x^{-3} + 2x^{-5}$; $(1, 6)$

(iv) $y = 3x^4 - 4 - 8x^{-3}$; $(2, 43)$

(v) $y = \sqrt{x} + 3x$; $(4, 14)$

(vi) $y = 4x^{-\frac{1}{2}}$; $(9, 1\frac{1}{3})$

3 (i) Use your knowledge of the shape of the curve $y = \dfrac{1}{x}$ to sketch the curve

$y = \dfrac{1}{x} + 2.$

(ii) Write down the co-ordinates of the point where the curve crosses the x axis.

(iii) Differentiate $y = \dfrac{1}{x} + 2.$

(iv) Find the gradient of the curve at the point where it crosses the x axis.

4 Given that $f(x) = 9x + \dfrac{4}{x}$, find the range of values of x for which the function is decreasing.

5 The sketch shows the graph of $y = \dfrac{4}{x^2} + x$.

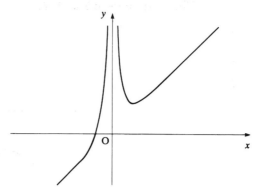

- **(i)** Differentiate $y = \dfrac{4}{x^2} + x$.
- **(ii)** Show that the point $(-2, -1)$ lies on the curve.
- **(iii)** Find the gradient of the curve at $(-2, -1)$.
- **(iv)** Show that the point $(2, 3)$ lies on the curve.
- **(v)** Find the gradient of the curve at $(2, 3)$.
- **(vi)** Relate your answer to (v) to the shape of the curve.

6 (i) Plot on the same axes the graphs with equations

$$y = \dfrac{1}{x^2} + 1 \quad \text{and} \quad y = -16x + 13 \quad \text{for} \quad -3 \leqslant x \leqslant 3.$$

- **(ii)** Show that the point $(0.5, 5)$ lies on both graphs.
- **(iii)** Differentiate $y = \dfrac{1}{x^2} + 1$ and find its gradient at $(0.5, 5)$.
- **(iv)** What can you deduce about the two graphs?

7 The sketch shows the graph of $y = \sqrt{x} - 1$.

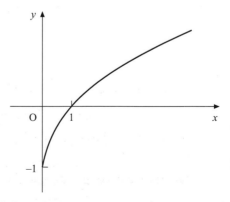

- **(i)** Differentiate $y = \sqrt{x} - 1$.
- **(ii)** Find the co-ordinates of the point on the curve $y = \sqrt{x} - 1$ at which the tangent is parallel to the line $y = 2x - 1$.
- **(iii)** Is the line $y = 2x - 1$ a tangent to the curve $y = \sqrt{x} - 1$? Give reasons for your answer.

8 The graph of $y = 3x - \dfrac{1}{x^2}$ is shown below.

The point marked P is $(1, 2)$.

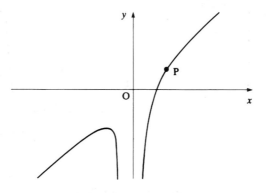

(i) Find the gradient function $\dfrac{dy}{dx}$.

(ii) Use your answer from (i) to find the gradient of the curve at P.

(iii) Use your answer from (ii), and the fact that the gradient of the curve at P is the same as that of the tangent at P, to find the equation of the tangent at P in the form $y = mx + c$.

9 The graph of $y = x^2 + \dfrac{1}{x}$ is shown below. The point marked Q is $(1, 2)$.

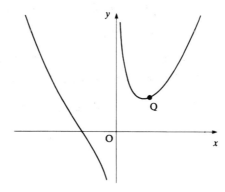

(i) Find the gradient function $\dfrac{dy}{dx}$.

(ii) Find the gradient of the tangent at Q.

(iii) Show that the equation of the normal to the curve at Q can be written as $x + y = 3$.

(iv) At what other points does the normal cut the curve?

10 For each of the following functions, find $\dfrac{dy}{dx}$ and $\dfrac{d^2y}{dx^2}$.

(i) $y = x^{-2}$ 　　　　　　(ii) $y = x^{\frac{3}{2}}$ 　　　　　　(iii) $y = x^4 - \dfrac{2}{x^3}$

11 Find any stationary points on the curves of the following functions and identify their nature. You do not need to sketch the curves but you should check your answers, if possible, using a graphic calculator.

(i) $y = x + \dfrac{1}{x}$ (ii) $y = x^3 + \dfrac{12}{x}$ (iii) $y = 6x - x^{\frac{3}{2}}$

12 For the function $y = x - 4\sqrt{x}$,

(i) find $\dfrac{dy}{dx}$ and $\dfrac{d^2y}{dx^2}$

(ii) find the co-ordinates of the turning point and determine its nature.

13 The equation of a curve is $y = 6\sqrt{x} - x\sqrt{x}$.

Find the x co-ordinate of the turning point and show that the turning point is a maximum.

14 For the curve $x^{\frac{5}{2}} - 10x^{\frac{3}{2}}$,

(i) find the values of x for which $y = 0$

(ii) show that there is a minimum turning point of the curve when $x = 6$ and calculate the y value of this minimum, giving the answer correct to 1 decimal place.

15 Charlie wants to add an extension with a floor area of 18m² to the back of his house. He wants to use the minimum possible number of bricks, so he wants to know the smallest perimeter he can use. The dimensions, in metres, are x and y as shown.

(i) Write down an expression for the area in terms of x and y.

(ii) Write down an expression, in terms of x and y, for the total length, T, of the outside walls.

(iii) Show that

$$T = 2x + \frac{18}{x}.$$

(iv) Find $\dfrac{dT}{dx}$ and $\dfrac{d^2T}{dx^2}$.

(v) Find the dimensions of the extension that give a minimum value of T, and confirm that it is a minimum.

16 A fish tank with a square base and no top is to be made from a thin sheet of toughened glass. The dimensions are as shown.

(i) Write down an expression for the volume V in terms of x and y.

(ii) Write down an expression for the total surface area A in terms of x and y.

The tank needs a capacity of $0.5\,\text{m}^3$ and the manufacturer wishes to use the minimum possible amount of glass.

(iii) Deduce an expression for A in terms of x only.

(iv) Find $\frac{\mathrm{d}A}{\mathrm{d}x}$ and $\frac{\mathrm{d}^2A}{\mathrm{d}x^2}$.

(v) Find the values of x and y that use the smallest amount of glass and confirm that these give the minimum value.

17 A closed rectangular box is made of thin card, and its length is three times its width. The height is $h\,\text{cm}$ and the width is $x\,\text{cm}$.

(i) The volume of the box is $972\,\text{cm}^3$.
Use this to write down an expression for h in terms of x.

(ii) Show that the surface area, A, can be written as $A = 6x^2 + \frac{2592}{x}$.

(iii) Find $\frac{\mathrm{d}A}{\mathrm{d}x}$ and use it to find a stationary point.

Find $\frac{\mathrm{d}^2A}{\mathrm{d}x^2}$ and use it to verify that the stationary point gives the minimum value of A.

(iv) Hence find the minimum surface area and the corresponding dimensions of the box.

Answers

9 (i) (a) £860

(b) £2390.65

(ii)

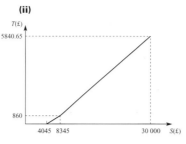

(iii) (a) $T = 0.2S - 809$

$4045 \leqslant S \leqslant 8345$

(b) $T = 0.23S - 1059.35$

$8345 \leqslant S \leqslant 30\,000$

(iv) (a) £791

(b) £3080.65

(c) £4690.65

10 (i)

(ii) $10P + N = 300$

(iii) £21.20

(iv) 63

11 (i)

(ii) $4I - 3S + 77 = 0$

(iii) £41 million

(iv) $10\frac{3}{4}\%$

12 (i)

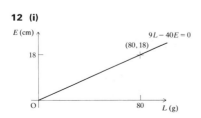

(ii) 10.8 cm

(iii) $44\frac{4}{9}$ g

(iv) $133\frac{1}{3}$ g

13 (i) $2x + y - 5 = 0$

(ii) 5 m

(iii) 5 m 59 cm

❓ (Page 56)

Attempting to solve the equations simultaneously gives 3 = 4 which is clearly false so there is no point of intersection. The lines are parallel.

Exercise 2D (Page 57)

1 (i) A (1, 1); B (5, 3); C (−1, 10)

(ii) BC = AC = $\sqrt{85}$

2 (i)

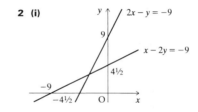

(ii) (−3, 3)

(iii) $2x - y = 3$; $x - 2y = 0$

(iv) (−6, −3); (5, 7)

3 (i) $y = \frac{1}{2}x + 1$, $y = -2x + 6$

(ii) Gradients = $\frac{1}{2}$ and $-2 \Rightarrow$ AC and BD are perpendicular. Intersection = (2, 2) = mid-point of both AC and BD.

(iii) AC = BD = $\sqrt{20}$

(iv) Square

4 (i)

(ii) A: (4, 0); B: (0,11); C: (2, 10)

(iii) 11

(iv) (−2, 21)

5 (i)

(ii) A: $2D - 5P + 5 = 0$

B: $3D - 5P = 0$

(iii) 5 km

(iv) A

6 (i) Supply: $L - 500W + 500 = 0$;

Demand: $L + 750W - 4750 = 0$

(ii) $L^* = 1600$; $W^* = 4.2$

(iii) Wage rate is the independent variable.

7 (i) (2, 4)

(ii) (0, 3)

8 (i)

(ii) £40; 28 articles

9 (i) $-\frac{1}{2}, \frac{3}{4}, -\frac{1}{2}, \frac{3}{4}$, parallelogram

(ii) 10

(iii) $-\frac{4}{3}$, $4x + 3y = 20$

(iv) (4.4, 0.8)

(v) 40 square units

10 (i) −3

(ii) $x - 3y + 5 = 0$

(iii) $x = 1$

(iv) (1, 2)

(vi) 3.75 square units

❓ (Page 60)

Even values of n: all values of y are positive; y axis is a line of symmetry.
Odd values of n: origin is the centre of rotational symmetry of order 2.

Activity 2.4 (Page 61)

$y = \dfrac{1}{x-1} + 2$

Asymptotes $x = 1$, $y = 2$.

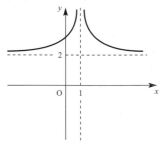

$y = \dfrac{1}{(x-1)^2} + 2$

Asymptotes $x = 1$, $y = 2$.

❓ (Page 62)

You need to ensure the same scale is used on the x and y axes for the curves to be displayed as circles.

❓ (Page 64)

Here are some hints:
For the angle in a semi-circle, join O to the vertex and use the fact that the triangles are isosceles, together with the angle sum of a triangle and the angle on a straight line.

For the perpendicular bisecting the chord, join O to both ends of the chord and prove that the triangles are congruent.
For the tangent and radius, use a symmetry argument.

❓ (Page 64)

The converse of p implies q is q implies p.
To prove the converses, look at your arguments for the last discussion point. Think whether 'implies' at each stage can be replaced by 'is implied by' or 'both implies and is implied by' and adapt your reasoning as necessary. (See also page 152.)

❓ (Page 66)

The radius of the circle, or the perpendicular distance of the centre from AB.

Exercise 2E (Page 66)

1   **(i)** $(x-1)^2 + y^2 = 16$

    (ii) $(x-2)^2 + (y+1)^2 = 9$

    (iii) $(x-1)^2 + (y+3)^2 = 25$

    (iv) $(x+2)^2 + (y+5)^2 = 1$

2   **(i)**   **(a)** $(0, 0)$

        (b)   3

    (ii)   **(a)** $(0, 2)$

        (b)   5

    (iii)   **(a)** $(3, -1)$

        (b)   4

    (iv)   **(ai)** $(-2, -2)$

        (b)   2

    (v)   **(a)** $(-4, 0)$

        (b) $\sqrt{8}$

3   $(x-1)^2 + (y-7)^2 = 169$

4

5   $r = 2$; $(-1, 2)$; 2

6   **(i)** $(2, 11)$; $\sqrt{10}$

    (ii) $(x-2)^2 + (y-11)^2 = 10$

7

    $(x-4)^2 + (y-4)^2 = 16$

8   $(x-5)^2 + (y-4)^2 = 25$ or
    $(x-5)^2 + (y+4)^2 = 25$

9   **(i)**   Centre: $(3, -1)$; B: $(5, 0)$

10   **(i)** $(8, 2)$

    (ii) $\sqrt{45}$

    (iii) $\sqrt{50}$

11   **(i)** $AB = \sqrt{20}$, $BC = \sqrt{45}$,
      $AC = \sqrt{65}$

    (ii) $AB^2 + BC^2 = 65 = AC^2$

        $\Rightarrow$ triangle ABC is right-angled, with the right angle at B (converse of Pythagoras' theorem)

        $\Rightarrow$ B is angle in a semi-circle (converse of the angle in a semi-circle is a right angle)

        i.e. AC is a diameter of the circle, as required.

    (iii)   15

12   **(i)** $y = 2$, $y = \frac{1}{3}x + 1$

    (ii) $(3, 2)$

    (iii) $(x-3)^2 + (y-2)^2 = 25$

13   $4x - 3y + 13 = 0$

❓ (Page 69)

        $(x-5)^2 + (0-8)^2 = 73$

$\Rightarrow$ $(x-5)^2 + 64 = 73$

$\Rightarrow$ $(x-5)^2 = 9$

$\Rightarrow \quad x - 5 = \pm 3$

$\Rightarrow \quad x = 5 + 3$ or $x = 5 - 3$

$\Rightarrow \quad x = 8$ or 2

❓ (Page 71)

Methods for finding the intersection of a curve and a line include:

1 solving simultaneous equations algebraically

2 drawing the graphs

   (i)   by hand

   (ii) using a graphic calculator, and using zoom and trace or an intersect function

   (iii) using a computer graphics package and using an intersect function

3 Listing values in a table then using trial and improvement (not recommended!).

Exercise 2F (Page 72)

1 $(2, 7)$

2 (ii)

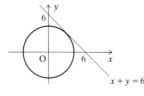

$(-3, -3); x + y = -6$

3

$x = -6, x = 2, y = -1, y = 7$

4 $(3, 5); (-1, -3)$

5 (i) $(1, 2); (-5, -10)$

6 $(0, 5); (-3, 4)$

7 $(0, 1); (1, 2); (2, 3)$

8 (i) 14 cm

   (ii) $x^2 + (y - 8)^2 = 100$

   (iii) 264 cm^2

9 (i) $(8, 0), (0, 6), (4, 3); 10$

   (ii) $(x - 4)^2 + (y - 3)^2 = 25$

   (iii) $\left(-10\frac{2}{7}, -7\frac{5}{7}\right)$

10 (i) $4x - 3y + 13 = 0$

   (ii) $(2, 7)$

   (iii) 5

   (iv) $(x - 2)^2 + (y - 7)^2 = 5^2$

   (v) $(-2, 10)$

11 (ii) $\frac{1}{2}, -2$

   (iii) 10 square units

   (iv) $y = 3x - 7$

   (vi) 0.27, 3.73

12 (i) 2

   (ii) $(6, 4)$

   (iii) $2x + y - 8 = 0$

   (iv) $(2.8, 2.4)$

   (v) $(x - 3)^2 + (y - 2)^2 = 13$

13 (i) $x = 7$

   (ii) $x + 3y = 10$

   (iv) $(x - 7)^2 + (y - 1)^2 = 50$

   (v) 2

   (vi) 30 square units

Chapter 3

❓ (Page 77)

For the solid curve you can try $y = f(x)$ where $f(x) = kx(x - 1)(x - 2)$. This passes through $(0, 0)$, $(0, 1)$ and $(2, 0)$ but its maximum is not quite when $x = \frac{1}{2}$. A value of k of 0.208 gives a maximum value of 0.08. The broken curve is then $y = -f(x)$. A better fit can be obtained by taking a two part function

$$f(x) = 0.32x(1 - x) \text{ for } 0 \leq x \leq 1$$

and $\quad f(x) = 0.32(x - 1)(x - 2)$

$$\text{for } 1 \leq x \leq 2.$$

Exercise 3A (Page 82)

1 (i) 3   **(ii)** 12   **(iii)** 7

2 $2x^3 - 4$

3 $x^4 + 4x^3 + 6x^2 + 4x + 1$

4 $x^3 + 2x^2 + 5x + 7$

5 $-x^2 + 15x + 18$

6 $2x^4 + 8$

7 $x^4 + 4x^3 + 6x^2 + 4x + 1$

8 $x^4 - 5x^2 + 4$

9 $x^4 - 10x^2 + 9$

10 $x^{11} - 1$

11 $2x - 2$

12 $10x^2$

13 4

14 $2x^2 - 2x$

15 $-8x^3 - 8x$

16 $x^2 - 2x - 3$

17 $x^2 + 3x$

18 $2x^2 - 5x + 5$

19 $x^3 + x^2 + 2x + 2$

20 $2x^2 + 3$

Activity 3.1 (Page 84)

$y = x^6 + \ldots$	$y = x^5 + \ldots$
$y = -x^6 + \ldots$	$y = -x^5 + \ldots$

Exercise 3B (Page 87)

1

2

3

4

5

6

7

8

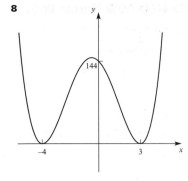

9 $y = (x + 1)^2 (x - 2)^2$

❓ (Page 87)

$(x - a)^3$: crosses the x axis at $(a, 0)$ but is flat at that point.

$(x - a)^4$: touches the x axis at $(a, 0)$.

The same results hold for any odd or even n for $(x - a)^n$.

❓ (Page 93)

Its order will be less than n.

Exercise 3C (Page 94)

1 (i) $0, 0, -8, -18, -24, -20, 0$

(ii) $(x + 3)(x + 2)(x - 3)$

(iii) $-3, -2$ or 3

(iv)

2 (i) $-15, 0, 3, 0, -3, 0, 15$

(ii) $x(x + 2)(x - 2)$

(iii) $-2, 0$ or 2

(iv)

3 (i) $30, 0, (x - 3)$

(ii) $p = 2, q = -15$

(iii) $-5, 2$ or 3

(iv)

4 (ii) $-2, 3$ or 4

(iii)

5 (i) 0

(ii) $-1 \pm \sqrt{2}$

(iii)

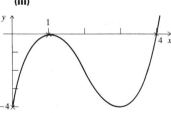

6 (i) -4

(ii) $(x - 1)^2$

(iii)

7 (i) $a = 2, b = 1, c = 2$

(ii) $0, \sqrt{3}$ or $-\sqrt{3}$

8 (i) $(x^2 - 4)(x^2 - 1)$

(ii) $(x + 2)(x - 2)(x^2 + 1)$

(iii) Two real roots: -2 and 2

9 (ii) 19

10 (i) $\pm 6, \pm 3, \pm 2, \pm 1,$

(ii) $-1, 2$ or 3

11 (i) $(x-1)(x-2)(x+2)$

 (ii) $(x+1)(x^2-x+1)$

 (iii) $(x-2)(x^2+2x+5)$

 (iv) $(x+2)(x^2-x+3)$

12 (ii) (a) -6

 (b) -2

 (c) $-2x-4$

13 -12

14 2 or -5

15 $-5; 4; 4$

16 $-1; -7; 1, -2$ or $\frac{3}{2}$

17 (i) $\left(\dfrac{8}{x^2}\right)$ m

 (iv) $4, 1.464$

18 (i) $-3, 2$

 (ii) $-3, 2, 2$

 (iii) -24

 (iv) $2, 16, -24$

19 (i) A quadratic has only one turning point and this curve has two.

 (ii) $1, 3, -2$

 (iii) $-2, 10, -14, 6$

 (iv) $f(2) = 2$ so a value of 1.9 is a good fit.

20 (i) This has two turning points and so does a cubic.

 (ii) $1, 2$

 (iii) 0.15

 (iv) The model predicts $y = 3.6$ when $x = 4$.

 Not a very good fit

 (v) $x = 3, y = 1: x = 4, y = 5$.

 A better fit

❓ (Page 99)

For $x^2 + bx + c$, the process makes it into $x^2 + bx + \left(\dfrac{b}{2}\right)^2 + \left(c - \left(\dfrac{b}{2}\right)^2\right)$.

This is $\left(x + \dfrac{b}{2}\right)^2 + \left(c - \dfrac{b^2}{4}\right)$ and so is of the form $(x+p)^2 + q$ with $p = \dfrac{b}{2}$ and $q = \left(c - \dfrac{b^2}{4}\right)$.

Exercise 3D (Page 100)

1 (i) (a) $(x+2)^2 + 5$

 (b) $x = -2; (-2, 5)$

 (c)
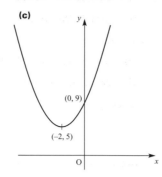

(ii) (a) $(x-2)^2 + 5$

 (b) $x = 2; (2, 5)$

 (c)
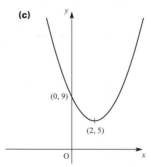

(iii) (a) $(x+2)^2 - 1$

 (b) $x = -2, (-2, -1)$

 (c)
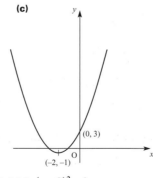

(iv) (a) $(x-2)^2 - 1$

 (b) $x = 2; (2, -1)$

 (c)

(v) (a) $(x+3)^2 - 10$

 (b) $x = -3; (-3, -10)$

 (c)
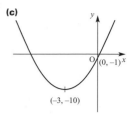

(vi) (a) $(x-5)^2 - 25$

 (b) $x = 5; (5, -25)$

 (c)
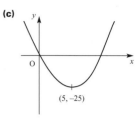

(vii) (a) $\left(x+\frac{1}{2}\right)^2 + 1\frac{3}{4}$

 (b) $x = -\frac{1}{2}; \left(-\frac{1}{2}, 1\frac{3}{4}\right)$

 (c)
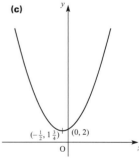

(viii) (a) $\left(x-1\frac{1}{2}\right)^2 - 9\frac{1}{4}$

 (b) $x = 1\frac{1}{2}; \left(1\frac{1}{2}, -9\frac{1}{4}\right)$

 (c)
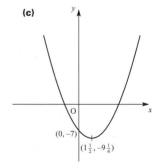

(ix) (a) $\left(x-\frac{1}{4}\right)^2 + \frac{15}{16}$

 (b) $x = \frac{1}{4}; \left(\frac{1}{4}, \frac{15}{16}\right)$

(c)

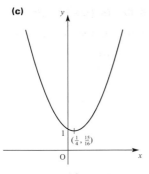

(x) **(a)** $(x + 0.05)^2 + 0.0275$

   (b) $x = -0.05$; $(-0.05, 0.0275)$

(c)

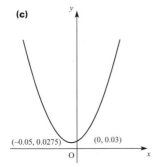

2 (i) $x^2 + 4x + 1$

   (ii) $x^2 + 8x + 12$

   (ii) $x^2 - 2x + 3$

   (iv) $x^2 - 20x + 112$

   (v) $x^2 - x + 1$

   (vi) $x^2 + 0.2x + 1$

3 (i) $2(x + 1)^2 + 4$

   (ii) $3(x - 3)^2 - 54$

   (iii) $-(x + 1)^2 + 6$

   (iv) $-2\left(x + \frac{1}{2}\right)^2 - 1\frac{1}{2}$

   (v) $5(x - 1)^2 + 2$

   (vi) $4\left(x - \frac{1}{2}\right)^2 - 5$

   (vii) $-3(x + 2)^2 + 12$

   (viii) $8\left(x + 1\frac{1}{2}\right)^2 - 20$

4 (i) $b = -6$, $c = 10$

   (ii) $b = 2$, $c = 0$

   (iii) $b = -8$, $c = 16$

   (iv) $b = 6$, $c = 11$

Activity 3.2 (Page 101)

See text that follows.

❓ (Page 104)

Completing the square uses an approach starting from the algebra of the equation in the form

$y = ax^2 + bx + c.$

Using transformations starts best from the graph, identifying the equation as $y = (x - p)^2 + q$.

❓ (Page 104)

Yes. An identity is true for all values of the variable so any particular values can be substituted to give an equation.

Activity 3.3 (Page 105)

(i)

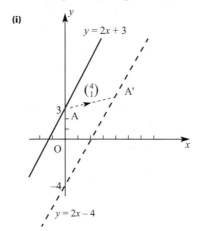

(ii) $(y - 1) = 2(x - 4) + 3$

   $y = 2x - 4$

Exercise 3E (Page 105)

1 (i) $\begin{pmatrix} 0 \\ 3 \end{pmatrix}$; $x = 0$

   (ii) $\begin{pmatrix} -4 \\ 0 \end{pmatrix}$; $x = -4$

   (iii) $\begin{pmatrix} 0 \\ -7 \end{pmatrix}$; $x = 0$

   (iv) $\begin{pmatrix} 1 \\ 0 \end{pmatrix}$; $x = 1$

   (v) $\begin{pmatrix} 2 \\ 10 \end{pmatrix}$; $x = 2$

   (vi) $\begin{pmatrix} -5 \\ 6 \end{pmatrix}$; $x = -5$

   (vii) $\begin{pmatrix} 1 \\ -1 \end{pmatrix}$; $x = 1$

   (viii) $\begin{pmatrix} 2 \\ -1 \end{pmatrix}$; $x = 2$

---

2 (i) $y = x^3 + 4$

   (ii) $y = (x - 4)^3$

   (iii) $y = (x + 3)^3$

   (iv) $y = x^3 - 20$

   (v) $y = (x - 5)^3 + 6$

   (vi) $y = (x + 7)^3 + 1$

3 $y = 3(x - 4)(x - 1)(x + 2)$

4 (i)

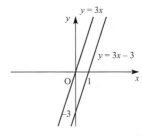

   (ii) -3

   (iii) 1

5 (i) $y = 2x + 6$

   (ii) $y = 2x + 16$

   (iii) $y = 2x$

6 (i) $a = -4$

   (ii)

7 $p = 3$, $q = 2$

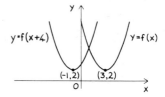

8 $y = x^2 + 20x + 91$

9 (i) (a) $y = g(x) + 1$

   (b) $y = g(x - 1) - 1$

   (ii)

10 (i)

(ii)

(iii)

11 (i)

(4,-2)

(ii)

(-2,4)

(ii)

12 (i) 9

(ii) 5

(iii) 1

(iv) 13

(v) 15

(vi) 3. 5

Activity 3.4 (Page 111)

(i) $\dfrac{n-1}{2}$

(ii) $\dfrac{n-2}{3}$

❓ (Page 114)

1.61051. This is $1 + 5 \times (0.1) + 10 \times (0.1)^2 + 10 \times (0.1)^3 + 5 \times (0.1)^4 + 1 \times (0.1)^5$ and 1, 5, 10, 10, 5, 1 are the binominal coefficients for $n = 5$.

Exercise 3F (Page 115)

1 (i) $x^4 + 4x^3 + 6x^2 + 4x + 1$

(ii) $1 + 7x + 21x^2 + 35x^3 + 35x^4 + 21x^5 + 7x^6 + x^7$

(iii) $x^5 + 10x^4 + 40x^3 + 80x^2 + 80x + 32$

(iv) $64x^6 + 192x^5 + 240x^4 + 160x^3 + 60x^2 + 12x + 1$

(v) $16x^4 - 96x^3 + 216x^2 - 216x + 81$

(vi) $8x^3 + 36x^2y + 54xy^2 + 27y^3$

2 (i) 6

(ii) 15

(iii) 20

(iv) 15

(v) 1

(vi) 220

(vii) 220

(viii) 1365

(ix) 1

3 (i) 56

(ii) 210

(iii) 673 596

(iv) −823 680

(v) 70

4 (i) $1 + 4x + 6x^2 + 4x^3 + x^4$

(ii) 1.008

(iii) 0.0024%

5 (i) $6x + 2x^3$

6 (i) $32 - 80x + 80x^2 - 40x^3 + 10x^4 - x^5$

(ii) 31.208

(iii) 0.000 13%

7 (i) and (ii)

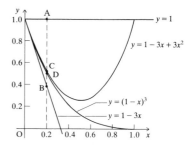

(iii) (a) AD

(b) BD

(c) CD

8 (i) £2570

(ii) True value = £2593.74

(iii) £23.74

9 (ii) $x = 0, -1$ and -2

10 (i) $(x-2), (x-2)(x^2 - 4x - 21)$

(ii) $(-3, 0), (2, 0), (7.0)$

(iii) $16 - 32x + 24x^2 - 8x^3 + x^4$

(iv) 0.2321

Chapter 4

❓ (Page 119)

No. Even to the nearest £1 million would be quite accurate and to the nearest month for the work.

❓ (Page 119)

Sarah's statement will often be true; Stephen's hardly ever.

❓ (Page 121)

The numerical difference between a calculated or measured value and the true value (which is often unknown).

Activity 4.1 (Page 122)

(i) (a) −4.51%

(b) 0.04%

(c) −0.05%

(d) 0.66%

(ii) (a) 27.3%

(b) −15.1%

(c) 10.3%

(d) −7.8%

(e) 6.3%

(f) −5.3%

❓ (Page 125)

To sketch $y = ax^2 + bx + c$, first solve the quadratic equation $ax^2 + bx + c = 0$ to find where the graph crosses the x axis. Try to solve by factorisation before using the formula if necessary. The sign of a tells you which way up the parabola is.

❓ (Page 125)

$$x^2 - 4x + 3 \leqslant 0$$

$$\Rightarrow \quad (x-1)(x-3) \leqslant 0$$

For the product of two numbers to be negative, one must be positive and the other must be negative.

$\Rightarrow \quad x - 1 \leqslant 0$ and $x - 3 \geqslant 0$

$\Rightarrow \quad x \leqslant 1$ and $x \geqslant 3$

$\Rightarrow \quad$ impossible

or

$\Rightarrow \quad x - 1 \geqslant 0$ and $x - 3 \leqslant 0$

$\Rightarrow \quad x \geqslant 1$ and $x \leqslant 3$

$\Rightarrow \quad 1 \leqslant x \leqslant 3$

So the answer is $1 \leqslant x \leqslant 3$.

❓ (Page 125)

It is easier to solve an equation than an inequality, and sketching a quadratic graph when you know where it crosses the x axis is then simple. The graphical method then shows clearly the required region rather than having to consider two cases separately, as in the algebraic method.

Exercise 4A (Page 126)

1 (i) $a > 6$

(ii) $b \leqslant 2$

(iii) $c > -2$

(iv) $d \leqslant -\frac{4}{3}$

(v) $e > 7$

(vi) $f > -1$

(vii) $g \leqslant 1.4$

(viii) $h < 0$

2 (i) $1 < p < 4$

(ii) $p \leqslant 1$ or $p \geqslant 4$

(iii) $-2 \leqslant x \leqslant -1$

(iv) $x < -2$ or $x > -1$

(v) $y < -1$ or $y > 3$

(vi) $-4 \leqslant z \leqslant 5$

(vii) $q \neq 2$

(viii) $y < -2$ or $y > 4$

(ix) $-2 < x < \frac{1}{3}$

(x) $y \leqslant -\frac{1}{2}$ or $y \geqslant 6$

(xi) $1 \leqslant x \leqslant 3$

(xii) $y < -\frac{1}{2}$ or $y > \frac{3}{5}$

Chapter 5

❓ (Page 127)

$a = 60; b = 28$

Exercise 5A (Page 130)

1 (i) $\sqrt{7}$

(ii) $\sqrt{3}$

(iii) $\sqrt{2} + 1$

(iv) 1

(v) $2(\sqrt{3} - \sqrt{2})$

2 (i) $8 + 3\sqrt{2}$

(ii) $5\sqrt{2}$

(iii) $19 + 16\sqrt{5}$

(iv) $8\sqrt{2} + 2\sqrt{5}$

(v) $6\sqrt{2}$

3 (i) $10 + \sqrt{2}$

(ii) $7 - 4\sqrt{3}$

(iii) $10 - 2\sqrt{5}$

(iv) -4

(v) $1 + \frac{1}{2}\sqrt{3}$

(vi) $3\sqrt{7} - 9$

(vii) 14

(viii) $\sqrt{30}$

(ix) 2

4 (i) $1 + \frac{1}{2}\sqrt{2}$

(ii) $\frac{1}{2}\left(3\sqrt{3} - 5\right)$

(iii) $1 - \frac{2}{5}\sqrt{5}$

(iv) $-\frac{1}{4}\left(1 + \sqrt{5}\right)$

(v) $-3 - \sqrt{3}$

(vi) $\frac{1}{3}\left(\sqrt{7} + 1\right)$

(vii) $\frac{1}{7}\left(9 + 4\sqrt{2}\right)$

(viii) $11 + 2\sqrt{30}$

❓ (Page 130)

As $T = kr^x$ where x is a number between 1 and 2.

❓ (Page 134)

Method 2 is usually preferable. For numbers greater than 1, finding the root first gives a smaller number to deal with, as shown in Example 5.9.

Exercise 5B (Page 136)

1 (i) 3^4

(ii) 3^0

(iii) 3^3

(iv) 3^{-3}

(v) $3^{\frac{1}{2}}$

(vi) 3^1

2 (i) 4^2

(ii) $4^{\frac{1}{2}}$

(iii) 4^{-1}

(iv) $4^{-\frac{1}{2}}$

(v) $4^{\frac{3}{2}}$

(vi) $4^{-\frac{3}{2}}$

3 (i) 10^3

(ii) 10^{-4}

(iii) 10^{-3}

(iv) $10^{\frac{3}{2}}$

(v) $10^{-\frac{1}{2}}$

(vi) 10^{-6}

4 (i) $\frac{1}{32}$

(ii) 3

(iii) $\frac{1}{3}$

(iv) 5

(v) $\frac{1}{5}$

(vi) 1

5 (i) x^{18}

(ii) x^{10}

(iii) x^{-2}

(iv) x^4

(v) $x^{-\frac{3}{2}}$

(vi) x^{-12}

(vii) x^2

(viii) x^2

(ix) $x^{\frac{1}{2}}$

(x) x^{-10}

6 (i) $12x^8y^3$

(ii) $4x^4y^{-1}$

(iii) $64x^{24}y^9$

(iv) $2x^{-2}y^{-1}$

(v) x^4y^0

7 (i) 9

(ii) 10

(iii) $\frac{1}{5}$

(iv) 1

(v) $5^5 = 3125$

(vi) 27

8 (i) 49

(ii) 3

(iii) 3

(iv) $3^6 = 729$

(v) 8

(vi) 4

9 (i) 4

(ii) 0

(iii) 0

(iv) $1\frac{15}{16}$

(v) 0

(vi) $2\frac{2}{3}$

10 (i) $3\sqrt{2}$

(ii) $-3\sqrt[3]{4}$

(iii) $43\sqrt{7}$

11 (i) $(2 + x)(1 + x)^{\frac{1}{2}}$

(ii) $(10 + 9x)(2 + 3x)^{\frac{1}{2}}$

(iii) $[6 - 5(x + y)](x + y)^{\frac{1}{2}}$

(iv) $\left(1 + \frac{1}{x}\right)\sqrt{x}$

(v) $(-2 + 2x - x^2)(x^2 - 2x + 3)^{\frac{1}{2}}$

Chapter 6

❓ (Page 138)

153. Airline flights, for example, connecting 18 major cities.

❓ (Page 140)

Yes.

❓ (Page 142)

To walk for 8 hours a day, not 24!

❓ (Page 143)

Recognise that the direct mileage of 874 miles is not the best walking route. More realistic are routes taking about 1100 miles.

Reduce her average speed figure to allow for hills, etc.

Allow for walking less than 8 hours each day, rest days, etc.

❓ (Page 143)

Step 1: How long will it take?

Step 2: Katie's initial assumptions of walking at 4 mph, etc.

Step 3: Using the formula, distance = speed × time.

Step 4: Finding the initial result.

Steps 5 and 7: Comparing the initial result with common sense to say that the time is still too short.

Step 8: Revising assumptions to use 8 hours rather than 24 for the walking time per day.

Steps 5, 6 and 7: Researching and comparing her results with actual results.

Step 8: Reviewing assumptions again.

Exercise 6A (Page 145)

1 (i) $p = 2(l + w)$; $A = lw$

(ii) (a) $p = 18$ feet;

$A = 18$ square feet

(b) $p = 36$ feet;

$A = 72$ square feet

(iii) $p = 3l$, $A = \frac{l^2}{2}$; $3 \leq l \leq 12$

2 (i) $500 - 8f - 6s$

(ii) The stamps cost more than £5.

(iii) $f \in \mathbb{Z}+$; $s \in \mathbb{Z}+$; $f > s$ and $s \geq 1$

3 (i) 30, 19.5, 12, 7.5, 6, 7.5, 12, 19.5, 30

(ii)

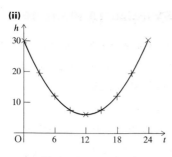

(iii) Unlikely: this implies heavy
demand from midnight to
6 am.

4 (i) $h = \sqrt{a^2 + b^2}$

(ii) (a) 5

(b) 17

(c) 29

(d) $\sqrt{2}$

(iii) No: see part (ii) (d)

5 (i) 1 hour 53 minutes

(ii) 7

6 (i) $A = lw - 4x^2$;
$V = x(l - 2x)(w - 2x)$

(ii) $A = 700$, $V = 1500$

(iii) x just over 1.2, V just under 33

7 (i) (a) £30

(b) £75

(ii) (a) 30p

(b) 7.5p

(iii) $\frac{2500 + 5n}{n}$ pence

(iv) Fixed £25; run-on 5p/card

(v) $n \in \mathbb{Z}+$

8 (i) $g = 8(4n - 1)$

(ii) 23 girders; length 184 m

(iii) (a) 5

(b) 5

(iv) $s = 8 \times$ (largest whole
number $\leqslant (m + 1)/4$)

9 (i) (a) £11 900

(b) £57 500

(c) £110 000

(ii) (a) £11 900

(b) £11 500

(c) £11 000

(iii) £$(12\,000 - 100n)$

(iv) The average price per car
continues to fall as you
increase the number ordered,
until for 120 cars the price
according to this formula is
zero. The dealer would soon
be out of business.

10 (i) $s = r + g,\ p = rg$

(ii) (a) 10, −4

(b) 24, −12

(iii) $s \in \{-4, -3, -2, -1, 0, 1, 2, 3,$
$4,\ 5, 6, 8, 10\},\ p \in \{-12, -8,$
$-6, -4, -2, -1, 0, 1, 2, 4, 12, 24\}$

? (Page 149)

Yes.

? (Page 150)

⇔

? (Page 151)

1 (i) Necessary: no, it could end
in 5.

(ii) Sufficient: yes

2 (i) Yes

(ii) No. You also need $a \neq 0$.

? (Page 151)

⇔

Exercise 6B (Page 151)

1 ⇒

2 ⇐

3 ⇔

4 ⇔

5 ⇒

6 ⇔

7 ⇐

8 ⇐

9 ⇒

10 ⇐

11 ⇒

12 ⇐

13 ⇔

14 ⇒

15 ⇔

? (Page 153)

1 Yes.

2 For example, if ABCD is a
rectangle then AB = CD.

Exercise 6C (Page 153)

1 (i) If a triangle has two angles
equal, then it has two sides
equal.

(ii) True

2 (i) If Alf is dead, then Alf was
murdered by Fred.

(ii) False

3 (i) If the square of a number is
an integer, then the number
is an integer.

(ii) True

4 (i) If each of the angles of ABCD
is 90°, then ABCD is a square.

(ii) False

5 (i) If $x^2 = y^2$, $x \neq y$ (e.g. $(-4)^2 =$
$(4)^2$ but $-4 \neq 4$).

(ii) False

6 (i) If $\angle PQR + \angle PSR = 180°$,
then P, Q, R and S all lie on
a circle.

(ii) True

7 (i) If Struan goes swimming,
then it is sunny.

(ii) False

8 (i) $\angle x = \angle y \Rightarrow l$ and m are parallel.

　(ii) True

9 (i) If $n > 2$, then n is an odd prime number.

　(ii) False

10 (i) If an equation has at least one root, then it is a cubic equation.

　(ii) False

11 (i) If a triangle has three equal angles, then it has three equal sides.

　(ii) True

12 (i) If a curve has one turning point, then it is the curve of a quadratic function.

　(ii) False

❓ (Page 155)

You need to check only the prime numbers 2, 3, 5 and 7.

Exercise 6D (Page 157)

1 True

2 True

3 False

4 False

5 True

6 True

7 False

8 True

9 True

10 False

11 (i) True　(ii) False

12 True

13 False

14 False

15 True

16 True

17 True

18 (i) True　(ii) True

19 True

Chapter 7

❓ (Page 160)

(i) (a) Avonford Savings

　(b) 80 000, 160 000, 320 000, …

　(c) Exponential geometric sequence

　(d) The sequence could go on but the family will not live forever.

(ii) (a) Fish & Chips opening hours

　(b) 10, 10, 10, 10, 12, …

　(c) They go in a cycle, repeating every 7

　(d) Go on forever (or a long time)

(iii) (a) Clock

　(b) 0, −3.5, −5, −3.5, 0, 3.5, …

　(c) A regular pattern, repeating every 8

　(d) Forever

(iv) (a) Steps

　(b) 120, 140, 160, …

　(c) Increasing by a fixed amount (arithmetic sequence)

　(d) The steps won't go on forever.

❓ (Page 166)

Check each others' sequences by using the definition of a_k you have found to generate the sequence.

Exercise 7A (Page 167)

1 (i) 19 22 25 28. Arithmetic with 1st term $a = 7$ and common difference $d = 3$.

　(ii) 4 3 2 1. Arithmetic: $a = 8$, $d = -1$.

　(iii) 810 2430 7290 21870. Geometric with 1st term $a = 10$ and common ratio $r = 3$.

　(iv) 4 2 1$\frac{1}{2}$. Geometric: $a = 64$, $r = \frac{1}{2}$.

　(v) 2 2 2 5. Periodic with period $p = 4$.

　(vi) 4 2 1 2. Periodic: $p = 8$

　(vii) −32 64 −128 256. Geometric, oscillating, non-periodic: $a = 1$, $r = -2$.

　(viii) 4 6 8 2. Periodic: $p = 4$.

　(ix) 3.3 3.1 2.9 2.7. Arithmetic: $a = 4.1$, $d = -0.2$.

　(x) 1.4641 1.61051 1.771561 1.9487171. Geometric: $a = 1$, $r = 1.1$.

2 (i) 3 5 7 9

　(ii) 6 12 24 48

　(iii) 4 8 14 24

　(iv) 1 $\frac{1}{2}$ $\frac{1}{3}$ $\frac{1}{4}$

　(v) 12 15 18 21

　(vi) −5 5 −5 5

　(vii) 72 36 18 9

　(viii) 4 6 4 6

　(ix) 4 6 4 6

　(x) 1 4 9 16

3 (i) 58

　(ii) 90

　(iii) 25

　(iv) 40

　(v) 8

4 (i) $\sum_{1}^{10} k$

(ii) $\sum_{1}^{10}(20 + k)$

(iii) $\sum_{1}^{10}(200 + 10k)$

(iv) $\sum_{1}^{10}(200 + 11k)$

(v) $\sum_{1}^{10}(200 - 10k)$

5 (i) 15

(ii) 400

(iii) −20

6 (i) 0 1 1 2 3. The sequence of differences, after the first term, is the same as the sequence itself.

(ii) 13 21 34

(iii) 1.0 2.0 1.5 1.667 1.6 1.625 1.615 1.619. The ratios are converging.

7 (i) 2 6 2 6 2 6

(ii) Oscillating periodic sequence, $p = 2$.

(iii) (a) 2 8 −4 20 −28 68. Diverging oscillating sequence.

(b) $3\frac{1}{2}$ $4\frac{1}{4}$ $3\frac{7}{8}$ $4\frac{1}{16}$ $3\frac{31}{32}$ $4\frac{1}{64}$. Oscillating sequence, converging towards 4.

8 (i) 0, −2, 2; $t_{100} = 2$

(ii) $2^2 - 2 = 2$; $t_1 = -1$

(iii) (a) Diverges

(b) Converges to −1

(c) Oscillates between $\frac{\sqrt{5}-1}{2}$ and $\frac{-\sqrt{5}-1}{2}$.

9 (i) 4.000 2.667 3.467 2.895 3.340 2.976 3.284 3.017.

(ii) The numbers appear to converge towards a value between 3.0 and 3.2.

10 (i) $\frac{1}{3} + \frac{1}{4} > \frac{1}{4} + \frac{1}{4} = \frac{1}{2}$;
$\frac{1}{5} + \frac{1}{6} + \frac{1}{7} + \frac{1}{8} > \frac{1}{8} + \frac{1}{8} + \frac{1}{8} + \frac{1}{8} = \frac{1}{2}$.
This is true for each bracket formed, so
$S > 1 + \frac{1}{2} + \frac{1}{2} + \frac{1}{2} + \dots$

(ii) $1 + \frac{1}{2} + \frac{1}{2} + \frac{1}{2} + \dots$ is clearly infinite, and S is greater than this.

Exercise 7B (Page 173)

1 (i) Yes: $d = 2$, $a_7 = 39$

(ii) No

(iii) No

(iv) Yes: $d = 4$, $a_7 = 27$

(v) Yes: $d = -2$, $a_7 = -4$

2 (i) 10

(ii) 37

3 (i) 4

(ii) 34

4 (i) 5

(ii) 850

5 (i) 16 18 20

(ii) 324

6 (i) 15

(ii) 1170

7 (i) First term 4, common difference 6

(ii) 12

8 (i) 3

(ii) 165

9 (i) 23p

(ii) £1.44

10 (i) 5000

(ii) 5100

(iii) 10 100

(iv) The 1st sum, 5000, and the 2nd sum, 5100, add up to the third sum, 10 100. This is because the sum of the odd numbers plus the sum of the even numbers from 50 to 150 is the same as the sum of all the numbers from 50 to 150.

11 (i) 22 000

(ii) The 17th term is the first negative term.

12 (i) $a_k = 3k + 4$; 23rd term

(ii) $\frac{n}{2}(11 + 3n)$; 63 terms

13 (i) $t_1 = 10$; difference 7; 35 650

(ii) $t_1 = 5$; $t_2 = 9$; $t_k = 4k + 1$

14 (i) £16 500

(ii) 8

15 (i) 49

(ii) 254.8 km

16 (i) 16

(ii) 2.5 cm

17 (i) 2

(ii) 40

(iii) $\frac{n}{2}(3n + 1)$

(iv) $\frac{n}{2}(9n + 1)$

18 (i) $a + 4d = 205$; $a + 18d = 373$

(ii) 12 tickets; 157

(iii) 28 books.

❓ (Page 179)

For example, in column A enter 1 in cell A1 and fill down a series of step 1; then in B1 enter
=0.2*5^(A1-1)
then fill down column B. Look for the value 390 635 in column B and read off the value of n in column A. An alternative approach is to use the IF function to find the correct value.

❓ (Page 180)

3.7×10^{11} tonnes. Less than 1.8×10^9; perhaps 10^8 for China.

❓ (Page 183)

The series does not converge so it does not have a sum to infinity.

Exercise 7C (Page 183)

1 (i) Yes: $r = 2$, $a_7 = 320$

   (ii) No

   (iii) Yes: $r = -1$, $a_7 = 1$

   (iv) Yes: $r = 1$, $a_7 = 5$

   (v) No

   (vi) Yes: $r = \frac{1}{2}$, $a_7 = \frac{3}{32}$

   (vii) No

2 (i) 384

   (ii) 765

3 (i) 4

   (ii) 81 920

4 (i) 9

   (ii) 10th term

5 (i) 9

   (ii) 4088

6 (i) 6

   (ii) 267 (to 3 s.f.)

7 (i) 2

   (ii) 3

   (iii) 3069

8 (i) $\frac{1}{2}$

   (ii) 8

9 (I) $\frac{1}{10}$

   (ii) $\frac{7}{9}$

10 (i) 0.9

   (ii) 45th

   (iii) 1000

   (iv) 44

11 (i) 0.2

   (ii) 1

12 (i) $r = 0.8$; $a = 25$

   (ii) $a = 6$; $r = 4$

13 (i) $\frac{16}{3}$

   (ii) (a) $x = -8$ or 2

   (b) $r = -\frac{1}{2}$ or 2

   (iii) (a) 256

   (b) $170\frac{2}{3}$

14 (i) $r = \frac{1}{3}$

   (ii) $54 \times \left(\frac{1}{3}\right)^{n-1}$

   (iii) $81\left(1 - \left(\frac{1}{3}\right)^n\right)$

   (iv) 81

   (v) 11 terms

15 (i) $a + ar + ar^2 = 4.88$; $\frac{a}{1-r} = 10$; $r = 0.8$, $a = 2$

   (ii) $11\frac{1}{9}$

16 (i) 20 10 5 2.5 1.25

   (ii) 0 10 15 17.5 18.75

   (iii) First series geometric, common ratio $\frac{1}{2}$. Second sequence not geometric as there is no common ratio.

17 (i) 68th swing is the first less than 1°

   (ii) 241° (to nearest degree)

18 (i) Height after nth impact = $10 \times \left(\frac{2}{3}\right)^n$

   (ii) 59.0 m (to 3 s.f.)

20 (i) Common ratio $r = 1.08$

   (ii) £29 985

   (iv) £1496 (nearest £)

21 (i) (a) 40

   (b) 1093

   (ii) £21 860

   (iii) £21 660; £180

   (iv) 16 months from the start

22 (i) $n(n + 4)$; 62 days

   (ii) (b) 72 days

   (c) 4000 is the sum to infinity of the series

23 (i) (a) $6(0.4)^{n-1}$

   (b) 9.993 446 4

   (ii) $15(0.4)^n$; 8

   (iii) $15[1 + 2(0.4) + 2(0.4)^2 + \ldots + 2(0.4)^{n-1}]$; 35 m

   (iv) $15\left[1 + 2\sum_{1}^{\infty}(0.4)^n\right]$

24 (i) $50\,000 \times 1.08^2 - P(1 + 1.08)$

   (ii) $50\,000 \times 1.08^n - P(1 + 1.08 + \ldots + 1.08^{n-1})$; $50\,000 \times 1.08^n - \frac{25P}{2}(1.08^n - 1)$; $P = £4441.37$

   (iii) $k = 3.32$

Chapter 8

Activity 8.1 (Page 192)

See text that follows.

Activity 8.2 (Page 194)

6.1;   6.01;   6.001.

Activity 8.3 (Page 195)

(i) 2   (ii) −4   (iii) 8

Gradient is twice the x co-ordinate.

Exercise 8A (Page 197)

2 $4x^3$

3

$f(x)$	$f'(x)$
x^2	$2x$
x^3	$3x^2$
x^4	$4x^3$
x^5	$5x^4$
x^6	$6x^5$
$\vdots$	
x^n	nx^{n-1}

❓ (Page 197)

When $f(x) = x^n$, then

$f(x + h)$

$= (x + h)^n$

$= x^n + nhx^{n-1} +$ terms of order h^2 and higher powers of h.

The gradient of the chord

$= \dfrac{f(x + h) - f(x)}{h}$

$= nx^{n-1} +$ terms of order h and higher powers of h.

As h tends to zero, the gradient tends to nx^{n-1}.

Hence the gradient of the tangent is nx^{n-1}.

Activity 8.4 (Page 198)

When $x = 0$, all gradients $= 0$

When $x = 1$, all gradients are equal.

i.e. for any x value they all have the same gradient.

Activity 8.5 (Page 199)

$y = x^3 + c \Rightarrow \dfrac{dy}{dx} = 3x^2$,

i.e. gradient depends only on the x co-ordinate.

Exercise 8B (Page 201)

1 (i) $5x^4$

(ii) $8x$

(iii) $6x^2$

(iv) $11x^{10}$

(v) $40x^9$

(vi) $15x^4$

(vii) 0

(viii) 7

(ix) $6x^2 + 15x^4$

(x) $7x^6 - 4x^3$

(xi) $2x$

(xii) $3x^2 + 6x + 3$

(xiii) $3x^2$

(xiv) $x + 1$

(xv) $6x + 6$

(xvi) $8\pi r$

(xvii) $4\pi r^2$

(xviii) $\frac{1}{2}t$

(xix) 2π

(xx) $3\ell^2$

Exercise 8C (Page 203)

1 (i)

(ii) $(-2, 0), (2, 0)$

(iii) $\dfrac{dy}{dx} = 2x$

(iv) At $(-2, 0), \dfrac{dy}{dx} = -4$;

at $(2, 0), \dfrac{dy}{dx} = 4$

2 (i)

(ii) $\dfrac{dy}{dx} = 2x - 6$

(iii) At $(3, -9), \dfrac{dy}{dx} = 0$

(iv) Tangent is horizontal: curve at a minimum.

3 (i)

(iii) $\dfrac{dy}{dx} = -2x$: at $(-1, 3), \dfrac{dy}{dx} = 2$

(iv) Yes: the line and the curve both pass through $(-1, 3)$ and they have the same gradient at that point.

(v) Yes, by symmetry.

4 (i)

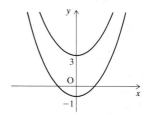

(Note: the image above appears at position 4(i))

(ii) $x = 1, 2$ and 3

(iii) $\dfrac{dy}{dx} = 3x^2 - 12x + 11$

(iv) $x = 1: \dfrac{dy}{dx} = 2; \ x = 2: \dfrac{dy}{dx} = -1;$

$x = 3: \dfrac{dy}{dx} = 2.$

The tangents at $(1, 0)$ and $(3, 0)$ are therefore parallel.

5 (i)

(ii) $\dfrac{dy}{dx} = 2x + 3$

(iii) $(1, 3)$

(iv) No, since the line does not go through $(1, 3)$.

6 (i)

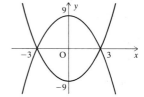

(ii) $\dfrac{dy}{dx} = 2x$

(iii) At $(2, -5), \dfrac{dy}{dx} = 4$;

at $(-2, -5), \dfrac{dy}{dx} = -4$

(iv) At $(2, 5), \dfrac{dy}{dx} = -4$;

at $(-2, 5), \dfrac{dy}{dx} = 4$

(v) A rhombus.

7 (i)

(ii) 4

(iv) $y = x^2 + c, c \in \mathbb{R}.$

8 (i) $4a + b - 5 = 0$

(ii) $12a + b = 21$

(iii) $a = 2$ and $b = -3$

9 (i) $\dfrac{dy}{dx} = -\dfrac{7x}{20}$

(ii) 0.8225 and -0.8225

(iii) $x = \frac{10}{7}$

10 (i) 8.01

(ii) Gradient of chord AB

(iii) Gradient of tangent at A

11 (i) $y + \delta y = 3x^2 + 6x\delta x + 3(\delta x)^2 + 1$

(ii) $\dfrac{\delta y}{\delta x} = 6x + 3\delta x$

12 (i) $2x - x^2 + 2\delta x - 2x\delta x - (\delta x)^2$

(ii) $\dfrac{\delta y}{\delta x} = 2 - 2x - \delta x$

(iii) $\dfrac{dy}{dx} = 2 - 2x$

Exercise 8D (Page 208)

1 (i) $\dfrac{dy}{dx} = 6 - 2x$

(ii) 4

(iii) $y = 4x + 1$

2 (i)

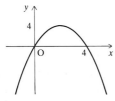

(ii) $\dfrac{dy}{dx} = 4 - 2x$

(iii) 2

(iv) $y = 2x + 1$

3 (i)

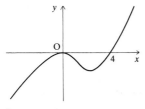

(ii) $\dfrac{dy}{dx} = 3x^2 - 8x$

(iii) −4

(iv) $y = -4x$

(v) $(0, 0)$

4 (i)

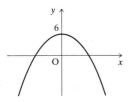

(ii) At $(-1, 5)$, $\dfrac{dy}{dx} = 2$;
at $(1, 5)$, $\dfrac{dy}{dx} = -2$

(iii) $y = 2x + 7$, $y = -2x + 7$

(iv) $(0, 7)$

5 (i)

(ii) $(-2, 0)$, $(0, 0)$, $(2, 0)$

(iii) $\dfrac{dy}{dx} = 4x^3 - 8x$;

at $(-2, 0)$,

$\dfrac{dy}{dx} = -16$;

at $(0, 0)$,

$\dfrac{dy}{dx} = 0$;

at $(2, 0)$, $\dfrac{dy}{dx} = 16$

(iv) Through $(-2, 0)$, $y = -16x - 32$;

through $(0, 0)$, $y = 0$;

through $(2, 0)$, $y = 16x - 32$

(v) Area = 64

6 (i)

(iii) $y = 4x$ is the tangent to the

curve at $(2, 8)$.

7 (i)

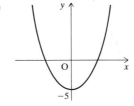

(ii) At $(-2, -1)$, $\dfrac{dy}{dx} = -4$;

at $(2, -1)$, $\dfrac{dy}{dx} = 4$

(iii) At $(-2, -1)$: $4y = x - 2$;

at $(2, -1)$: $4y = -x - 2$

(iv) $\left(0, -\dfrac{1}{2}\right)$

8 (i) $f(x) = x(x + 1)(x + 2)$;

$x = 0, -1$ or -2

(ii) $\dfrac{dy}{dx} = 3x^2 + 6x + 2$

(iii) At $(-2, 0)$: $2y = -x - 2$;

at $(-1, 0)$: $y = x + 1$;

at $(0, 0)$: $2y = -x$

(iv) The normals do not intersect
in one point: two of them are
parallel and the other one
crosses them.

9 (i) $y = 6x + 28$

(ii) $(3, 45)$

(iii) $6y = -x + 273$

10 (i) $\dfrac{dy}{dx} = 3x^2 - 8x + 5$

(ii) 4

(iii) 8

(iv) $y = 8x - 20$

(v) $8y = -x + 35$

(vi) $x = 0$ or $\dfrac{8}{3}$

11 (i)

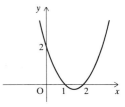

A$(1, 0)$; B$(2, 0)$ or vice versa

(ii) At $(1, 0)$, $\dfrac{dy}{dx} = -1$;
at $(2, 0)$, $\dfrac{dy}{dx} = 1$

(iii) At $(1, 0)$, tangent is $y = -x + 1$,
normal is $y = x - 1$;
at $(2, 0)$, tangent is $y = x - 2$,
normal is $y = -x + 2$.

(iv) A square.

12 (i) $(1, -7)$ and $(4, -4)$

(ii) $\dfrac{dy}{dx} = 4x - 9$. At $(1, -7)$,
tangent is $y = -5x - 2$;
at $(4, -4)$, tangent is
$y = 7x - 32$.

(iii) $(2.5, -14.5)$

(iv) No.

13 (i) $\dfrac{dy}{dx} = 3x^2 - 1$

(ii) $y = 6$

(iii) $\dfrac{dy}{dx} = 2$

(iv) $y = 2x + 8$

(v) $(1, 6)$

(vi) $x + 2y - 13 = 0$

Activity 8.6 (Page 210)

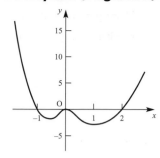

(i) 3

(ii) 0

(iii) (0, 0) maximum;

minima to left and right of this.

(iv) No

(v) No

(vi) About –2.5

Exercise 8E (Page 215)

1 (i) $\frac{dy}{dx} = 2x + 8$;

$\frac{dy}{dx} = 0$ when $x = -4$.

(ii) Minimum

(iv)

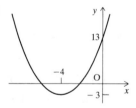

2 (i) $\frac{dy}{dx} = 2x + 5$;

$\frac{dy}{dx} = 0$ when $x = -2\frac{1}{2}$

(ii) Minimum

(iii) $y = -4\frac{1}{4}$

(iv)

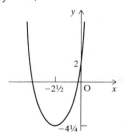

3 (i) $\frac{dy}{dx} = 3x^2 - 12$;

$\frac{dy}{dx} = 0$ when $x = -2$ or 2

(ii) Minimum at $x = 2$,

maximum at $x = -2$

(iii) When $x = -2$, $y = 18$;

when $x = 2$, $y = -14$

(iv)

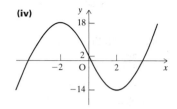

4 (i) A maximum at (0, 0),

a minimum at (4, –32)

(ii)

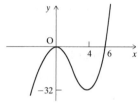

5 $\frac{dy}{dx} = 3x^2 - 1$

6 (i) $\frac{dy}{dx} = 3x^2 + 4$

7 (i) $\frac{dy}{dx} = 3(x + 3)(x - 1)$

(ii) $x = -3$ or 1

(v)

8 (i) $\frac{dy}{dx} = -3(x + 1)(x - 3)$

(ii) Minimum when $x = -1$,

maximum when $x = 3$.

(iii) When $x = -1$, $y = -5$;

when $x = 3$, $y = 27$

(iv)

9 (i) Maximum at $\left(-\frac{2}{3}, 4\frac{13}{27}\right)$,

minimum at (2, –5).

(ii)

10 (i) Maximum at (0, 300),

minimum at (3, 165),

minimum at (–6, –564)

(ii)

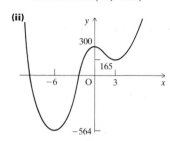

11 (i) $\frac{dy}{dx} = 3(x^2 + 1)$

(ii) There are no turning points.

(iii)

x	–3	–2	–1	0	1	2	3
y	–36	–14	–4	0	4	14	36

(iv)

12 (i) $\frac{dy}{dx} = 4x^3 - 16x$

(ii) Maximum at (0, 16),

minima at (2, 0) and (–2, 0).

(iii)

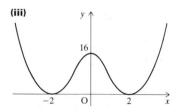

(iv) $x^4 - 8x^2 + 16 = (x^2 - 4)^2$

$= (x - 2)^2 (x + 2)^2$

(v) The factorised form shows

that the graph touches the

x axis twice (repeated roots at

373

$x = -2$ and $+2$). The *unfactorised* version shows behaviour for large positive and negative x values, and shows where the graph crosses the y axis. By symmetry this must be a turning point.

13 (i) $\dfrac{dy}{dx} = 6x^2 + 6x - 72$

(ii) $y = 18$

(iii) $\dfrac{dy}{dx} = 48$; $y = 48x - 174$

(iv) $(-4, 338)$ and $(3, -5)$

14 (i) $\dfrac{dy}{dx} = 3x^2 - 12$

(ii) $(-2, 21)$ and $(2, -11)$

(iii) sign change of $\dfrac{dy}{dx}$

(v)

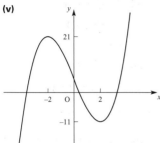

(iv) $12x + y - 5 = 0$

15 (i) $y = 39$; $y = 164$

(ii) $\dfrac{dy}{dx} = 6x^2 - 6x - 36$

(iii) $(-2, 164)$ and $(3, 39)$

(iv) max at $(-2, 164)$; min at $(3, 39)$

(v) $39 < k < 164$

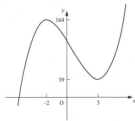

? (Page 219)

There will be points of inflection between consecutive bends that go in opposite directions. A driver will need to change the direction of lock on the steering wheel as he passes through the points of inflection.

Exercise 8F (Page 220)

1 (i) $\dfrac{dy}{dx} = (3x + 1)(x - 1)$

(ii) $x = -\frac{1}{3}$ or 1

(iii) Maximum at $x = -\frac{1}{3}$, minimum at $x = 1$

(iv) When $x = -\frac{1}{3}$, $y = 4\frac{5}{27}$; when $x = 1$, $y = 3$

(v)

2 (i) $\dfrac{dy}{dx} = 12x^2(x - 1)$

(ii) $x = 0$ or 1

(iii) Point of inflection when $x = 0$; minimum when $x = 1$

(iv) When $x = 0$, $y = 0$; when $x = 1$, $y = -1$

(v) A: $(0, 0)$; B: $(1, -1)$; C: $(\frac{4}{3}, 0)$

3 (i) $\dfrac{dy}{dx} = 12x(x - 1)^2$

(ii) Minimum at $(0,2)$; point of inflection at $(1,3)$

(iii)

Activity 8.7 (Page 221)

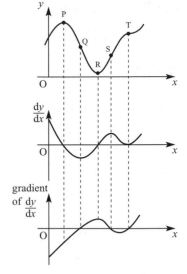

At P (max.) the gradient of $\dfrac{dy}{dx}$ is negative.

At R (min.) the gradient of $\dfrac{dy}{dx}$ is positive.

At T (stationary point of inflection) the gradient of $\dfrac{dy}{dx}$ is 0.

At Q and S (non-stationary points of inflection) the gradient of $\dfrac{dy}{dx}$ is 0.

Activity 8.8 (Page 224)

At the point of inflection the gradient is negative but neither increasing nor decreasing.
$\dfrac{dy}{dx} < 0, \dfrac{d^2y}{dx^2} = 0$.

The gradient is negative but increasing.
$\dfrac{dy}{dx} < 0, \dfrac{d^2y}{dx^2} > 0$.

The gradient is negative and decreasing.
$\dfrac{dy}{dx} < 0, \dfrac{d^2y}{dx^2} < 0$.

Exercise 8G (Page 226)

1 (i) $\frac{dy}{dx} = 3x^2; \frac{d^2y}{dx^2} = 6x$

(ii) $\frac{dy}{dx} = 5x^4; \frac{d^2y}{dx^2} = 20x^3$

(iii) $\frac{dy}{dx} = 8x; \frac{d^2y}{dx^2} = 8$

2 (i) $(-1, 3)$, minimum

(ii) $(3, 9)$, maximum

(iii) $(-1, 2)$, maximum and
$(1, -2)$, minimum

(iv) $(0, 0)$, maximum and
$(-1, -1)$, minimum;

(v) $(-1, 2)$, minimum;
$(-\frac{3}{4}, 2.02)$, maximum;
$(1, -2)$, minimum.

3 (i) $4x(x + 2)(x - 2)$

(ii) $4(3x^2 - 4)$

(iii) $(-2, -16)$, minimum;
$(0, 0)$, maximum;
$(2, -16)$, minimum

(iv)

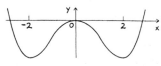

4 (i) $\frac{dy}{dx} = 5x^4$

(ii) Point of inflection at $(0, -3)$

(iii)

5 (i) Point of inflection at $(0, -8)$;
maximum at $(3, 19)$

(ii)

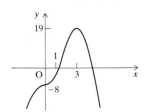

6 (i) Points of inflection at $(-1, -8)$
and $(1, 8)$

(ii)

7 (i) $\frac{dy}{dx} = (3x - 7)(x - 1)$

(ii) Maximum at $(1, 0)$;
minimum at $(2\frac{1}{3}, -1\frac{5}{27})$

(iii)

8 (i) $\frac{dy}{dx} = 4x(x - 1)(x - 2)$

(ii) Minimum at $(0, 0)$;
maximum at $(1, 1)$;
minimum at $(2, 0)$

(iii)

9 (i) $p + q = -1$

(ii) $3p + 2q = 0$

(iii) $p = 2$ and $q = -3$

10 (i) $\frac{dy}{dx} = 12x^2(x + 1)$

(ii) $(0, 0)$ and $(-1, -1)$

(iii) Minimum at $(-1, -1)$;
point of inflection at $(0, 0)$

(iv)

Exercise 8H (Page 230)

1 (i) $y = 60 - x$

(ii) $A = 60x - x^2$

(iii) $\frac{dA}{dx} = 60 - 2x;$

$\frac{d^2A}{dx^2} = -2$

Dimensions 30 m by 30 m,
area 900 m^2

2 (i) $V = 4x^3 - 48x^2 + 144x$

(ii) $\frac{dV}{dx} = 12x^2 - 96x + 144;$

$\frac{d^2V}{dx^2} = 24x - 96$

3 (i) $y = 8 - x$

(ii) $S = 2x^2 - 16x + 64$

(iii) 32

4 (i) $2x + y = 80$

(ii) $A = 80x - 2x^2$

(iii) $x = 20, y = 40$

5 (i) $x(1 - 2x)$

(ii) $V = x^2 - 2x^3$

(iii) $\frac{dV}{dx} = 2x - 6x^2;$

$\frac{d^2V}{dx^2} = 2 - 12x$

(iv) All dimensions $\frac{1}{3}$ m (a cube);
volume $\frac{1}{27}$ m^3

6 (i) (a) $(4 - 2x)$ cm

(b) $(16 - 16x + 4x^2)$ cm^2

(iii) $x = 1.143$

(iv) A = 6.857

7 (i) $P = 2\pi r, r = \frac{15 - 2x}{\pi}$

(iii) $x = \frac{30}{4 + \pi}$ cm: lengths $\approx$
16.8 cm and 13.2 cm

8 (i) $r^2 = \frac{4\ell^2 - h^2}{16}$

(ii) $V = \frac{\pi h}{16}(4\ell^2 - h^2)$

(iii) $h = \frac{2}{\sqrt{3}}\ell$

9 (i) $h = \frac{125}{r} - r$

(ii) $V = 125\pi r - \pi r^3$

(iii) $\frac{dV}{dr} = 125\pi - 3\pi r^2;$

$\frac{d^2V}{dx^2} = -6\pi r$

(iv) $r = 6.45$ cm; $h = 12.9$ cm
(to 3 s.f.)

Chapter 9

❓ (Page 234)

The gradient depends only on the x co-ordinate. This is the same for all four curves so at points with the same x co-ordinate the tangents are parallel.

Exercise 9A (Page 237)

1 (i) $y = 2x^3 + 5x + c$

  (ii) $y = 2x^3 + 5x + 2$

2 (i) $y = 2x^2 + 3$

  (ii) 5

3 (i) $y = 2x^3 - 6$

4 (ii) $t = 4$. Only 4 is applicable here.

5 (i) $y = 5x + c$

  (ii) $y = 5x + 3$

  (iii)

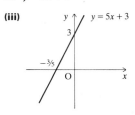

6 (i) $x = 1$ (minimum) and $x = -1$ (maximum)

  (ii) $y = x^3 - 3x + 3$

  (iii)

7 (i) $y = x^2 - 6x + 9$

  (ii) The curve passes through $(1, 4)$

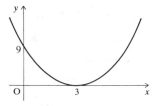

8 (i) $y = \frac{9}{32}\left(\frac{x^3}{3} - 2x^2\right) + 3$

  (ii)

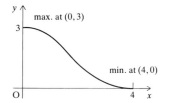

  (iii) The slide starts off fairly flat, then becomes steep, and finally flattens out again.

  (iv) Yes, in middle section of slide

9 (i) $y = x^3 - x^2 - x + 1$

  (ii) $\left(-\frac{1}{3}, -1\frac{5}{27}\right)$ and $(1, 0)$

  (iii)

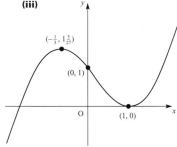

10 (i) $y = x^3 - 4x^2 + 5x + 3$

  (ii) max $(1, 5)$, min $\left(1\frac{2}{3}, 4\frac{23}{27}\right)$

  (iii) $4\frac{23}{27} < k < 5$

  (iv) $1 < x < 1\frac{2}{3}$; $x = 1\frac{1}{3}$

Activity 9.1 (Page 243)

The bounds converge on the value $A = 45\frac{1}{3}$.

Activity 9.2 (Page 246)

(i) Area $= \frac{1}{2}[3 + (b+3)]b - \frac{1}{2}[3 + (a+3)]a$

$= \frac{1}{2}[6b + b^2 - 6a - a^2]$

(ii) $= \left[\frac{b^2}{2} + 3b\right] - \left[\frac{a^2}{2} - 3a\right]$

$= \left[\frac{x^2}{2} + 3x\right]_a^b$

(iii) $\int_a^b (x + 3)\,\mathrm{d}x = \left[\frac{x^2}{2} + 3x\right]_a^b$

Exercise 9B (Page 247)

1 (i) $x^3 + c$

  (ii) $x^5 + x^7 + c$

  (iii) $2x^3 + 5x + c$

  (iv) $\frac{x^4}{4} + \frac{x^3}{3} + \frac{x^2}{2} + x + c$

  (v) $x^{11} + x^{10} + c$

  (vi) $x^3 + x^2 + x + c$

  (vii) $\frac{x^3}{3} + 5x + c$

  (viii) $5x + c$

  (ix) $2x^3 + 2x^2 + c$

  (x) $\frac{x^3}{5} + x^3 + x^2 + x + c$

2 (i) 3

  (ii) 9

  (iii) 27

  (iv) $10\frac{1}{2}$

  (v) 12

  (vi) 15

  (vii) 114

  (viii) $\frac{1}{6}$

  (ix) $2\frac{9}{20}$

  (x) 0

  (xi) $-105\frac{3}{4}$

  (xii) 5

3 (i) A: $(2, 4)$; B: $(3, 6)$

  (ii) 5

  (iv) In this case the area is not a trapezium since the top is curved.

4 (i)

(ii) $2\frac{1}{3}$

5 (i)

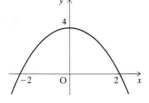

(ii) $-2 < x < 2$

(iii) $10\frac{2}{3}$

6 (i)

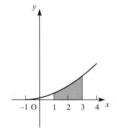

(ii) $2\frac{2}{3}$ sq. units

7 (i)

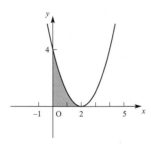

(ii) $18\frac{2}{3}$ sq. units

8 (i)

(ii) $y = x^2$

(iii) $y = x^2$: area $= \frac{1}{3}$;

  $y = x^3$: area $= \frac{1}{4}$

(iv) Expect $\int_1^2 x^3 \, dx > \int_1^2 x^2 \, dx$,

  since the curve $y = x^3$ is

  above the curve $y = x^2$

  between 1 and 2.

  Confirmation: $\int_1^2 x^3 \, dx = 3\frac{3}{4}$

  and $\int_1^2 x^2 \, dx = 2\frac{1}{3}$

9 (i)

(ii) $1\frac{1}{3}$

(iii)

(iv) $1\frac{1}{3}$

(v) The answers are the same,

  since the second area is a

  translation of the first.

10 (i)

(ii) 24

11 (i)

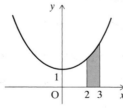

(ii) $7\frac{1}{3}$

(iii) $7\frac{1}{3}$, by symmetry

(iv) $7\frac{1}{3}$

12 (i)

(ii) $\int_0^4 (x^2 - 2x + 1) \, dx$ larger, as

  area between 3 and 4 is larger

  than area between -1 and 0.

(iii) $\int_{-1}^3 (x^2 - 2x + 1) \, dx = 5\frac{1}{3}$;

  $\int_0^4 (x^2 - 2x + 1) \, dx = 9\frac{1}{3}$

13 (i) and (ii)

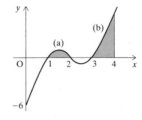

(iii) (a) $\frac{1}{4}$ **(b)** $2\frac{1}{4}$

(iv) 0.140625. The maximum lies

  before $x = 1.5$.

14 (i) $\frac{dy}{dx} = -2x + 2$

(ii) max $y = 4$

(iii) 6 m^2

15 (i) 9 m

(ii) Yes: distance in 3rd second

  was $6\frac{1}{3}$ m; distance in first 2

  seconds was $2\frac{2}{3}$ m.

16 Blue: 2; red: 3; green: 8;

  black: 3; pink: 10

Exercise 9C (Page 253)

1 (i)

  $20\frac{1}{4}$

(ii)

9

(iii)

$2\frac{1}{6}$

(iv)

1

(v)

$\frac{4}{15}$

(vi)

$2\frac{1}{16}$

(vii)

$\frac{1}{6}$

(viii)

$8\frac{1}{6}$

(ix)

$11\frac{1}{12}$

(x)

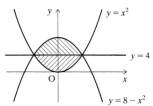

$8\frac{1}{6}$

2 (i) $\frac{dy}{dx} = 20x^3 - 5x^4$;

(0, 0) and (4, 256)

(ii) $520\frac{5}{6}$ square units

(iii) 0. Equal areas above and below the x axis.

Exercise 9D (Page 256)

1 (i) A: $(-3, 9)$; B: $(3, 9)$

2 (i)

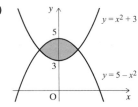

(ii) $(-1, 4)$ and $(1, 4)$

(iii) $2\frac{2}{3}$

3 (i)

(ii) $(-2, -8)$, $(0, 0)$ and $(2, 8)$

(iii) 8

4 (i)

(ii) $(0, 0)$ and $(2, 4)$

(iii) $2\frac{2}{3}$

5 (i)

(ii) $10\frac{2}{3}$

(iii) $10\frac{2}{3}$

(iv) $21\frac{1}{3}$

6 (i)

(ii) $(1, -5)$ and $(5, -5)$

(iii) $10\frac{2}{3}$

7 (i)

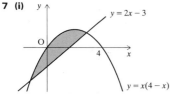

(ii) $(-1, -5)$, $(3, 3)$

(iii) $10\frac{2}{3}$

8 72

9 $1\frac{1}{3}$

10 (i)

(ii) 8 (4 each)

11 (i)

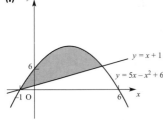

(ii) $(-1, 0)$ and $(5, 6)$

(iii) 36 square units

12 (i) $\dfrac{dy}{dx} = 6x - 6x^2 - 4x^3$

(ii) $4x + y - 4 = 0$

(iv) 8.1 square units

13 (i) $\left(\frac{1}{2}, -1\right)$

(ii) $8x^3 - 36x^2 + 54x - 27$

(iii) $\frac{1}{8}\int_{\frac{3}{2}}^{\frac{5}{2}}(8x^3 - 36x^2 + 54x - 27)dx$

(iv) $\frac{1}{4}$ square units

(v) 3 square units

14 (i) $\dfrac{dy}{dx} = 4 - 3x^2$; $8x + y - 16 = 0$

(ii) $(-4, 48)$

(iii) 108 square units

Exercise 9E (Page 260)

1 (i) 6   **(ii)** $6\frac{2}{3}$

(iii) 4

(iv) $8\frac{2}{3}$

(v) $6\frac{1}{5}$

(vi) 20

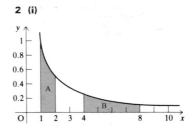

Activity 9.3 (Page 263)

For example

32 strips:	8.398
50 strips:	8.409
100 strips:	8.416
1000 strips:	8.420

❓ (Page 263)

The curve is part of the circle centre $\left(2\frac{1}{2}, 0\right)$, radius $2\frac{1}{2}$.

Area required is half a major segment $= 8.4197\,\text{units}^2$.

Error from 16 strip estimate is about 0.7%.

❓ (Page 264)

(i) Underestimates – all trapezia below the curve

(ii) Impossible to tell

(iii) Overestimates – all trapezia above the curve

Exercise 9F (Page 264)

1 (i) 2 strips: 2.6286; 4 strips: 2.5643; 8 strips: 2.5475. Overestimate, even 1 decimal place uncertain.

(ii) 2 strips: 5.1667; 4 strips: 5.1167; 8 strips: 5.1032. Overestimate, correct to 1 decimal place.

(iii) 2 strips: 1.2622; 4 strips: 0.9436; 8 strips: 0.8395. Overestimate, even 1 decimal place uncertain.

2 (i)

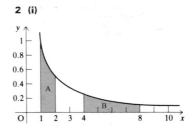

(ii) Both A and B: 2 strips: 0.7083; 4 strips: 0.6970; 8 strips: 0.6941

(iii) The same

3 (i) 458 m

(ii) A curve is approximated by a straight line. The speeds are not given to a high level of accuracy.

4 (i) 3.1349...

(ii) 3.1399..., 3.1411...

(iii) 3.14

5 (i) 7.3

(ii) overestimate

6 (i)

x	2	3	4	5	6	7
y	2	2.2361	2.4495	2.6458	2.8284	3

(ii) 12.6598; too small

(iii) $2\frac{1}{3}$ square units

(iv) $12\frac{2}{3}$ square units, 0.054%

7 (i) 1.05101 ; 1.53862

0.535644

(ii) $1 + 5x^2 + 10x^4 + 10x^6 + 5x^8 + x^{10}$;

0.527147

(iii) Estimate in (i) too high
(curve below chords)
Estimate in (ii) too low
(positive terms ignored)

(iv) more strips in (i) and more
terms in (ii)

Chapter 10

❓ (Page 270)

1 Angle of elevation and height of
lighthouse.

2 Lengths of all sides of the
pentagon and the lengths of the
dotted lines.

3 Angle between train and
mountain at each point, the
angles of elevation of the point
on the mountain as viewed from
the train and the speed of the
train, hence the distance between
the points.

❓ (Page 274)

When looking at the gradient of a
tangent to a curve it was considered
as the limit of a chord as the width of
the chord tended to zero. Similarly,
the region between a curve and an
axis was considered as the limit of a
series of rectangles as the width of
the rectangles tended to zero.

Activity 10.1 (Page 276)

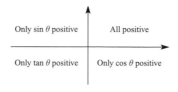

❓ (Page 278)

1 The oscillations continue to the
left.

$y = \sin\theta$

$y = \cos\theta$

2 $y = \sin\theta$:
- reflect in $\theta = 90°$ to give the
curve for $90° \leqslant \theta \leqslant 180°$
- rotate the curve for
$0 \leqslant \theta \leqslant 180°$ through $180°$,
centre $(180°, 0)$ to give the
curve for $180° \leqslant \theta \leqslant 360°$.

$y = \cos\theta$:
- translate $\begin{pmatrix} -90° \\ 0 \end{pmatrix}$ and reflect in
y axis to give the curve for
$0 \leqslant \theta \leqslant 90°$
- rotate this through $180°$, centre
$(90°, 0)$ to give the curve for
$90° \leqslant \theta \leqslant 180°$
- reflect the curve for $0 \leqslant \theta \leqslant 180°$
in $\theta = 180°$ to give the curve
for $180° \leqslant \theta \leqslant 360°$.

Activity 10.2 (Page 279)

$y = \sin\theta$

$y = \cos\theta$

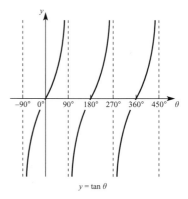

$y = \tan\theta$

❓ (Page 281)

The tangent graph repeats every $180°$
so, to find more solutions, keep
adding or subtracting $180°$.

Exercise 10A (Page 283)

1 (i) Converse of Pythagoras'
theorem

(ii) $\frac{8}{17}, \frac{15}{17}, \frac{8}{15}$

2 (i), (ii)

(ii) $30°, 150°$

(iii) $30°, 150°$ ($\pm$ multiples of $360°$)

(iv) -0.5

3 (i), (ii)

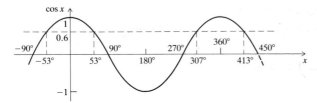

(ii) $x = -53°, 53°, 307°, 413°$

   (to nearest 1°)

(iii), (iv)

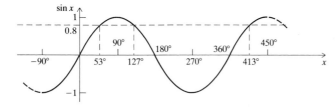

(iv) $x = 53°, 127°, 413°$

   (to nearest 1°)

(v) For $0 \leqslant x \leqslant 90°$, $\sin x = 0.8$ and $\cos x = 0.6$ have the same root. For $90° \leqslant x \leqslant 360°$, $\sin x$ and $\cos x$ are never both positive.

4 (Where relevant, answers are to the nearest degree.)

(i) $45°, 225°$

(ii) $60°, 300°$

(iii) $240°, 300°$

(iv) $135°, 315°$

(v) $154°, 206°$

(vi) $78°, 282°$

(vii) $194°, 346°$

(viii) $180°$

5 (i) $\dfrac{\sqrt{3}}{2}$

(ii) $\dfrac{\sqrt{1}}{2}$

(iii) 1

(iv) $\frac{1}{2}$

(v) $-\frac{1}{2}$

(vi) 0

(vii) $\frac{1}{2}$

(viii) $\dfrac{\sqrt{3}}{2}$

(ix) -1

7 (i) $-60°$

(ii) $-155.9°$

(iii) $54.0°$

8 (i)

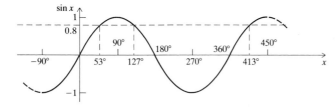

shaded areas are congruent

(ii) (a) False

    (b) True

    (c) False

    (d) True

9 (i) a between $0°$ and $90°$, $360°$ and $450°$, $720°$ and $810°$, etc. (and corresponding negative values).

(ii) No: since $\tan a = \dfrac{\sin a}{\cos a}$, all must be positive or one positive and two negative.

(iii) No: $\sin a = \cos a \Rightarrow a = 45°$, $225°$, etc. but $\tan a = \pm 1$ for these values of a, and $\sin a = \cos a = \dfrac{1}{\sqrt{2}}$

10 (i) $5.7°, 174.3°$

(ii) $60°, 300°$

(iii) $116.6°, 296.6°$

(iv) $203.6°, 336.4°$

(v) $0°, 90°, 270°, 360°$

(vi) $90°, 270°$

(vii) $0°, 180°, 360°$

(viii) $54.7°, 125.3°, 234.7°, 305.3°$

(ix) $60°, 300°$

(x) $18.4°, 71.6°, 198.4°, 251.6°$

11 $A = (38.2°, 0.786)$,

    $B = (141.8°, -0.786)$

Exercise 10B (Page 288)

1 (i)   8.0 cm

(ii)   7.4 cm

(iii) 10.4 cm

(iv) 9.1 cm

2 (i)   42.8°

(ii)   47.9°

    The diagram shows that θ is acute, so 132.1° is irrelevant.

(iii) 47.7°

(iv) 71.3°

    The diagram shows that θ is acute, so 108.7° is irrelevant.

3 $C = 65°$, $a = 5.45$ cm, $b = 8.85$ cm

Exercise 10C (Page 291)

1 (i)   10.14 cm

(ii)   5.57 cm

(iii) 4.72 cm

(iv) 10.72 cm

2 (i)   57.1°

(ii)   97.4°

(iii) 63.1°

(iv) 120°

3 (i)   5 cm

(ii)   90.7°

4 (i) 87°

(ii) 5.29 km

Exercise 10D (Page 293)

1 114 m

2 AD = 148.2 m, CD = 181.4 m, height = 121.4 m

3 8.8 km

4 14.6 km h⁻¹

5 (i)

(ii) 64.7 km

(iii) 27.7 km h⁻¹

6 10.7 km

7 3.28 km

8 (i) 18.6°

(ii) 76.9 m

(iii) 35.6 m

9 (i) 3.72 km

(ii) 3.32 km

(iii) 94.8 km h⁻¹

10 (i)

(ii) 837 m

(iii) 556 m

11 (i) 1011 m

(ii) 1082 m

(iii) 065° m

12 (i) 1.6 m

(ii) 93°

Exercise 10E (Page 297)

1 (i) 7.21 cm²

(ii) 8.45 cm²

(iii) 6.77 cm²

(iv) 6.13 cm²

2 (i) 2.25 m²

(ii) 0.3375 m³

3 27.4°, 152.6°

4 77.94 cm²

5 (i) 72°

(ii) 11 011 m²

6 (i) 4.35 m

(ii) 7.38 m

(iii) 47.38 m²

(iv) 7.29 m

7 5412 m²

Exercise 10F (Page 302)

1 (i) $\frac{\pi}{4}$

(ii) $\frac{\pi}{2}$

(iii) $\frac{2\pi}{3}$

(iv) $\frac{5\pi}{12}$

(v) $\frac{5\pi}{3}$

(vi) 0.4 rad

(vii) $\frac{5\pi}{2}$

(viii) 3.65 rad

(ix) $\frac{5\pi}{6}$

(x) $\frac{\pi}{25}$

2 (i) 18°

(ii) 108°

(iii) 114.6°

(iv) 80°

(v) 540°

(vi) 300°

(vii) 22.9°

(viii) 135°

(ix) 420°

(x) 77.1°

3 (i) $\frac{1}{\sqrt{2}}$

(ii) $\sqrt{3}$

(iii) $\frac{\sqrt{3}}{2}$

(iv) −1

(v) −1

(vi) $\frac{\sqrt{3}}{2}$

(vii) $\sqrt{3}$

(viii) $-\frac{1}{\sqrt{2}}$

(ix) $\frac{1}{2}$

(x) $\frac{1}{2}$

4 (i) $\frac{\pi}{6}, \frac{11\pi}{6}$

(ii) $\frac{\pi}{4}, \frac{5\pi}{4}$

(iii) $\frac{\pi}{4}, \frac{3\pi}{4}$

(iv) $\frac{7\pi}{6}, \frac{11\pi}{6}$

(v) $\frac{3\pi}{4}, \frac{5\pi}{4}$

(vi) $\frac{\pi}{3}, \frac{4\pi}{3}$

5 (i) 0.201 rads, 2.940 rads

(ii) −0.738 rads, 0.738 rads

(ii) −1.893 rads, 1.249 rads

(iv) −2.889 rads, −0.253 rads

(v) −1.982 rads, 1.982 rads

(vi) −0.464 rads, 2.678 rads

6 0 rads, 0.730 rads, 2.412 rads, 3.142 rads

Exercise 10G (Page 305)

1

r (cm)	θ	s	A(cm²)
5	$\frac{\pi}{4}$	$\frac{5\pi}{4}$	$\frac{25\pi}{8}$
8	1	8	32
4	$\frac{1}{2}$	2	4
$1\frac{1}{2}$	$\frac{\pi}{3}$	$\frac{\pi}{2}$	$\frac{3\pi}{8}$
5	$\frac{4}{5}$	4	10
1.875	0.8	1.5	1.41
3.46	$\frac{2\pi}{3}$	7.26	4π

2 (i) (a) $\frac{20\pi}{3}$ cm²

(b) 4 cm²

(c) 16.9 cm²

(ii) 19.7 cm²

3 (i) 1.98 mm^2

   (ii) 43.0 mm

5 (i) 140 yards

   (ii) 5585 square yards

6 1.05 cm^3

7 (i) 5.16 m

   (ii) 3.11 m^2

   (iii) $\frac{9\pi}{8}$ (3.53) m^2

   (iv) $\frac{40\pi}{3}$ (41.89) m^2

   (v) 32.14 m^2

8 (i) 147.8 cm

   (ii) 65.1 cm

   (iii) 2.17 rad; 124°

9 (i) $200 - \pi r$

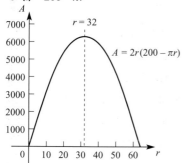

   (iii) $(x - 50)^2 + y^2 = 32^2$

   (iv) $k = 30.24$ or 9.76

   Length = 121 m,

   breadth = 60.5 m.

❓ (Page 309)

White – he started at the North Pole.

Activity 10.3 (Page 311)

See text that follows.

Activity 10.4 (Page 312)

See text that follows.

Exercise 10H (Page 315)

1 (i) Translation $\begin{pmatrix} 90° \\ 0 \end{pmatrix}$

   (ii) One-way stretch parallel to
   x axis of s.f. $\frac{1}{3}$

   (iii) One-way stretch parallel to y
   axis of s.f. $\frac{1}{2}$

   (iv) One-way stretch parallel to
   x axis of s.f. 2

   (v) Translation $\begin{pmatrix} 0 \\ 2 \end{pmatrix}$

2 (i) Translation $\begin{pmatrix} -60° \\ 0 \end{pmatrix}$

   (ii) One-way stretch parallel to
   y axis of s.f. $\frac{1}{3}$

   (iii) Translation $\begin{pmatrix} 0 \\ 1 \end{pmatrix}$

   (iv) One-way stretch parallel to
   x axis of s.f. $\frac{1}{2}$

3 (i) (a)

   (b) $y = \sin x$

   (ii) (a)

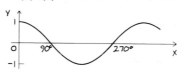

   (b) $y = \cos x$

   (iii) (a)

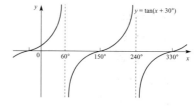

   (b) $y = \tan x$

   (iv) (a)

   (b) $y = \sin x$

   (v) (a)

   (b) $y = -\cos x$

4 (i) One-way stretch s.f. 4
   parallel to the y axis or
   one-way stretch s.f. $\frac{1}{2}$ parallel
   to the x axis.

   (ii) One-way stretch s.f. $\frac{1}{3}$
   parallel to the y axis or
   one-way stretch s.f. $\sqrt{3}$
   parallel to the x axis

5 (i) $y = 2x^3$

   (ii) $y = \frac{1}{8} x^3$

   (iii) $y = 3x^3$

   (iv) $y = 8x^3$

6 (i) $y = \tan x + 4$

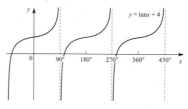

   (ii) $y = \tan (x + 30°)$

   (iii) $y = \tan (0.5x)$

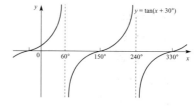

7 (i) $y = 4\sin x$

   (ii) $-2\sqrt{3}$

8 (i)

(ii)

(iii)

9 (i) (a) $y = 2g(x)$

　　(b) $y = g\left(\frac{x}{3}\right)$

(ii)

10 (i)

(ii)

(iii)

Chapter 11

❓ (Page 319)

Without using logarithms, you would probably use trial and improvement to find x where $x^3 = 500$.

❓ (Page 322)

The advantages include speed and accuracy.

Activity 11.1 (Page 323)

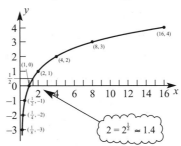

❓ (Page 324)

- $a^0 = 1$, $\log_a 1 = 0$

- $a^m = x > 0$ (for $a > 0$) so
  $\log_a(x) = m$ is defined only for
  $x > 0$

- Putting $x = \frac{1}{y}$ in $\log\left(\frac{1}{y}\right) = -\log y$
  $\Rightarrow \log x = -\log\left(\frac{1}{x}\right)$: as $x \to 0$,
  $-\log\left(\frac{1}{x}\right) \to -\infty$

- There is no limit to m in $a^m = x$
  and $\log_a x = m$

- $\log_a a = 1$

Exercise 11A (Page 325)

1 (i) $x = \log_3 9$, 2

　　(ii) $x = \log_4 64$, 3

　　(iii) $x = \log_2 \frac{1}{4}$, -2

　　(iv) $x = \log_5 \frac{1}{5}$, -1

　　(v) $x = \log_7 1$, 0

　　(vi) $x = \log_{16} 2$, $\frac{1}{4}$

2 (i) $3^y = 9$, 2

　　(ii) $5^y = 125$, 3

　　(iii) $2^y = 16$, 4

　　(iv) $6^y = 1$, 0

　　(v) $64^y = 8$, $\frac{1}{2}$

　　(vi) $5^y = \frac{1}{25}$, -2

3 (i) 4

　　(ii) -4

　　(iii) $\frac{1}{2}$

　　(iv) 0

　　(v) 4

　　(vi) -4

　　(vii) $\frac{3}{2}$

　　(viii) $\frac{1}{4}$

　　(ix) $\frac{1}{2}$

　　(x) -3

4 (i) $\log 10$

　　(ii) $\log 2$

　　(iii) $\log 36$

　　(iv) $\log \frac{1}{7}$

　　(v) $\log 3$

　　(vi) $\log 4$

　　(vii) $\log 4$

　　(viii) $\log \frac{1}{3}$

　　(ix) $\log \frac{1}{2}$

　　(x) $\log 12$

5 (i) $2\log x$

　　(ii) $3\log x$

　　(iii) $\frac{1}{2}\log x$

　　(iv) $\frac{11}{6}\log x$

　　(v) $6\log x$

　　(vi) $\frac{5}{2}\log x$

6 $\log_{10} \frac{x^2}{7}$, $x = 21$

7 (i) $x - 19.93$

　　(ii) $x = -9.97$

　　(iii) $x = 9.01$

　　(iv) $x = 48.32$

　　(v) $x = 1375$

8 9

9 (i) 25

　　(ii) 17

10 11

Exercise 11B (Page 331)

The techniques in this exercise involve drawing a line of best fit by eye. Consequently your answers may reasonably vary a little from those given.

1 (i) If the relationship is of the form $R = kT^n$, the graph of $\log R$ against $\log T$ will be a straight line.

(ii) $\log R$ 5.46 5.58 5.72 6.09 6.55
$\log T$ 0.28 0.43 0.65 1.20 1.90

(iii) $k = 1.8 \times 10^5$, $n = 0.690$

(iv) 0.7 days

2 (ii) Plotting $\log A$ against t will test the model: if it is a straight line the model fits the data.

(iii) $b = 1.4$, $k = 0.89$

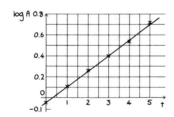

(iv) (a) $t = 2.4$ days

(b) $A = 3.0$ cm^2

(v) Exponential growth

3 (i) The deforestation started in 1910, when there were 3 200 000 trees.

(ii) The constant k is the original number of trees.
The value of a will be less than 1 because the number of trees is decreasing.

(iv) $k = 3.2 \times 10^6$, $a = 0.98$

(t measured in years since 1910)

(v) In the year 2002.

4 (i) The model $s = kt^n$ can be written as $\log s = \log k + n\log t$, so if this model is appropriate the graph of $\log s$ against $\log t$ will be a straight line. Since the points do lie in a straight line, the model is appropriate.

(ii) $k = 1100$, $n = 1.6$

(iii) $s = 2500$ m

(iv) The train would not continue to accelerate like this through-out its journey. After 10 minutes it would probably be travelling at constant speed, or possibly even slowing down.

5 Taking logs of both sides,
$\log y = \log A + B\log x$.
Plotting $\log y$ against $\log x$ gives a straight line of gradient B and intercept $\log A$.
This gives $A = 1.5$, $B = 0.78$.
The value of y that is wrong is 6.21. If x is 5.07, y should be 5.32 according to the equation.

6 $\log y = B \log x + \log A$.
He should plot $\log y$ against $\log x$.
If this gives a straight line, there is a relationship of the form $y = Ax^B$. If there is no such relationship, the points will not be in a straight line.
The value of $\log A$ is given by the intercept on the $\log y$ axis. The value of B is the gradient of the line.

From the graph, $A = 1.5$, $B = 0.5$.
The formula is therefore $y = 1.5x^{0.5}$.

7 (iii) $A = 2.0$, $n = 1.5$

8 (iii) Approximate values $n = -1.9$, $k = 12\,000$.

(iv) Not without evidence that the human body can withstand dives to such depths.

9 (iv) $n \approx 5.2$, $k \approx 0.003$; but notice that the value of k is very sensitive to the value taken for n.

(v) The model does not apply as far as $V = 15$.

10 (iii) $a \approx 3$, $b \approx 2$

(v) Just over 3 million.

11 (ii)

$\log_{10}t$	$\log_{10}d$
0.32	2.88
0.41	2.91
0.51	2.94
0.60	2.97
0.68	3.00
0.75	3.02
0.77	3.05
0.79	3.07

(iii) $D \approx 1050$

(iv) $n = 3$

(v) $d = 840$ (nearest 10)

12 (i) $a = 15.3, b = 2.7; a = $ sag from weight of beam alone.

(ii) 39.6 m

(iv) $c \approx 1.46, k \approx 12.3.$

(v) The second model gives a closer fit to the data.

Chapter 12

❓ (Page 339)

Differentiating $y = x^2$ gives $m_A = 2x.$
Using the symmetry of the curves and the fact that $\tan(90 - \theta) = \dfrac{1}{\tan\theta}$ it can be shown that $m_B = \dfrac{1}{2y}.$
For formal differentiation, see the contents of this chapter.

Exercise 12A (Page 341)

1 (i) $-\dfrac{4}{x^5}$

(ii) $-20x^{-6}$

(iii) $-42x^{-7}$

(iv) $-\dfrac{6}{x^3}$

(v) $-\dfrac{15}{x^6}$

(vi) $-\dfrac{2}{x^2} + 3x^2$

(vii) $-\dfrac{15}{x^4} + \dfrac{2}{x^2}$

(viii) $\frac{1}{4}x^{-\frac{3}{4}}$

(ix) $2x^{-\frac{2}{3}}$

(x) $\frac{3}{4}x^{-\frac{1}{4}}$

(xi) $-\frac{2}{3}x^{-\frac{5}{3}}$

(xii) $-\frac{1}{2}x^{-\frac{3}{2}}$

(xiii) $\frac{1}{5}x^{-\frac{4}{5}}$

(xiv) $\frac{1}{2}x^{-\frac{1}{2}} - 3x^{-4} + 2$

(xv) $\frac{4}{3}x^{\frac{1}{3}}$

2 (i) (a) $-2x^{-3}$

(b) -128

(ii) (a) $-x^{-2} - 4x^{-5}$

(b) 3

(iii) (a) $-12x^{-4} - 10x^{-6}$

(b) -22

(iv) (a) $12x^3 + 24x^{-4}$

(b) 97.5

(v) (a) $\dfrac{1}{2\sqrt{x}} + 3$

(b) $3\frac{1}{4}$

(vi) (a) $-2x^{-\frac{3}{2}}$

(b) $-\dfrac{2}{27}$

3 (i)

(ii) $\left(-\frac{1}{2}, 0\right)$

(iii) $-\dfrac{1}{x^2}$

(iv) -4

4 $-\frac{2}{3} < x < \frac{2}{3}$

5 (i) $-\dfrac{8}{x^3} + 1$

(iii) 2

(v) 0

(vi) There is a minimum point at $(2, 3).$

6 (i)

(iii) $-\dfrac{2}{x^3}; -16$

(iv) The line $y = -16x + 13$ is a tangent to the curve $y = \dfrac{1}{x^2} + 1$ at $(0.5, 5).$

7 (i) $\dfrac{1}{2\sqrt{x}}$

(ii) $\left(\frac{1}{16}, -\frac{3}{4}\right)$

(iii) No. The point $\left(\frac{1}{16}, -\frac{3}{4}\right)$ does not lie on the line $y = 2x - 1.$

8 (i) $3 + \dfrac{2}{x^3}$

(ii) 5

(iii) $y = 5x - 3$

9 (i) $2x - \dfrac{1}{x^2}$

(ii) 1

(iv) $(-2.4, 5.4), (0.4, 2.6)$

10 (i) $\dfrac{dy}{dx} = -2x^{-3}; \dfrac{d^2y}{dx^2} = 6x^{-4}$

(ii) $\dfrac{dy}{dx} = \frac{3}{2}x^{\frac{1}{2}}; \dfrac{d^2y}{dx^2} = \frac{3}{4}x^{-\frac{1}{2}}$

(iii) $\dfrac{dy}{dx} = 4x^3 + \dfrac{6}{x^4}; \dfrac{d^2y}{dx^2} = 12x^2 - \dfrac{24}{x^5}$

11 (i) $(1, 2)$, minimum and $(-1, -2)$, maximum

(ii) $(\sqrt{2}, 8\sqrt{2})$, minimum and $(-\sqrt{2}, -8\sqrt{2})$, maximum

(iii) $(16, 32)$, maximum

12 (i) $1 - \dfrac{2}{\sqrt{x}}; \quad x^{-\frac{3}{2}}$

(ii) $(4, -4)$, minimum

13 2

14 (i) 0, 10

(ii) -58.8

15 (i) Area $= xy = 18$

(ii) $T = 2x + y$

(iv) $\dfrac{dT}{dx} = 2 - \dfrac{18}{x^2}; \dfrac{d^2T}{dx^2} = \dfrac{36}{x^3}$

(v) $x = 3$ and $y = 6$

16 (i) $V = x^2y$

(ii) $A = x^2 + 4xy$

(iii) $A = x^2 + \dfrac{2}{x}$

(iv) $\dfrac{dA}{dx} = 2x - \dfrac{2}{x^2}; \dfrac{d^2A}{dx^2} = 2 + \dfrac{4}{x^3}$

(v) $x = 1$ and $y = \frac{1}{2}$

17 (i) $h = \dfrac{324}{x^2}$

(iii) $\dfrac{dA}{dx} = 12x - \dfrac{2592}{x^2}$; stationary point when $x = 6$ and $h = 9$

(iv) Minimum area $= 648$ cm^2. Dimensions: 6 cm $\times$ 18 cm $\times$ 9 cm.

18 (i) $y = \dfrac{24}{x}$

(ii) $A = 3x + 30 + \dfrac{48}{x}$

(iii) $A = 54$ m^2

19 (i) $h = \dfrac{1}{8r^2}$

(iii) $\dfrac{dA}{dr} = 2\pi r - \dfrac{\pi}{4r^2}$;

$\dfrac{d^2A}{dx^2} = 2\pi + \dfrac{\pi}{2r^3}$;

$r = \frac{1}{2}\,\text{m};\ h = \frac{1}{2}\,\text{m}$

(iv) Minimum area $= \dfrac{3\pi}{4}\,\text{m}^2$

$(= 2.36\,\text{m}^2\ \text{to 3 s.f.})$

20 (i) Time taken $= \dfrac{100}{v}$

(ii) $C = 80v + \dfrac{200\,000}{v^2}$

(iii) $v = 17\,\text{km}\,\text{h}^{-1}$

(iv) £2052 (to nearest £)

21 (ii) $r = 0.683\,\text{m}$ (to 3 s.f.)

22 (i) $y = \dfrac{16}{x}$

(ii) $S = x^2 + \dfrac{256}{x^2}$

(iii) 32

(iv) $4\sqrt{2}\,\text{cm} = 5.66\,\text{cm}$ (to 3 s.f.)

Exercise 12B (Page 350)

1 (i) $-\frac{10}{3}x^{-3} + c$

(ii) $x^2 + x^{-3} + c$

(iii) $2x + \frac{1}{4}x^4 - \frac{5}{2}x^{-2} + c$

(iv) $2x^3 + 7x^{-1} + c$

(v) $4x^{\frac{5}{4}} + c$

(vi) $-\dfrac{1}{3x^3} + c$

(vii) $\frac{2}{3}x^{\frac{3}{2}} + c$

(viii) $\dfrac{2x^5}{5} + \dfrac{4}{x} + c$

(ix) $-12x^{-\frac{1}{2}} + c$

(x) $\frac{2}{5}x^{\frac{5}{2}} + c$

2 (i) $2\frac{1}{4}$

(ii) $\frac{3}{4}$

(iii) 41.4

(iv) $\frac{7}{12}$

(v) $-2\frac{2}{3}$

(vi) $\frac{4}{3}$

(vii) 3.68

(viii) 30.5

3 (i) $21\frac{1}{3}$

4 (i) P(−4, 3); Q(−2, 0); R(2, 0); S(4, 3)

(ii) 8

5 (i) (4, 2)

(ii) and (iii)

(iv) 6.77 (to 3 s.f.)

6 (ii) B(1, −2)

(iii) $1\frac{1}{4}$

7 (i) $y = -\dfrac{2}{x} - 3x + c$

(ii) $y = -\dfrac{2}{x} - 3x + 17$

8 $y = \frac{2}{3}x^{\frac{3}{2}} + c;\ y = \frac{2}{3}x^{\frac{3}{2}} + 2$

9 $11\frac{1}{4}$

10 $\frac{3}{4}$

11 $v = 5 + 4\sqrt{t}$

12 (i) 4 seconds, $20\,\text{ms}^{-1}$

(ii)

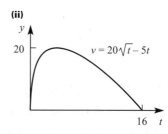

(iii) $213\frac{1}{3}$

Index